Modern Trends in
Multi-Agent Systems

Modern Trends in Multi-Agent Systems

Editors

Agostino Poggi
Martin Kenyeres
Ivana Budinská
Ladislav Hluchy

Basel • Beijing • Wuhan • Barcelona • Belgrade • Novi Sad • Cluj • Manchester

Editors
Agostino Poggi
Department of Engineering
and Architecture
University of Parma
Parma
Italy

Martin Kenyeres
Institute of Informatics
Slovak Academy of Sciences
Bratislava
Slovakia

Ivana Budinská
Institute of Informatics
Slovak Academy of Sciences
Bratislava
Slovakia

Ladislav Hluchy
Institute of Informatics
Slovak Academy of Sciences
Bratislava
Slovakia

Editorial Office
MDPI
St. Alban-Anlage 66
4052 Basel, Switzerland

This is a reprint of articles from the Special Issue published online in the open access journal *Future Internet* (ISSN 1999-5903) (available at: www.mdpi.com/journal/futureinternet/special_issues/Modern_Trends_Multi-Agent_Systems).

For citation purposes, cite each article independently as indicated on the article page online and as indicated below:

Lastname, A.A.; Lastname, B.B. Article Title. *Journal Name* **Year**, *Volume Number*, Page Range.

ISBN 978-3-7258-0526-6 (Hbk)
ISBN 978-3-7258-0525-9 (PDF)
doi.org/10.3390/books978-3-7258-0525-9

© 2024 by the authors. Articles in this book are Open Access and distributed under the Creative Commons Attribution (CC BY) license. The book as a whole is distributed by MDPI under the terms and conditions of the Creative Commons Attribution-NonCommercial-NoDerivs (CC BY-NC-ND) license.

Contents

About the Editors vii

Martin Kenyeres, Ivana Budinská, Ladislav Hluchý and Agostino Poggi
Modern Trends in Multi-Agent Systems
Reprinted from: *Future Internet* 2024, 16, 54, doi:10.3390/fi16020054 1

Martin Kenyeres and Jozef Kenyeres
Comparative Study of Distributed Consensus Gossip Algorithms for Network Size Estimation in Multi-Agent Systems
Reprinted from: *Future Internet* 2021, 13, 134, doi:10.3390/fi13050134 4

Barry Dowdeswell, Roopak Sinha and Stephen G. MacDonell
Architecting an Agent-Based Fault Diagnosis Engine for IEC 61499 Industrial Cyber-Physical Systems
Reprinted from: *Future Internet* 2021, 13, 190, doi:10.3390/fi13080190 26

Grigorios Kakkavas, Vasileios Karyotis and Symeon Papavassiliou
Topology Inference and Link Parameter Estimation Based on End-to-End Measurements [†]
Reprinted from: *Future Internet* 2022, 14, 45, doi:10.3390/fi14020045 51

Domenico Lembo, Valerio Santarelli, Domenico Fabio Savo and Giuseppe De Giacomo
Graphol: A Graphical Conceptual Modeling Language Equivalent to OWL 2
Reprinted from: *Future Internet* 2022, 14, 78, doi:10.3390/fi14030078 68

Mattia Pellegrino, Gianfranco Lombardo, Stefano Cagnoni and Agostino Poggi
High-Performance Computing and ABMS for High-Resolution COVID-19 Spreading Simulation
Reprinted from: *Future Internet* 2022, 14, 83, doi:10.3390/fi14030083 97

Mahdi Zargayouna
On the Use of the Multi-Agent Environment for Mobility Applications
Reprinted from: *Future Internet* 2022, 14, 132, doi:10.3390/fi14050132 120

Sana Sahar Guia, Abdelkader Laouid, Mohammad Hammoudeh, Ahcène Bounceur, Mai Alfawair and Amna Eleyan
Co-Simulation of Multiple Vehicle Routing Problem Models
Reprinted from: *Future Internet* 2022, 14, 137, doi:10.3390/fi14050137 136

Giuseppe Vizzari and Thomas Cecconello
Pedestrian Simulation with Reinforcement Learning: A Curriculum-Based Approach
Reprinted from: *Future Internet* 2022, 15, 12, doi:10.3390/fi15010012 152

Sean Grimes and David E. Breen
A Multi-Agent Approach to Binary Classification Using Swarm Intelligence
Reprinted from: *Future Internet* 2023, 15, 36, doi:10.3390/fi15010036 177

František Čapkovič
Dealing with Deadlocks in Industrial Multi Agent Systems
Reprinted from: *Future Internet* 2023, 15, 107, doi:10.3390/fi15030107 204

About the Editors

Agostino Poggi

Agostino Poggi is a full-time professor of computer engineering at the Dipartimento di Ingegneria dell'Informazione of the University of Parma and teaches Advanced Software Engineering, Computer Networks, and Distributed and Agent Systems at the Faculty of Engineering. Agostino Poggi received a Laurea degree cum laude in Electronic Engineering in 1987 and a Ph.D. in Computer and Electronic Engineering in 1992, both from the University of Genoa. From 1993 to 1998, he was an assistant professor at the Dipartimento di Ingegneria dell'Informazione of the University of Parma, and from 1998 to 2001, he was an associate professor at the same university. His research is primarily focused on agent-, web-, and object-oriented technologies and their use to develop distributed and complex systems. In these research areas, he has been involved both in national and international projects, coordinating the research of his department on different projects funded by public and private organizations. In particular, he participated in the following EU-funded research projects: COLLABORATOR, IST-2000-30045, (2001–2003), of which he was the scientific coordinator; CoMMA, IST-1999-12217, (2000–2002); LEAP, IST-1999-10211, (2000–2002); AGENTCITIES: RTD, IST-2000-28385, (2001–2003); and ALIS TECNET, ALA/2002/049-055, (2003–2006), where he acted as the coordinator of the research unit of the University of Parma. Moreover, he was one of the authors of JADE, an "open source" software development framework for multi-agent systems, which has become the international reference software for developing multi-agent applications.

Martin Kenyeres

Martin Kenyeres is a research scientist (IIa since 2022) at the Institute of Informatics of the Slovak Academy of Sciences (Slovakia) and a doctoral advisor at the Faculty of Electrical Engineering and Information Technology of the Slovak University of Technology in Bratislava (Slovakia). He received his M.Sc. from the Slovak University of Technology in Bratislava and his Ph.D. from the Brno University of Technology (Czech Republic). His primary research interests include distributed algorithms for data aggregation in multi-agent systems and wireless sensor networks. He has authored/co-authored almost 50 scientific papers (indexed in Scopus) in these areas. In 2013, he was with the Vienna University of Technology (Austria), where he participated in the NFN SISE project under Professor Markus Rupp's supervision. Since 2018, Martin has been with the Institute of Informatics of the Slovak Academy of Sciences. In 2019, Martin Kenyeres received the Stefan Schwarz Supporting Fund (prolonged in 2021). In addition, he has handled plenty of national and international projects and completed several foreign internships. Martin is also a member of the editorial/reviewer/topics board of several prestigious journals and a guest editor of Special Issues related to his expertise.

Ivana Budinská

Ivana Budinská is a senior researcher working with the Modeling and Simulation of Discrete Processes Department at the Institute of Informatics of the Slovak Academy of Sciences. Also, she is a member of the Presidium of the Slovak Academy of Sciences and a supervisor and consultant for PhD studies at the Slovak University of Technology in Bratislava. Her research interests include discrete systems modeling and simulation, multi-agent systems, artificial intelligence, complex systems, and system theory. Recently, she has been interested in bio-inspired method applications in various domains, e.g., manufacturing, production line optimization, supply chain management, the control and coordination of a group of mobile agents, and swarm robotics.

Ladislav Hluchy

Ladislav Hluchý (Associated Professor, M.Sc., Ph.D.) has been the head of the Parallel and Distributed Information Processing Department and former Director of the Institute of Informatics, Slovak Academy of Sciences (IISAS), for over 20 years. He received both his M.Sc. and Ph.D. in computer science. He is an R&D Project Manager, Work-Package Leader, and Coordinator in many 4th, 5th, 6th, 7th, and H2020 EU IST RTD projects, as well as Slovak R&D projects (VEGA, APVV, SPVV). His research topics are focused on parallel and distributed computing, large-scale applications, cluster/grid/cloud computing, service-oriented computing, and knowledge-oriented technology. His highlighted research works are within EU IST RTD projects EGI-Engage H2020-654142 Engaging the research community towards an Open Science Commons, EGI-InSPIRE FP7-261323, EGEE IIIFP7-222667, EGEE II FP6 RI-031688, EGEE FP6 INFSO-RI-508833, REDIRNET FP7-607768, VENIS FP7-284984, SeCriCom FP7-218123, Commius FP7-213876, ADMIREFP7-215024, DEGREE FP6-034619, INTAS FP6 06-1000024-9154, int.eu.grid FP6 RI-031857, K-Wf Grid FP6-511385, MEDIGRID FP6 GOCE-CT-2003-004044, CROSSGRIDFP5 IST-2001-32243, PELLUCID FP5 IST-2001-34519, ANFAS FP5 IST-1999-11676, SEIHPC, SEPP, and HPCTI, as well as in international and Slovak national research projects. He is a member of the IEEE, e-IRG, and EGI Councils and the Editor-in-Chief of the current contents (CC) journal Computing and Informatics (CAI). He is also the (co-)author of scientific books, numerous scientific papers (more than 300), contributions, and invited lectures at international scientific conferences and workshops. He is a supervisor and consultant for Ph.D. studies at the Slovak University of Technology (STU) in Bratislava.

 future internet

Editorial

Modern Trends in Multi-Agent Systems

Martin Kenyeres [1,*], Ivana Budinská [1], Ladislav Hluchý [1] and Agostino Poggi [2]

1. Institute of Informatics, Slovak Academy of Sciences, 845 07 Bratislava, Slovakia; budinska.ui@savba.sk (I.B.); hluchy.ui@savba.sk (L.H.)
2. Department of Engineering and Architecture, University of Parma, 43124 Parma, Italy; agostino.poggi@unipr.it
* Correspondence: martin.kenyeres@savba.sk; Tel.: +421-2-5941-1194

The term "multi-agent system" is generally understood as an interconnected set of independent entities that can effectively solve complex and time-consuming problems exceeding the individual abilities of common problem solvers. The coordinated entities forming these systems regularly interact with each other to solve various massive problems in numerous technical/non-technical applications (e.g., grid computing, bioinformatics, business, monitoring, resource management, controlling, computational biology, education, military, space research, etc.). In many modern multi-agent systems, the entities are required to be fully autonomous, to provide global decisions based on local knowledge, and to be able to work effectively in a decentralized way. The design of robust, energy-efficient, and high-performance algorithms for MASs, therefore, poses a demanding challenge for the wider scientific community. Thus, significant attention has been paid by many scientists to optimizing the operation of multi-agent systems in many respects (e.g., routing, data aggregation, communication, coordination, consensus achievement, synchronization, etc.) over recent decades.

The paper [1] addresses an extensive analysis of five frequently applied distributed consensus gossip-based algorithms for network size estimation in multi-agent systems (namely, the randomized gossip algorithm, the geographic gossip algorithm, the broadcast gossip algorithm, the push–sum protocol, and the push–pull protocol). The performance of the algorithms with bounded execution is examined in random geometric graphs, in two scenarios, and by applying two metrics used to evaluate the precision and rate of the algorithms. In the paper, it is identified which algorithms are applicable to estimating the network size, which algorithm is the best performing, how the leader selection affects the performance of the algorithms, and how to optimally configure the used stopping criterion to border the algorithms.

In [2], the authors present the software architecture for an agent-based fault diagnostic engine that equips agents with domain knowledge of IEC 61499 [3]. Using sound architectural design approaches and documentation methods, coupled with rigorous evaluation and prototyping, this paper demonstrates how quality attributes, risks, and architectural trade-offs were identified and mitigated before the construction of the engine commenced.

The authors of [4] deal with the design, implementation, experimental validation, and evaluation of a network tomography approach for performing inferential monitoring based on indirect measurements. Additionally, the authors address the problems of inferring the routing tree topology (both logical and physical) and estimating the links' loss rate and jitter based on multicast end-to-end measurements from a source node to a set of destination nodes using an agglomerative clustering algorithm. Finally, the authors implement and present a motivating practical application of the proposed algorithm that combines monitoring with change point analysis to realize performance anomaly detection.

Lembo et al. [5] study a fully graphical language Graphol, which is inspired by standard formalisms for conceptual modeling, similar to the UML class diagram and the

Citation: Kenyeres, M.; Budinská, I.; Hluchý, L.; Poggi, A. Modern Trends in Multi-Agent Systems. *Future Internet* 2024, *16*, 54. https://doi.org/10.3390/fi16020054

Received: 4 February 2024
Accepted: 6 February 2024
Published: 8 February 2024

Copyright: © 2024 by the authors. Licensee MDPI, Basel, Switzerland. This article is an open access article distributed under the terms and conditions of the Creative Commons Attribution (CC BY) license (https:// creativecommons.org/licenses/by/ 4.0/).

ER model, but equipped with formal semantics. The authors also present several usability studies indicating that Graphol is suitable for quick adoption by conceptual modelers.

The paper [6] is focused on an approach for the modeling and simulation of the spread of COVID-19 based on agent-based modeling and simulation. The primary achievement of this paper consists of the effective modeling of 10 million concurrent agents, each one mapping an individual behavior with a high resolution in terms of social contacts, mobility, and contribution to the virus spreading. Moreover, the authors analyze the forecasting ability of our framework to predict the number of infections being initialized with only a few days of real data. The proposed approach outperforms state-of-the-art solutions.

In [7], the author provide a comprehensive discussion about the relevance of the multi-agent environment in mobility applications and describe different use cases in simulation and optimization.

The authors of [8] present the Vehicle Routing Problem simulation results in several aspects, where the main goal is to satisfy several client demands. The executed experiments show the performance of the proposed Vehicle Routing Problem multi-model and carry out its improvement in terms of computational complexity.

In the paper [9], the authors explore the possibility of applying reinforcement learning to pedestrian simulations. The learned pedestrian behavioral model is applicable to situations not presented to the agents in the training phase, and seems therefore reasonably general. This paper describes the basic elements of the approach, the training procedure, and an experimentation within a software framework employing Unity and ML-Agents (the employed ML-Agents version the authors adopted was 0.25.1 for Python and 1.0.7 for Unity).

The authors of [10] demonstrate that Wisdom-of-Crowds-Bots are competitive with other top classification methods on three datasets and apply their system to a real-world sport betting problem, producing a consistent return on investment from 1 January 2021 to 15 November 2022 on most major sports.

Two methods based on Petri nets are presented in [11] based on (i) P-invariants and (ii) Petri net siphons and traps. The intended result of the usage of these methods is to find a supervisor which allows for deadlock-free activity of the global multi-agent systems. While the former method yields results in analytical terms, the latter one needs computation of siphons and traps.

Author Contributions: Conceptualization, M.K., I.B., L.H. and A.P.; methodology, M.K., I.B., L.H. and A.P.; writing—original draft preparation, M.K.; writing—review and editing, M.K., I.B., L.H. and A.P.; visualization, M.K.; supervision, M.K., I.B., L.H. and A.P. All authors have read and agreed to the published version of the manuscript.

Acknowledgments: We would like to thank all the authors for submitting their interesting contributions, the reviewers for their precise and insightful reviews, and the involved editorial staff from Future Internet for their professional work.

Conflicts of Interest: The author declares no conflicts of interest.

References

1. Kenyeres, M.; Kenyeres, J. Comparative Study of Distributed Consensus Gossip Algorithms for Network Size Estimation in Multi-Agent Systems. *Future Internet* **2021**, *13*, 134. [CrossRef]
2. Dowdeswell, B.; Sinha, R.; MacDonell, S.G. Architecting an Agent-Based Fault Diagnosis Engine for IEC 61499 Industrial Cyber-Physical Systems. *Future Internet* **2021**, *13*, 190. [CrossRef]
3. IEC. *Function Blocks–Part 1: Architecture*; IEC: Geneva, Switzerland, 2013.
4. Kakkavas, G.; Karyotis, V.; Papavassiliou, S. Topology Inference and Link Parameter Estimation Based on End-to-End Measurements. *Future Internet* **2022**, *14*, 45. [CrossRef]
5. Lembo, D.; Santarelli, V.; Savo, D.F.; De Giacomo, G. Graphol: A Graphical Language for Ontology Modeling Equivalent to OWL 2. *Future Internet* **2022**, *14*, 78. [CrossRef]
6. Pellegrino, M.; Lombardo, G.; Cagnoni, S.; Poggi, A. High-Performance Computing and ABMS for High-Resolution COVID-19 Spreading Simulation. *Future Internet* **2022**, *14*, 83. [CrossRef]
7. Zargayouna, M. On the Use of the Multi-Agent Environment for Mobility Applications. *Future Internet* **2022**, *14*, 132. [CrossRef]

8. Guia, S.S.; Laouid, A.; Hammoudeh, M.; Bounceur, A.; Alfawair, M.; Eleyan, A. Co-Simulation of Multiple Vehicle Routing Problem Models. *Future Internet* **2022**, *14*, 137. [CrossRef]
9. Vizzari, G.; Cecconello, T. Pedestrian Simulation with Reinforcement Learning: A Curriculum-Based Approach. *Future Internet* **2023**, *15*, 12. [CrossRef]
10. Grimes, S.; Breen, D.E. A Multi-Agent Approach to Binary Classification Using Swarm Intelligence. *Future Internet* **2023**, *15*, 36. [CrossRef]
11. Čapkovič, F. Dealing with Deadlocks in Industrial Multi Agent Systems. *Future Internet* **2023**, *15*, 107. [CrossRef]

Disclaimer/Publisher's Note: The statements, opinions and data contained in all publications are solely those of the individual author(s) and contributor(s) and not of MDPI and/or the editor(s). MDPI and/or the editor(s) disclaim responsibility for any injury to people or property resulting from any ideas, methods, instructions or products referred to in the content.

Article
Comparative Study of Distributed Consensus Gossip Algorithms for Network Size Estimation in Multi-Agent Systems

Martin Kenyeres [1,*] and Jozef Kenyeres [2]

[1] Institute of Informatics, Slovak Academy of Sciences, Dúbravská cesta 9, 845 07 Bratislava, Slovakia
[2] EBCONT Proconsult GmbH, Millennium Tower, Handelskai 94-96, 1200 Vienna, Austria; jozef.kenyeres@ebcont.com
* Correspondence: martin.kenyeres@savba.sk

Citation: Kenyeres, M.; Kenyeres, J. Comparative Study of Distributed Consensus Gossip Algorithms for Network Size Estimation in Multi-Agent Systems. *Future Internet* **2021**, *13*, 134. https://doi.org/10.3390/fi13050134

Academic Editor: Ivan Serina

Received: 9 April 2021
Accepted: 14 May 2021
Published: 18 May 2021

Publisher's Note: MDPI stays neutral with regard to jurisdictional claims in published maps and institutional affiliations.

Copyright: © 2021 by the authors. Licensee MDPI, Basel, Switzerland. This article is an open access article distributed under the terms and conditions of the Creative Commons Attribution (CC BY) license (https://creativecommons.org/licenses/by/4.0/).

Abstract: Determining the network size is a critical process in numerous areas (e.g., computer science, logistic, epidemiology, social networking services, mathematical modeling, demography, etc.). However, many modern real-world systems are so extensive that measuring their size poses a serious challenge. Therefore, the algorithms for determining/estimating this parameter in an effective manner have been gaining popularity over the past decades. In the paper, we analyze five frequently applied distributed consensus gossip-based algorithms for network size estimation in multi-agent systems (namely, the Randomized gossip algorithm, the Geographic gossip algorithm, the Broadcast gossip algorithm, the Push-Sum protocol, and the Push-Pull protocol). We examine the performance of the mentioned algorithms with bounded execution over random geometric graphs by applying two metrics: the number of sent messages required for consensus achievement and the estimation precision quantified as the median deviation from the real value of the network size. The experimental part consists of two scenarios—the consensus achievement is conditioned by either the values of the inner states or the network size estimates—and, in both scenarios, either the best-connected or the worst-connected agent is chosen as the leader. The goal of this paper is to identify whether all the examined algorithms are applicable to estimating the network size, which algorithm provides the best performance, how the leader selection can affect the performance of the algorithms, and how to most effectively configure the applied stopping criterion.

Keywords: consensus algorithms; count; data aggregation; distributed algorithms; distributed computing; gossip algorithms; information fusion; network size; network size estimation; sensor fusion

1. Introduction

1.1. Theoretical Background into Multi-Agent Systems

The term "multi-agent system" (MAS) is defined as a computer-based environment formed potentially by hundreds to thousands of interacting intelligent entities referred to as agents [1]. As the literature review shows [2–4], numerous experts from the computer science community provide various definitions of what the term "agent" means. In general, an agent of MAS is considered to be a part of a software/hardware computer-based system that exchanges messages with its peers as well as interacting with its surrounding environment [5,6]. Thus, the agents are able to learn novel actions and contexts, thereby being capable to make autonomous decisions [6]. One of the greatest advantages of the agents is their significant flexibility, making MASs applicable in many various fields such as diagnostics, civil engineering, power system restoration, market simulation, network control, etc. [3,6]. Besides, an agent of MAS is also characterized by other valuable features such as low cost, high efficiency, reliability, etc. and can take various forms—it is a software, hardware, pr hybrid (i.e., a combination of two previous) component [6] (see Figure 1 for a general structure of an agent forming MAS) [6].

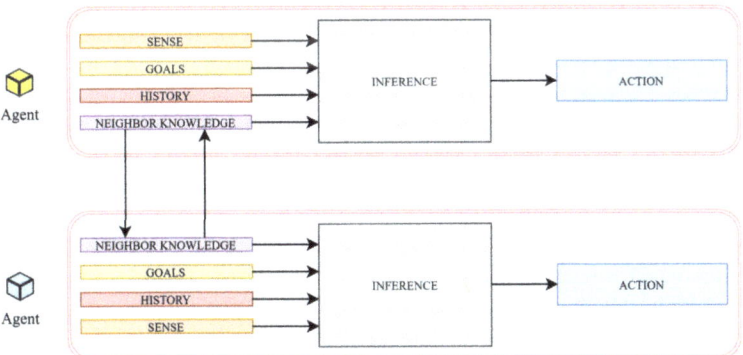

Figure 1. General structure of agent forming multi-agent system.

Furthermore, as stated in [5], the agents of MASs can be characterized by four main features:

- Autonomy is the ability to operate without any human interaction and to control its own actions/inner state.
- Reactivity is the ability to react to a dynamic surrounding environment.
- Social ability is the ability to communicate with other agents or human beings.
- Pro-activeness is the ability to act as an initiative entity and not only to respond to an external stimulus.

All the mentioned benefits of the agents allow MASs to be applied to solving time-demanding and complex problems (often unsolvable by an individual agent) by splitting them into several simpler subtasks [6,7]. Thus, MAS can be understood as an interconnected computerized system of multi-functional entities interacting with each other in order to solve various complex problems in an effective manner. Therefore, MASs have been significantly gaining importance over the past decades [7].

1.2. Data Aggregation in Multi-Agent Systems

In our modern era, the amount of information is rapidly being increased in numerous industries whereby many modern systems benefit from the application of algorithms for data aggregation [8,9]. Data aggregation is a multidisciplinary research field addressing how to integrate data from independent multi-data sources into a more precise, consistent, and suitable form [10–12]. As stated in [9] and shown in Figure 2, there are many ways to classify the data aggregation methods.

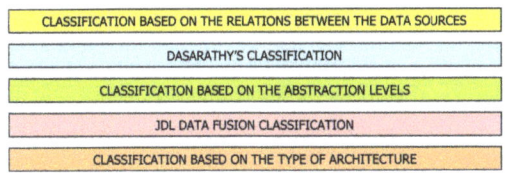

Figure 2. Various classifications of data aggregation methods.

In this paper, we turn our attention to the classification based on the type of the system architecture. In this case, the data aggregation methods are divided into categories according to where (i.e., on which system component) data aggregation is executed. Namely, these four categories are defined by the authors of [9]:

- *Centralized architecture*: Data aggregation is carried out by the fusion node, which collects the raw data from all the other agents in the system. Thus, all the agents measure the quantity of interest and are only required to deliver this information to the fusion node subsequently. Therefore, this approach is not too appropriate for real-world systems since it is characterized by a significant time delay, a massive transmitted information amount, high vulnerability to potential threats, etc.
- *Decentralized architecture*: In this approach, there is no single point of data aggregation in contrast to the centralized architecture. In this case, each agent autonomously aggregates its local information with data obtained from its peers. Despite many advantages, decentralized architecture also has several shortcomings, e.g., communication costs, poor scalability, etc.
- *Distributed architecture*: Each agent in a system independently processes its measurement; therefore, the object state is executed only according to the local information. This approach is characterized by a significant reduction of communication and communication cost, thereby gaining in popularity and finding a wide application in real-world systems over recent years [13–16].
- *Hierarchical architecture*: This architecture (also referred to as hybrid architecture) is a combination of the decentralized and the distributed architecture, executing data aggregation at different levels at the hierarchy.

Even though the decentralized and the distributed architecture seem to be similar to one another, there are several differences between these two categories [9,17]. In this part, we turn the readers' attention to the most significant contrasts. One of them is the fact that the measured data are pre-processed in the distributed architecture. Subsequently, a vector of features, which is then aggregated, is created as a result of this process. However, in the decentralized architecture, the data aggregation is completely executed at every agent in MAS whereby each agent can provide a globally aggregated output. Furthermore, in the decentralized architecture, information is commonly communicated, while, in the distributed one, the common notion of some states (position, identity, etc.) is shared. Besides, in decentralized architecture, it is an easy process to separate old information from the new one in contrast to the distributed one. On the other hand, the implementation of the decentralized architecture is generally considered to be more difficult. However, as shown in the literature [17,18], these two terms are often understood as synonyms and are therefore used as equivalents.

Note that one may find more general classifications according to the type of the system architecture [19]. As stated above, we focus our attention on distributed data aggregation mechanisms, a modern solution preferred in numerous modern applications (see Figure 3 for an example of the distributed architecture).

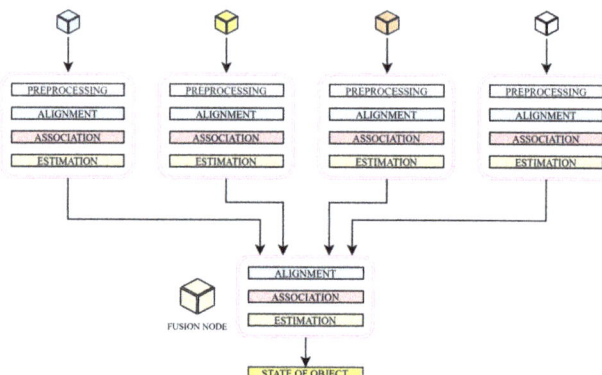

Figure 3. Example of distributed architecture.

1.3. Consensus Theory

The problem of consensus achievement, an active research field with a long history in computer science, has been attracting great attention from both academia and industry over recent years [20]. In general, the term "consensus" means achieving an agreement upon a certain value determined by the inner states of all the agents in MAS [20,21]. In MASs, the term "consensus algorithm" (sometimes referred to as a consensus protocol) is understood as a set of rules specifying how the agents in MAS interact with their neighbors [20]. The goal of distributed consensus algorithms is to ensure agreement among a set of independent autonomous entities interconnected by potentially faulty networked systems [21]. Over the past decades, the consensus algorithms have found a wide range of applications in various fields such as wireless sensor networks, robotic systems, unmanned air vehicles, clustered satellites, etc. [19,21]. In this paper, we focus our attention on the distributed consensus algorithms, which are iterative schemes for determining/estimating various aggregate functions (e.g., the arithmetic mean, the sum, the graph order, the extreme, etc.).

The authors of [22] defined two categories of distributed consensus algorithms:

- *Deterministic* algorithms include the Metropolis–Hastings algorithm, the Max-Degree weights algorithm, the Best Constant weights algorithm, the Convex Optimized weights algorithm, etc.
- *Gossip* algorithms include the Push-Sum protocol, the Push-Pull protocol, the Randomized gossip algorithm, the Broadcast gossip algorithm, etc.

1.4. Our Contribution

In this paper, we analyze five frequently applied distributed consensus gossip algorithms with bounded execution for network size estimation. Namely, we choose these five algorithms for evaluation:

- *Randomized gossip algorithm (RG)*;
- *Geographic gossip algorithm (GG)*;
- *Broadcast gossip algorithm (BG)*;
- *Push-Sum protocol (PS)*; and
- *Push-Pull protocol (PP)*.

Our contribution is motivated by the lack of papers concerned with the applicability of these algorithms to network size estimation and their comparison. Our goal is to identify whether all the examined algorithms are applicable to estimating the network size, which algorithm is the best performing approach, how the leader selection can affect the performance of the algorithms, and how to most effectively configure the applied stopping criterion. In our analyses, the initial configuration of the applied stopping criterion is varied, either the best-connected or the worst-connected agent is the leader, and also the way to stop the algorithms differs. The algorithms are tested over 100 random geometric graphs (RGGs) each with a unique topology. The performance of the algorithms is quantified by applying two metrics, namely the number of sent messages required for consensus achievement and the estimation precision. Besides, the distribution of the number of sent messages is examined for each algorithm. Finally, we compare our conclusions made according to the presented experimental results with papers published by other authors and addressing the same algorithms.

1.5. Paper Organization

In Section 2, we provide papers published by other authors where the five examined algorithms are compared and analyzed. In Section 3, we present the used model of MAS. In Section 4, the analyzed algorithms are introduced. In Section 5, we present the applied research methodology and the metrics used to evaluate the performance of the analyzed algorithms. In Section 6, we present the results from the numerical experiments and compare our conclusion with related papers. Section 7 briefly summarizes the outputs of our research.

2. Related Work

In this section, we deal with papers concerned with distributed consensus gossip-based algorithms published by other authors. We focus our attention on papers (or their parts) where the algorithms that we analyze in this paper are compared.

The authors of [23] compared *BG* and *RG* using the simulator Castalia and by applying several metrics, namely the communication overhead, the latency, the energy consumption, the normalized absolute error, and the standard deviation. In addition, three different sets of the initial states are assumed in the presented research. They identified that *BG* in general achieves a greater performance than *RG*. *BG* achieves low performance only in terms of the normalized absolute error. As in the previously discussed manuscript, *BG* and *RG* are also compared in [24], however, under quantized communication in this case. In this paper, it is identified that *BG* outperforms *RG* in terms of the time required to achieve the quantized consensus over various network types, namely random geographical spatial networks with the same connectivity radius, small-world networks, and scale-free networks. The authors of [25] also focused their attention on a comparison of *BG* with *RG* and identified that *BG* outperforms *RG* in both the convergence time and the number of radio transmissions regardless of the network size. In [26], the authors examined and compared three gossip algorithms (*BG*, *RG*, and *GG*) by applying several metrics. They identified that *BG* outperforms the two other examined algorithms in terms of the per-node variance. It is furthermore concluded in the paper that *GG* performs better in terms of the mentioned metric than *RG* in large-scale networks. However, in smaller networks, *RG* achieves better performance than *GG*. In the paper, an analysis of the algorithms in terms of the per-node mean square error is also provided. In this case, an interesting phenomenon is identified by the authors: the error of *BG* does not drop below a specific threshold in contrast to the two other algorithms, the precision of which is increased with no bound as the number of radio transmissions increases. For fewer radio transmissions, *BG* outperforms the two other algorithms, but, for higher values, it is the worst-performing algorithm among the analyzed ones—in this case, *RG* achieves the lowest per-node mean square error. The same conclusion regarding the per-node variance as in the previous paper was also reported by Spano [27]. Wang [28] compared *RG* and *GG* in terms of the error in estimation. They identified that *GG* outperforms *RG* regardless of the network size except for the scenarios where low energy is spent. Moreover, it is identified in the paper that the more energy is spent, the higher precision of the estimation is achieved. In [29], *RG* and *GG* are compared in terms of the relative error under various initial inner states over RGGs and grid graphs. In RGGs, *GG* outperforms *RG* in all the realized scenarios except for low values of the number of transmissions. In grid topologies, *GG* is better for each value of the number of the transmission.

In this paragraph, we turn our attention to papers dealing with *PS* and *PP*. In [30], the authors compared the mentioned algorithms in terms of the convergence rate expressed as the root mean square error as a function of rounds under asynchronous and potentially faulty environments. They identified that *PS* is slightly outperformed by *PP* for a lower number of rounds. However, when the round number is equal to approximately 60, *PS* achieves higher performance than *PP*. In [31], very similar research to the one from [30] is carried out. In [31], *PS* outperforms *PP* also for lower values of iterations. Spano [32] compared *PP* and *PS* by applying the mean percentage error and the variance. It can be observed in the paper that *PP* outperforms *PS* for a lower number of rounds, but *PS* performs better for a greater number of rounds. The variance is greater in the case of *PS*. The authors of [33] identified that *PS* outperforms *PP* in terms of the mean least absolute percent error. Moreover, they showed that *PS* achieves worse performance only in large-scale networks with a low mean degree. *PS* is better than *PP* also in terms of the mean number of rounds except for large-scale networks with a high mean degree. It is furthermore shown in the paper that *PS* outperforms *PP* in terms of the mean number of wasted rounds in each analyzed scenario. In terms of the number of sent messages, *PS* achieves a greater performance than *PP* in all the executed scenarios.

In [34], the authors introduced a distributed algorithm based on Extrema Propagation, which is general considered to be a fast and fault-tolerant approach for estimating the network size. In the presented algorithm, each agent generates a vector containing random numbers (generated data have a known probability distribution). Then, the data are aggregated (an obtained value has a distribution dependent on the network size) over the whole network by applying a pointwise minimum, an idempotent operation. Afterward, the resulting vector as a sample is used to infer the number of the nodes. In contrast to this approach, PP is used to estimate the arithmetic mean, from which the network size is then estimated (it is equal to the inverse value of the arithmetic mean estimate). In this algorithm, the initial inner states are equal to either "1" or "0", and one of the agents has to be selected as the leader. Thus, in [34], it is shown that there are also other ways to estimate the network size.

As shown in [35,36], network size estimation is an important process in many areas such as charging electric vehicles, social Internet of vehicles, etc.

Thus, as seen in the provided literature review, the papers addressing distributed consensus gossip algorithms are primarily focused on the problem of distributed averaging. Thus, there is a lack of papers concerned with an analysis of RG, GG, and BG for network size estimation. The two other chosen algorithms (i.e., PS and PP) for this purpose are briefly discussed in [30,34,37–42]. However, in none of these papers, a comprehensive analysis of these algorithms applied to estimating the network size is provided. Besides, a deep comparison of all the five algorithms is not found in the literature.

3. Mathematical Model of Multi-Agent Systems

In this paper, MASs are modeled as simple finite undirected unweighted graphs labeled as G and determined by two time-invariant sets, namely the vertex set $\mathbf{V}$ and the edge set $\mathbf{E}$ ($G = (\mathbf{V}, \mathbf{E})$) [43,44]. The vertex set $\mathbf{V}$ consists of all the graph vertices representing the agents in MAS. The cardinality of this set determines the graph order (labeled as n), i.e., the number of agents in MAS. Each vertex from $\mathbf{V}$ is allocated a unique index, a positive integer value from the range $[1, n]$, i.e., $\mathbf{V} = \{v_1, v_2, \ldots, v_n\}$. The other set, the edge set $\mathbf{E} \subset \mathbf{V} \times \mathbf{V}$, is formed by all the graph edges, which represent a direct link between two vertices. The cardinality of the edge set $\mathbf{E}$ determines the size of the corresponding graph G, i.e., the overall number of direct connections in MAS. The direct link between two agents v_i and v_j (i.e., their distance is one hop) is indicated by the existence of an edge in G labeled as e_{ij}. Every two vertices directly linked to one another are said to be neighbors. Subsequently, the set containing all the neighbors of an agent v_i can be defined as:

$$\mathcal{N}_i = \{v_j : e_{ij} \in \mathbf{E}\} \qquad (1)$$

In this paper, we examine the chosen algorithms over RGGs, graphs that represent spatial MASs with n randomly deployed agents [43,44] (see Figure 4 for an example of RGGs (one of 100 RGGs applied in our research is shown in this figure to illustrate what the network topology of the used graphs looks like) and Table 1 containing the graph parameters (the average value of each parameter of 100 applied graphs is shown)). In these graphs, the agents are placed uniformly at random over a square area of finite size. Subsequently, two agents are directly linked to one another, provided their distance is not greater than the transmission radius (each agent has the same transmission radius). In the case that there is a path between each pair of two vertices, we say that this graph is connected. If not, the graph is disconnected, thereby being composed of two or more components. Different connectivity in a graph can be ensured by modifying the value of the transmission radius. As shown in the literature [22,34,45,46], this graph type is often applied to modeling real-world systems such as wireless sensor networks, ad-hoc IoT networks, social networks, etc. The algorithm used to generate RGGs applied in our research can be described as follows: in the beginning, we have a blank working area formed by 150 points on both the x- and the y-axis. Thus, there are 150^2 coordinates (x,y) in the working area. Then, the first vertex is placed uniformly at random on one of these coordinates (i.e., it can be placed on each coordinate with the same probability equal to $1/150^2$). Afterward, the other vertices (one by one) are placed on free coordinates—one coordinate can be allocated to only one vertex. Once all the vertices are distributed over the working area (200 vertices in overall in our case), edges linking all the adjacent vertices are added to the graph. As mentioned earlier, two vertices are linked to one another, provided that their distance is not greater than their transmission radius.

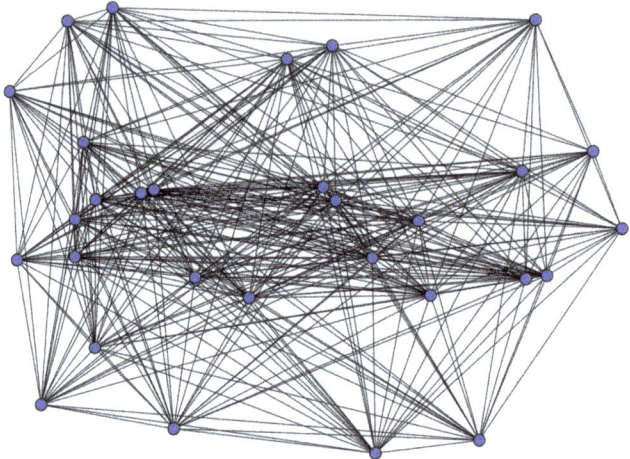

Figure 4. Example of random geometric graphs used in our experiments.

Table 1. Graph parameters of 100 RGGs used in our experiments.

Graph Parameter	Numerical Value
Graph order	30
Median degree	25.21
Max degree	29
Min degree	16.17
Diameter	2
Graph size	371.43

4. Examined Distributed Consensus Gossip-Based Algorithms

In this section, we introduce all the distributed consensus gossip-based algorithms chosen for evaluation in our research presented in this paper. We analyze five frequently cited approaches primarily proposed for estimating arithmetic mean, namely we examine these algorithms:

☐ *Randomized gossip algorithm (RG)*: see Section 4.1.
☐ *Geographic gossip algorithm (GG)*: see Section 4.2.
☐ *Broadcast gossip algorithm (BG)*: see Section 4.3.
☐ *Push-Sum protocol (PS)*: see Section 4.4.
☐ *Push-Pull protocol (PP)*: see Section 4.5.

Furthermore, as stated above, we compare these five algorithms for not very frequently applied functionality—distributed network size estimation. In each algorithm, the agents of MAS initiate their inner state (or the variable sum in the case of *PS*) with, e.g., locally measured information in the case of distributed averaging or distributed summing. The vector gathering the inner states (representing arithmetic mean estimates) of all the agents at a time instance k is labeled as $\mathbf{x}(k)$, the inner state of v_i at a time instance k is labeled as $x_i(k)$, and $x_i(0)$ is a label of the initial inner state of v_i. However, in the case of distributed network size estimation, exactly one of the agents has to be selected as the leader—for example, the agent at which the query is inserted [47]. The initial inner state of the leader is equal to "1", while all other agents set their initial inner state to "0". In our experiments, either the best-connected or the worst-connected agent is chosen as the leader in order to identify the impact of the leader selection on the performance of the algorithms. Thus, the inner states of all the agents approach $\frac{1}{n}$ (n is equaled to 200 in our experiments) as the number of time instances is increased. Thus, the agent can easily estimate the network size at each time instance as follows:

$$NSE_i(k) = \frac{1}{x_i(k)} \qquad (2)$$

Thus, in our experiments, NSE_i approaches 200 and $x_i(k)$ 1/200. The vector gathering all the estimates at a kth time instance is labeled as **NSE**(k). We refer to the states/the estimates after the consensus among all the agents in MAS is achieved as the final inner states/the final estimates. Figure 5 shows an example of how the inner states/the network size estimates differ before and after any examined algorithm for network size estimation is executed.

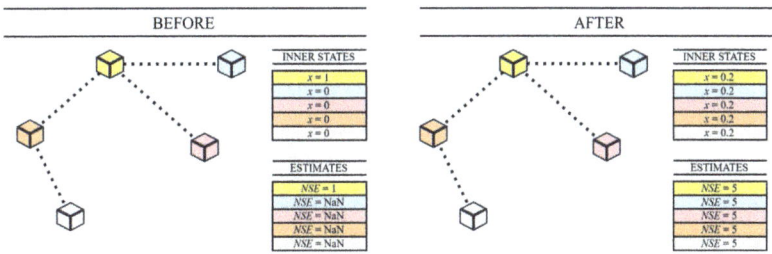

Figure 5. Comparison of inner states/arithmetic mean estimates before and after consensus is achieved in multi-agent system.

4.1. Randomized Gossip Algorithm

The first analyzed algorithm is *RG*, where one of the agents is woken up (this agent is selected from all the agents in MAS uniformly at random—let us label it as v_i) at each time instance k and chooses one of its adjacent neighbors (i.e., one of the agents from $\mathcal{N}_i$—let it be labeled as v_j) [22,26,48]. Subsequently, these two agents exchange their current inner and execute the pairwise averaging operation [22]:

$$x_i(k+1) = x_j(k+1) = \frac{x_i(k) + x_j(k)}{2} \qquad (3)$$

The inner states of the agents that do not send/receive any message at a time instance are not updated at this time instance. Thus, all other agents except for those that perform the pairwise averaging operation (3) use their current inner state also for the next time instance. In [48], it is identified that the consensus is achieved, provided that the graph is strongly connected on average. As stated in [26], this algorithm poses a vulnerable and communication-demanding approach.

4.2. Geographic Gossip Algorithm

Another analyzed approach is *GG*, the principle of which lies in the combination of gossiping with geographic routing mechanisms [28]. As in the case of the previous algorithm, at each time instance k, one of the agents is woken up and selects one of the agents from the whole network (except for itself) uniformly at random [26,28]. Subsequently, these two agents perform the pairwise averaging operation (3). Thus, the main idea of this approach is that an agent can perform the pairwise averaging operation with agents further than one hop [28]. Thus, one of the most serious drawbacks of this approach is the necessity to know the geographical information about the agents [26,28]. However, the diversity of pairwise exchanges is significantly increased compared to the previous algorithm whereby data aggregation is assumed to be optimized [26]. In our experiments, we assume the optimal routing, i.e., the messages are always transported to the addressee by the shortest path.

4.3. Broadcast Gossip Algorithm

The next examined algorithm is *BG*, whose principle can be described as follows: at each time instance k, one of the agents (let us refer to it as v_i) is selected uniformly at random [22,26]. Subsequently, this agent broadcasts its current inner states to all its neighbors, which updates their inner states as follows [26]:

$$x_j(k+1) = \gamma x_j(k) + (1-\gamma)x_i(k) \text{ for } \forall j \in \mathcal{N}_i \quad (4)$$

Here, γ is the mixing parameter taking a value from the following interval [26]:

$$\gamma \in (0,1) \quad (5)$$

In our analyses, its value is set to 0.9. The inner state of all the other agents (including the broadcasting one) for the next time instance is determined as follows [26]:

$$x_j(k+1) = x_j(k) \text{ for } \forall j \notin \mathcal{N}_i \quad (6)$$

Thus, this algorithm does not require a pairwise communication whereby it is significantly simplified in contrast to the two previous approaches. However, as shown in [26], the precision of *BG* can be much lower than the precision of concurrent approaches as the inner states may not approach the value of the estimated aggregate function.

4.4. Push-Sum Protocol

In this paper, *PS* is also chosen for evaluation. In this algorithm, every agent has to store and update two variables [47]:

☐ *sum* s_i (initiated with either "1" (leader) or "0" (other agents) when the network size is estimated); and
☐ *weight* w_i (each agent sets its value to "1").

The principle of this algorithm can be described as follows [47]: at each time instance k, each agent in a system selects one of its neighbors uniformly at random and sends it half of its sum and half of its weight, both for the current time instance (we assume that the agents are synchronized; therefore, no collisions may occur while the messages are sent). In addition, the same values are stored in its memory. Each agent v_i can estimate the arithmetic mean (labeled as $x_i(k)$—this parameter is equivalent to the inner states in the other algorithms) at each time instance k as follows:

$$x_i(k) = \frac{s_i(k)}{w_i(k)} \quad (7)$$

The sum s_i for the next time instance (i.e., $s_i(k+1)$) is determined by the sum of all the received sums from other agents at a time instance k with half of its own sum at a time instance k. Analogically, the weight for the next time instance (i.e., $w_i(k+1)$) is equal to the sum of all the received weights from other agents at a time instance k with half of its own weight at a time instance k. As stated in [47], the proper operation of *PS* is ensured, provided that the total system mass is preserved constant. Thus, losing messages causes that algorithm to not operate correctly [34].

4.5. Push-Pull Protocol

The last analyzed algorithm is *PP*, where each agent periodically (i.e., at each time instance k) sends a message containing its current inner state (referred to as a Push message) to one of its neighbors chosen uniformly at random [3,34]. The message receiver answers with its current inner state (a so-called Pull message) so that these two agents can perform the pairwise averaging operation [3,34]. Similar to the previous approach, *PP* is very sensitive to losing messages [34]. Again, the agents are assumed to be synchronized, so no collisions may occur while the messages are sent.

4.6. Comparison of Distributed Gossip Consensus Algorithms with Deterministic Ones

As mentioned above, we focus our attention on the gossip algorithms, where the message receivers are chosen randomly in contrast to the deterministic algorithms. Thus, many parameters of the gossip algorithms vary over the runs—in Figure 6, we provide the evolution of arithmetic mean estimates of the Push-Sum protocol (gossip algorithm) and the Max-Degree weights algorithm (deterministic algorithm) for three independents runs of the algorithms in order to demonstrate differences between these two categories.

The Max-Degree weights algorithm is s a deterministic distributed consensus algorithm operating in synchronous mode [49]. It requires the exact value of the maximum degree of a graph Δ (i.e., the degree of the best-connected agent in MAS) for the proper operation. In this algorithm, this parameter determines the value of the mixing parameter ϵ, i.e., all the graph edges are set to the value of this parameter. The update rule of this algorithm is defined as follows [49]:

$$\mathbf{x}(k+1) = \mathbf{W}(k)\mathbf{x}(k) \quad (8)$$

Here, **W** is the weight matrix of this algorithm, a doubly-stochastic matrix defined as follows [49]:

$$[W]_{ij}^{MD} = \begin{cases} \frac{1}{\Delta}, & \text{if } e_{ij} \in \mathbf{E} \\ 1 - d_i \frac{1}{\Delta}, & \text{if } i = j \\ 0, & \text{otherwise} \end{cases} \quad (9)$$

Here, d_i is the degree of v_i. The principle of this algorithm can be described as follows: at each time instance, each agent broadcasts its current inner states to all its neighbors as well as receiving the inner states from them. Subsequently, it multiplies all received data and its current inner state with the allocated weights (as shown in (9)). The sum of all these values represents its inner state for the next time instance.

Figure 6 shows that the evolution of the estimates is the same for each run in the case of the deterministic Max-Degree weights algorithm, while the estimates may differ in the case of the Push-Sum protocol. In both cases, the estimates, however, approach the value of the arithmetic mean (=3 in this case), which is the most important fact.

In Figure 7, we show the distribution of the convergence rates (a stopping criterion is applied) for 100,000 runs for both algorithms. As seen, the convergence rates are the same for each run in the case of the Max-Degree weights algorithm. However, when the Push-Sum Protocol is applied, the convergence rates may differ from each other for various runs, and the distribution evokes a Gaussian distribution.

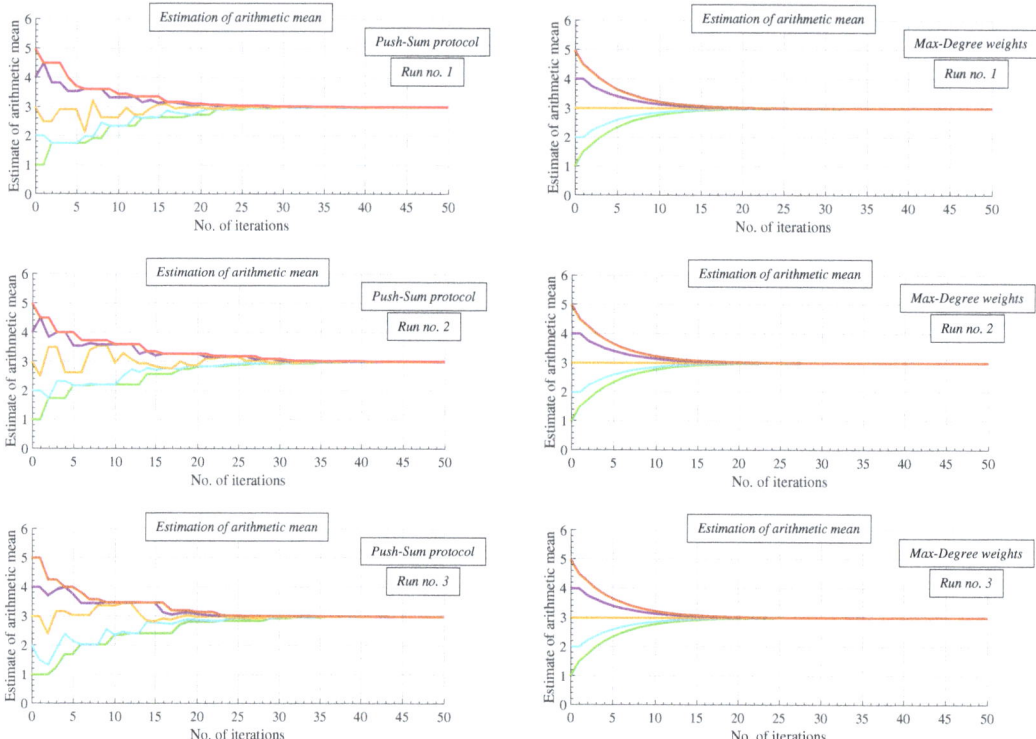

Figure 6. Comparison of gossip Push-Sum protocol with deterministic Max-Degree weights algorithm over three runs—evolution of arithmetic mean estimates.

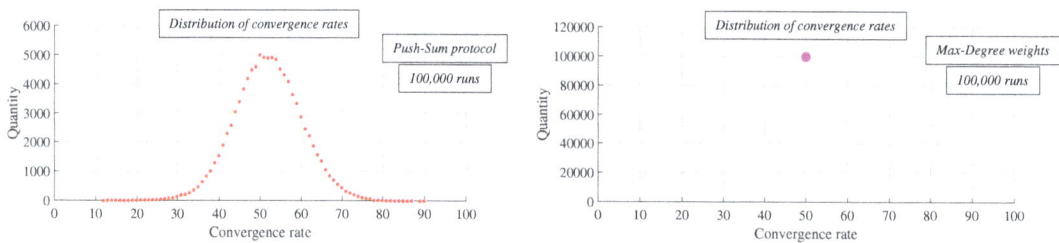

Figure 7. Comparison of gossip Push-Sum protocol with deterministic Max-Degree weights algorithm—distribution of convergence rate over 100,000 runs.

5. Applied Research Methodology

In this section, we draw our attention to the methodology applied in our research and the metrics used to evaluate the performance of the algorithms chosen for an examination.

As mentioned above we carry out two extensive experiments differing from each other in the way to bound the algorithms:

- *Scenario 1:* In this scenario, the value of the current inner states is relevant in the decision about whether or not to stop an algorithm at the current time instance. This stopping criterion is defined in (10), meaning that an algorithm is stopped at the time instance when (10) is met for the first time.

- *Scenario 2*: In the case of applying the other applied stopping criterion, the values of the current network size estimates are checked instead of the inner states. In this scenario, the consensus is considered to be achieved when (11) is met.

The time instance when (10) or (11) is met for the first time is labeled as k_l. Once the conditions (10) and (11) are met, the agents forming MAS are said to have achieved consensus. Thus, the algorithms are completed.

$$| max\{\mathbf{x}(k)\} - min\{\mathbf{x}(k)\} | < P \tag{10}$$

$$| max\{\mathbf{NSE}(k)\} - min\{\mathbf{NSE}(k)\} | < P \tag{11}$$

Here, P is the parameter determining when to stop an algorithm. Its higher values mean that the difference between the inner states/the network size estimates is greater after the consensus is achieved. In our experiments, it takes the following values: $\{0.1, 0.01, 0.001, 0.0001\}$.

In this paragraph, we justify why we choose these two scenarios for evaluation. In Scenario 1, the arithmetic mean is estimated, and then network size estimates are determined by applying (2). Thus, the consensus achievement among the agents is conditioned by the arithmetic mean estimates. In this scenario, the consensus among the agents is achieved, provided that the difference in the absolute value between the maximum and the minimum from all the current arithmetic mean estimates is smaller than the parameter P. Unlike this scenario, consensus achievement is conditioned by the current network size estimates in Scenario 2. Therefore, in this case, consensus among the agents is achieved if the difference in the absolute value between the maximum and the minimum from all the current network size estimates is smaller than the parameter P.

In Figures 8 and 9, we compare RG in both scenarios. The figures show that the algorithm is faster in Scenario 1, but the precision of the final estimates of the network size (the network size is 5 in this case) is lower than in Scenario 2.

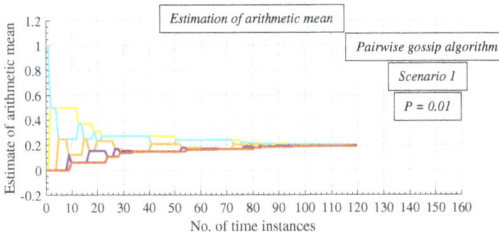 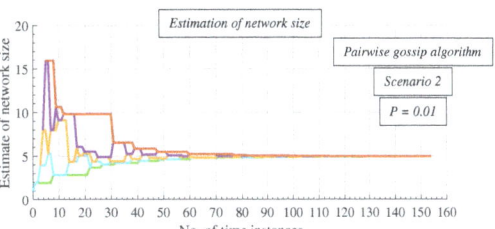

Figure 8. Comparison of evolution of arithmetic mean estimates with evolution of network size estimates—pairwise gossip algorithm is applied.

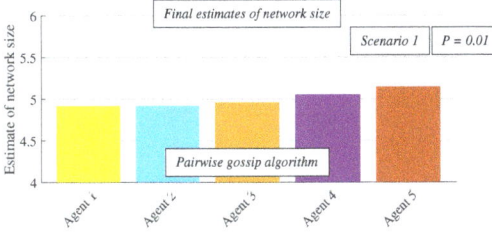 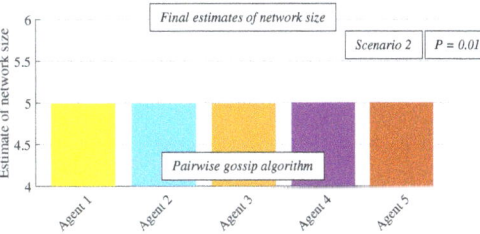

Figure 9. Comparison of final network size estimates in both examined scenarios—pairwise gossip algorithm is applied.

As shown in [50], where distributed deterministic consensus algorithms are analyzed, the selection of the leader can affect the performance of algorithms for the network size estimation. Thus, we carry out two analyses in order to examine the impact of the leader selection on the performance of the examined algorithms:

- ☐ The best-connected agent is the leader.
- ☐ The worst-connected agent is the leader.

To evaluate the performance of the chosen algorithms, we apply two metrics, namely the number of sent messages required for consensus achievement and the median deviation of the final estimates from the real value of the network size. We do not apply the frequently applied metric—the number of time instances for consensus—as the number of sent messages per time instance differs for various algorithms. In the case of RG, two messages are sent at each time instance. When GG is used, the number of sent messages per time instance is equal to twice the distance between the two agents performing the pairwise averaging operation. If BG is applied, the number of sent messages per time instance equals one. In the case of PS, n messages are sent per time instance, and twice n messages are transmitted when PP is used. The precision of estimation is determined as the median deviation of the final estimates of all the agents from the real network size (the median is chosen instead of the average since the final inner state of some agents can be equal to zero whereby their final estimate is NaN). Its formula (for each algorithm same) is defined as follows:

$$Deviation\ of\ estimation = median(\mathbf{NSE}(k_l) - n) \qquad (12)$$

As the algorithms are gossip, both metrics vary over runs; therefore, each algorithm is repeated 100 times in each graph. Subsequently, the median of these values is chosen as a representative of a corresponding metric in a graph.

In addition, as mentioned above, we analyze the algorithms over RGGs—to ensure high credibility of our research, we generate 100 graphs of unique topology each and with the graph order $n = 30$. All generated graphs are connected because the algorithms can be applied to estimating the network size only under this circumstance (in the disconnected graphs, the size of the components is estimated instead of the network size). In Figures 10–13, we show the median of representatives of both metrics over 100 graphs.

In the last experiment, the results of which are shown in Figure 14, each algorithm is repeated 10,000 times in one of the graphs (each algorithm in the same graph) in order to examine the distribution of the number of sent messages required for consensus achievement.

Regarding the value of the mixing parameter γ of BG, we set this value to 0.9 as this configuration ensures the highest estimation precision compared to the other mixing parameters to the nearest tenth.

As shown in [51], the algorithms can also be analyzed by applying the topological distance. This kind of analysis is involved in our future plans.

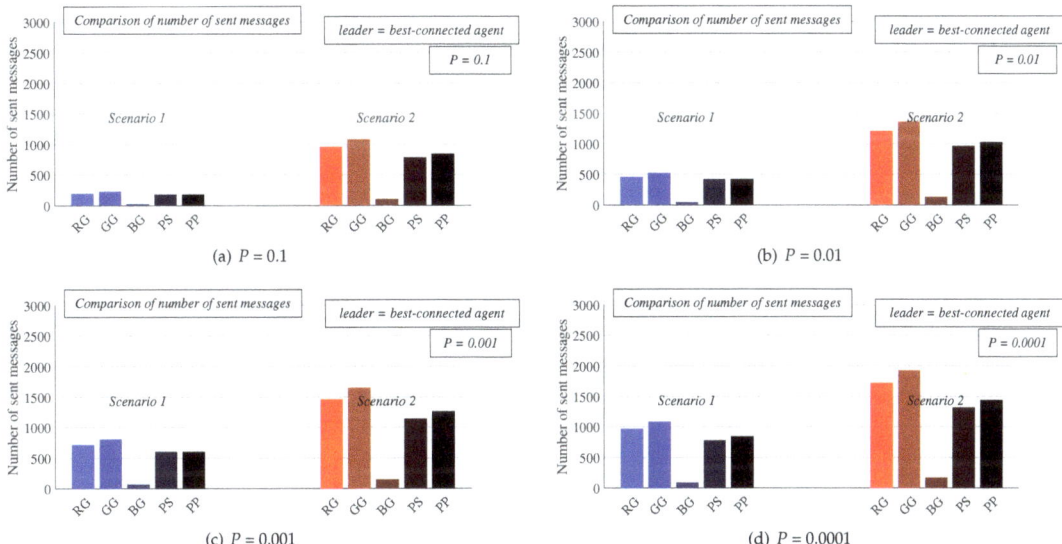

Figure 10. Comparison of the number of sent messages required for consensus achievement of all algorithms in both scenarios for various configurations of implemented stopping criterion—best-connected agent is leader.

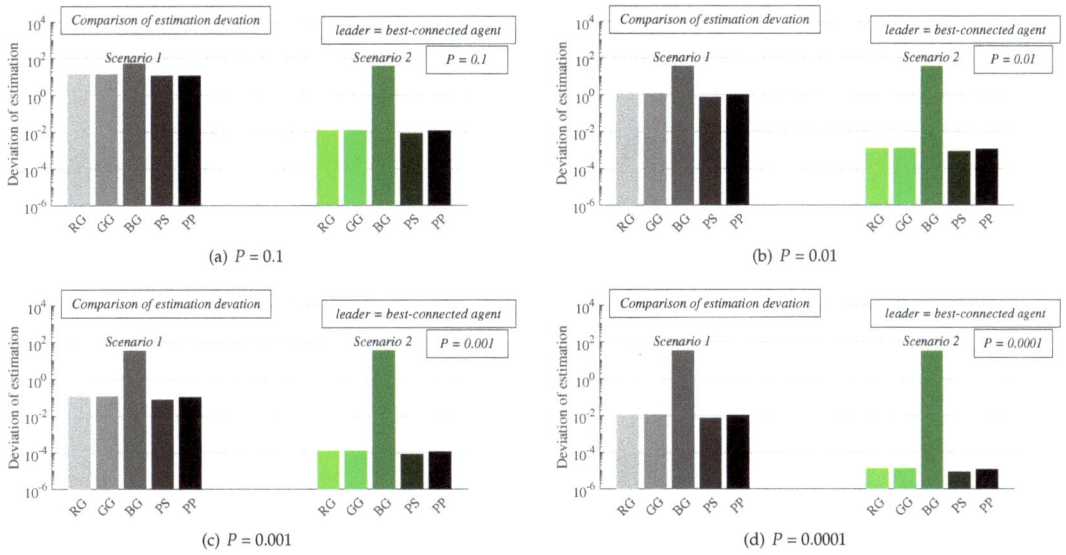

Figure 11. Comparison of the estimation precision of all algorithms in both scenarios for various configurations of implemented stopping criterion—best-connected agent is leader.

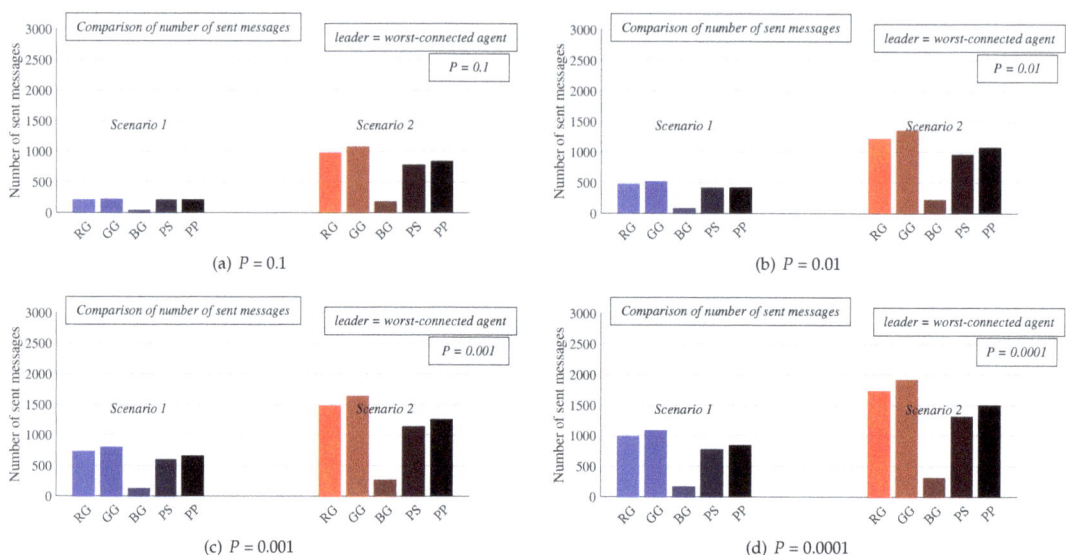

Figure 12. Comparison of the number of sent messages required for consensus achievement of all algorithms in both scenarios for various configurations of implemented stopping criterion—worst-connected agent is leader.

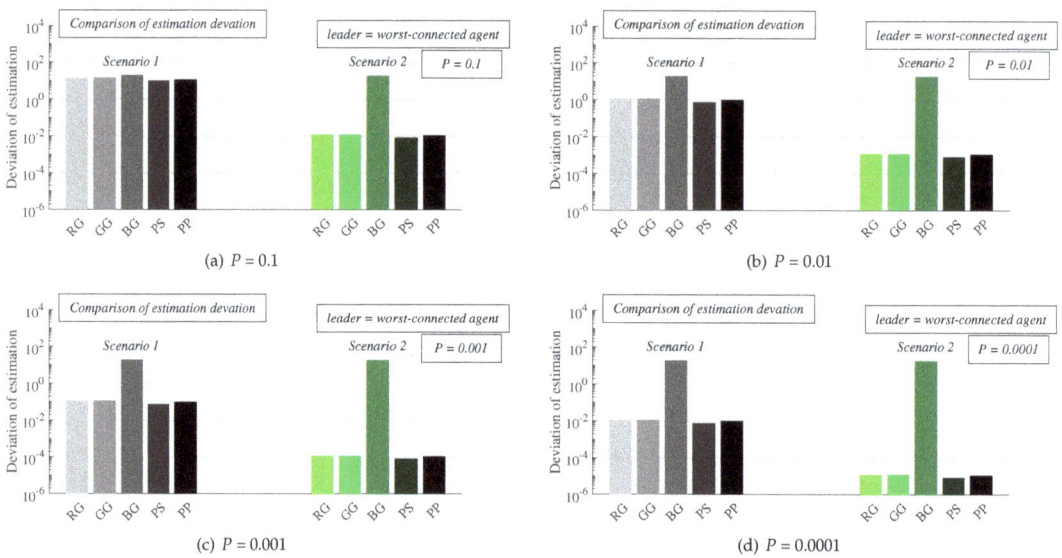

Figure 13. Comparison of the estimation precision of all algorithms in both scenarios for various configurations of implemented stopping criterion—worst-connected agent is leader.

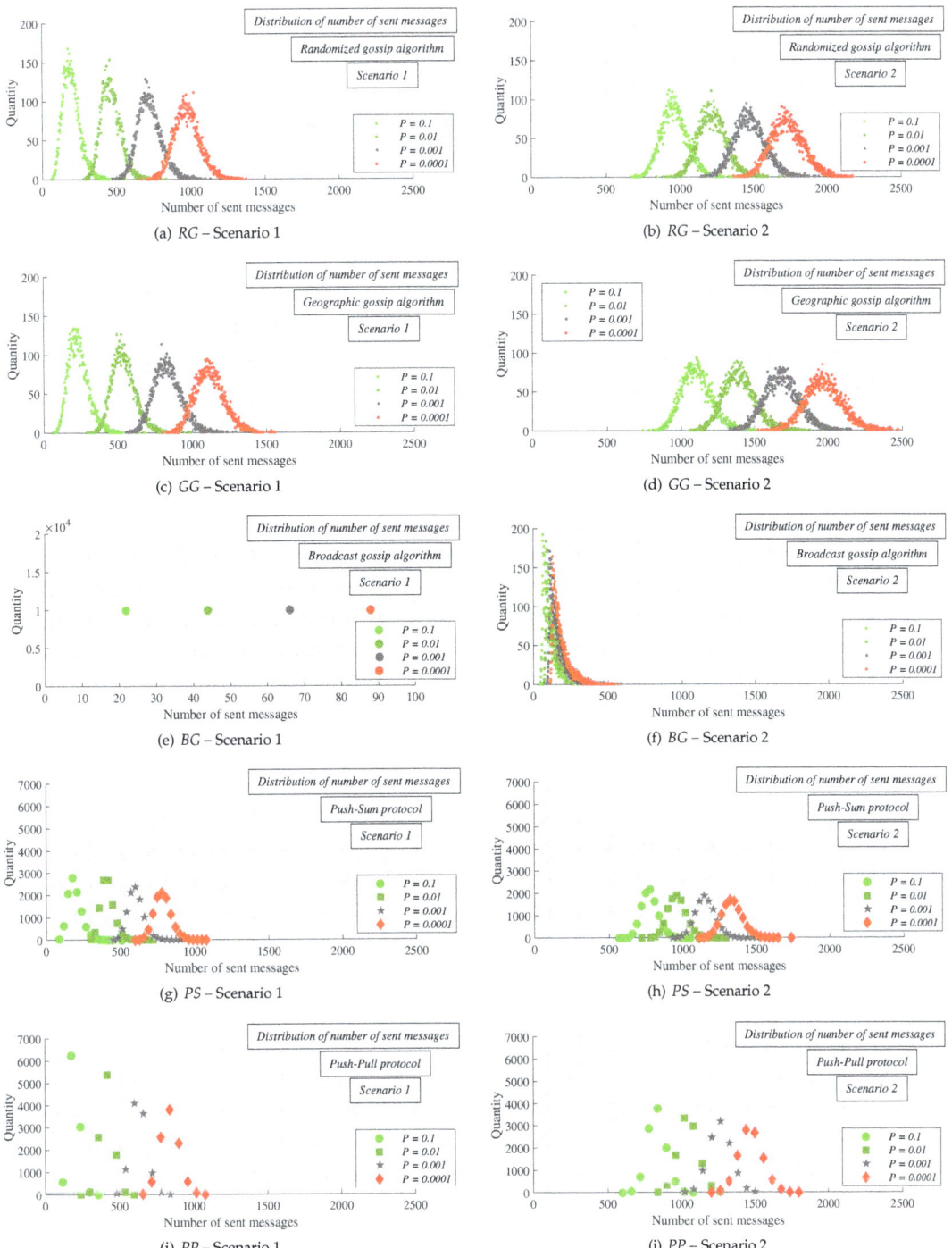

Figure 14. Distribution of number of sent messages in both scenarios for various configurations of implemented stopping criterion and with the best-connected agent as leader.

6. Experiments and Discussion

In this section, we present and discuss the results of numerical experiments executed in Matlab 2018a. We use either software proposed by the authors of this paper or Matlab built-in functions. This section is partitioned into two subsections:

☐ *Experiments*: In this subsection, we present the results from numeral experiments for each examined algorithm. In Figures 10 and 11, we provide the number of sent messages for consensus and the estimation precision, respectively, in both scenarios, for four values of the parameter P, and with the best-connected agent selected as the leader. In Figures 12 and 13, the results obtained in experiments with the worst-connected agent as the leader are provided. In Figure 14, the distribution of the sent messages over 10,000 runs for each algorithm, in both scenarios, for each value of P, and with the best-connected agent selected as the leader is provided.

☐ *Discussion*: In this subsection, we compare the results presented in Section 6.1 with conclusions presented in the papers from Section 2.

6.1. Experiments

In our experiments, we assume that there are no potential failures negatively affecting the execution of the algorithms (e.g., communication breakdowns, deaths of agents, misbehavior of agents, etc.), and the communication is not affected by any noise worsening the quality of the transmitted messages. In addition, all the agents are assumed to be homogenous in the transmission range, communication, computation capabilities, and other aspects affecting the execution of the algorithms.

At first, we focus our attention on an analysis of the number of sent messages in Scenario 1 with the best-connected agent selected as the leader. From the results depicted in Figure 10 (blue bars), it can be seen that a decrease in P results in an increase in the number of sent messages for each analyzed algorithm. Thus, the best performance of all examined algorithms in terms of the number of sent messages is achieved when the value of P is equal to 0.1. In addition, the highest performance is achieved by BG, which significantly outperforms all the other algorithms for each value of P. Besides, a decrease in P has only a marginal impact on the performance of BG in contrast to the other algorithms—the sent messages take the values from this interval $[22, 88]$. In addition, a decrease in P ensures that the difference in the performance between BG and the other algorithms is increased. The second-best performing algorithm is PS followed by PP, the third-best performing algorithm. However, the difference between these two algorithms in the number of sent messages required for consensus is almost negligible except for lower values of P. The sent messages are from the interval $[180, 780]$ in the case of PS and from $[180, 840]$ in the case of PP. Thus, these algorithms require much more messages for consensus than previously discussed BG. The fourth best-performing is RG, the sent messages of which are from the following interval $[193.5, 968]$. The worst performance is achieved by GG, whose sent messages take the following values $[225, 1085]$. Moreover, it is seen that a decrease in P causes that the difference in the performance between these algorithms and the difference between these two algorithms and the others to increase.

As mentioned above, we compare two scenarios determining the way to bound the algorithms in order to identify whether it is better to stop the algorithms according to the current arithmetic mean estimates or the current network size estimates. The results presented in this paragraph and their comparison with those from the previous one help identify the optimal way to bound the algorithms. In the following, we turn our attention to Scenario 2, and the sent messages required for consensus achievement with the best-connected agent selected as the leader are analyzed again. Thus, in this paragraph, we present the results of the same experiments as in the previous one with the difference that the stopping criterion (11) is applied instead of (10). The purpose of this analysis is to identify the optimal way to bound the algorithms. The results for Scenario 2 are shown in Figure 10 (red bars). Again, it is seen that a decrease in P results in an increase in the number of sent messages regardless of the applied algorithm. As in Scenario 1, the best performance is achieved by *BG* (the number of sent messages is from the interval [100.5, 167.5], and the value of *P* has only a marginal impact on the performance of *BG*), the second-best by *PS* ([780, 1320]), the third-best by *PP* ([840, 1440]), the fourth-best by *RG* ([955, 1717]), and the worst performance is achieved by *GG* ([1078, 1923]). Again, a decrease in *P* causes that the difference in the performance between the algorithms to increase. Compared to Scenario 1, the algorithms require many more sent messages for consensus—in the case of *RG*, the difference between Scenario 1 and Scenario 2 in the number of sent messages is around 750 messages, around 840 in the case of *GG*, around 80 when *BC* is applied, around 540 if *PS* is used, and around 630 in the case of *PP*. Moreover, it is observed that the value of *P* has only a marginal impact on the value of this difference.

We next turn the readers' attention to the precision of the network size estimation (see Figure 11). As mentioned above, we quantify this parameter by applying the median deviation defined in (12). At first, we focus on Scenario 1 with the best-connected agent as the leader (grey bars)—from the results, we can see that a decrease in *P* ensures a lower deviation of each analyzed algorithm whereby a higher precision of the final estimates is achieved. In contrast to the previous analyses, the algorithm requiring the lowest number of sent messages for consensus achievement, *BG*, is significantly outperformed by all the four other algorithms. Its deviation is from the range [32.95, 52.25] agents; therefore, its precision is so low that this algorithm is not applicable to estimating the network size for any *P* in Scenario 1. The four other algorithms do not significantly differ from each other in the estimation precision, but their precision is also very low (the median deviation is around 12 agents) for $P = 0.1$. In the case of $P = 0.01$, the median deviation is around one agent, which is a significantly more precise estimation compared to the previous case. Nevertheless, even this configuration is not appropriate for real-world applications requiring the exact value of the network size. Very high precision of the final estimates is achieved in the case of $P = 0.001$ (the median deviation is equal to around 0.1 agents) and $P = 0.0001$ (the median deviation is approximately 0.01 agents). Thus, only these two configurations of the stopping criterion can ensure estimation of the network size with high precision in Scenario 1.

We next focus on the precision of the final estimates in Scenario 2 with the best-connected agent as the leader (see green bars in Figure 11). As seen from the results, a decrease in *P* ensures a higher precision of the final estimates as in Scenario 1. In this scenario, the precision of *BG* is higher (the deviation is from the interval [32.52, 37.66] agents) compared to Scenario 1, but it is still very low. Thus, *BG* is useless in both scenarios and is, therefore, not applicable to estimating the network size at all. Conversely, the precision of the four other algorithms is very high for each *P* in this scenario, and, again, there is no significant difference between these algorithms in terms of the estimation precision. Even for $P = 0.1$, the deviation is low—the median deviation is approximately 0.01 agents. The lowest deviation is achieved for $P = 0.0001$, taking the value around 10^{-5} agent. Thus, the estimation precision is much greater in Scenario 2 than in Scenario 1—except for *BG*, the deviation is about three orders of magnitude lower, and *P* has only a marginal impact on this difference.

In Figures 12 and 13, the same experiments are repeated, but the worst-connected agent is selected as the leader instead of the best-connected one. As seen, the number of sent messages is slightly increased compared to scenarios with the best-connected agent chosen as the leader, while the deviation of the final estimates from the real network size is slightly decreased. However, there is no significant difference in the values of both applied metrics when the worst-connected agent is selected as the leader instead of the best-connected one. As further observed from the results, the most affected algorithms are *RG* and *BG*. Thus, the selection of the leader has only a marginal impact on the performance of distributed consensus gossip algorithms in contrast to deterministic ones, the performance of which is intensively affected by the leader selection, as identified in [50].

In the last part, we analyze the distribution of the number of sent messages—the algorithms are carried out in one of the graphs 10,000 times in both scenarios and for each value of P as mentioned above. Since the number of sent messages is only marginally affected by the leader selection, we carry out only Scenario 1 (i.e., with the best-connected agent selected as the leader). The goal of this experiment is to identify how the number of sent messages differs over various runs of the algorithms. From the results shown in Figure 14, we can see that the number of sent messages in the cases of RG (Figure 14a,b) and GG (Figure 14c,d) has a Gaussian distribution in both scenarios and for each P. In addition, this distribution is slightly skewed to the right in all four figures. In addition, the data in each figure are more spread as the value of P is decreased. The next analyzed algorithm is BG (Figure 14e,f), in which case we can see an interesting phenomenon—the number of sent messages does no differ over various runs in Scenario 1. Such behavior is usually observed when a distributed deterministic consensus algorithm is analyzed (Figure 7). However, in Scenario 2, the data differ for various runs as in the case of the two previous algorithms and has a significantly right-skewed Gaussian distribution. As in the cases of the two previously analyzed algorithms, a decrease in P causes that data are more spread, but not as significantly as in the cases of RG and GG. Finally, the two remaining algorithms, PS and PP (see Figure 14g–j), are analyzed. It can be seen in the figures that the data of both algorithms have a Gaussian distribution, again with right skewness. Compared to RG and GG, the data do not vary for various runs as significantly as in the case of the first two analyzed algorithms. Again, as in the case of the three previous algorithms, lower values of P result in greater data dispersion.

6.2. Discussion

In this section, we discuss the results presented in Section 6.1 and compare them with those from Section 2 in order to compare the examined algorithms for distributed averaging with their application to distributed network size estimation.

As shown in [23–29], BG outperforms RG and GG in terms of numerous various metrics. However, in [26], it is identified that the error of BG cannot drop below a threshold value whereby BG is outperformed by RG and GG for a higher number of time instances. This fact causes that BG requires the lowest number of sent messages for consensus achievement (significantly lower than the other algorithms), but its estimation precision is so low that this algorithm cannot be applied to estimating the network size—very low precision is achieved in all our experiments. Thus, a high convergence rate of BG at the cost of lower estimation precision can be beneficial if the arithmetic mean is estimated. However, in the case of network size estimation, its low precision makes this algorithm inapplicable to estimating the network size. Furthermore, it is shown in many papers that GG performs better than RG in numerous scenarios. However, in our analyses, GG requires the most sent messages for consensus achievement and thus is worse for network size estimation than RG. In GG, many redundant messages are often transmitted as two agents many hops away from one another with zero inner states perform the pairwise averaging operation (3). In our experiments, it is identified that these two algorithms achieve high precision in general and therefore can be used to estimate the network size in real-world systems.

As shown above, a comparison of PS and PP both for distributed averaging is provided in [30–33]. Generally, it is identified that PS outperforms PP except for several scenarios. In addition, the application of these algorithms to estimating network size is discussed in [30,34,37–42], but a comprehensive analysis is provided in none of them. In our research, it is identified that there is no significant difference between these two algorithms (PS performs a bit better), their precision is high in general, and they require fewer messages for consensus than RG and GG.

In addition, our research identifies that the selection of the leader has only a marginal impact on the performance of all the five algorithms. According to the presented results, we can conclude that the best-performing algorithm for network size estimation is PS, which requires the second-lowest number of sent messages for consensus, and its estimation precision is very high (except for cases when P takes high values in Scenario 1). The best performance of all the four applicable algorithms is achieved for $P = 0.001$ in Scenario 1, where the estimation precision is high, and the number of sent messages is lower than in Scenario 2 or in Scenario 1 with $P = 0.0001$. It is further identified that the precision in Scenario 2 is much higher than in Scenario 1 but at the cost of a significant increase in the number of sent messages.

7. Conclusions

In this paper, we analyze five frequently cited distributed consensus gossip algorithms (RG, GG, BG with $\gamma = 0.9$, PS, and PP), which are bounded by a stopping criterion determined by the parameter P, for minor application—distributed network size estimation. We analyze their performance over RGGs in two scenarios—the consensus achievement is conditioned by either the inner states (Scenario 1) or the network size estimates (Scenario 2). Besides, in both scenarios, either the best-connected or the worst-connected agent is selected as the leader. From the results presented in Section 6.1, it can be seen that a decrease in P ensures higher estimation precision of every analyzed algorithm, however, at the cost of an increase in the number of sent messages for consensus in both scenarios. The lowest number of sent messages for consensus is required by BG, but the precision of this algorithm is very low. Thus, this algorithm is not applicable to estimating the network size in any of the analyzed scenarios. All four other algorithms achieve high precision except for two configurations of the applied stopping criterion: $P = 0.1$ in Scenario 1 and $P = 0.01$ in Scenario 1. Overall, the best performance is achieved by PS, whose precision is the highest (a bit greater than the precision of RG, GG, and PP), and the number of sent messages is the second-lowest among the examined algorithms. In addition, we identify that the algorithms are more precise in Scenario 2 but require many more sent messages for consensus than in Scenario 1. Besides, it is shown that the selection of the leader has only a marginal impact on all the analyzed algorithms. Regarding the distribution of the sent messages, all the examined algorithms have a Gaussian distribution skewed to the right except for BG in Scenario 1, where the number of sent messages does not differ over runs. Moreover, it is identified that lower values of P cause a greater dispersion. According to the presented results and their analysis, we conclude that the best performance for all the four applicable algorithms is achieved for $P = 0.001$ in Scenario 1. Thus, this configuration is recommended by us for real-world systems.

Author Contributions: Conceptualization, M.K. and J.K.; methodology, M.K.; software, M.K.; validation, M.K., and J.K.; formal analysis, M.K. and J.K.; investigation, M.K.; resources, M.K.; data curation, M.K. and J.K.; writing—original draft preparation, M.K.; writing—review and editing, M.K. and J.K.; visualization, M.K.; supervision, J.K.; project administration, M.K.; and funding acquisition, M.K. All authors have read and agreed to the published version of the manuscript.

Funding: This work was supported by the VEGA agency under the contract No. 2/0155/19 and by the project CHIST ERA III (SOON) "Social Network of Machines". Since 2019, Martin Kenyeres has been a holder of the Stefan Schwarz Supporting Fund.

Data Availability Statement: The data presented in this study are available on request from the corresponding author.

Acknowledgments: We would like to thank the anonymous reviewers of this paper for their supportive and insightful comments.

Conflicts of Interest: The authors declare no conflict of interest.

Abbreviations

The following abbreviations are used in this manuscript:

BG	Broadcast gossip algorithm
GG	Geographic gossip algorithm
MAS	Multi-agent system
NaN	Not a Number
PP	Push-Pull protocol
PS	Push-Sum protocol
RG	Randomized gossip algorithm
RGG	Random geometric graph

References

1. Zheng, Y.; Zhao, Q.; Ma, J.; Wang, L. Second-order consensus of hybrid multi-agent systems. *Syst. Control Lett.* **2019**, *125*, 51–58. [CrossRef]
2. McArthur, S.; Davidson, E.M.; Catterson, V.M.; Dimeas, A.L.; Hatziargyriou, N.D.; Ponci, F.; Funabashi, T. Multi-agent systems for power engineering applications—Part I: Concepts, approaches, and technical challenges. *IEEE Trans. Power Syst.* **2007**, *22*, 1743–1752. [CrossRef]
3. Shames, I.; Charalambous, T.; Hadjicostis, C.N.; Johansson, M. Distributed Network Size Estimation and Average Degree Estimation and Control in Networks Isomorphic to Directed Graphs. In Proceedings of the 50th Annual Allerton Conference on Communication, Control, and Computing, Allerton, Monticello, IL, USA, 1–5 October 2012; pp. 1885–1892.
4. Seda, P.; Seda, M.; Hosek, J. On Mathematical Modelling of Automated Coverage Optimization in Wireless 5G and beyond Deployments. *Appl. Sci.* **2020**, *10*, 8853. [CrossRef]
5. Wooldridge, M.; Jennings, N.R. Intelligent agents: Theory and practice. *Knowl. Eng. Rev.* **1995**, *10*, 115–152. [CrossRef]
6. Dorri, A.; Kanhere, S.S.; Jurdak, R. Multi-Agent Systems: A Survey. *IEEE Access* **2018**, *6*, 28573–28593. [CrossRef]
7. Rocha, J.; Boavida-Portugal, I.; Gomes, E. Introductory Chapter: Multi-Agent Systems. In *Multi-Agent Systems*; IntechOpen: Rijeka, Croatia, 2017.
8. Li, M.; Zhang, X. Information fusion in a multi-source incomplete information system based on information entropy. *Entropy* **2017**, *19*, 570. [CrossRef]
9. Castanedo, F. A review of data fusion techniques. *Sci. World J.* **2013**, *2013*, 704504. [CrossRef]
10. Skorpil, V.; Stastny, J. Back-propagation and k-means algorithms comparison. In Proceedings of the 2006 8th International Conference on Signal Processing, ICSP 2006, Guilin, China, 16–20 November 2006; pp. 374–378.
11. Zacchigna, F.G.; Lutenberg, A. A novel consensus algorithm proposal: Measurement estimation by silent agreement (MESA). In Proceedings of the 5th Argentine Symposium and Conference on Embedded Systems, SASE/CASE 2014, Buenos Aires, Argentina, 13–15 August 2014; pp. 7–12.
12. Zacchigna, F.G.; Lutenberg, A.; Vargas, F. MESA: A formal approach to compute consensus in WSNs. In Proceedings of the 6th Argentine Conference on Embedded Systems, CASE 2015, Buenos Aires, Argentina, 12–14 August 2015; pp. 13–18.
13. Merezeanu, D.; Nicolae, M. Consensus control of discrete-time multi-agent systems. *U. Politeh. Buch. Ser. A* **2017**, *79*, 167–174.
14. Antal, C.; Cioara, T.; Anghel, I.; Antal, M.; Salomie, I. Distributed Ledger Technology Review and Decentralized Applications Development Guidelines. *Future Int.* **2021**, *13*, 62. [CrossRef]
15. Merezeanu, D.; Vasilescu, G.; Dobrescu, R. Context-aware control platform for sensor network integration. *Stud. Inform. Control* **2016**, *25*, 489–498. [CrossRef]
16. Vladyko, A.; Khakimov, A.; Muthanna, A.; Ateya, A.A.; Koucheryavy, A. Distributed Edge Computing to Assist Ultra-Low-Latency VANET Applications. *Future Int.* **2019**, *11*, 128. [CrossRef]
17. Xiao, L.; Boyd, S.; Lall, S. A Scheme for robust distributed sensor fusion based on average consensus. In Proceedings of the 4th International Symposium on Information Processing in Sensor Networks, IPSN 2005, Los Angeles, CA, USA, 25–27 April 2005; pp. 63–70.
18. Hlinka, O.; Sluciak, O.; Hlawatsch, F.; Djuric, P.M.; Rupp, M. Likelihood consensus and its application to distributed particle filtering. *IEEE Trans. Signal Process.* **2012**, *60*, 4334–4349. [CrossRef]
19. Xiao, L.; Boyd, S. Fast linear iterations for distributed averaging. *Syst. Control. Lett.* **2004**, *53*, 65–78. [CrossRef]
20. Mahmoud, M.S.; Oyedeji, M.O.; Xia, Y. *Advanced Distributed Consensus for Multiagent Systems*; Academic Press: Cambridge, MA, USA, 2020.
21. Kenyeres, M.; Kenyeres, J. Average consensus over mobile wireless sensor networks: Weight matrix guaranteeing convergence without reconfiguration of edge weights. *Sensors* **2020**, *20*, 3677. [CrossRef]
22. Gutierrez-Gutierrez, J.; Zarraga-Rodriguez, M.; Insausti, X. Analysis of Known Linear Distributed Average Consensus Algorithms on Cycles and Paths. *Sensors* **2018**, *18*, 968. [CrossRef] [PubMed]

23. Yu, J.Y.; Rabbat, M. Performance comparison of randomized gossip, broadcast gossip and collection tree protocol for distributed averaging. In Proceedings of the 5th IEEE International Workshop on Computational Advances in Multi-Sensor Adaptive Processing, CAMSAP 2013, Montreal, QC, Canada, 15–18 December 2013; pp. 93–96.
24. Liu, Z.W.; Guan, Z.H.; Li, T.; Zhang, X.H.; Xiao, J.W. Quantized consensus of multi-agent systems via broadcast gossip algorithms. *Asian J. Control* **2012**, *14*, 1634–1642. [CrossRef]
25. Baldi, M.; Chiaraluce, F.; Zanaj, E. Performance of gossip algorithms in wireless sensor networks. *Lect. Notes Electr. Eng.* **2011**, *81*, 3–16.
26. Aysal, T.C.; Yildiz, M.E.; Sarwate, A.D.; Scaglione, A. Broadcast gossip algorithms for consensus. *IEEE Trans. Signal Process.* **2009**, *57*, 2748–2761. [CrossRef]
27. Aysal, T.C.; Yildiz, M.E.; Sarwate, A.D.; Scaglione, A. Broadcast gossip algorithms. In Proceedings of the IEEE Information Theory Workshop, ITW, Porto, Portugal, 5–9 May 2008; pp. 343–347.
28. Dimakis, A.A.G.; Sarwate, A.D.; Wainwright, M.J.; Scaglione, A. Geographic gossip: Efficient averaging for sensor networks. *IEEE Trans. Signal Process.* **2008**, *56*, 1205–1216. [CrossRef]
29. Aysal, T.C.; Yildiz, M.E.; Sarwate, A.D.; Scaglione, A. Broadcast gossip algorithms: Design and analysis for consensus. In Proceedings of the 47th IEEE Conference on Decision and Control, CDC 2008, Cancun, Mexico, 9–11 December 2008; pp. 4843–4848.
30. Jesus, P.; Baquero, C.; Almeida, P.S. Dependability in Aggregation by Averaging. *arXiv* **2010**, arXiv:1011.6596.
31. Jesus, P.; Baquero, C.; Almeida, P.S. A study on aggregation by averaging algorithms (poster). In Proceedings of the EuroSys 2007–2nd EuroSys Conference, Lisbon, Portugal, 21–23 March 2007; p. 1.
32. Blasa, F.; Cafiero, S.; Fortino, G.; Di Fatta, G. Symmetric push-sum protocol for decentralised aggregation. In Proceedings of the 3rd International Conference on Advances in P2P Systems, AP2PS 2011, Lisbon, Portugal, 20–25 November 2011; pp. 27–32.
33. Huang, W.; Wang, Y.; Provan, G. Comparing Asynchronous Distributed Averaging Gossip Algorithms over Scale-free Graphs. Available online: http://www.cs.ucc.ie/~gprovan/Provan/comparegossip.pdf (accessed on 16 May 2021).
34. Cardoso, J.C.S.; Baquero, C.; Almeida, P.S. Probabilistic Estimation of Network Size and Diameter. In Proceedings of the 4th Latin-American Symposium on Dependable Computing, LADC 2009, Joao Pessoa, Brazil, 1–4 September 2009; pp. 33–40.
35. García-Magariño, I.; Palacios-Navarro, G.; Lacuesta, R.; Lloret, J. ABSCEV: An agent-based simulation framework about smart transportation for reducing waiting times in charging electric vehicles. *Comput. Netw.* **2018**, *138*, 119–135. [CrossRef]
36. García-Magariño, I.; Sendra, S.; Lacuesta, R.; Lloret, J. Security in Vehicles with IoT by Prioritization Rules, Vehicle Certificates, and Trust Management. *IEEE Internet Things J.* **2019**, *6*, 5927–5934. [CrossRef]
37. Baquero, C.; Almeida, P.S.; Menezes, R.; Jesus, P. Extrema Propagation: Fast Distributed Estimation of Sums and Network Sizes. *IEEE Trans. Parallel Distrib. Syst.* **2012**, *23*, 668–675. [CrossRef]
38. Kennedy, O.; Koch, C.; Demers, A. Dynamic Approaches to In-Network Aggregation. In Proceedings of the 25th IEEE International Conference on Data Engineering, ICDE 2009, Shanghai, China, 29 March–2 April 2009; pp. 1331–1334.
39. Jesus, P.; Baquero, C.; Almeida, P.S. A Survey of Distributed Data Aggregation Algorithms. *IEEE Commun. Surveys Tuts.* **2015**, *17*, 381–404. [CrossRef]
40. Nyers, L.; Jelasity, M. A comparative study of spanning tree and gossip protocols for aggregation. *Concurr. Comp.* **2015**, *27*, 4091–4106. [CrossRef]
41. Nyers, L.; Jelasity, M. Spanning tree or gossip for aggregation: A comparative study. In Proceedings of the European Conference on Parallel Processing, Euro-Par 2014, Porto, Portugal, 25–29 August 2014; pp. 379–390.
42. Nyers, L.; Jelasity, M. A practical approach to network size estimation for structured overlays. *Lect. Notes Comput. Sci.* **2008**, *5343*, 71–83.
43. Fraser, B.; Coyle, A.; Hunjet, R.; Szabo, C. An Analytic Latency Model for a Next-Hop Data-Ferrying Swarm on Random Geometric Graphs. *IEEE Access* **2020**, *8*, 48929–48942. [CrossRef]
44. Gulzar, M.M.; Rizvi, S.T.H.; Javed, M.Y.; Munir, U.; Asif, H. Multi-agent cooperative control consensus: A comparative review. *Electronics* **2018**, *7*, 22. [CrossRef]
45. Qurashi, M.A.; Angelopoulos, C.M.; Katos, V.; Munir, U.; Asif, H. An Architecture for Resilient Intrusion Detection in IoT Networks. In Proceedings of the 2020 IEEE International Conference on Communications, ICC 2020, Dublin, Ireland, 7–11 June 2020; pp. 1–7.
46. Mustafa, A.; Islam, M.N.U.; Ahmed, S. Dynamic Spectrum Sensing under Crash and Byzantine Failure Environments for Distributed Convergence in Cognitive Radio Networks. *IEEE Access* **2021**, *9*, 23153–23167. [CrossRef]
47. Kempe, D.; Dobra, A.; Gehrke, J. Gossip-based computation of aggregate information. In Proceedings of the 44th Annual IEEE Symposium on Foundations of Computer Science, FOCS 2003, Cambridge, MA, USA, 11–14 October 2003; pp. 482–491.
48. Boyd, S.; Ghosh, A.; Prabhakar, B.; Shah, D. Randomized gossip algorithms. *IEEE Trans. Inf. Theory* **2006**, *52*, 2508–2530. [CrossRef]
49. Avrachenkov, K.; Chamie, M.E.; Neglia, G. A local average consensus algorithm for wireless sensor networks. In Proceedings of the 7th IEEE International Conference on Distributed Computing in Sensor Systems, DCOSS'11, Barcelona, Spain, 27–29 June 2011; pp. 1–6.
50. Kenyeres, M.; Kenyeres, J.; Budinska, I. On Performance Evaluation of Distributed System Size Estimation Executed by Average Consensus Weights. *Fuzziness Soft Comput.* **2021**, *403*, 15–24.
51. Shang, Y.; Bouffanais, R. Consensus reaching in swarms ruled by a hybrid metric-topological distance. *Eur. Phys. J. B* **2014**, *87*, 1–7. [CrossRef]

 future internet

Article

Architecting an Agent-Based Fault Diagnosis Engine for IEC 61499 Industrial Cyber-Physical Systems

Barry Dowdeswell *, Roopak Sinha and Stephen G. MacDonell

Department of Computer Science and Software Engineering School of Engineering, Computer and Mathematical Sciences, Auckland University of Technology, Private Bag 92006, Auckland 1142, New Zealand; roopak.sinha@aut.ac.nz (R.S.); stephen.macdonell@aut.ac.nz (S.G.M.)
* Correspondence: barry.dowdeswell@aut.ac.nz

Abstract: IEC 61499 is a reference architecture for constructing Industrial Cyber-Physical Systems (ICPS). However, current function block development environments only provide limited fault-finding capabilities. There is a need for comprehensive diagnostic tools that help engineers identify faults, both during development and after deployment. This article presents the software architecture for an agent-based fault diagnostic engine that equips agents with domain-knowledge of IEC 61499. The engine encourages a Model-Driven Development with Diagnostics methodology where agents work alongside engineers during iterative cycles of design, development, diagnosis and refinement. Attribute-Driven Design (ADD) was used to propose the architecture to capture fault telemetry directly from the ICPS. A Views and Beyond Software Architecture Document presents the architecture. The Architecturally-Significant Requirement (ASRs) were used to design the views while an Architectural Trade-off Analysis Method (ATAM) evaluated critical parts of the architecture. The agents locate faults during both early-stage development and later provide long-term fault management. The architecture introduces dynamic, low-latency software-in-loop Diagnostic Points (DPs) that operate under the control of an agent to capture fault telemetry. Using sound architectural design approaches and documentation methods, coupled with rigorous evaluation and prototyping, the article demonstrates how quality attributes, risks and architectural trade-offs were identified and mitigated early before the construction of the engine commenced.

Citation: Dowdeswell, B.; Sinha, R.; MacDonell, S.G. Architecting an Agent-Based Fault Diagnosis Engine for IEC 61499 Industrial Cyber-Physical Systems. *Future Internet* **2021**, *13*, 190. https://doi.org/10.3390/fi13080190

Academic Editors: Agostino Poggi, Ivana Budinská, Martin Kenyeres and Ladislav Hluchy

Received: 29 June 2021
Accepted: 16 July 2021
Published: 23 July 2021

Publisher's Note: MDPI stays neutral with regard to jurisdictional claims in published maps and institutional affiliations.

Copyright: © 2021 by the authors. Licensee MDPI, Basel, Switzerland. This article is an open access article distributed under the terms and conditions of the Creative Commons Attribution (CC BY) license (https://creativecommons.org/licenses/by/4.0/).

Data Set: 10.17632/5skpwjh3sw.2

Data Set License: CC BY 4.0

Keywords: industrial cyber-physical systems; IEC 61499; function blocks; quality-driven architectures; fault diagnostics; multi-agent systems

1. Introduction

Embedded Control Systems (ECSs), augmented with communications and sophisticated sensors, have led to the development of powerful new mechanisms known as Industrial-scale Cyber-Physical Systems (ICPS). ICPS control their electro-mechanical parts by using on-board processors and transducers, the sensors and mechanical actuators that enable them to sense and interact with their physical environment. This blending of their "cyber" software parts and their "physical" mechanical and environmental aspects extends them beyond the capabilities of earlier generations of ECSs. It is at this intersection, not the union, between the cyber and the physical that we must understand these entities more deeply [1].

This paper presents the software architecture of our Fault Diagnostic Engine, referred to in this paper as *"the engine"*.

The scale, diversity and complexity of ICPS used in transportation, medical and manufacturing systems demands innovative approaches to fault diagnostics. The engine is a stand-alone, multi-platform application that can identify and diagnose faults in applications created with IEC 61499 Function Blocks (FBs) [2]. The architecture employs software agents that are hosted within the GORITE (Goal ORIented TEams) Multi-Agent Framework [3–5]. The Belief-Desire-Intention (BDI) paradigm embodied in GORITE allows teams of agents to respond to changes in the FBs under examination, adopting a range of analysis strategies when faults are uncovered.

Current IEC 61499 Integrated Development Environments (IDEs) have limited design-time fault-finding capabilities. While some IDEs allow single FBs to be exercised, sets of connected blocks cannot be diagnosed together [6,7]. Engineers need to be able to quickly build semi-automated fault identification capabilities that can be reused throughout the life-cycle of an IEC 61499 Function Block application (FB application). The engine described here addresses that need by facilitating a Model-Driven Development with Diagnostics methodology that supports engineers while they are creating or reusing FBs to construct their ICPS with IEC 61499 [8].

This paper focuses primarily on the architectural design of the software agents and the way in which they have been provided with domain-specific knowledge of IEC 61499. This equips them with the abilities they need to interact with FB applications that are operating nominally, are failing, or have failed. GORITE provides a framework upon which to create new agent designs, but it does not include templates of pre-built agents. The architectural design of the agents, their skills and beliefs was therefore framed by four research questions:

RQ1: *How do we equip an agent with the ability to distinguish between normal function block activities and misbehaviour that indicates that a fault may have occurred?* A scoping survey on industrial-scale fault diagnostics for ICPS was published before the architectural design commenced [9]. This examined fault identification and diagnostic techniques across a range of domains where robust fault management has become critical. The findings that relate to the design of the engine are discussed in Section 2, including the underlying concepts of ICPS, function blocks, faults and agents.

RQ2: *How do we architect a software agent to observe the data that is flowing between function blocks so that it can recognise fault evidence?* Agents exhibit intentional behaviors that enable them to pursue goals and make decisions that modify their actions. To reason about faults, agents need to be able to capture information flowing between FBs. Section 3.4 explores the Diagnostic Point (DPs) that are a key feature of the engine, explaining how the agents autonomously deploy these custom FBs into an FB application to capture real-time fault telemetry.

RQ3: *How can a fault diagnostic engine that implements the features identified in RQ1 and RQ2 be architected?* Section 3 profiles the architecture in detail, showing how the Views and Beyond methodology [10] was used to guide and document the design.

RQ4: *How do we evaluate the architectural decisions made to satisfy RQ1 and RQ2?* The ATAM evaluation and the prototyping of key parts of the engine are discussed in Section 4. These processes refined both the agents themselves and the way they exchange information with the FBs being examined. This led to a more robust and versatile architecture. The ATAM presents scenarios that show how the features of the architecture satisfy both the functional and quality requirements for the engine. It demonstrates how the risks, sensitivities and trade-offs uncovered drove the architectural design choices that were made.

This paper illustrates how Attribute-Driven Design (ADD) [11] and the Views and Beyond methodology were coupled with prototyping to architect the engine through iterative design steps. By creating a range of complementary artefacts that present features as distinct *views*, architects make it easier for stakeholders to understand the reasons why features should be implemented in the ways proposed. Thinking about non-functional requirements as Quality Attributes (QAs) that can be evaluated empirically led to the creation of a more robust architecture. The complete Software Architecture Document (SAD) is available on Mendeley Data [12] to complement the exploration of the architecture presented in this article. Each recommended section of the Views and Beyond document template was carefully replicated as an exemplar to help other practitioners. The resulting document illustrates the scope and maturity of ADD and Views and Beyond, which has continued to guide the on-going development of the engine.

The primary contribution of this paper is its presentation of the architecture for a fault detection engine in a well-structured Software Architecture Document that draws on recognized industry standards. It describes the way the agents apply domain-specific knowledge during fault finding for ICPS. When agents are deployed by the engine, they first explore the IEC 61499 application definition files of the ICPS that will be diagnosed. They then build sets of beliefs about the FBs and how they are connected to each other. This creates a navigable in-memory representation of the FB application that captures what they believe. This later guides their search through fault paths while they determine if each FB is performing nominally. The agents deploy DPs by wiring them dynamically into the data and event streams of a FB. Each DP operates as a native FB, passing data transparently through itself while also relaying that data back to the agent that is monitoring the DP. When commanded by an agent, sets of DPs can isolate or *gate* sections of the FB application. The agents then examine either individual or logical groups of FBs that are exhibiting fault symptoms, exercising them with pre-defined diagnostic tests. The DPs exhibit low-latency and impose a minimal overhead on the FB application. This approach illustrates how agents can dynamically investigate systems, reconfiguring the control layer from the agent's execution layer. This represents a significant enhancement of the interaction scheme employed in Kalachev et al. [13], Jarvis et al. [14] and Christensen [15]. In their approaches, execution layer agents only initiated function block controlled actions. Our approach was chosen to satisfy the quality attributes that the presence of DPs should not adversely impact the normal operation of the individual FBs. Hence, the agents are responsible for managing the fault-finding activities while the primary role of the DPs is to gather telemetry and inject test values into function blocks.

2. Background

The design of fault diagnostic engines has to address many of the challenges common to ICPSs [16]. By the start of the 1960s, the first general-purpose ECSs had been developed for General Motors' automotive assembly lines [17,18]. Referred to as Programmable Logic Controllers (PLCs), they controlled individual machines in isolation. Industrial plants rapidly became *systems-of-systems* [19], with connected production planning and management that demanded up-to-date information from the factory floor. Increasingly sophisticated manufacturing processes required more complex PLC capabilities. However, connecting multiple PLCs together and co-ordinating them was in itself complex. The term Cyber-Physical System (CPS) originated in the work of Bagheti and Gill in 2006 to describe the new device architectures that were emerging to network devices together to better control their environments [20]. As the scale of CPS architectures expanded, the term Industrial Cyber-Physical System (ICPS) was adopted to distinguish them from simpler consumer CPSs [21].

ICPSs bridge the divide between their "cyber" computational parts and their "physical" real-world environments. At this boundary, the discrete behavior of computational programs has to co-exist with the non-discrete, time-critical behaviors that drive real-world activities [22]. Figure 1 shows a typical entity in an ICPS, a Franka Emika Panda Collaborative Robot [23]. Collaborative Robots or "cobots" often share production line assembly operations with humans. Cobots perform a wide range of pre-programmed tasks but can autonomously modify their behavior in real-time. They detect the presence of nearby objects in their work area and capture feedback from their environment. They make control decisions, often exchanging telemetry over networks. Sensors convert physical characteristics such as orientation, proximity and velocity into electrical signals that can be processed by their control computers [24].

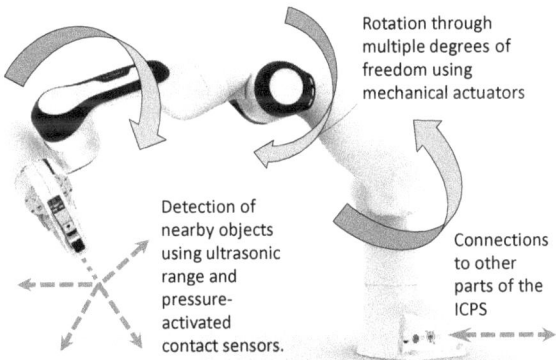

Figure 1. A Franka Emika Panda Collaborative Robot operating as part of an ICPS.

Mechanical actuators are transducers that enable an ICPS to move physical objects in its environment [1]. Motors are special classes of actuators that create translational or rotational movement. They allow cobots to rotate through multiple degrees of freedom with high precision. At all times, cobots have to honor hazard prevention protocols when working in close collaboration with humans or other cobots. This ability to operate in safety-critical environments is a core requirement demanded of many ICPSs. Alur comments that the emergence of distributed ICPSs and CPSs is far more ubiquitous [25]. The same cyber-physical concepts that implement large-scale ICPSs also apply to smaller, less complex consumer and medical CPSs.

2.1. The IEC 61499 Function Block Reference Architecture

At present, no single reference software architecture for the creation of ICPSs dominates. The capabilities of PLCs grew rapidly as industry began to find innovative ways of automating manufacturing operations. That demanded more robust, fault-tolerant software architectures to run PLC applications on. The IEC 61499 standard introduced in 2005 addresses the limitations of the earlier IEC 61131 standard [26] by providing an object-oriented, event-driven architecture that scales well [2]. Figure 2 shows a custom FB that has been developed from a standard Basic Function Block (BFB) type definition. This FB processes a temperature reading in degrees Fahrenheit that is received from another FB that interfaces with a temperature sensor. The IEC 61499 standard defines a convention that *Data Inputs* such as TEMP_F are drawn on the left side of the function block symbol. When new data have been made available from another connected FB to the input TEMP_F, the *Input Event* REQ is triggered. Each function block implements its own Moore-type finite state machine [27]. The *Output Events* and *Data Outputs* shown on the right of the FB symbol depend only on the current state and the values of the Data Inputs it has received. The IEC 61499 *Execution Control Chart* (ECC) [28] shown in Figure 2 details the states and state transitions possible for this FB. For each state transition, one or more software algorithms are triggered to process the data and make control decisions. After the algorithms have executed, the converted temperature is output via TEMP_C and the output event CNF is triggered. If the temperature cannot be converted, the ECC transitions to the error state and the output event ERROR is triggered. This event-driven behaviour and the ability to encapsulate both state management and algorithms in an FB facilitates loose-coupling and scalability. However, event-driven systems present issues when interactive diagnostic approaches are used since the actions of the diagnoser can interfere with the timing of the ICPS.

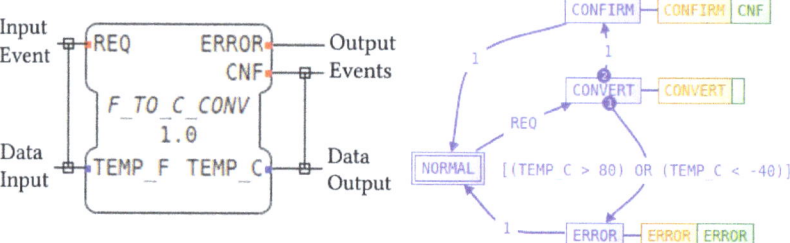

Figure 2. IEC 61499 Function Block that converts temperatures with its ECC.

Hehenberger comments that one of the advantages of ICPSs is the cost saving that modularity, adaptability and re-usability offer when implementing larger, distributed systems [29]. IEC 61499 provides a way to encapsulate capabilities in reusable units that are wired together to create event-driven logic and control. Encapsulation encourages component re-use by enabling developers to craft new FB applications from well-proven resources. The standard function block type definitions provides templates that are used to craft specialized FBs from. The custom Service Interface Function Block template interfaces well to physical sensors and actuators. In this way, trusted libraries evolve as generations of FBs share and refine field-proven resources. IEC 61499 also supports partitioning of applications to work collaboratively on separate, distributed platforms, providing scalability and redundancy. The IEC 61499 architecture has gained wide acceptance, being used in PLCs for industrial automation [30] and in the Intelligent Electronic Devices (IEDs) of Smart Electricity Grids [31,32].

2.2. Fault Identification and Diagnosis in ICPS

ICPS demand sophisticated fault management if they are to operate for the maximum possible uptime without interruption [33,34]. Self-managing fault diagnostic engines now ensure the reliability of interplanetary spacecraft and smart factories, often in situations where humans are not able to be present when things go wrong [35,36]. A *fault* is defined as any change in the operation of an ICPS that leads to unacceptable behavior or degraded performance [37]. Diagnostic strategies must enable fault-management software to be able to recognise what constitutes both normal and abnormal behavior by the devices that operate in the ICPS. If the cobot in the example above pauses because it cannot complete a task when an obstruction is blocking its path, that is not a fault. It is the ICPS adapting appropriately to a change in its environment. However, failing to halt is a fault, possibly caused by a damaged sensor or a programming error.

Sophisticated smart sensors contain in-built electronics to pre-process readings and transmit them to the ICPS they are connected to. Faults in such sensors can include failures in electronic components, both intermittent and permanent, as well as calibration errors that cause them to return false readings. Actuators such as those that move aircraft flight control surfaces rely on feedback from multiple position sensors to determine if they are orientated correctly. Since many sensors and actuators have their own embedded processors, software faults can lead to operational failures. The recent failure of the airspeed and angle of attack sensors on the Boeing MAX 8 led to the incorrect operation of the on-board MCAS flight stability software, resulting in catastrophic behavior of the aircraft [38]. Zolghadri et al. [39] note how the number of sensors being monitored for faults affects both the design and worst-case performance of diagnostic approaches. Dearden et al. [40] comment that many ICPS devices are designed for low power consumption and have limited computational capabilities. Hence, external fault diagnostic systems rather than built-in fault-finding ensures that these ICPSs are not overloaded by fault management and diagnostic processes.

Physics-Based Modeling of faults relies on models of behavior that can be used to recognise misbehavior. Model-invalidation techniques recognize deviations in the ICPS telemetry from the values predicted in the model [41,42]. Noise discrimination is required since the differences may be small when the device is appearing to perform nominally [43,44]. However, creating models is labor-intensive and they require careful calibration to enable them to determine when the ICPS has deviated from expected behaviors [41,45].

In contrast, Model-Free approaches use Artificial Intelligence (AI) where the correct operation of the ICPS is learnt by observation during a training period. While the effort to create a pre-defined model is not required, fault engines that rely on AI techniques must be trained on a system that is able to demonstrate what nominal operation is. In the prior scoping survey [9], variations of Model-Based approaches in the aerospace sector were encountered in 85% of the studies while AI featured in 30% of the studies. Hybrid techniques that combine aspects of both approaches were found in 36% of these studies. This predominance of Model-Based techniques reflects a conservative approach typical of safety-critical environments.

Christensen [15] proposed a model of fault diagnosis applicable to IEC 61499 that extends the Model-View-Controller (MVC) pattern to include diagnostics and fault recovery. The approach proposed an additional layer of custom FBs that monitored activities of the other blocks it is connected to in that region. Hametner et al. propose a Unit-Test framework for IEC 61499 using FBs that surround the block to be examined [46]. They generate a test framework automatically; however, the scope of this approach is design-time testing rather than Christensen's goal of longer-term fault detection.

2.3. Intentional Agents for Fault Finding

Agents were originally conceived as a way of computerizing tasks and processes in the way that humans typically might address them. Milis et al. discuss cognitive agents who are able to apply expert reasoning, mimicking the activities of human investigators [45]. Like humans, agents are able to adapt their strategies autonomously to cope with changes in the environment they perceive. Agents have emerged as a promising approach to creating large distributed and self-adaptive systems including ICPSs [47,48]. Bratman [49] and Wooldridge [50] provided an early background to intentional agents, introducing the concepts of Beliefs, Desires and Intentions (BDI). They described how agents form beliefs about the environment they are observing. Reasoning about those beliefs leads to the formation of desires to achieve goals that are fulfilled by pursuing intentional tasks. While ICPSs are deterministic, the world they operate in is not. Agents are one approach to working with devices that must bridge that temporal divide.

Diagnostic approaches encountered employed agents in both Model-Based [41,45] and Model-Free Artificial Intelligence fault-finding techniques [44,51]. The most common scenarios describe agents capturing diagnostic data, reasoning about evidence and then facilitating fault management [52,53]. Modest and Thielecke discuss encapsulating avionics domain knowledge for agents to create standard libraries of resources and techniques [54]. These are captured in failure–indicator matrices. They envisage the use of agent techniques to create a set of standard functions and interfaces that can be deployed as rule-based expert systems.

A number of alternative agent frameworks have emerged since Bratman and Wooldridge's original work. Jones and Wray [55] provide a comparison of multi-agent frameworks including GOMS [56] and Soar [57]. Both of these architectures approach agent interactions from a computational intelligence perspective. Later work by Jarvis, Rönnquist and Jain led to the development of the GORITE (Goal ORIented TEams) Multi-Agent Framework [3,5]. GORITE implements intentions as explicit activities and makes no distinction between goals and plans. This approach simplifies the specification of goals that can be shared by multiple agents and then executed independently. However, representing environment information in a format agents can use is complex [58,59]. Jarvis et al. comment that there is a need to be able to describe the activities required from agents more concisely using appropriate Domain-Specific Languages (DSLs) [3].

3. Architecting the Engine

RQ3 asks how a fault diagnostic engine can best be architected. Attribute-Driven Design is a systematic methodology for designing the architecture of software-intensive systems [11]. It relies on having sufficient, well-defined functional requirements before the architectural design phase can proceed. IEEE Standard 610 defines a requirement as a *"condition or capability needed by a user to achieve an objective"* ([60], p. 65). However, requirements for software-intensive systems such as the engine quickly become highly-detailed. This can lead to ambiguity when multiple interpretations of the same need are possible [61–63]. Architects address this by identifying and focusing on those functional requirements that are Architecturally-Significant Requirements (ASRs) [10]. ASRs describe the functionality that will have a significant influence on or constrain the architectural design choices that can be made [64].

Chen et al. outline an approach for identifying ASRs among the requirements [65]. Table 1 details two of the ASRs for the engine categorized using their criteria. ASRs often affect multiple parts of the system rather than just the functionality they are describing. A characteristic that makes them significant is the high cost of changing that feature later [66]. Requirements that are *Strict* limit the architectural choices available while *Trade-offs* are the compromises that the designer must make to balance one desired property or quality against another. *Trade-off Points* occur where no single architectural approach satisfies all the requirements of that feature. Chen et al. give the example of a functional requirement for an application to display temperatures in both Fahrenheit and Celsius. In contrast, the quality requirement for the uptime of the system to be "99.999 percent" embodies the ISO 25010 Quality Attribute of Availability [67]. Fulfilling the requirement for displaying a reading in degrees Fahrenheit and Celsius requires additional software functions to be written. In contrast, achieving the quality characteristic of High Application Availability requires architectural decisions regarding fail-over to alternative hardware or the choice of different sensors with higher reliability.

Table 1. Chen et al. criteria for being architecturally significant.

ID	Requirement	Wide Impact?	Requires Trade-Offs?	Strict?	Breaks Assumptions?	Difficult to Achieve?	Architecturally Significant?
1	The agents must be able to interact with multiple, distributed parts of the system that is under diagnosis.	Yes	Yes	No	No	Yes	Yes
2	The operation of the Diagnostic Points shall not degrade the performance of the system under diagnosis by more than 5%.	No	Yes	Yes	No	Yes	Yes

Neither of the two examples break assumptions made during the original requirements' elicitation. However, the requirement to be able to interact with multiple, distributed IEC 61499 applications has a wide impact on how information is exchanged and collated from different parts of the application. It also requires trade-offs that are related to the design of the DPs and how they gather telemetry. This requirement is also deemed to be difficult to achieve, leading to the decision that this requirement is an ASR. In contrast, the performance of the DPs is critical, but does not have a wide-impact; the DPs are self-contained. However their development is complex, leading to them also being classified as an ASR.

While functional requirements are goals that define what a feature must do, *quality attributes* describe qualities the feature must possess. They specify characteristics such as how suitable, how modifiable, or how reliable that feature must be. ISO Standard 25010 defines and standardizes categories of quality attributes so that they can be used consistently by architects and understood by stakeholders [67]. While architecting the engine, the desired quality attributes were established by working alongside stakeholders in structured Quality Attribute Workshops (QAWS) [68]. The architecture was then evaluated through scenarios that were created using the Architectural Trade-off Analysis Method (ATAM) [69]. The ATAM provides a step-by-step method of validating an architecture empirically.

The IEEE Standard 610 qualifies this definition of a requirement further, asserting that a requirement should be a "documented representation" of a need ([60], p. 65). Clements et al. caution that all the effort put in by the architects is wasted if the documentation they produce cannot be understood later by developers [10]. By describing the structure of each architecturally-significant feature, architectures provide the framework needed to reason about the elements that make up a system, how they interact and how well they meet the objectives demanded of them [66]. Hence, the role of a software architect is to propose and document a solution by blending different, well-proven architectural styles. The Views and Beyond approach was used to create the Software Architecture Document (SAD) [70].

Applications such as the engine are too complex to be captured in any single diagram. Architects address this complexity by delivering a set of *Views*, structured descriptions of subsets of related architectural features. Each view is presented from the perspective or *Viewpoint* of a particular stakeholder. Since stakeholders have different concerns and interests, a view illustrates how that part of the architecture addresses their needs. Figure 3 illustrates how in Views and Beyond, Bass et al. extend the 4 + 1 Views Model of Architecture proposed by Kruchten [71] to incorporate Rozanski and Woods seven distinct architectural viewpoints [72]. The Viewpoint Catalogue of Rozanski and Woods is explored in more detail in Section 1.3 of the SAD. The diagram shows how the stakeholders' viewpoints are considered in the light of the ASRs. The *View Packets* are the smallest piece of information a stakeholder requires, presented from a particular viewpoint [73]. They are detailed on the right of the diagram, showing the view packets contained in the SAD that detail an aspect of the architecture. Inside each view packet, the rationale behind each feature is explained, providing diagrams that present each element used in the architecture [64].

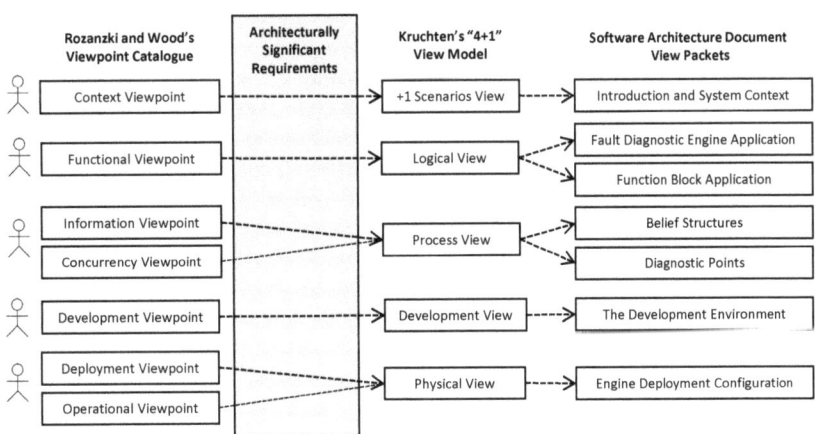

Figure 3. From viewpoints, architecturally-significant requirements and views to view packets.

SysML diagrams were adopted as a way of of presenting the elements of an architectural feature in a consistent way. SysML is an extension of the UML modeling language defined in the ISO 19514 standard [74,75]. SysML extends the range of UML diagrams to add Activity, Requirement and Block diagram types which are ideal for describing systems-of-systems architectures such as the engine. UML and SysML both encourage systematic naming conventions for elements and the diagrams which contain them.This makes it easier to build the Views and Beyond Element Catalogues in the SAD that describe each view. For every view in the Kruchten 4 + 1 model, there are well-known UML or SysML diagrams that have been adopted to document the elements appropriately in that view. The SAD is intended to provide a single-source of truth to capture the needs of the stakeholders and propose architectural solutions to those needs. In doing that, the architects carefully tread a fine line between providing just enough detail without over-architecting the design. Doing so would constrain the ability of the developers to make their own decisions about how the code should implement the design. Architecture is concerned with the external characteristics of elements. In contrast, developers create the internal implementation of elements to realize those external characteristics. The SAD should therefore present an unambiguous architectural design, without unnecessary internal implementation details.

3.1. The System Context View of the Engine

The introductory sections of SAD present the agents and the engine in-context with the diagnostic needs they satisfy. Figure 4 illustrates the activities the agents can perform and the subsystems the engine is constructed from in this context. The view does this by presenting the relations, dependencies and interactions between the engine subsystems. Doberkat [76] explains that a *relation* links an input to an element to a corresponding output or a state. Relations can imply hierarchies and dependencies that define which modules provide support or inherit their capabilities from other elements. The view corresponds to the +1 Scenario View proposed by Kruchten [71]. The Context View is a high-level overview, designed to present the purpose and business drivers that underpin the architectural decisions made about the engine. The view also describes the needs of the stakeholders who either use or will develop the engine. Stakeholders have differing concerns, so alternative view packets address their individual needs in more detail. For example, Software Engineers are concerned with operational features of the engine and the agents while they use the system to help them develop FB applications. Their needs include interactive fault-finding sessions during early-stage development. In contrast, Maintenance Engineers use the engine, configured with different agent goals, for longer-term fault monitoring and management.

The engine is a stand-alone system that interacts with a separate FB application. Design resources created in the IDE during the creation of the FB application are available to the agents. They use this structural information to configure the telemetry connections they need to interact with the FBs during fault-finding. Each of the subsequent views details the subsystems shown in this diagram in more detail from differing viewpoint perspectives. Constraints that drove architectural decisions are discussed in each context. Views and Beyond creates a framework in which each view or view packet includes a description of each architectural element the subsystem relies on as well as the interfaces they provide.

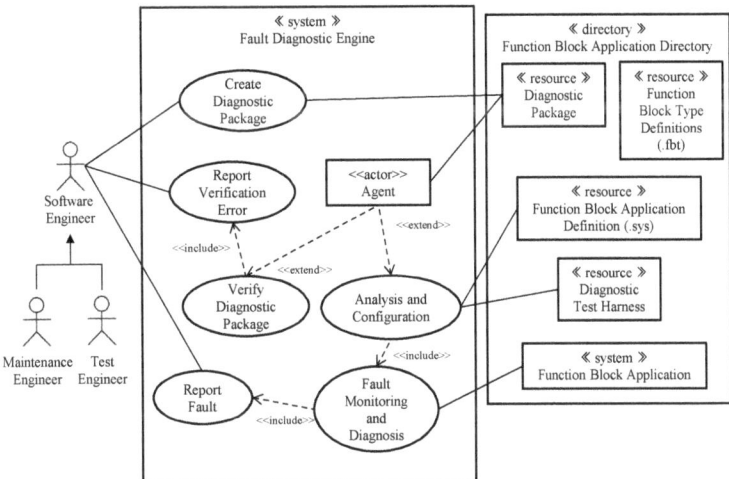

Figure 4. The system context view of the fault diagnostic engine.

3.2. The Logical View

Figure 5 presents the Logical View of the engine from the Rozanski and Woods Functional Viewpoint. A layered architectural style was chosen since the self-contained GORITE Team Manager subsystem provides the primary interface to the diagnostic agents. The refinement of the agent subsystem is discussed further in Section 3.3. This was driven by later evaluations that identified the need to multi-thread agents to better manage their scheduling and resources. The engines' communication subsystem operates in the agent layer, providing the interface to the separate FB application layer. Sub-applications of the FB application can run on their own hardware platforms as distributed device instances in this lower layer.

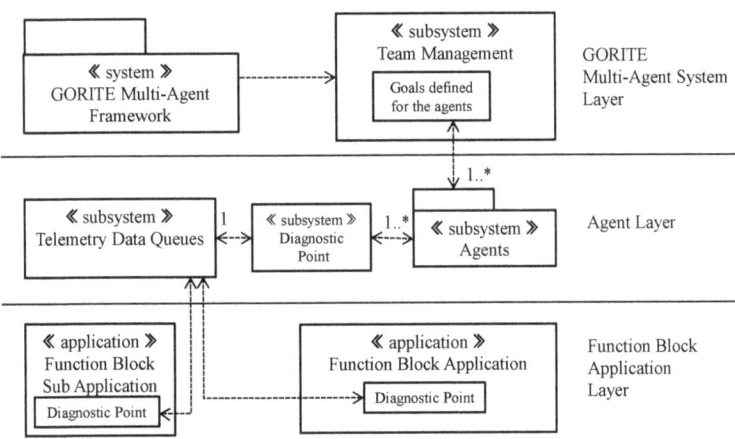

Figure 5. The layered architectural style of the fault diagnostic engine.

While agents are often created using object-oriented design patterns, there is a distinct difference in the way agents interact with other components in multi-agent frameworks. Objects implement methods and functions and cannot refuse to execute when called by a component that holds a reference to an instance of that object. In contrast, an agent operates in a contract or agreement with other subsystems. When requested to perform a task or provide a service, an agent will evaluate its current priorities and only comply if it can [50,77]. An *active agent* encompasses its own thread of control [50]. Unlike object instances which can only undergo a change of state when one of their methods is called, agents can initiate a state change based on their own deliberations. Adapting the notation of Kidney and Denzinger [78], an active agent ag can be defined as:

Definition 1 (Active Agent). $ag = \langle Sit, Act, Dat, f_{sit} \rangle$ *is a tuple where:*

1. *Sit is the set of situations that an agent can be in. The characteristics of the agents' situation $sit_j \in Sit$ is defined by the nature of the goal it is pursuing or an individual task within that goal it is performing.*
2. *Act is the set of actions that an agent can perform in that environment.*
3. *Dat is the set of internal data the agent maintains about its state and the environment it is situated in.*
4. *f_{sit} is a function defined for the current situation over the data values that allows the agent to determine its next actions such that $f_{sit} : Sit \times Dat \rightarrow Act$.*

Within GORITE, teams of agents are assembled and allocated goals. A goal that an agent attempts to achieve is defined in terms of the set of actions Ga that the agent can perform to work towards a desired outcome. Jarvis et al. make no distinction between the traditional BDI concept of a plan and a goal; a plan in GORITE is just an explicit goal [3]. The pursuit of a goal is evidenced as a set of *behaviors*. The behavior *Beh* of an individual agent ag_i is described by the set of actions that it takes in its environment while it is attempting to achieve a particular goal:

Definition 2 (Behaviour). $Beh_{task} = \{act_1, act_2, \ldots, act_t\}$ *where*

1. *$act_n \in Act$, are the actions the agent ag_i is capable of performing, and*
2. *act_t is the action that causes the agent to terminate its operations when that task is completed. Since agents have the ability to self-determine what the appropriate course of action might be in a given environment, it is possible that a number of different behaviors could be exhibited that still achieve the same outcome.*

Since agents have the ability to choose from a number of alternatives what the appropriate course of action might be in a given situation or environment, and it is possible that a number of different behaviors could be exhibited that still achieve the same outcome.

Agents only begin executing activities when they are assigned a goal to pursue. The GORITE *execute*() method provides a function body in which to implement the code to allow an agent to perform tasks as it works towards fulfilling the goal. Goals are designed to execute until the agent either completes, suspends, or fails the goal. A goal in GORITE is defined as:

Definition 3 (Goal). *Given an agent ag, a goal is specified as the tuple $Goal = \langle N, Ga, gs_w \rangle$ where:*

1. *N is a unique identifier that names the goal, and*
2. *Ga is the set of actions the agent can perform while pursuing the goal where $Ga \subset Act$, and*
3. *gs_w is the current state of the goal where $gs_w \in Gs$, the set of defined GORITE goal states.*

GORITE defines the following goal states that can be returned from the customized *execute*() function defined for a goal:

- PASSED: The current goal has been completed successfully by the *DiagnosticAgent*. This usually results in the *TeamManagerAgent* assigning a new goal if there is a subsequent task that follows on from the goal that has just been completed.
- STOPPED: The agent cannot complete the current goal at the present time. This usually signifies that there has been some sort of obstruction in the environment

that is stopping the agent working on the goal. The agent is recommending to the *TeamManagerAgent* that the goal should be re-scheduled to be attempted again at a later time.
- FAILED: The agent cannot complete the current goal and has determined that further attempts to re-start and complete the goal would be futile. The *TeamManagerAgent* will not attempt to re-schedule this goal again during the current fault diagnostic session.

3.3. The Process View

The Process View of the architecture focuses on processes that execute in the engine that support fault-finding. The view corresponds to Rozanski and Woods Information and Concurrency Viewpoint, detailed in Section 1.5 of the SAD. The SAD presents the operation of the agents and the DPs in two separate view packets.

Prototyping the agents and DPs during the ATAM evaluation of the architecture led to significant refinements. The *DiagnosticTeam* component is responsible for creating the team of agents and assigning goals to them. However, the Open Source version of GORITE does not provide a way of implementing multiple agent instances that can be multi-threaded. Each goal is implemented as a class with an *execute()* function that is designed to operate until the status of the goal changes. That implies that different agents cannot perform their goals in parallel if they are both operating on the current GORITE thread. The prototype single agent performed three goals successfully that included the configuration of the FB application, watching for simple faults and then reporting them. The ATAM identified that this did not address the quality attributes including Concurrency and Scalability. These could not be satisfied by executing agents on a single execution thread. The agents also need to be able to persist their own private copies of resource objects, each with their own state management requirements. Instantiating agents on their own threads demanded a Trade-Off that led to a different goal structure for the Team manager. Figure 6 details the revised interaction between the Team Manager Agent and the Diagnostic Agents.

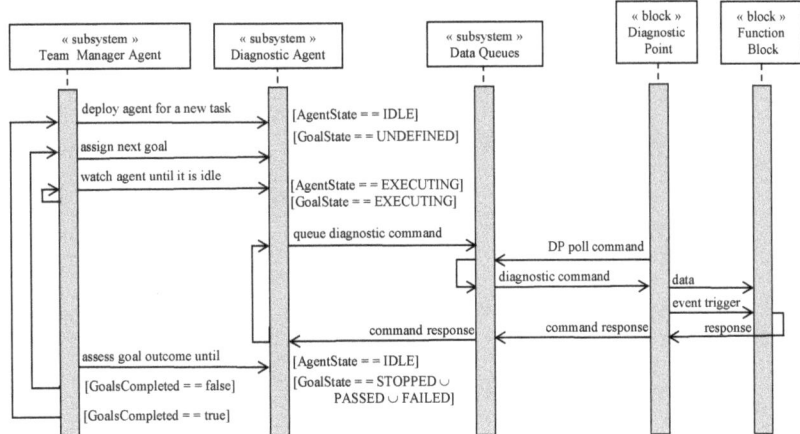

Figure 6. GORITE Team, agent, and diagnostic point processes across the execution layers.

This included the extension of the set of GORITE Goals states to include a new *EXECUTING* status. The Team Manager Agent executes a set of GORITE Sequence Goals named *Manage* where the role of the team manager is to assign goals to available agents and monitor their progress. Each named agent instance provides a set of thread-safe synchronized methods that ensure the setting and reading of the *AgentState* and *GoalState* agent properties are interleaved appropriately. Agents execute goals such as *Configure*, *Monitor*, *Diagnose* and *Analyse*, transitioning from first configuring the FB application, then watching the telemetry streams and intervening whenever fault evidence is observed. Each transition to a new goal is initiated by reporting via the *AgentState* that the current goal is no longer being executed, whereupon the Team Manager Agent evaluates the goal status reported by the agent in *GoalState* and assigns a new goal. Five agents were prototyped for an ATAM scenario and evaluated with GORITE on its own thread and its own set of management goals. No collisions or conflicts were observed. This new configuration now positions the Team Manager as an agent in its own right, co-ordinating multiple agents and freeing each agent to manage the state of the resources it instantiates. ATAMs do not usually involve a prototyping phase; however, the prototypes provided valuable quantitative feedback to justify the architectural changes needed that the ATAM had identified.

3.4. Diagnostic Points and Telemetry

Telemetry is defined as the in situ collection of measurements or other types of data at remote points and the transmission of that data back to receiving equipment [79]. The agents treat FBs as black-boxes whose behavior or misbehavior can be inferred from the data they exchange with each other. In most practical instances, the engine is deployed on its own hardware, separate from the platform the FB application is executing on. The rational for creating stand-alone fault management engines is discussed in depth in Benowitz's description of the NASA Curiosity Mars Rover [36]. Goupil et al. present a similar rational for the Airbus fault engine [80]. These engines have to keep functioning even when the applications they are managing are failing. Hence, the DPs in our engine need to provide remote data capture and interaction points that can operate as software-in-the-loop entry points within the FB application, exchanging telemetry via managed network connections to the platform that the agents are operating on.

Figure 7 shows the construction of the DP function block DP. This is a Composite Function Block (CFB) that contains an instance of the AGENT_GATE Service Interface Function Block (SIFB). The DP block is used to break and re-connect the data and event lines that connect FBs together.

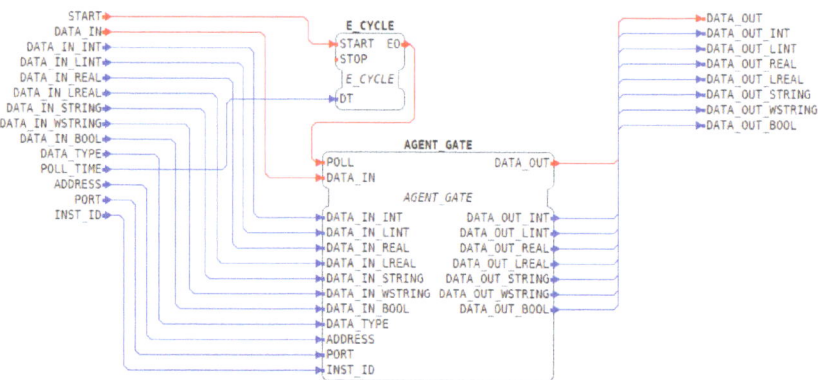

Figure 7. Diagnostic point composite function block.

CFBs expose a single input and output interface that encapsulates a more complex internal configuration. The configuration parameters include a *POLL_TIME* parameter that allows the performance of the DPs to be fine-tuned by the agent during the configuration of the diagnostic test harness. DPs initially pass all data and events through transparently after the agent has instructed them to operate in their *PASSTHROUGH_ENABLED* mode. Each data value is also sent back to the agent as it passes through the DP. The AGENT_GATE block implements a TCP client connection to a single named non-blocking I/O gateway component called *NIOserver* that is hosted on the engine. A TCP server listener socket handover then assigns a unique socket to maintain the connection between the agent and the client DP. The agent communicates with the DP wired into the FB application via an in-memory object interface, also referred to as a *DiagnosticPoint*, established within the engine. The agents exchange telemetry with the DP using First-In-First Out (FIFO) data queues and the packet structure detailed in Figure 8.

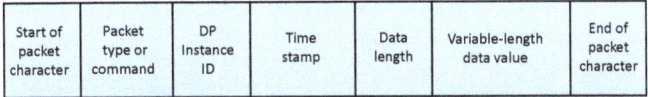

Figure 8. Definition of the Data Packet structure used to exchange telemetry.

The start and end of packet characters are used to ensure that the packet has not been malformed and to allow multiple variable-length packets to be unpacked from the input buffer reliably in a single read from a TCP port. The data type is inferred by the agent since it was established during the set up of the DP. The input DATA_TYPE is used by the block to determine the format conversion needed into and out of the string format that is carried in the data packet. TCP addresses and the Host listener port are also specified on input parameters. Table 2 details the packet commands supported by the DP and the agents. The DP provides input and output data ports for each defined IEC 61499 data type. These range from Boolean types through to long and short Integers, Real Numbers and Strings. An efficient type conversion in C++ with rounding to a specified number of decimal places was implemented in the blocks to ensure that data were processed rapidly and packed efficiently into the data packets.

Table 2. Packet Type Commands used to control and exchange data with Diagnostic Points.

Packet Type Enum	Description
SAMPLED_DATA_VALUE	A typed data value sent to the agent that has been either captured from an input or an output port on the function block.
PASSTHROUGH_ENABLED	Command received from the agent to switch the DP to its transparent pass-through mode.
POLL_AGENT	The DP is polling the agent, signaling that it is ready to receive a new data value to inject into the function block. The value is returned in a Post-Back from the NIOserver.
TRIGGER_ENABLED	Command received from the agent to switch from its transparent pass-through mode and begin requesting and injecting test data values. Used in conjunction with the GATE_OPEN and GATE_CLOSE commands.
GATE_OPEN	Instructs the DP to open the gate to traffic from other function blocks after switching back to its PASSTHROUGH_ENABLED mode.
GATE_CLOSE	Instructs the DP to close the gate, blocking traffic to and from other function blocks after switching to its TRIGGER_ENABLED mode.
TRIGGER_DATA_VALUE	A typed data value received from the agent to inject into the function block input and event ports.

The *gate*() functionality allows the agent to dynamically isolate either a single FB or a set of related blocks to exercise them. Data and events are blocked from passing into or out of a ring-fenced area to allow the blocks to be tested in isolation, unaffected by other parts of the FB application. The agent can then restore the pass-through mode of those blocks and move on to investigate other blocks of interest. In this way, the agent can walk through an entire application, listening, probing, and then moving on to the next section of interest. This improvement was driven by the ATAM evaluation and resulted in a more dynamic and resilient approach that allows the agents to change the type of interventions they choose to make without needing to re-wire additional DPs at runtime.

The Reliability quality attribute was addressed by making the DP function blocks fault-tolerant to network issues by ensuring that they manage their own TCP client connections. In the event of a loss of connection, the DP re-establishes a new connection by itself. Since the data packets carry a unique DP instance identifier, the matching *DiagnosticPoint* instance in the engine automatically re-routes the packets to and from the correct FIFO packet queue via the new socket. This ensures that all network interruptions are handled asynchronously by the *NIOserver* component and the *DiagnosticPoint* subsystems. In this sense, the *DiagnosticPoint* instance shown in the Agent layer of Figure 5 acts like a Digital Twin of the DP FB within the FB application [81]. Later, this made the creation of the diagnostic scripts the agents use to execute their goals easier to construct since the instance references to the collection of DPs marshaled by the agent do not change in the event of a network issue.

3.5. Managing Agent Beliefs

The Process View also details the beliefs an agent forms. These are stored in an in-memory structure that provides a model of the domain the agents operate in [4]. An *atomic belief* is an opinion about one characteristic of the ICPS or its environment, formed from evidence that the agent holds at a given time. The ability to revise a belief is one of their key skills that allows them to maintain an up-to-date model when situations change or when the weight of evidence alters the agents' perceptions. Dennett defines a First-Order Intentional system as one that has beliefs and desires, but no beliefs and desires about its beliefs and desires [82]. This corresponds to the initial BDI concept proposed by Bratman [83]. Dennett then defines a Second-Order Intentional system as one that has formed beliefs, desires and intentional states about the beliefs and desires of other systems as well as its own. The beliefs formed by each agent in the engine are First-Order. Definition 4 is the primary definition of a belief that all the subsequent beliefs used by the agents are built upon:

Definition 4 (Beliefs). *Every agent ag contains a set of beliefs $B = \{b_1, \ldots, b_n\}$ such that each belief $b \in B$ is a tuple $\langle \triangle, v \rangle$ where:*

- *$\triangle$ is a skill that the agent can use and*
- *v is the veracity of the belief held by the agent about the skill. This may be true, false, or undetermined.*

The veracity v is defined as the degree to which a concept or unit of information conforms to the truth or known facts [84]. The quantities assigned to v can range from true, false, or undetermined, supported by numeric values or percentages that indicate how much a behavior is deviating from expected norms. A fault diagnosis is understood to be a summary and evaluation of the set of beliefs held by an agent. When the application is performing nominally, this diagnosis could be a No Fault Found (NFF) belief on the part of the agent. Within the engine, agents can maintain three types of beliefs: *interaction* beliefs, *system-under-diagnosis (SUD)* beliefs and *dynamic diagnostics* beliefs.

Interaction beliefs capture an agent's knowledge about an ability they possess to interact with either other agents or the FB application to perform goals.

Definition 5 (Interaction belief). *A belief $b = \langle \triangle, v \rangle$ is an interaction belief when $\triangle$ describes a pair (ag, S), where ag represents an agent and the S is the signature of a method that can be used by that agent to interact with the function block application and other agents.*

An example of a skill is the ability of an agent to communicate with the DPs, open and close control gates, and trigger inputs on an FB of interest. This belief structure models IEC 61499-specific domain knowledge needed to interact with the FB application being diagnosed.

Figure 9 shows a set of DPs that an agent has wired between Z_TEMPERATURE and the F_TO_C_CONV. When the agent performs a *rewire()* interaction, the DP1 and DP2 FB instances are inserted into the event and data paths. Later, the *gateClose()* command isolates this incoming information path from Z_TEMPERATURE so that a *trigger()* command can inject test values. These are captured further down the path by DP2 using the *read()* command. Note that, if a DP is capturing the input side of a FB, the *gateClose()* function must close only the inbound side. Conversely, when the DP is capturing an output, only the outbound data and events should be blocked from being sent onto the next connected FB.

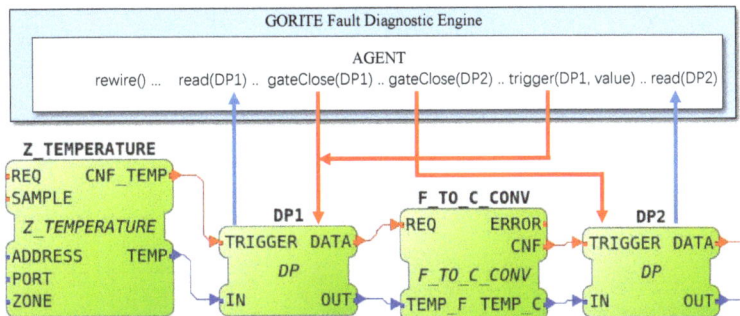

Figure 9. Capturing and triggering Diagnostic Points.

While other belief sets are dynamic, the capabilities captured in this first set are static, intrinsic skills since they are core domain-specific abilities of the agent. Hence, the veracity of interaction beliefs is always true unless for some reason the agent is blocked from wielding that ability. Before the diagnostic goals are assigned, a second belief structure is made available to the agent that provides knowledge about the FB application and its structure.

Figure 10 shows the implementation of this belief structure created by restructuring the FB application as a Directed Graph. This is referred to as the System-Under-Diagnosis belief structure.

Definition 6 (System-Under-Diagnosis belief). *A belief $b = \langle \triangle, v \rangle$ is called a system-under-diagnosis belief when $\triangle$ is described by the triple $\langle FB_1, trg, FB_2 \rangle$. FB_1 where:*

- FB_2 *are function block instances in the system under diagnosis, and*
- *trg represents the conditions (events and variable values) under which a transition can be triggered by the agent from FB_1 to FB_2.*

The fault diagnostic engine adopts a model-based rather than a machine-learning approach. Manually creating models is labour and time-intensive, since models need to be calibrated [41,45]. IEC 61499 offers a formally-defined application structure file that allows the engine to autonomously construct an in-memory model of the function block application it has been assigned to monitor and diagnose. As engineers change their designs, the engine is able to update its model using its domain knowledge of the IEC 61499 architecture.

IEC 61499 Application Definition files are optimized to work with development IDEs such as 4diac [6] and nxtCONTROL [85]. However, the XML structure of these files is hard for an agent to navigate dynamically since the parameters for each FB are stored in different parts of the file. The five FB instances are stored as *FunctionBlock* nodes and the connections between them as directed edges stored in the *Connections* object. The name of an edge corresponds to the output event or data output on the FB the node describes. This structure is easier for the agents to navigate when rewiring the FBs to insert DPs. Agents are also able to access this belief structure during fault finding by referencing a single node where all its details are available as properties.

The *FunctionBlockApp* class provides an $update()$ method so that, if changes are made to the copy of the function block or the connection, the entry in the list of block nodes can be updated. This architectural approach using an indexed list of objects means that new methods and data can be added to the structure without complicated changes to the interface.

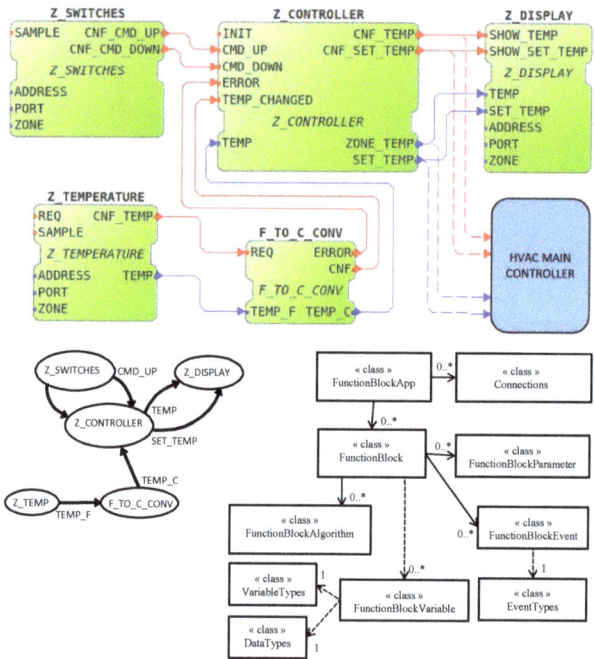

Figure 10. An FB application as a Directed Graph and the Function Block Node structure.

Each node of this belief structure provides the agent with detailed knowledge to allow it to reliably interact with each FB. Agents are responsible for determining by themselves how to interact with a particular FB, verifying input and output data types so they can provide type-safe test values. The Directed Graph structure also allows agents to navigate fault paths autonomously, making decisions about the next possible fault location they should investigate. System beliefs are dynamic, providing the agents with a way to remember the result of diagnosing a FB as they traverse the FB application and update their beliefs about what they have observed.

During the design phase, an engineer will create a package of information that identifies the DPs that are available for each FB. These *Diagnostic Packages* contain sets of test values associated with data pathways through the FB that can be used during diagnosis to determine if the FB is performing correctly. The agent interprets these diagnostic packages while iterating each FB as it builds its application belief structure. A *Diagnostic Harness* is then created by inserting all the DP instances into the function block using the agents' *rewire()* interaction belief.

Model-based approaches rely on techniques of fault-finding that involve invalidating one or more aspects of the model. The engine architecture facilitates this with interaction belief skills and domain knowledge of the IEC 61499 function block architecture, enabling the agents to build their own model of the application they are examining. This addresses some of the concerns that creating models is labor-intensive [41,45]. For fault diagnosis,

First-Order beliefs such as these are sufficient to form this model of the ICPS that the agents are examining.

The third belief structure captures dynamic diagnostic beliefs. As an agent investigates a fault, it forms new beliefs as it observes the FB application that is executing and interacts with it. It may also modify existing beliefs to better align them with new evidence.

Definition 7 (Dynamic diagnostics belief). *A belief $b = \langle \triangle, v \rangle$ is a dynamic diagnostics belief if $\triangle$ is represented as a pair (FB_i, f_q) where*

- *FB_i is a function block instance of the system under diagnosis, and*
- *f_q is a valid fault code for FB_i, obtained from a set of fault codes F.*

In this belief structure, a belief about what is happening is a fuzzy logic opinion about a particular FB, sensor, actuator, or algorithm in the FB application. The set $B = \{b_0, b_1, \ldots, b_n\}$ captures the agent's beliefs, where b_i represents either a single BFB or a network of BFBs connected as a CFB. A BFB or CFB represents the smallest unit of functionality an agent can test and hence beliefs are atomic at this level.

Before the Team Manager shown in Figure 6 instructs the agent to begin operating, it provides a set of goals that can include monitoring for fault signatures and executing diagnostic plans. The agent is also provided with a definition of what constitutes normal behavior for each FB via the set of diagnostic packages. One example of normal behavior is the appearance of temperature readings at 500 ms intervals from Z_TEMPERATURE TEMP. These propagate through the controller to appear at Z_CONTROLLER ZONE_TEMP. The agent then pursues its *Monitor* goal, watching for normal temperature fluctuations. All DP instances pass events and data through transparently to other FBs as well as back to the agent. The agent continues pursuing this goal until one or more of its primary beliefs about normal operation are invalidated. The agent establishes an initial belief for the *Monitor* goal such that:

$$b_0 = \langle FB_{\text{Z\_TEMPERATURE}}, v_{\text{undetermined}}, f_0 \rangle$$

For an agent, the pursuit of its *Monitor* goal is the repeated re-evaluation of each of its beliefs by observing or performing prescribed tests at defined intervals. Whenever the agent determines that the FB is operating within tolerance, it reinforces its belief so that $v_{\text{undetermined}} \rightarrow v_{\text{true}}$. Other primary beliefs track and remember what is being observed in different parts of the FB application.

Invalidating any one of these beliefs in B causes the agent to signal the Team Manager Agent that it has completed its primary *Monitor* goal successfully by finding a potential fault. The Team Manager Agent will then assign the agent a *Diagnostic* goal. The agent then adopts a divide-and-conquer strategy for diagnosing faults in the temperature sensor subsystem described earlier in Figure 9. A range of nominal Fahrenheit temperatures are injected via DP1 and captured as Celsius values at DP2. Out-of-range values such as absolute zero (-459.67 F) should trigger the ERROR event, captured by another DP. If all test values are converted and captured correctly, the agent updates the v of the $b_{F\_TO\_C\_CONV}$ to *true*. The agent continues down the fault path checking each subsequent FB, updating its beliefs until all FBs have been tested. This process caters for the possibility of multiple fault candidates. In subsequent *Analyse* and *Report* goals, the agent proposes a diagnosis after iterating each belief to examine its veracity.

4. Evaluating the Architecture of the Engine

Software Engineering, and Software Architecture in particular, are reflective disciplines [86]. Once an architecture is proposed, it should be presented in a well-structured document. The design decisions made should then be considered carefully to ensure they will meet the quality criteria identified for them. Conclusions and recommendations from the evaluation are used to refine the architecture before the application is constructed.

An ATAM [69] frames these evaluations in a set of scenarios that examine significant features of the architecture. The goal of the ATAM is to understand the consequences of architectural decisions. Kazman et al. define *risks* as architectural decisions which are potentially problematic. In contrast, they describe *non-risks* as good design decisions. A *sensitivity point* is an aspect of the architecture where one or more quality attributes are highly-correlated with the architectural choices made. Changes to that part of the architecture might compromise other qualities with undesirable consequences. *Trade-offs* are decisions that balance both the risks and sensitivities inherent in an element. They often occur in features that have multiple sensitivity points. ATAM *scenarios* propose ways that an aspect of the architecture can be evaluated in the light of the qualities it embodies, the known risks, the sensitivities and the trade-offs made. By following a structured process, the results are consistent and repeatable: architectural evaluation is an iterative process.

Barcelos and Travassos comment that a SAD visualizes the application with a high degree of abstraction [87]. They suggest that the ATAM process is highly subjective and that there is a need to identify more concrete implications of the architectural decisions made. This helps to prevent defects propagating from the design down into the application. Bass et al. note that rectifying defects early is usually less costly than remediation work later [66]. However, Reijonen et al. were concerned that there is a steep learning curve between understanding the theory of the ATAM and then applying it to obtain meaningful outcomes [88]. While scenarios are widely used in business, its application in software development is less evident. Scenarios propose situations that would exercise parts of the architecture and are driven by questions that probe the implications of an architectural decision. Information from the scenarios also influences the scope of the diagnostic tests. Reijonen et al. also comment that the original ATAM approach does not include preparation or post-work. This was addressed when evaluating the engine after the creation of the first draft of the SAD by the prototyping relevant parts of the architecture to investigate issues uncovered during the ATAM.

4.1. Constructing the ATAM Utility Tree

RQ4 was partially addressed by constructing a Utility Tree. These are used during the ATAM to present quality attributes in a hierarchical tree structure that highlights the importance and risk of each attribute. Figure 11 shows part of the Utility Tree constructed during our ATAM showing quality attributes derived from ISO 25010. The main branch Functional Suitability leads to the sub-qualities identified for the engine in Section 2.1.3 of the SAD. Each of the sections gives examples that evaluate the SAD views against these qualities, identifying the risks, sensitivities and trade-offs and proposing scenarios to evaluate suggested changes.

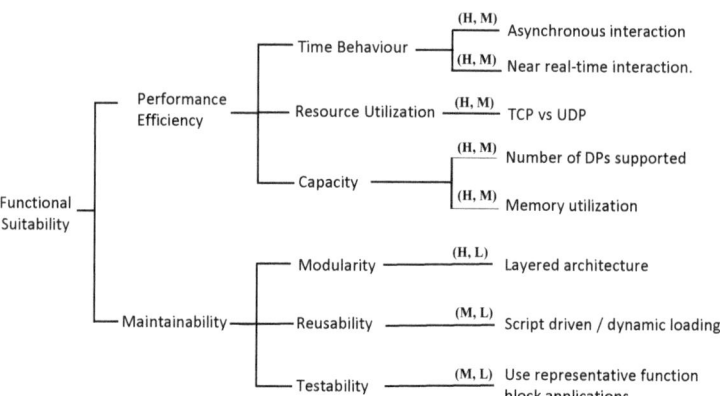

Figure 11. The ATAM utility tree for the engine.

4.2. ISO 4.2.2 Performance Efficiency

Efficiency for the engine is defined in terms of how well it uses the resources of the platform it is deployed on. QAS 2 in he SAD requires that the agents must be able to operate faster than the FB application. While the diagnostic point only has to mediate the flow of data to and from the engine, the agent also has to analyze the data streams from multiple DPs and execute diagnostic strategies preemptively. QAS 5 requires the engine to be able to be run natively on the same hardware as the FB application. However, that is unlikely to be a viable option in most cases. Separate and redundant fault diagnostic engines that operate reliably while other systems are failing are the norm in avionic and aerospace control systems [36,80]. Where large ICPS are being diagnosed, the engine must provide sufficient resources to ensure that the agents can perform all tasks within the required time window.

4.3. ISO 4.2.8 Portability

The engine uses Java and C++ as development languages to address the Portability sub-qualities of Adaptability and Installability. The GORITE engine and the agents are implemented in Java to ensure they can operate on a desktop, server and embedded system platforms. The DPs are custom FBs implemented in C++ for compatibility with the FORTE function block runtime [89]. DPs were converted to C# to run with the nxtCONTROL runtime [85]. The engine is considered low risk for these qualities. This also partially satisfies RQ2 by helping to ensure that the DPs can operate in the same way in multiple environments.

4.4. ISO 4.2.5 Reliability

Reliability is also addressed by running the engine on its own hardware. QAS 4 requires the engine to operate reliably even when the FB application is failing or has failed. The sub-category of Recoverability is addressed by the DP ability to re-connect automatically if they lose their connection to the engine. Data is exchanged asynchronously between the agent and the DPs it is capturing data from or sending test data to. A First-In, First-Out (FIFO) queue structure is used by the engine. A non-blocking socket TCP socket protocol was implemented rather than use UDP. Transmission Control Protocol (TCP) [90] is a connection-oriented protocol that provides guaranteed packet delivery and error correction. In contrast, the User Datagram Protocol (UDP) [91] is a raw, connectionless protocol that provides no error checking or guarantee of delivery. The quality attribute trade-offs of reliability and performance were considered between the extra overhead of TCP versus the simplicity of packet management that guaranteed, reliable delivery provided. TCP does not require additional packet buffering for the FIFO queue manager since only complete packets are received. This also simplified the client C++ code for the DP function blocks. Further scenario testing is recommended with a large number of DPs to evaluate the latency of high-traffic environments.

4.5. ISO 4.2.6 Security

Security is partially addressed by running the engine on its own platform. However, in the current design, the data exchanged between the DPs and the agents are not encrypted. This presents risks when the diagnostic harness is deployed on a function block application that is operating in a production environment rather than in design or testing. DPs are TCP clients and the data exchange packet structure is available publicly. This poses problems if the engine is impersonated by a rogue application. In that scenario, it would be possible to inject false data into the function block application and route it through to other function blocks that are not gated at the time. Tanveer et al. [92] propose a secure-by-design approach that implements encrypted data streams using custom function blocks and security keys that are applicable to this architecture.

5. Conclusions and Future Work

The model-based invalidation approach presented here addresses RQ1 by providing the agent with a way of distinguishing normal operation from misbehavior. The use of domain-specific agents in the GORITE framework also provides a scope for implementing model-free or machine-learning approaches during subsequent research. The proliferation of hybrid techniques encountered in the literature suggests that a blend of fault detection methods is viable. The use of the DPs addresses RQ2 by providing feeds of not only telemetry from FBs but also control over their operations during fault investigations.

The application of Views and Beyond coupled with ADD was used to address RQ3. The ATAM evaluations that addressed RQ4 are usually performed after the first version of the architecture has been documented. Our approach demonstrated the value of performing brief, focused and iterative ATAMs that led to the findings presented in the evaluation section. Adhering to a sound architectural documentation methodology, rigorous evaluation with the ATAM and validation with prototypes led to important architectural refinements. These are continuing to improve the resilience, performance and reliability of the engine during the subsequent on-going development.

Model-Driven Development with Diagnostics suggests a more collaborative and resilient approach to fault management needs early in the architectural design. The engine offers a way to automate many of the fault diagnostic tasks that are not possible in the current IEC 61499 IDEs. The dynamic nature of DPs capitalises on the existing reconfigurability features of the 4diac FORTE runtime environment. Running the engine on its own platform with multiple agents addresses scalability concerns that traditional Built-In-Self-Test (BITS) approaches to fault diagnostics and testing do not. However, engines such as these need to deliver practical advantages if they are to see adoption in the IEC 61499 community. At present, the diagnosis presented by the agents to the engineers does not include deep reasoning about the evidence captured. The belief structures presented here suggest ways of doing that which is being investigated in our current research. This is leading to the implementation of *pragmatic* agents that reason more deeply about the faults they have observed using their domain knowledge as a basis for their deliberations. There is also further work on a Domain Specific Language used to write the diagnostic routines [3]. A level of compliance with products such as Selenium would help to standardize the way diagnostic commands are expressed by the agents, making adoption easier for users [93].

The architecture will continue to evolve through subsequent iterations as the engine is being implemented by our team. We intend to publish further articles that include empirical evaluations of the architecture supported by appropriate FB applications that illustrate the full scope of the engines' capabilities.

Author Contributions: Conceptualization, B.D. and R.S.; methodology, B.D., R.S. and S.G.M.; software, B.D.; validation, B.D. and R.S.; writing—original draft preparation, B.D.; review and editing, B.D. and R.S.; supervision, R.S. and S.G.M. All authors have read and agreed to the published version of the manuscript.

Funding: This research received no external funding.

Conflicts of Interest: The authors declare no conflict of interest.

Glossary

ADD	Attribute-Driven Design method [11].
ATAM	Architectural Trade-off Analysis Method [69].
CFB	Composite Function Block [2].
DP	Diagnostic Point [8].
FB	Function Block [2].
ICPS	Industrial Cyber-Physical System.
PLC	Programmable Logic Controller.

QAW	Quality Attribute Workshop
ASR	Architecturally-Significant Requirement.
BFB	Basic Function Block [2].
CPS	Cyber-Physical System [20].
ECS	Embedded Control System.
FDE	Fault Diagnostic Engine.
IDE	Integrated Development Environment.
QA	Quality Attribute.
SAD	Software Architecture Document.

References

1. Lee, E.A.; Seshia, S.A. *Introduction to Embedded Systems: A Cyber-Physical Systems Approach*; MIT Press: Cambridge, MA, USA, 2016.
2. IEC. *Function Blocks–Part 1: Architecture*; IEC: Geneva, Switzerland, 2013.
3. Jarvis, D.; Jarvis, J.; Rönnquist, R.; Jain, L.C. Multi-Agent Systems. In *Multiagent Systems and Applications*; Springer: Berlin/Heidelberg, Germany, 2013; pp. 1–12. [CrossRef]
4. Ganzha, M.; Jain, L.C.; Jarvis, D.; Jarvis, J.; Rönnquist, R. *Multiagent Systems and Applications*; Springer: Berlin/Heidelberg, Germany, 2013.
5. Rönnquist, R. The Goal Oriented Teams (GORITE) framework. In *International Workshop on Programming Multi-Agent Systems*; Springer: Berlin/Heidelberg, Germany, 2007; pp. 27–41.
6. Strasser, T.; Rooker, M.; Ebenhofer, G.; Zoitl, A.; Sünder, C.; Valentini, A.; Martel, A. Framework for distributed industrial automation and control (4DIAC). In Proceedings of the 2008 6th IEEE International Conference on Industrial Informatics, Daejeon, Korea, 13–16 July 2008; pp. 283–288.
7. Zoitl, A.; Strasser, T.; Ebenhofer, G. Developing modular reusable IEC 61499 control applications with 4DIAC. In Proceedings of the 2013 11th IEEE International Conference on Industrial Informatics (INDIN), Bochum, Germany, 29–31 July 2013; pp. 358–363.
8. Dowdeswell, B.; Sinha, R.; MacDonell, S.G. Diagnosable-by-Design Model-Driven Development for IEC 61499 Industrial Cyber-Physical Systems. In Proceedings of the IECON 2020 46th International Conference of the IEEE Industrial Electronics Society, Singapore, 18–21 October 2020.
9. Dowdeswell, B.; Sinha, R.; MacDonell, S.G. Finding faults: A scoping study of fault diagnostics for Industrial Cyber-Physical Systems. *J. Syst. Softw.* **2020**, *168*, 110638. [CrossRef]
10. Clements, P.; Garlan, D.; Little, R.; Nord, R.; Stafford, J. Documenting software architectures: Views and Beyond. In Proceedings of the 25th International Conference on Software Engineering, Portland, OR, USA, 3–10 May 2003; pp. 740–741. [CrossRef]
11. Wojcik, R.; Bachmann, F.; Bass, L.; Clements, P.; Merson, P.; Nord, R.; Wood, B. *Attribute-Driven Design (ADD), Version 2.0.*; Technical Report; Software Engineering Institute (SEI), Carnegie-Mellon University: Pittsburg, PA, USA, 2006.
12. Dowdeswell, B.; Sinha, R.; MacDonell, S. Mendeley Dataset: A Software Architecture for a Fault Diagnostic Engine. *Mendeley Data* **2020**. [CrossRef]
13. Kalachev, A.; Zhabelova, G.; Vyatkin, V.; Jarvis, D.; Pang, C. Intelligent mechatronic system with decentralised control and multi-agent planning. In Proceedings of the IECON 2018-44th Annual Conference of the IEEE Industrial Electronics Society, Washington, DC, USA, 21–23 October 2018; pp. 3126–3133. [CrossRef]
14. Jarvis, D.; Jarvis, J.; Kalachev, A.; Zhabelova, G.; Vyatkin, V. PROSA/G: An architecture for agent-based manufacturing execution. In Proceedings of the 2018 IEEE 23rd International Conference on Emerging Technologies and Factory Automation (ETFA), Turin, Italy, 4–7 September 2018; Volume 1, pp. 155–160. [CrossRef]
15. Christensen, J.H. Design Patterns, Frameworks, and Methodologies. In *Distributed Control Applications: Guidelines, Design Patterns, and Application Examples with the IEC 61499*; CRC Press: Boca Raton, FL, USA, 2017; p. 27. [CrossRef]
16. Samad, T.; Parisini, T.; Annaswamy, A. Systems of systems. *Impact Control. Technol.* **2011**, *12*, 175–183.
17. Laughton, M.A.; Say, M.G. *Electrical Engineer's Reference Book*; Elsevier: Amsterdam, The Netherlands, 2013.
18. Parr, E.A. *Industrial Control Handbook*; Industrial Press Inc.: New York, NY, USA, 1998.
19. Boem, F.; Ferrari, R.M.; Parisini, T. Distributed fault detection and isolation of continuous-time nonlinear systems. *Eur. J. Control.* **2011**, *17*, 603–620. [CrossRef]
20. Baheti, R.; Gill, H. Cyber-physical systems. *Impact Control. Technol.* **2011**, *12*, 161–166.
21. Leitao, P.; Karnouskos, S.; Ribeiro, L.; Lee, J.; Strasser, T.; Colombo, A.W. Smart agents in industrial cyber–physical systems. *Proc. IEEE* **2016**, *104*, 1086–1101. [CrossRef]
22. Cremona, F.; Lohstroh, M.; Broman, D.; Lee, E.A.; Masin, M.; Tripakis, S. Hybrid co-simulation: its about time. *Softw. Syst. Model.* **2019**, *18*, 1655–1679. [CrossRef]
23. Workers, W. Franka Emika Panda Research Robot Manual. 2020. Available online: https://www.franka.de/ (accessed on 21 July 2021).
24. Jazdi, N. Cyber physical systems in the context of Industry 4.0. In Proceedings of the 2014 IEEE International Conference on Automation, Quality and Testing, Robotics, Cluj-Napoca, Romania, 22–24 May 2014; pp. 1–4. [CrossRef]
25. Alur, R. *Principles of Cyber-Physical Systems*; MIT Press: Cambridge, MA, USA, 2015.
26. IEC. *Function Blocks–Part 1: Programmable Controllers. General Information*; IEC: Geneva, Switzerland, 2003; p. 61131.

27. Moore, E.F. Gedanken-experiments on sequential machines. *Autom. Stud.* **1956**, *34*, 129–153.
28. Lindgren, P.; Lindner, M.; Lindner, A.; Vyatkin, V.; Pereira, D.; Pinho, L.M. A real-time semantics for the IEC 61499 standard. In Proceedings of the 2015 IEEE 20th Conference on Emerging Technologies & Factory Automation (ETFA), Luxembourg, 8–11 September 2015; pp. 1–6. [CrossRef]
29. Hehenberger, P.; Vogel-Heuser, B.; Bradley, D.; Eynard, B.; Tomiyama, T.; Achiche, S. Design, modelling, simulation and integration of cyber physical systems: Methods and applications. *Comput. Ind.* **2016**, *82*, 273–289. [CrossRef]
30. Atmojo, U.D.; Blech, J.O.; Vyatkin, V. A Plug and Produce-inspired Approach in Distributed Control Architecture: A Flexible Assembly Line and Product Centric Control Example. In Proceedings of the 2020 IEEE International Conference on Industrial Technology (ICIT), Buenos Aires, Argentina, 26–28 February 2020; pp. 271–277. [CrossRef]
31. Yang, C.W.; Zhabelova, G.; Vyatkin, V.; Nair, N.K.C.; Apostolov, A. Smart Grid automation: Distributed protection application with IEC61850/IEC61499. In Proceedings of the IEEE 10th International Conference on Industrial Informatics, Beijing, China, 25–27 July 2012; pp. 1067–1072. [CrossRef]
32. NOJA. NOJA Power Smart Grid Automation Software. 2015. Available online: https://www.nojapower.com.au/tags/smart-grid-automation-software (accessed on 21 July 2021).
33. Khairullah, S.S.; Elks, C.R. Self-repairing hardware architecture for safety-critical cyber-physical-systems. *IET Cyber-Phys. Syst. Theory Appl.* **2020**, *5*, 92–99. [CrossRef]
34. Jackson, S. A multidisciplinary framework for resilence to disasters and disruptions. *J. Integr. Des. Process. Sci.* **2007**, *11*, 91–108.
35. Holzmann, G.J. Mars Code. *Commun. ACM* **2014**, *57*, 64–73. [CrossRef]
36. Benowitz, E. The Curiosity Mars Rover's Fault Protection Engine. In Proceedings of the 2014 IEEE International Conference on Space Mission Challenges for Information Technology, Laurel, MD, USA, 24–26 September 2014; pp. 62–66. [CrossRef]
37. Thombare, T.R.; Dole, L. Review on fault diagnosis model in automobile. In Proceedings of the 2014 IEEE International Conference on Computational Intelligence and Computing Research, Coimbatore, India, 18–20 December 2014; pp. 1–4. [CrossRef]
38. Ragheb, M. Fault Tree Analysis and Alternative Configurations of Angle of Attack (AOA) Sensors as Part of Maneuvering Characteristics Augmentation System (MCAS). 2019. Available online: https://www.mragheb.com (accessed on 20 July 2021).
39. Zolghadri, A.; Cieslak, J.; Efimov, D.; Henry, D.; Goupil, P.; Dayre, R.; Gheorghe, A.; Leberre, H. Signal and model-based fault detection for aircraft systems. *IFAC-PapersOnLine* **2015**, *48*, 1096–1101. [CrossRef]
40. Dearden, R.; Willeke, T.; Simmons, R.; Verma, V.; Hutter, F.; Thrun, S. Real-time fault detection and situational awareness for rovers: Report on the mars technology program task. In Proceedings of the 2004 IEEE Aerospace Conference Proceedings (IEEE Cat. No. 04TH8720), Big Sky, MT, USA, 6–13 March 2004; Volume 2, pp. 826–840. [CrossRef]
41. Provan, G. A Contracts-Based Framework for Systems Modeling and Embedded Diagnostics. In Proceedings of the International Conference on Software Engineering and Formal Methods, Grenoble, France, 1–5 September 2014; Springer: Berlin/Heidelberg, Germany, 2014; pp. 131–143. [CrossRef]
42. Harirchi, F.; Ozay, N. Guaranteed model-based fault detection in cyber–physical systems: A model invalidation approach. *Automatica* **2018**, *93*, 476–488. [CrossRef]
43. Koitz, R.; Lüftenegger, J.; Wotawa, F. Model-based diagnosis in practice: interaction design of an integrated diagnosis application for industrial wind turbines. In Proceedings of the International Conference on Industrial, Engineering and Other Applications of Applied Intelligent Systems, Arras, France, 27–30 June 2017; Springer: Berlin/Heidelberg, Germany, 2017; pp. 440–445. [CrossRef]
44. Sankavaram, C.; Kodali, A.; Pattipati, K. An integrated health management process for automotive cyber-physical systems. In Proceedings of the 2013 International Conference on Computing, Networking and Communications (ICNC), San Diego, CA, USA, 28–31 January 2013; pp. 82–86. [CrossRef]
45. Milis, G.M.; Eliades, D.G.; Panayiotou, C.G.; Polycarpou, M.M. A cognitive fault-detection design architecture. In Proceedings of the 2016 International Joint Conference on Neural Networks (IJCNN), Vancouver, BC, Canada, 24–29 July 2016; pp. 2819–2826. [CrossRef]
46. Hametner, R.; Hegny, I.; Zoitl, A. A unit-test framework for event-driven control components modeled in IEC 61499. In Proceedings of the 2014 IEEE Emerging Technology and Factory Automation (ETFA), Barcelona, Spain, 16–19 September 2014; pp. 1–8. [CrossRef]
47. Calvaresi, D.; Marinoni, M.; Sturm, A.; Schumacher, M.; Buttazzo, G. The challenge of real-time multi-agent systems for enabling IoT and CPS. In Proceedings of the International Conference on Web Intelligence, Leipzig, Germany, 23–26 August 2017; ACM: New York, NY, USA, 2017; pp. 356–364. [CrossRef]
48. Braberman, V.; D'Ippolito, N.; Kramer, J.; Sykes, D.; Uchitel, S. Morph: A reference architecture for configuration and behaviour self-adaptation. In Proceedings of the 1st International Workshop on Control Theory for Software Engineering, Bergamo, Italy, 31 August 2015. [CrossRef]
49. Bratman, M.E.; Israel, D.J.; Pollack, M.E. Plans and resource-bounded practical reasoning. *Comput. Intell.* **1988**, *4*, 349–355. [CrossRef]
50. Wooldridge, M. *An Introduction to Multiagent Systems*; John Wiley & Sons: Hoboken, NJ, USA, 2009.
51. Wu, D.; Liu, S.; Zhang, L.; Terpenny, J.; Gao, R.X.; Kurfess, T.; Guzzo, J.A. A fog computing-based framework for process monitoring and prognosis in cyber-manufacturing. *J. Manuf. Syst.* **2017**, *43*, 25–34. [CrossRef]
52. Janasak, K.M.; Beshears, R.R. Diagnostics to Prognostics—A product availability technology evolution. In Proceedings of the 2007 Annual Reliability and Maintainability Symposium, Orlando, FL, USA, 22–25 January 2007; pp. 113–118. [CrossRef]

53. Klar, D.; Huhn, M. Interfaces and models for the diagnosis of cyber-physical ecosystems. In Proceedings of the 2012 6th IEEE International Conference on Digital Ecosystems and Technologies (DEST), Campione d'Italia, Italy, 18–20 June 2012; pp. 1–6. [CrossRef]
54. Modest, C.; Thielecke, F. SPYDER: A software package for system diagnosis engineering. *CEAS Aeronaut. J.* **2016**, *7*, 315–331. [CrossRef]
55. Jones, R.M.; Wray, R.E. Comparative analysis of frameworks for knowledge-intensive intelligent agents. *AI Mag.* **2006**, *27*, 57. [CrossRef]
56. Card, S.K.; Newell, A.; Moran, T.P. *The Psychology of Human-Computer Interaction*; CRC Press: Boca Raton, FL, USA, 1983.
57. Laird, J.E.; Newell, A.; Rosenbloom, P.S. Soar: An architecture for general intelligence. *Artif. Intell.* **1987**, *33*, 1–64. [CrossRef]
58. Fröhlich, P.; Móra, I.; Nejdl, W.; Schröder, M. Diagnostic agents for distributed systems. In *ModelAge Workshop on Formal Models of Agents*; Springer: Berlin/Heidelberg, Germany, 1997; pp. 173–186. [CrossRef]
59. Santos, F.; Nunes, I.; Bazzan, A.L. Model-driven agent-based simulation development: A modeling language and empirical evaluation in the adaptive traffic signal control domain. *Simul. Model. Pract. Theory* **2018**, *83*, 162–187. [CrossRef]
60. IEEE. IEEE Standard Glossary of Software Engineering Terminology. *Office* **1990**, *121990*, 1.
61. Ribeiro, C.; Berry, D. The Prevalence and Severity of Persistent Ambiguity in Software Requirements Specifications: Is a Special Effort Needed to Find Them? *Sci. Comput. Program.* **2020**, *195*, 102472. [CrossRef]
62. Sabriye, A.O.J.; Zainon, W.M.N.W. An Approach for Detecting Syntax and Syntactical Ambiguity in Software Requirement Specification. *J. Theor. Appl. Inf. Technol.* **2018**, *96*, 2275–2284.
63. Segal, S. A framework for removing ambiguity from software requirements. *IIOAB J.* **2017**, *8*, 43–46.
64. Van Heesch, U.; Avgeriou, P.; Hilliard, R. A documentation framework for architecture decisions. *J. Syst. Softw.* **2012**, *85*, 795–820. [CrossRef]
65. Chen, L.; Babar, M.A.; Nuseibeh, B. Characterizing architecturally significant requirements. *IEEE Softw.* **2012**, *30*, 38–45. [CrossRef]
66. Bass, L.; Clements, P.; Kazman, R. *Software Architecture in Practice*, 3rd ed.; Addison-Wesley: Boston, MA, USA, 2013.
67. ISO. *Systems and Software Engineering: Systems and Software Quality Requirements and Evaluation (SQuaRE): System and Software Quality Models*; International Organization for Standardization: Geneva, Switzerland, 2011.
68. Barbacci, M.R.; Ellison, R.J.; Lattanze, A.J.; Stafford, J.A.; Weinstock, C.B. *Quality Attribute Workshops (QAWA)*; Technical Report; Carnegie-Mellon University: Pittsburgh, PA, USA, 2003.
69. Kazman, R.; Klein, M.; Clements, P. *ATAM: Method for Architecture Evaluation*; Technical Report; Software Engineering Institute, Carnegie-Mellon University: Pittsburgh, PA, USA, 2000.
70. Mellon, C. *Views and Beyond: The SEI Approach for Architecture Documentation*; Carnegie Mellon University: Pittsburgh, PA, USA, 2018.
71. Kruchten, P.B. The 4 + 1 View Model of Architecture. *IEEE Softw.* **1995**, *12*, 42–50. [CrossRef]
72. Rozanski, N.; Woods, E. *Software Systems Architecture: Working with Stakeholders Usin Viewpoints and Perspectives*; Addison-Wesley: Boston, MA, USA, 2011.
73. May, N. A survey of software architecture viewpoint models. In Proceedings of the Sixth Australasian Workshop on Software and System Architectures, Brisbane, Australia, 29 March 2005; pp. 13–24.
74. ISO. *ISO Standard 19514:2017 Information Technology—The Object Management Group Systems Modeling Language (OMG SysML)*; ISO: Geneva, Switzerland, 2019.
75. ISO. *ISO Standard 19501:2005 Information Technology—The Unified Modeling Language (OMG UML)*; ISO: Geneva, Switzerland, 2019.
76. Doberkat, E.E. Pipelines: Modelling a software architecture through relations. *Acta Inform.* **2003**, *40*, 37–79. [CrossRef]
77. Shehory, O.M. *Architectural Properties of Multi-Agent Systems*; The Robotics Institute, Carnegie Mellon University: Pittsburgh, PA, USA, 1998.
78. Kidney, J.; Denzinger, J. Testing the limits of emergent behavior in MAS using learning of cooperative behavior. *Front. Artif. Intell. Appl.* **2006**, *141*, 260.
79. Carden, F.; Jedlicka, R.P.; Henry, R. *Telemetry Systems Engineering*; Artech House: Norwood, MA, USA, 2002.
80. Goupil, P.; Boada-Bauxell, J.; Marcos, A.; Cortet, E.; Kerr, M.; Costa, H. AIRBUS efforts towards advanced real-time fault diagnosis and fault tolerant control. *IFAC Proc. Vol.* **2014**, *47*, 3471–3476. [CrossRef]
81. Kritzinger, W.; Karner, M.; Traar, G.; Henjes, J.; Sihn, W. Digital Twin in manufacturing: A categorical literature review and classification. *IFAC-PapersOnLine* **2018**, *51*, 1016–1022. [CrossRef]
82. Dennett, D. Intentional Systems Theory. In *The Oxford Handbook of Philosophy of Mind*; Oxford University Press: Oxford, UK, 2009; pp. 339–350.
83. Bratman, M. *Intention, Plans, and Practical Reason*; Harvard University Press: Cambridge, MA, USA, 1987; Volume 10. [CrossRef]
84. Merriam-Webster. Veracity Dictonary Definition. 2021. Available online: https://www.merriam-webster.com/dictionary/veracity (accessed on 20 July 2021).
85. nxtControl GmbH. The nxtCONTROL Development Environment. 2020. Available online: https://www.nxtcontrol.com/en/engineering/ (accessed on 20 July 2021).
86. Hazzan, O. The reflective practitioner perspective in software engineering education. *J. Syst. Softw.* **2002**, *63*, 161–171. [CrossRef]

87. Barcelos, R.F.; Travassos, G.H. *Evaluation Approaches for Software Architectural Documents: A Systematic Review*; CIbSE: London, UK, 2006; pp. 433–446.
88. Reijonen, V.; Koskinen, J.; Haikala, I. Experiences from scenario-based architecture evaluations with ATAM. In Proceedings of the European Conference on Software Architecture, Copenhagen, Denmark, 23–26 August 2010; Springer: Berlin/Heidelberg, Germany, 2010; pp. 214–229. [CrossRef]
89. 4DIAC-RTE (FORTE): IEC 61499 Compliant Runtime Environment. 2019. Available online: https://www.eclipse.org/4diac/en_rte.php (accessed on 20 July 2021)
90. Defense Advanced Research Projects Agency. *RFC 793 Transmission Control Protocol*; Defense Advanced Research Projects Agency: Arlington County, VA, USA, 1981. Available online: https://datatracker.ietf.org/doc/html/rfc793 (accessed on 20 July 2021).
91. DARPA. *RFC 768 User Datagram Protocol*; DARPA: Arlington County, VA, USA, 1980. Available online: https://www.ietf.org/rfc/rfc768 (accessed on 20 July 2021).
92. Tanveer, A.; Sinha, R.; MacDonell, S.G. On Design-time Security in IEC 61499 Systems: Conceptualisation, Implementation, and Feasibility. In Proceedings of the 2018 IEEE 16th International Conference on Industrial Informatics (INDIN), Porto, Portugal, 18–20 July 2018; pp. 778–785. [CrossRef]
93. The Selenium Testing Environment. 2020. Available online: https://developer.mozilla.org/en-US/docs/Learn/Tools_and_testing/Cross_browser_testing/Your_own_automation_environment (accessed on 20 July 2021).

Article

Topology Inference and Link Parameter Estimation Based on End-to-End Measurements [†]

Grigorios Kakkavas [1], Vasileios Karyotis [1,2] and Symeon Papavassiliou [1,*]

[1] School of Electrical and Computer Engineering, National Technical University of Athens, Iroon Polytechniou 9, 15780 Athens, Greece; gkakkavas@netmode.ntua.gr (G.K.); karyotis@ionio.gr (V.K.)
[2] Department of Informatics, Ionian University, 49100 Corfu, Greece
[*] Correspondence: papavass@mail.ntua.gr; Tel.: +30-210-772-2550
[†] This paper is an extended version of our paper published in the Proceedings of ICC 2020—2020 IEEE International Conference on Communications (ICC), A Distance-Based Agglomerative Clustering Algorithm for Multicast Network Tomography, Dublin, Ireland, 7–11 June 2020.

Abstract: This paper focuses on the design, implementation, experimental validation, and evaluation of a network tomography approach for performing inferential monitoring based on indirect measurements. In particular, we address the problems of inferring the routing tree topology (both logical and physical) and estimating the links' loss rate and jitter based on multicast end-to-end measurements from a source node to a set of destination nodes using an agglomerative clustering algorithm. The experimentally-driven evaluation of the proposed algorithm, particularly the impact of the employed reduction update scheme, takes place in real topologies constructed in an open large-scale testbed. Finally, we implement and present a motivating practical application of the proposed algorithm that combines monitoring with change point analysis to realize performance anomaly detection.

Keywords: network tomography; agglomerative clustering; end-to-end measurements; topology inference; link parameters; change point analysis

Citation: Kakkavas, G.; Karyotis, V.; Papavassiliou, S. Topology Inference and Link Parameter Estimation Based on End-to-End Measurements. *Future Internet* 2022, 14, 45. https://doi.org/10.3390/fi14020045

Academic Editors: Agostino Poggi, Martin Kenyeres, Ivana Budinská and Ladislav Hluchy

Received: 8 January 2022
Accepted: 27 January 2022
Published: 28 January 2022

Publisher's Note: MDPI stays neutral with regard to jurisdictional claims in published maps and institutional affiliations.

Copyright: © 2022 by the authors. Licensee MDPI, Basel, Switzerland. This article is an open access article distributed under the terms and conditions of the Creative Commons Attribution (CC BY) license (https://creativecommons.org/licenses/by/4.0/).

1. Introduction

Nowadays, due to the proliferation of network architectures and technologies, advanced network management requires successfully addressing the challenge of collecting and analyzing massive volumes of data. Network monitoring refers to systems that constantly monitor computer networks for problematic components or abnormal traffic variations, and either notify (via dedicated alarm mechanisms) and/or aid network administrators in troubleshooting and recovering normal operations. Considerable effort has been invested in network monitoring, especially lately, leading to the emergence of radical approaches and disruptive technologies like In-band Network Telemetry (INT) [1] and Programmable Forwarding Engine (PFE) accelerated telemetry systems [2]. These approaches address different challenges and operate in diverse, inter-connected environments, such as legacy, wireless, and SDN-enabled infrastructures.

Among them, Network Tomography (NT) has been proposed as an efficient and lightweight methodology for inferential network monitoring based on indirect measurements [3]. Broadly speaking, NT can be classified into the following three categories [4]:

(i) *link-level NT* that regards the estimation of per link Quality of Service (QoS) parameters (e.g., loss rates, delays, jitter) based on end-to-end path measurements,
(ii) *path-level NT* that concerns the estimation of the origin-destination (OD) traffic intensity matrix based on link-level measurements [5], and
(iii) *topology inference* for reconstructing the topology of the network itself, which is considered unknown.

It can also be categorized as active (injecting probes) or passive (observing existing traffic), depending on the employed measurement methodology. Compared to conventional monitoring techniques that involve the direct measurement of all objects of interest, NT does not require the special-purpose cooperation of all intermediate network elements and reduces the measurement traffic overhead. In this paper, we jointly consider topology inference and link-level NT, aiming at a "minimally-required knowledge" holistic monitoring tool that needs only end-to-end measurements, obtained at the edge through active multicast probing. Our objective is to present and experimentally validate the proposed approach in a generic context, going beyond network monitoring in itself and providing a motivating example of a representative practical application of the developed clustering algorithm.

Over the years, multicast-based NT has received a lot of research attention [6–10]. Compared to these studies, our approach makes use of additive metrics, recovers both the unknown topology and link performance parameters, requires only the pairwise joint empirical distribution of the outcome variables at the destination nodes as input, and is easier to implement since it comprises a heuristic recursive algorithm. Furthermore, it does not employ maximum likelihood estimators, which are not computationally efficient for large-size networks because they involve finding the roots of polynomials whose degrees depend on the number of outgoing links at the internal nodes. Finally, given that the required pairwise distances between terminal nodes can be calculated using unicast packet stripe probing as well, the proposed method is not only feasible under multicast probing. The grouping algorithms presented in [11,12] are the most relevant to our work. However, by incorporating the use of nearest neighbor chains into the agglomerative clustering algorithm, we manage to further reduce the computational complexity of the proposed approach from $O(n^2 \log n)$ to $O(n^2)$. Moreover, all aforementioned works infer the logical routing trees, where paths with no branches are represented as a single logical link. Contrary to that, our method can successfully identify all single-child nodes.

This work builds on [13] and provides important advances compared to what has been published so far. Although the aforementioned initial study forms the basis and the starting point of our current research, the present work has been vastly improved in terms of technical content, analysis, evaluation, and presentation, in a way that complements and significantly extends the contribution of the preliminary conference version. The main differences between the current article and the partial preliminary conference version can be briefly summarized as presenting new ideas (recovery of physical topologies, alternative reduction update formulas), additional experimentation (examining and quantifying a larger number of features and comparing with conventional tools), and a tangible application of the devised clustering algorithm. In greater detail, an important new feature of the proposed and implemented network tomography utility is the ability to infer not only logical routing trees but also the underlying physical routing trees by incorporating information about hop counts. Furthermore, we demonstrate that the reduction update formula, which is used at every iteration of the clustering algorithm for calculating the distances between the newly generated parent and the rest nodes, has a significant impact on the estimation of the link performance parameters. Taking that into consideration, we explore and experimentally compare several reduction update formulas that guarantee the correctness of the agglomerative algorithm, not being limited to only fixed schemes but also including an adaptive scheme that is tailored to the discovered hierarchy, since it depends on the number of offspring of the involved nodes. Finally, we go beyond simply presenting a modified nearest neighbor (NN) chain-extended agglomerative clustering algorithm. We design, implement, and experiment with a tangible application of the proposed inferential method that combines network tomography (NT)-based monitoring with change point analysis to realize performance anomaly detection over an actual topology constructed in an open large-scale testbed.

Overall, through the extended experimentally-driven analysis, we demonstrate the feasibility of our approach, and we provide a more detailed performance evaluation by examining and quantifying a larger number of features while also underlining a number of practical tools that can be used in the development and testing of network services. By designing, implementing, and presenting a tangible application that leverages the devised algorithm and the described extensions/modifications, we demonstrate the practical value of our approach, motivate implementation-driven deployments of similar utilities, and provide insights and good practices that can be adopted by researchers and developers working in related problems. To summarize, the key contributions of this article are the following:

- The logical routing tree can be considered as the "skeleton" of the underlying physical topology, including only its intermediate branching points. To infer physical routing trees, we extend the nearest neighbor (NN) chain-enhanced agglomerative clustering algorithm [13] by incorporating information about hop counts.
- The reduction update formula, which is used at every iteration for calculating the distances between the newly generated parent and the rest nodes, is a critical feature of clustering algorithms. Taking that into consideration, we explore several reduction update formulas that guarantee the correctness of the proposed algorithm, and we examine their impact on the estimation accuracy of the link performance parameters.
- We implement the proposed clustering algorithm with all extensions and alternative options discussed in this paper, creating a complete command-line-based network tomography tool. We publish [14] the source code under a permissive free software license, along with detailed documentation.
- We extensively evaluate the performance of the proposed algorithm, over a comprehensive set of criteria, with real topologies constructed in an open large-scale testbed.
- We design and implement a practical application of the proposed NN-extended clustering algorithm that combines the NT-based monitoring with change point analysis for performance anomaly detection. The respective source code is also publicly available [14].

The remainder of this article is organized as follows. In Section 2, we introduce the network and probing model, along with the considered inference problem. Section 3, describes in detail the proposed algorithm, analyzes the extensions needed for inferring physical routing trees, and explores a variety of alternative reduction update formulas. In Section 4, we present the employed experimental setup and we report the respective performance evaluation results. Finally, Section 5 presents the practical application of the clustering algorithm and Section 6 concludes the paper.

2. Network Model and Problem Formulation

In this work, we focus on tree network topologies that are formed in the case of active probing from a single source. In essence, a designated root node (i.e., the source) actively sends probes to the leaves (i.e., the destination nodes), where traffic is monitored. To facilitate the collection of end-to-end measurements in our experiments using the tools described in Section 4.1, we design the examined networks with the root having only one child. The internal nodes can have exactly two children, in which case the resulting tree is binary, or two or more children, in which case the resulting tree is general. In greater detail, assuming that during the measurement period the underlying routing algorithm determines a unique path from a source to each destination that is reachable from it, the physical routing topology from a source node to a set of destination nodes is a tree called *physical routing tree*. The *logical routing tree* consists of the source node (root), the destination nodes (leaves), and the branching points (i.e., nodes with two or more outgoing links) of the physical routing tree, along with the logical links between them. Consequently, a logical link comprises a sequence of one or more consecutive physical links and the degree of every internal node of the logical routing tree is at least three. The root (i.e., source node) has only one child (therefore a degree of one), and the leaves (i.e., destination nodes) none (therefore a degree of one). Figure 1 presents an indicative topology example of both the physical and the corresponding logical routing trees.

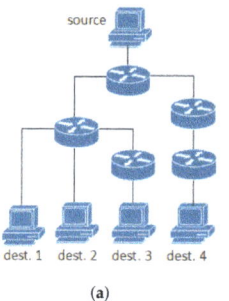 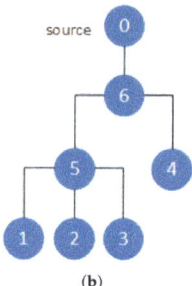

Figure 1. Example of corresponding physical and logical routing trees. (**a**) Physical routing tree. (**b**) Logical routing tree.

Let $T(s, D) = (V, E)$ denote the logical routing tree from source s to a set of destination nodes D, which consists of node set V and edge set E. Every node $k \in V \setminus \{s\}$ has a parent $f(k) \in V$ such that link $e_k \equiv (f(k), k) \in E$. Additionally, every node $k \in V \setminus D$ has a set of children $c(k) = \{j \in V : f(j) = k\}$. Each link $e \in E$ is associated with a performance parameter θ_e (e.g., loss rate, jitter). Finally, the unique path (i.e., sequence of links) that connects nodes i and j on the logical routing tree is denoted by $p(i, j)$. The network inference problem that we consider in this paper regards using aggregate end-to-end measurements obtained at the terminal nodes (i.e., $k \in \{s\} \cup D$) for: (i) inferring the routing tree topology and (ii) estimating the fine-grained network characteristics, i.e., the individual link parameters θ_e (loss rates or jitter).

2.1. Probing Model

In this work, we use source-specific multicast (SSM) due to its effectiveness and efficiency for our purposes. In particular, the multicast probing technique inherently provides sufficient packet-level correlations, which are required to infer the topology and link performance parameters. When a node receives a given multicast probe packet, it forwards a copy of the packet to its children. Therefore, the multicast packets of the same probe observed at various terminal points experience the same network conditions in their shared paths (performance contribution from links in shared paths is identical). Another advantage of multicast probing is that it can scale better compared to its unicast counterpart, given that for the latter back-to-back or even larger stripes of closely spaced unicast packets are required to emulate a multicast probe.

The main drawback of multicasting is that it is not widely deployed and readily available on the Internet. Nevertheless, as previously mentioned, the proposed algorithm can also function without any change or modification under striped unicast probing, albeit with an impact on the probing overhead scalability. The probes are only leveraged to estimate the distances between the terminal nodes, which are given as input to the algorithm. Back-to-back or even larger stripes of closely spaced unicast packets can be used to emulate a multicast probe. Of course, the emulated packet-level correlations achieved using unicast probes cannot be perfect. Therefore, multicast probing is considered the best-case experimental setting for our approach. For every probe traversing the tree, the state of each link of the routing tree is represented by the set of link state variables Y_e, $\forall e \in E$. Similarly, the set of outcome variables X_k, $\forall k \in V$ denotes the (random) outcome of the probe at each node. Clearly, the outcome at node k (i.e., X_k) is determined by the outcome at the node's parent (i.e., $X_{f(k)}$) and the state of the link $e_k = (f(k), k)$ that connects them (i.e., Y_{e_k}).

2.2. Multicast Additive Metrics

Additive link metrics are extremely important in the field of network tomography and have been widely used over the years. Under such formulations, the end-to-end measurements corresponding to paths between terminal nodes are the sums of the individual component link metrics. Delay is an example of an inherent additive link metric, whereas loss rates and other multiplicative metrics can be transformed into additive using a logarithmic scale. The network tomography inference problem can then be expressed as the inverse problem of solving the system of linear equations $y = A \cdot x$, where x is the vector of unknown link parameters, A is the routing or measurement matrix representing the network topology, and y is the vector of observed path-level end-to-end measurements. The goal is to estimate the unobserved vector x given the aforementioned linear model and the known vector of measurements y. The difficulty lies in the fact that the system of linear equations is heavily under-determined.

Using the previously described notation, an additive metric $d : V \times V \to \mathbb{R}^+$ on tree $T = (V, E)$ is a non-negative function such that:

- $0 < d(e) < \infty$, $\forall e \in E$,
- $d(i, j) = 0$ if and only if $i = j$, and
- $d(i, j) = d(j, i) = \sum_{e \in p(i,j)} d(e)$, otherwise.

The topology and the link lengths $d(e), \forall e \in E$ of a tree $T(s, D) = (V, E)$ can be recovered by the pairwise distances $\mathcal{D} = \{d(i, j) : i, j \in \{s\} \cup D\}$ between the terminal nodes under an additive metric [15]. Assuming that the link states are independent and stationary during the measurement period, we can construct the following additive metrics:

- $d(e) = -\log(\theta_e), \forall e \in E$, where θ_e is the success rate (i.e., the complement of loss rate) of link e.
- $d(e) = \theta_e = \text{Var}(Y_e), \forall e \in E$, where Y_e is a random variable that expresses the random queuing delay of link e and θ_e is the square of jitter of link e, with jitter defined as the standard deviation of delay $\sigma(Y_e)$ in order to be additive.

In the first case, the link-state variable Y_e is equal to one (or zero) with probability θ_e (or $1 - \theta_e$), if the probe traverses successfully (or is lost on) link e, and the outcome variable X_k takes value 1, if the probe reaches node k, and value 0 otherwise. Then, the outcome variable at a particular node can be expressed as the product of the link-state variables corresponding to the links comprising the path from the source to that specific node. Furthermore, the probability that this outcome variable takes value one can be computed as the product of the success rates corresponding to the links along that same path. Therefore, we can construct an additive tree metric with a link length equal to the negative logarithm of the complement of the packet loss rate. In the second case, the link-state variable Y_e expresses the random queuing delay of link e and the outcome variable X_k represents the cumulative end-to-end queuing delay that is experienced by the probe on its way to node k. Then, the outcome variable at a particular node can be expressed as the sum of the link-state variables corresponding to the links comprising the path from the source to that specific node. Moreover, given that the variance of a sum of independent random variables is the sum of their variances, the variance of this outcome variable can be computed as the sum of the performance parameters associated with the links along that same path. Consequently, we can construct an additive tree metric with a link length equal to the square of jitter. Accordingly, the pairwise distances between the terminal nodes for the aforementioned additive metrics can be calculated as follows [13]:

$$d(s, i) = \log\left(\frac{1}{\mathbb{P}(X_i = 1)}\right) = -\log(\mathbb{P}(X_i = 1)), \forall i \in D \quad (1)$$

$$d(i,j) = \log\left(\frac{\mathbb{P}(X_i=1)\cdot\mathbb{P}(X_j=1)}{[\mathbb{P}(X_iX_j=1)]^2}\right), \forall i,j \in D \qquad (2)$$

for the loss-based metric, and

$$d(s,i) = \mathrm{Var}(X_i), \forall i \in D \qquad (3)$$

$$d(i,j) = \mathrm{Var}(X_i) + \mathrm{Var}(X_j) - 2\cdot\mathrm{Cov}(X_i,X_j), \forall i,j \in D \qquad (4)$$

for the delay-based metric. Assuming source s sends n probes to the destination nodes D, the outcome variables at the terminal nodes

$$\left(X_k^{(t)}: k \in \{s\}\cup D \text{ and } t=1,2,\cdots,n\right)$$

can be observed. Then, according to the employed additive metric, we can estimate the above pairwise distances leveraging the fact that the maximum likelihood estimator (MLE) of the probability that a Bernoulli random variable takes value one is equal to the sample mean and using the unbiased sample variance (with lost packets ignored) as follows:

$$\hat{d}(s,i) = -\log(\overline{X_i}) \qquad (5)$$

$$\hat{d}(i,j) = \log\left(\frac{\overline{X_i}\cdot\overline{X_j}}{\overline{X_iX_j}^2}\right), \forall i,j \in D \qquad (6)$$

for the loss-based metric, and

$$\hat{d}(s,i) = \widehat{\mathrm{Var}}(X_i), \forall i \in D \qquad (7)$$

$$\hat{d}(i,j) = \widehat{\mathrm{Var}}(X_i) + \widehat{\mathrm{Var}}(X_j) - 2\widehat{\mathrm{Cov}}(X_i,X_j), \forall i,j \in D \qquad (8)$$

for the delay-based metric, where

$$\overline{X_i} = \frac{1}{n}\sum_{t=1}^n X_i^{(t)}, \quad \overline{X_iX_j} = \frac{1}{n}\sum_{t=1}^n X_i^{(t)}X_j^{(t)},$$

$$\widehat{\mathrm{Var}}(X_i) = \frac{1}{n-1}\sum_{t=1}^n \left(X_i^{(t)} - \overline{X_i}\right)^2, \text{ and}$$

$$\widehat{\mathrm{Cov}}(X_i,X_j) = \frac{1}{n-1}\sum_{t=1}^n \left(X_i^{(t)} - \overline{X_i}\right)\left(X_j^{(t)} - \overline{X_j}\right).$$

3. Topology Inference and Estimation of Link Parameters

In this section, we present in detail the nearest neighbor (NN) chain-extended agglomerative clustering algorithm and the modifications/extensions we incorporate to fulfill our objectives.

3.1. Distance-Based Agglomerative Hierarchical Clustering

In order to infer the logical routing tree using the estimated pairwise distances between terminal nodes under the previously described additive metrics, we employ an agglomerative hierarchical clustering algorithm with $O(n^2)$ complexity [13], where n is the number of network nodes. Furthermore, given that there is a one-to-one mapping between the returned edge lengths $d(e), \forall e \in E$ and the underlying link performance parameters $\theta_e, \forall e \in E$ (see Section 2.2), we can also estimate the latter from the former as follows:

- loss rate of link $e = 1 - \theta_e = 1 - 10^{-d(e)}$, and

- jitter of link $e = \sqrt{\theta_e} = \sqrt{d(e)}$, $\forall e \in E$.

Broadly speaking, the employed clustering algorithm operates in a bottom-up manner, starting with a set including all destination nodes, each one in its own cluster, and selecting at each iteration two nodes that are joined and replaced in the set by a new node designated as their parent. This process continues recursively on this reduced set until there is only one node left, which will be the (single) child of the root (source) s. A high-level overview of the algorithm is presented in Figure 2.

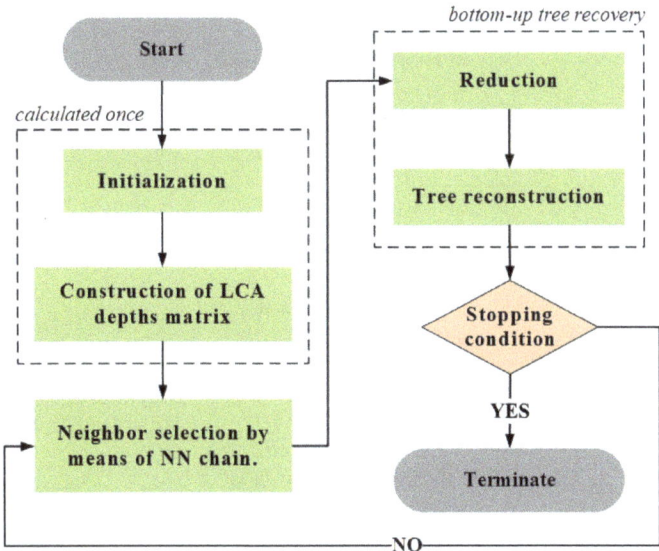

Figure 2. High-level overview of the proposed clustering algorithm.

In the following, we discuss the specifics of the functionality and the detailed operation of each depicted step:

- The *input* of the algorithm is the source node s, the set of destination nodes D, and the estimated pairwise distances between terminal nodes $\hat{\mathcal{D}} = \{\hat{d}(i,j) : i,j \in \{s\} \cup D\}$, calculated as described in Section 2.2.
- The *output* of the algorithm is the logical routing tree $T(s, D) = (V, E)$ and the link lengths $d(e), \forall e \in E$, from which we can obtain the link parameters $\theta_e, \forall e \in E$.
- At *initialization*, we start by adding the source and the destinations to the set of nodes, $V = \{s\} \cup D$, and we initialize the set of edges equal to the empty set, $E = \emptyset$.
- For every pair of nodes i and j of the routing tree, the lowest common ancestor, $\text{LCA}(i,j)$, is the node that is located the farthest from the root and has both nodes as descendants. The depth of the lowest common ancestor, $\ell(i,j) = d(s, \text{LCA}(i,j))$, expresses the length of the shared path from s to i and j. Given that there is a one-to-one mapping between the pairwise distances and the LCA depths, we can equivalently employ the latter to infer the routing tree and estimate the link parameters. To that end, at the step *construction of LCA depths matrix*, we compute the $|D| \times |D|$ matrix of LCA depths $\mathbf{L} = [\ell(i,j)]$, $\forall i,j \in D$ using the equations

$$\ell(i,j) = \frac{1}{2}[d(s,i) + d(s,j) - d(i,j)], \ \forall i,j \in D \text{ and} \tag{9}$$

$$\ell(i,i) = d(s,i), \ \forall i \in D. \tag{10}$$

- At the *neighbor selection* step, we choose the two nodes that are deemed siblings and are about to be joined. Taking into account that the LCA depth of two nodes expresses the length of their shared path, we select the nodes i and j that are *mutual or reciprocal nearest neighbor* (RNNs), meaning that, for each one, their LCA depth is the largest among all others: $\forall k \neq i, j,\ \ell(i,j) \geq \ell(i,k), \ell(j,k)$. The idea is that two siblings must have the largest shared path with one another, compared to all other nodes. Such RNNs can be found efficiently by constructing *nearest neighbor* (NN) chains [16]. Essentially, a NN chain follows paths in the nearest neighbor graph of the clusters, until the paths terminate in a pair of RNNs. It starts at an arbitrary initial node, and it is iteratively extended from the current node at the top of the chain, say i, to its nearest neighbor j such that $\ell(i,j) = \max\limits_{k \neq i} \ell(i,k)$, until it necessarily terminates at a pair of RNNs. After joining the discovered RNNs, the rest NN chain is still valid and, therefore, it is not discarded. Each node (either destination or intermediate created parent) enters the NN chain only once, where it remains until it is joined with another node.
- At *reduction* step, we create node u as the parent of the previously found RNNs i and j, and we calculate its LCA depth with the remaining nodes $\ell(u,k),\ \forall k \in D,\ k \neq u, i, j$. The choice of the employed reduction update formula is a crucial issue, which we analyze in Section 3.3.
- *Tree reconstruction* regards the update of the data structures related to the part of the tree that has been recovered up to this moment. In greater detail, we remove the found RNNs i and j from set D, $D = D \setminus \{i,j\}$; we add the newly created parent node u to sets V and D, $V = V \cup \{u\}$ and $D = D \cup \{u\}$; we add the two new edges to set E, $E = E \cup \{(u,i),(u,j)\}$; and we connect i and j to u with link lengths $d(u,i) = \ell(i,i) - \ell(i,j)$ and $d(u,j) = \ell(j,j) - \ell(i,j)$.
- Finally, if there is only one node left in set D (stopping condition $|D| = 1$), we connect that remaining node with the source and we terminate the algorithm, otherwise we return to the neighbor selection step and we repeat the process.

Given that a pair of RNNs is selected as siblings at every iteration, the output of the algorithm will be a binary inferred tree. To successfully apply the algorithm to general routing trees, nodes can be grouped as if the tree was binary, and then the "extra" edges of approximately zero length (excluding the edge between the root and its single child) can be removed at a post-processing step.

3.2. Inferring Physical Routing Trees

As previously mentioned, the output of the algorithm presented in Section 3.1 is the logical routing tree, which consists of the branching points of the physical topology. However, internal nodes where no branching of traffic occurs (i.e., nodes with a single child) do not appear in the logical tree and long paths with no branches might be represented as a single logical link. Therefore, the logical tree might differ significantly from the underlying physical routing tree. To infer more accurately the physical routing tree, in this work we incorporate into the algorithm information regarding the number of hops needed for reaching each node starting from the source. Assuming that we only have access to the network edge and not to the internal nodes, such information can be readily obtained simply by capturing the employed probes at the destination nodes using a packet analyzer tool and examining their time-to-live (TTL) fields. The idea is that two nodes that are siblings must have the same TTL value. At each iteration, the TTL value of the newly created parent of the selected RNNs is calculated based on the TTL value of its children.

In more detail, we start by extracting the TTL values corresponding to each destination node from the realized end-to-end measurements. Then, we modify the neighbor selection step as follows. After selecting a pair of RNNs, we check the respective TTL values of the two nodes. If they are equal, we proceed to the next step. Otherwise, we can deduce that the node with the smaller TTL value is located in a path with no branching points. To rectify this, we assign this node as the single child of a newly created parent, with a properly adjusted TTL value (i.e., incremented by one). We continue adding such parent nodes until the new TTL value becomes equal to that of the other RNN. Following that in the next step, we properly set (i.e., increment by one) the TTL value of the node that is designated as the parent of the two siblings (i.e., the two RNNs in the first case, or the head of the no branching path and the remaining RNN in the second case), and we proceed to the rest of the algorithm as before.

3.3. Reduction Update Formulas

Contrary to the conventional greedy agglomerative approach that repeatedly joins the two overall "closest" nodes (in our context, the nodes with the overall largest LCA depth), the proposed NN chain-enhanced algorithm joins any pair of RNNs as it is found. Consequently, the order of the cluster merges might be different. However, provided that the reduction update formula satisfies two certain properties, the resulted hierarchy will be the same [17]. Such suitable reduction update schemes are:

- the *single* reduction update formula:

$$\ell(u,k) = \min\{\ell(i,k), \ell(j,k)\} \quad (11)$$

- the *complete* reduction update formula:

$$\ell(u,k) = \max\{\ell(i,k), \ell(j,k)\} \quad (12)$$

- the *average* reduction update formula:

$$\ell(u,k) = \frac{1}{n_i + n_j}\left[n_i \cdot \ell(i,k) + n_j \cdot \ell(j,k)\right] \quad (13)$$

- the *weighted* reduction update formula:

$$\ell(u,k) = \frac{1}{2}[\ell(i,k) + \ell(j,k)] \quad (14)$$

$\forall k \in D$, $k \neq u, i, j$, where i and j are the pair of RNNs, u is the newly created parent, and n_i, n_j, n_k are the sizes of clusters i, j and k, which in our context can be interpreted as the number of the descendants of the respective nodes. As can be seen, the single, complete, and weighted schemes are "conservative" in the sense that they are fixed and do not adapt to the discovered hierarchy, whereas the average scheme depends also on the number of offspring of the involved nodes, thus being better tailored to each particular case. In [13], the use of the weighted and complete update formulas has been examined. Here, we comparatively explore all of the aforementioned schemes, as well as the generic convex formula analyzed in Section 4.2.

4. Performance Evaluation

The experiments presented in this article take place in a fully-controlled testbed to demonstrate the feasibility of our ideas. Exploring how our methods can be further fine-tuned and adapted to specific types of networks (e.g., cloud, overlay, or data center networks) and their particular characteristics is left for future work.

4.1. Experimental Setup

To evaluate the performance of the proposed algorithm in topology inference and estimate the link loss rates and jitter, we constructed several binary (i.e., all internal nodes have exactly two children) and general (i.e., internal nodes have two or more children) physical routing trees, following the network model described in Section 2, over bare-metal hardware in the Virtual Wall [18] testbed of the Fed4FIREPlus [19] federation. Routing was realized using the *Quagga* software suite and network impairment (i.e., loss and jitter) on links were configured on software using the *netem* kernel module and the *tc* utility. In particular, we employed the *ospfd* and *pimd* quagga routing daemons, implementing the OSPF, PIM-SSM, and IGMP protocols, while the links' loss rates and jitter values were chosen in the ranges 0–20% and 0–400 ms, respectively. The *iperf* traffic tool was used for performing multicast active probing and the required end-to-end measurements were obtained at the outgoing interface of the source node and the incoming interfaces of the destination nodes using the *tcpdump* command-line packet analyzer. For every routing tree, three different numbers of probes were examined, namely probes 2128, 5105, and 10,207.

4.2. Results and Discussion

The command-line network tomography tool has been developed in Python 3 and accepts as arguments the tcpdump output (since we do not need the detailed content of probe packets, we do not use pcap files) captured at the outgoing link of the source and the incoming links of the destinations. The binary routing trees are inferred correctly for all the conducted experimental scenarios. The extension of the algorithm to general routing trees is somewhat more complicated since it requires the selection of a suitable threshold that may vary from case to case due to the accumulated estimation errors of link lengths. For every examined experimental scenario, there is a fitting threshold under which the general routing tree is reconstructed correctly. However, in practice, it is more realistic to use a single predetermined hard-coded threshold. In this case, 48 out of 48, and 36 out of 48 experimental configurations (i.e., combinations of topology type, number of probes, and reduction update scheme) result in a correctly recovered tree under the loss-based metric and the jitter-based metric, respectively.

Table 1 lists the aggregated errors of the conducted experiments, to evaluate the accuracy of the link performance parameter estimation for several physical routing trees. The first column indicates the type of the studied topology (either binary or general physical routing tree) and the number of its nodes. The rest columns present the aggregated estimation errors of the respective test networks for each examined reduction update formula presented in Section 3.3 and for three different numbers of multicast probes (namely, 2128, 5105, and 10,207 probes) generated using iperf. In particular, we calculate and report the Root Mean Square Error (RMSE) for every experimental scenario (i.e., combination of topology, employed reduction formula, and the number of probes) according to the following equation:

$$\text{RMSE} = \sqrt{\frac{1}{|E|-1} \sum_{e \in E \setminus \{(s,c(s))\}} (y_e - \hat{y}_e)^2} \qquad (15)$$

where $\hat{y}_e$ is the estimate of the loss rate (or jitter) of link e, and y_e is the respective ground truth (i.e., the argument of tc). In other words, we consider the arguments that we passed to the tc utility during the experimental setup as the ground truth for the actual values of the links' loss rates and jitter that are compared to the estimations returned by our model. Loss rates are written as percentages, and jitter is measured in milliseconds. As can be seen, even though the estimation accuracy improves as the number of employed probes increases, the reported errors are relatively small for all configurations. Furthermore, despite being one of the "fixed" schemes, the weighted formula gives the better estimations for the majority of the experiments, followed closely by the average scheme, the only "adaptive" option.

Conventional network monitoring tools based on traditional IP-based mechanisms (e.g., ping, traceroute) are device-centric hop-by-hop approaches that rely on exchanging traffic (e.g., ICMP packets) with intermediate nodes and involve the direct measurement and observation of all entities of interest. Consequently, they require the special-purpose cooperation and participation of all network elements, which is not always feasible in large-scale IP networks due to administrative or security considerations (e.g., many nodes are configured to ignore ICMP packets altogether). Additionally, contrary to the proposed inferential approach, they assume knowledge of the exact topology of the examined network. Another important benefit of the presented NT-based method compared to traditional tools is the ability to provide a global overview of the network state without collecting fine-grained individual statistics but using end-to-end measurements realized at the network edge. As such, it reduces the computational and traffic overhead of the measurement process by decreasing the generated probing load and the consumption of valuable network resources (e.g., bandwidth, CPU, and memory).

Table 1. Estimation errors of the conducted experimental scenarios.

Physical Routing Tree		Single			Complete			Average			Weighted		
		2k	5k	10k	2k	5k	10k	2k	5k	10k	2k	5k	10k
Type	# Nds	Root Mean Square Error for Loss Rate Estimation (%)											
Bin.	8	0.6369	0.4859	0.3879	0.5892	0.3714	0.4061	0.6124	0.4248	0.3961	0.6124	0.4248	0.3961
Bin.	16	1.1824	0.6066	0.4431	1.8491	0.7492	0.4333	1.2346	0.6496	0.3912	1.2189	0.6442	0.3902
Bin.	24	1.2486	0.4924	0.4086	1.2859	0.5643	0.4939	1.1297	0.4881	0.4152	1.1393	0.5087	0.3963
Bin.	32	1.5678	0.9790	0.7226	1.5692	0.9542	0.5588	1.1749	0.8423	0.4649	1.1980	0.8354	0.4399
Gen.	10	0.7798	0.3335	0.4609	0.7787	0.3172	0.6394	0.6826	0.3180	0.5238	0.6627	0.3177	0.5357
Gen.	20	1.1571	0.5012	0.3354	0.9676	0.6972	0.3640	0.9334	0.5398	0.3079	0.8770	0.5344	0.3173
Gen.	30	0.9128	0.5867	0.6108	0.8889	0.5476	0.4623	0.7308	0.5169	0.4707	0.7432	0.5157	0.4718
Gen.	40	1.2380	0.8134	0.6406	1.2977	0.8368	0.6924	1.0557	0.6950	0.5111	1.1451	0.6597	0.5120
Type	# Nds	Root Mean Square Error for Jitter Estimation (ms)											
Bin.	8	2.2884	2.2625	1.8829	2.4840	2.3450	1.9747	2.3589	2.2891	1.9122	2.3589	2.2891	1.9122
Bin.	16	10.7957	5.1186	3.3833	7.5524	4.7407	4.0048	7.7135	4.7855	3.6110	7.1554	4.7276	3.3867
Bin.	24	9.0789	5.2434	4.0306	8.9049	4.7218	3.4756	7.7404	4.7545	3.6221	7.6445	4.6965	3.4926
Bin.	32	13.4703	7.4144	4.4306	14.6285	10.1443	6.5357	10.9308	7.0454	4.3438	11.0575	6.7905	4.4002
Gen.	10	1.9835	1.5422	1.4080	3.6359	1.5546	1.5469	1.8689	1.3350	1.4610	2.1025	1.3607	1.4249
Gen.	20	7.7615	4.5666	3.2201	9.3203	5.8837	3.8564	6.0876	4.7976	3.1658	5.7866	4.7219	3.1139
Gen.	30	7.3599	6.0090	3.2523	12.8225	8.3969	5.1931	7.4152	5.2917	3.5243	6.8374	5.2616	3.4022
Gen.	40	11.8077	6.4343	5.0352	14.0348	7.7253	6.7969	10.3950	5.2412	4.4222	10.2611	5.1472	4.2874

Assuming ideal conditions for the conventional tools (i.e., a priori known topology and unobstructed access to all intermediate nodes) and focusing only on link parameter estimation, we demonstrate the relation between measurement overhead and estimation accuracy for the NT-based approach and a representative conventional monitoring tool by selecting the general physical routing tree topology with 10 nodes and measuring the links' loss rates with the iperf tool using UDP probes (running an iperf server and client at the endpoints of the links). In particular, iperf was configured to send 1022, 1532, and 2042 probes at each link, resulting in 8176, 12,256, and 16,336 probes in total over the entire network. The achieved RMSE (the average of three measurements) was 0.5970, 0.4277, and 0.3335, respectively. As can be seen by comparing the respective results listed in Table 1, our approach can yield comparable estimation errors while utilizing a smaller number of probes, even in such a small-scale sample network.

In order to demonstrate the impact of the reduction update scheme to the estimation accuracy, we consider the following generic formula:

$$\ell(u,k) = \alpha\ell(i,k) + (1-\alpha)\ell(j,k), \text{ with } 0 \leq \alpha \leq 1, \forall k \in D, k \neq u, i, j. \tag{16}$$

Equation (16) can be employed during the reduction step of the clustering algorithm to compute the LCA depth of the newly created parent node u with every other node k as a convex combination of the LCA depths of that node with the two selected RNNs (i.e., nodes i and j). Since the coefficients of a convex combination must be non-negative and must sum to 1, in our case, α takes a value within the range 0—1. We select one of the experimental scenarios (Bin. 32) and we plot the resulting RMSE in relation to the value of α (Figure 3) under the loss-based metric. As can be seen, the error varies significantly as the employed update formula changes. In this particular case, it appears that the best result is obtained for $\alpha = 0.79$.

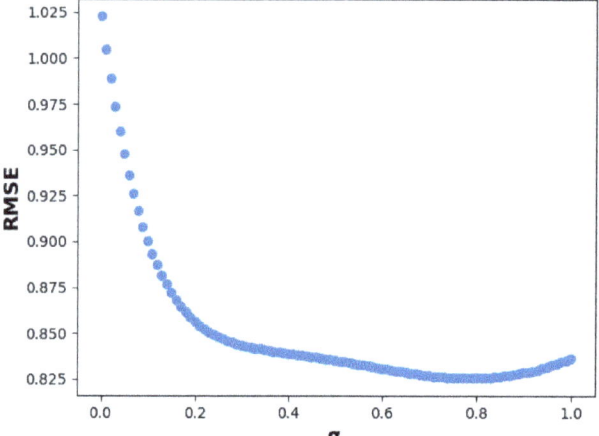

Figure 3. RMSE for different values of α.

Finally, Table 2 lists the execution time (in seconds) for the various experimental scenarios, as recorded in a reference machine with the following specifications: Intel Core i5-6500 @4x 3.6 GHz CPU and 16 GB DDR4 2133 MHz RAM. These measurements were taken using 5105 multicast probes, which were transmitted in 60 s (a time period that is not considered in this table). As it is evident, although no special optimizations have been made to that end, the required times are indeed rather small and depend on the size of the examined topology (the differences between alternative configurations applied to each examined tree are negligible). Nevertheless, an implementation in a compiled language is expected to further reduce the execution time, if so desired.

Table 2. Execution time of experimental scenarios.

Physical Tree		Single	Complete	Average	Weighted
Type	# Nds	\multicolumn{4}{c}{Loss Rate Estimation Execution Time (s)}			
Bin.	8	0.2665	0.2614	0.2592	0.2645
Bin.	16	0.3005	0.3042	0.2988	0.2989
Bin.	24	0.3950	0.3940	0.4008	0.3976
Bin.	32	0.4626	0.4586	0.4578	0.4555
Gen.	10	0.2879	0.2847	0.2876	0.2878
Gen.	20	0.3669	0.3655	0.3699	0.5344
Gen.	30	0.4797	0.4857	0.4798	0.4793
Gen.	40	0.5346	0.5285	0.5357	0.5281

Table 2. *Cont.*

Physical Tree		Single	Complete	Average	Weighted
Type	# Nds	Jitter Estimation Execution Time (s)			
Bin.	8	0.3229	0.3257	0.3212	0.3272
Bin.	16	0.4459	0.4515	0.4459	0.4448
Bin.	24	0.6800	0.6871	0.6803	0.6816
Bin.	32	0.9027	0.9021	0.9127	0.9140
Gen.	10	0.3823	0.3783	0.3830	0.3809
Gen.	20	0.6514	0.6620	0.6668	0.6620
Gen.	30	1.0172	1.0143	1.0189	1.0104
Gen.	40	1.3413	1.3435	1.3496	1.3294

5. Motivating Detection Application

As previously mentioned, one of the main objectives of this work is to go beyond validating the feasibility of the proposed clustering algorithm to designing, implementing, and presenting an actual application that leverages the devised inferential monitoring approach for performing a tangible task in a real testing network. The reasons for pursuing this direction are manifold:

1. We want to demonstrate the practical value of our technical content and point out that it is not limited to theoretical contributions.
2. We aim to motivate the adoption and further extension of our methods by researchers and developers working on related problems by providing a ready-to-use open-source implementation of an NT-enabled network service.
3. We try to highlight some representative tools and outline the overall process that can be followed for performing validation trials and experiments with real equipment.

Monitoring and identifying unusual or anomalous activity is essential for ensuring the efficient operation of network infrastructures. Hereinafter, we combine the proposed clustering algorithm with change point analysis [20] for detecting the occurrence of performance anomalies (i.e., abrupt changes to loss events). The topology employed in our experiments is illustrated in Figure 4, and for change point detection we have leveraged the methods provided by the ruptures [21] library. In particular, the approach we follow consists of the following steps:

(i) execute active multicast probing at the periphery of the network,
(ii) apply the NN-extended clustering algorithm to estimate the loss rates of all links,
(iii) repeat the previous two steps at regular intervals/rounds and record the obtained estimates in a multivariate time series, and
(iv) perform offline change point analysis on the multivariate time series to detect the breakpoints, i.e., the rounds where the loss rates' distribution changes significantly.

To coordinate the probing process and the required traffic captures, a node that can reach all terminal nodes is appointed as a controller. This controller is also charged with collecting all capture files and estimating the links' loss rates via network tomography at every round/iteration, to create a multivariate time series. The interactions between the controller and the terminal nodes (i.e., source and destinations) in every round/iteration are depicted in Figure 5. All communications between the nodes are realized with the ZeroMQ [22] asynchronous messaging library (following the request-reply messaging pattern) and, after constructing the multivariate time series, the linearly penalized segmentation (Pelt) algorithm [23] is employed for detecting the change points.

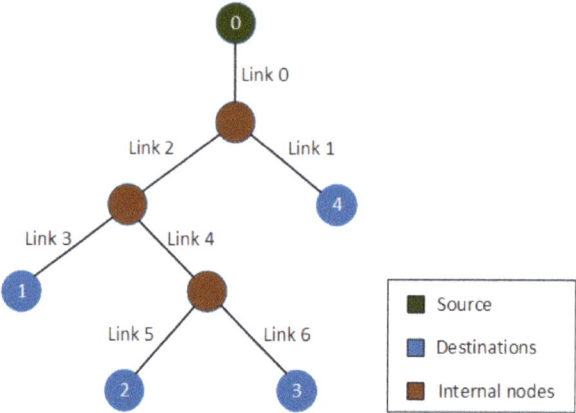

Figure 4. Employed experimental topology.

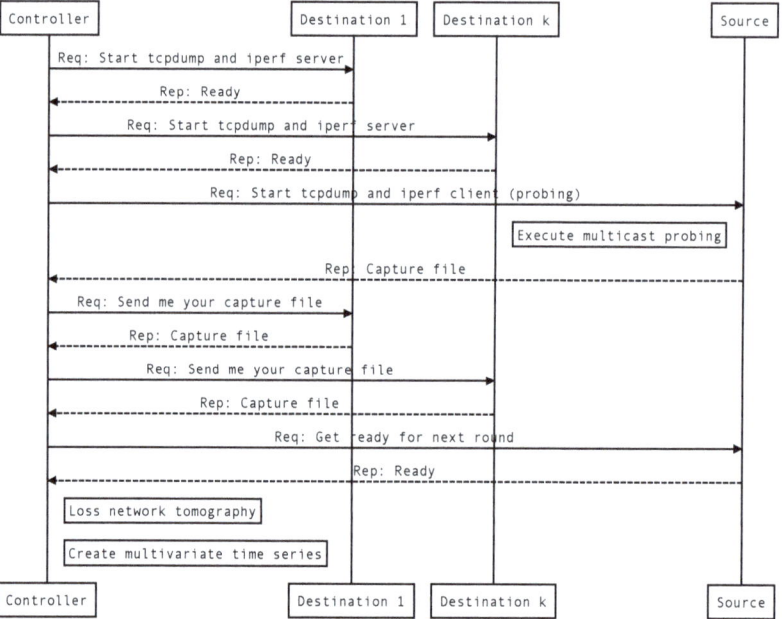

Figure 5. Sequence diagram of the interactions among the nodes in one round.

Figure 6 illustrates the loss rate estimates for every link of the topology (obtained using the proposed algorithm) across 250 iterations/rounds. The change of color indicates the real breakpoints (i.e., the iterations when the underlying distribution of the links' loss rates was changed during the experiment—the ground truth) and the dashed lines denote the breakpoints that were detected by applying the offline change-point algorithm to the obtained estimates. As can be seen, the two sets of breakpoints are indistinguishable.

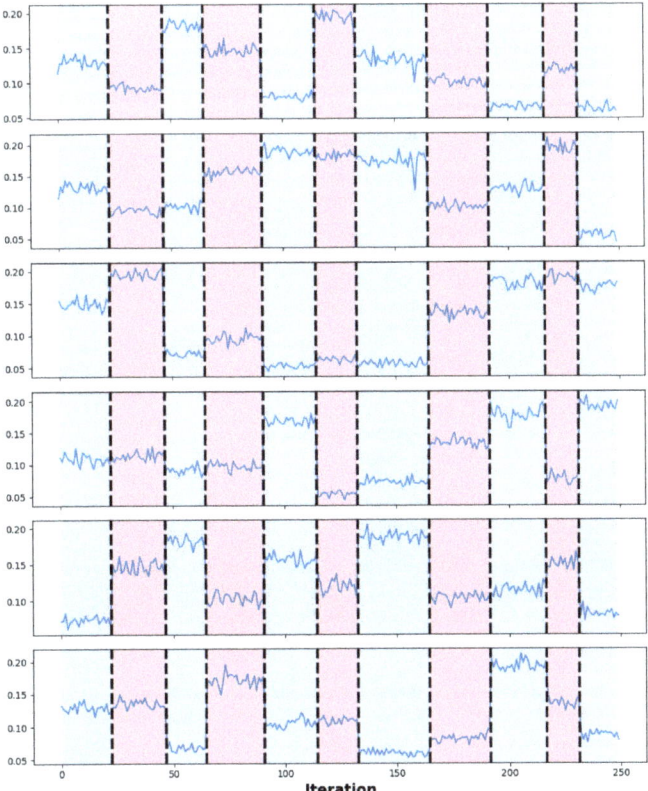

Figure 6. Loss rate estimates and detected change points.

6. Conclusions

In this article, we presented and implemented a clustering algorithm for performing inferential network monitoring based on multicast end-to-end measurements. Specifically, we addressed the problems of inferring the routing tree topology (both logical and physical) and estimating two link performance parameters (i.e., loss rate and jitter). The experimental results regarding the accuracy and the execution time of the proposed algorithm, as well as the presented motivating application leveraging change point analysis, demonstrated its promising potential as a close to real-time monitoring tool and an enabler of performance anomaly detection.

Regarding future work, we plan to explore and experimentally validate more applications of the proposed NT monitoring approach. One such example is the development of a utility-based framework enabling advanced decision-making. The envisaged utility function can incorporate network-centric QoS parameters provided and updated by the clustering algorithm to promote informed decisions based on network utility maximization.

Author Contributions: All authors contributed to the conceptualization of the paper. G.K. and V.K. outlined the structure of the article. G.K. was responsible for software development, performance evaluation, and preparation of the original draft. V.K. and S.P. performed the critical review and overall consistency check. All authors have read and agreed to the published version of the manuscript.

Funding: This work was supported by the European Commission in the framework of the H2020-ICT-19-2019 project 5G-HEART (Grant Agreement No. 857034).

Data Availability Statement: Not Applicable, the study does not report any data.

Conflicts of Interest: The authors declare no conflict of interest.

Abbreviations

The following abbreviations are used in this manuscript:

INT	In-band Network Telemetry
PFE	Programmable Forwarding Engine
SDN	Software Defined Networking
NT	Network Tomography
QoS	Quality of Service
OD	Origin-Destination
NN	Nearest Neighbor
SSM	Source-Specific Multicast
MLE	Maximum Likelihood Estimator
LCA	Lowest Common Ancestor
RNNs	Reciprocal Nearest Neighbor
TTL	Time-To-Live
RMSE	Root Mean Square Error

References

1. Haxhibeqiri, J.; Isolani, P.H.; Marquez-Barja, J.M.; Moerman, I.; Hoebeke, J. In-Band Network Monitoring Technique to Support SDN-Based Wireless Networks. *IEEE Trans. Netw. Serv. Manag.* **2021**, *18*, 627–641. [CrossRef]
2. Sonchack, J.; Michel, O.; Aviv, A.J.; Keller, E.; Smith, J.M. Scaling Hardware Accelerated Network Monitoring to Concurrent and Dynamic Queries with *Flow. In Proceedings of the 2018 USENIX Annual Technical Conference (USENIX ATC 18), Boston, MA, USA, 11–13 July 2018; pp. 823–835.
3. Kakkavas, G.; Stamou, A.; Karyotis, V.; Papavassiliou, S. Network Tomography for Efficient Monitoring in SDN-Enabled 5G Networks and Beyond: Challenges and Opportunities. *IEEE Commun. Mag.* **2021**, *59*, 70–76. [CrossRef]
4. Kakkavas, G.; Gkatzioura, D.; Karyotis, V.; Papavassiliou, S. A Review of Advanced Algebraic Approaches Enabling Network Tomography for Future Network Infrastructures. *Future Internet* **2020**, *12*, 20. [CrossRef]
5. Kakkavas, G.; Kalntis, M.; Karyotis, V.; Papavassiliou, S. Future Network Traffic Matrix Synthesis and Estimation Based on Deep Generative Models. In Proceedings of the 2021 International Conference on Computer Communications and Networks (ICCCN), Athens, Greece, 19–22 July 2021. [CrossRef]
6. Caceres, R.; Duffield, N.G.; Horowitz, J.; Towsley, D.F. Multicast-based inference of network-internal loss characteristics. *IEEE Trans. Inf. Theory* **1999**, *45*, 2462–2480. [CrossRef]
7. Duffield, N.; Horowitz, J.; Presti, F.L.; Towsley, D. Multicast topology inference from measured end-to-end loss. *IEEE Trans. Inf. Theory* **2002**, *48*, 26–45. [CrossRef]
8. Presti, F.L.; Duffield, N.; Horowitz, J.; Towsley, D. Multicast-based inference of network-internal delay distributions. *IEEE/ACM Trans. Netw.* **2002**, *10*, 761–775. [CrossRef]
9. Liang, G.; Yu, B. Maximum pseudo likelihood estimation in network tomography. *IEEE Trans. Signal Process.* **2003**, *51*, 2043–2053. [CrossRef]
10. Duffield, N.; Horowitz, J.; Presti, F.L.; Towsley, D. Explicit Loss Inference in Multicast Tomography. *IEEE Trans. Inf. Theory* **2006**, *52*, 3852–3855. [CrossRef]
11. Ni, J.; Xie, H.; Tatikonda, S.; Yang, Y. Efficient and Dynamic Routing Topology Inference from End-to-End Measurements. *IEEE/ACM Trans. Netw.* **2010**, *18*, 123–135. [CrossRef]
12. Ni, J.; Tatikonda, S. Network Tomography Based on Additive Metrics. *IEEE Trans. Inf. Theory* **2011**, *57*, 7798–7809. [CrossRef]
13. Kakkavas, G.; Karyotis, V.; Papavassiliou, S. A Distance-based Agglomerative Clustering Algorithm for Multicast Network Tomography. In Proceedings of the ICC 2020—2020 IEEE International Conference on Communications (ICC), Dublin, Ireland, 7–11 June 2020. [CrossRef]
14. Kakkavas, G. Inferential Network Monitoring. Available online: https://gitlab.com/gkakkavas/lca-rnn-extension (accessed on 7 January 2022).
15. Buneman, P. The Recovery of Trees from Measures of Dissimilarity. In *Mathematics the Archeological and Historical Sciences*; Edinburgh University Press: Edinburgh, UK, 1971; pp. 387–395.
16. Murtagh, F.; Contreras, P. Algorithms for hierarchical clustering: An overview, II. *WIREs Data Min. Knowl. Discov.* **2017**, *7*. [CrossRef]
17. Müllner, D. Modern hierarchical, agglomerative clustering algorithms. *arXiv* **2011**, arXiv:1109.2378.
18. Virtual Wall. Available online: https://doc.ilabt.imec.be/ilabt/virtualwall/ (accessed on 7 January 2022).
19. Federation For Fire Plus. Available online: https://www.fed4fire.eu/ (accessed on 7 January 2022).

20. Aminikhanghahi, S.; Cook, D.J. A survey of methods for time series change point detection. *Knowl. Inf. Syst.* **2016**, *51*, 339–367. [CrossRef] [PubMed]
21. Truong, C.; Oudre, L.; Vayatis, N. Selective review of offline change point detection methods. *Signal Process.* **2020**, *167*, 107299. [CrossRef]
22. Hintjens, P. ØMQ—The Guide. Available online: https://zguide.zeromq.org/ (accessed on 5 January 2022).
23. Killick, R.; Fearnhead, P.; Eckley, I.A. Optimal Detection of Changepoints with a Linear Computational Cost. *J. Am. Stat. Assoc.* **2012**, *107*, 1590–1598. [CrossRef]

Article

GRAPHOL: A Graphical Language for Ontology Modeling Equivalent to OWL 2

Domenico Lembo [1,*], Valerio Santarelli [2], Domenico Fabio Savo [3,*] and Giuseppe De Giacomo [1]

1. Department of Computer, Control and Management Engineering, Sapienza Università di Roma, Via Ariosto 25, 00185 Roma, Italy; degiacomo@diag.uniroma1.it
2. OBDA Systems S.R.L., Via di Casal Boccone, 00137 Roma, Italy; santarelli@obdasystems.com
3. Department of Management, Information and Production Engineering (DIGIP), Università degli Studi di Bergamo, Via A. Einstein 2, 24044 Dalmine, Italy
* Correspondence: lembo@diag.uniroma1.it (D.L.); domenicofabio.savo@unibg.it (D.F.S.)

Abstract: In this paper we study GRAPHOL, a fully graphical language inspired by standard formalisms for conceptual modeling, similar to the UML class diagram and the ER model, but equipped with formal semantics. We formally prove that GRAPHOL is equivalent to OWL 2, i.e., it can capture every OWL 2 ontology and vice versa. We also present some usability studies indicating that GRAPHOL is suitable for quick adoption by conceptual modelers that are familiar with UML and ER. This is further testified by the adoption of GRAPHOL for ontology representation in several industrial projects.

Keywords: ontology and conceptual modeling; OWL; description logics; graphical modeling languages

Citation: Lembo, D.; Santarelli, V.; Savo, D.F.; De Giacomo, G. GRAPHOL: A Graphical Language for Ontology Modeling Equivalent to OWL 2. *Future Internet* **2022**, *14*, 78. https://doi.org/10.3390/fi14030078

Academic Editors: Agostino Poggi, Martin Kenyeres, Ivana Budinská and Ladislav Hluchy

Received: 18 January 2022
Accepted: 25 February 2022
Published: 28 February 2022

Publisher's Note: MDPI stays neutral with regard to jurisdictional claims in published maps and institutional affiliations.

Copyright: © 2022 by the authors. Licensee MDPI, Basel, Switzerland. This article is an open access article distributed under the terms and conditions of the Creative Commons Attribution (CC BY) license (https://creativecommons.org/licenses/by/4.0/).

1. Introduction

There is a long tradition in many areas of computer science of conceptualizing domains of interest in terms of classes and relationships using a graphical or diagrammatic model. Consider, for example, ER (entity–relationship) diagrams [1], ubiquitously used in databases, or UML class diagrams [2], the de facto standard in software engineering for information modeling (when used as conceptual models rather than to represent software components). While often such diagrams are used in a semi-formal way to help communication, it is well-recognized that having precise semantics is actually needed to avoid ambiguities in design.

Interestingly, the very first conceptual languages developed in AI were also graphical, most prominently semantic networks [3,4]. However, most work on knowledge representation in AI has focused more on automated reasoning, and has gradually abandoned the graphical conceptual languages in favor of logical languages. This process has started with the famous paper "What's in a link" [5], which questioned the inherent ambiguity of graphical conceptual languages of the time, and has continued with the work on KL-ONE [6], then followed by the introduction of modern description logics (DLs) [7]. Nevertheless, by the early 1990s, a research program started to emerge: not to disregard, but to try to logically reconstruct graphical conceptual models used in many fields, such as software development and information systems, in order to enable automated reasoning on them [8–10]. This program has actually been one of the thrusts towards more and more expressive DLs [11] that ultimately led to the development of OWL and OWL 2 [12].

In this paper we bring about a novel contribution to this program: we study a graphical formalism, called GRAPHOL, which resembles ER and UML class diagrams, but has inherent formal semantics based on DLs and is able to fully capture the ontology language OWL 2. Our proposal comes after a few years of experience in ontology modeling in IT organizations that are knowledgeable on information systems and software engineering, so are familiar with UML and ER, but have only a technological view of ontology languages such as OWL 2 (e.g., [13–15]). In these contexts, people often struggle to effectively use the logical formalisms through which ontologies are typically specified, thus slowing down the adoption of semantic technologies. GRAPHOL mitigates this problem, since it provides IT people with a formalism for specifying and reading ontologies rooted in conceptual modeling languages they are used to. Indeed, its usage has helped substantially in taking up semantic technologies in the industrial use cases [16–21].

We point out that we have also developed tools for drawing GRAPHOL diagrams and translating them into standard OWL 2 ontology format. These tools, however, are not treated in depth in this paper, and we refer the reader to [22,23] and to the Github repository of the Eddy ontology editor (https://github.com/obdasystems/eddy, accessed on 17 January 2022) for the details. Here, instead, we study GRAPHOL as a language, and focus on its formal properties. Specifically, we give its mathematical semantics, based on DLs, and show that GRAPHOL diagrams can be translated into OWL 2 ontologies and vice versa. Furthermore, we describe a user evaluation study we carried out to verify the usability of our language. A preliminary version of some of the contributions given in this paper can be found in [24].

1.1. Introducing the GRAPHOL Language

To obtain an idea of GRAPHOL and its relation with UML and ER, in Figure 1 we model a simple situation about students and courses they attend, using a UML class diagram, a GRAPHOL diagram, and a set of DL axioms, all expressible in OWL 2. We assume that the reader is familiar with UML class diagrams [2], DLs [11], and OWL 2 [12]. Furthermore, since we adopt the DL notation throughout the paper to express logical axioms, we use the DL terminology for ontology predicates, e.g., we use "concept" to denote a set of objects (i.e., a "class" in OWL parlance), "role" to denote a binary relationship between concepts (i.e., an "ObjectProperty" in OWL parlance), and "attribute" to denote a binary relationship between a concept and a domain of values (i.e., a "DataProperty" relating objects to datatypes in OWL parlance). In all the three versions of the model, we use the same alphabet for predicates. The model states that a student must attend at least a course, that university students are students, that graduate courses are courses, and that university students can only attend graduate courses. One can see that, in GRAPHOL, concepts are represented through rectangles, analogously to UML, while, as in ER, diamonds are used for roles. Furthermore, solid directed arrows represent inclusions, as in UML and ER (cf. the inclusion between UniversityStudent and Student). However, differently from UML and ER, in GRAPHOL they do not need to involve only named concepts. The use of a diamond to represent a role, i.e., a "node" in the diagram, allows us indeed to depict, in a simple graphical way, concept expressions over the domain and the range of a role, i.e., over its first or second component, by connecting the role to possibly labeled blank and solid boxes, respectively. For example, in Figure 1, the blank box labeled with "forall" and linked to the role attends denotes the set of individuals that attend only graduate courses. The inclusion drawn between UniversityStudent and this concept expression specifies that a university student can only attend graduate courses, which corresponds to the DL inclusion axiom UniversityStudent $\sqsubseteq$ $\forall$attends.GraduateCourse. We remark that this property is not directly expressible in a graphical way in UML, where we need to specify it as an external constraint (cf. the note in the diagram), possibly expressed in a logical language such as OCL.

We notice that the idea of extending or adapting UML or ER to capture OWL is indeed not new. However, GRAPHOL is distinguished from the other proposals with precise semantics, such as [25–29] by its ability to capture any OWL 2 ontology in a completely graphical way. Indeed, previous UML-inspired approaches typically require to annotate diagrams with formulas corresponding to complex OWL expressions. Clearly, this hinders both the diagrammatic representation of the ontology and its intuitive understanding. A more in depth discussion on related work is given in Section 2.

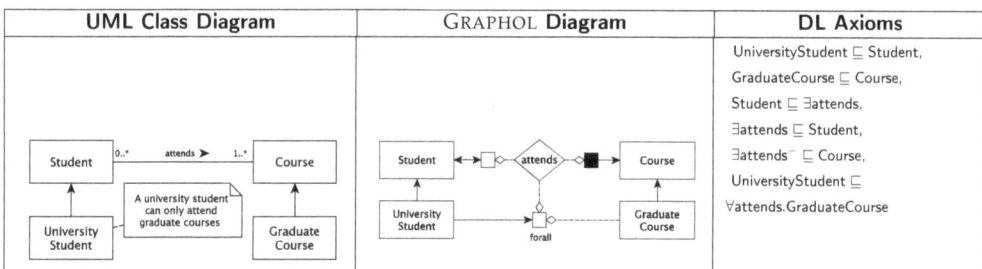

Figure 1. Introductory example.

1.2. Paper Organization and Contributions

The rest of the paper is organized as follows. As stated, we first provide an overview of related work on graphical languages for ontology design and visualization. Then, we give some preliminaries on DLs, which we use as formal tool for defining the semantics of GRAPHOL constructs and for establishing the correspondence between GRAPHOL and OWL 2, which also has a DL counterpart. Next, in Section 4, we give the formal syntax of the language (Section 4.1), its semantics (Section 4.2), and show its equivalence with OWL 2 (Section 4.4), i.e., we prove that every GRAPHOL diagram corresponds to an OWL 2 ontology, and, conversely, that every OWL 2 ontology corresponds to a GRAPHOL diagram. Then, in Section 5, we discuss the relationship between GRAPHOL and UML, and finally, in Section 6, we provide some user evaluations of our language. Our study shows that GRAPHOL can be adopted by non-expert modelers introducing only a minimal overhead with respect to the use of standard conceptual languages such as UML and ER, and that this overhead pays off when the UML/ER diagrams need logical annotation to fully capture the ontology of interest. More interestingly, the evaluations we carried out show that GRAPHOL can be adopted by expert conceptual modelers with ease, greatly facilitating the adoption of a full-fledged ontology language, such as OWL 2, as a formal conceptual modeling language. We conclude the paper in Section 7.

2. Related Work

The growing use of ontologies in information systems and throughout the semantic web has made effective ontology representation and management a necessity. In this section we provide a brief description of the main tools and graphical languages that have been proposed over the years for these purposes. We point out that many of the proposals we review in the following have been discontinued to date. Nonetheless, they testify the huge effort carried on by the community in this direction and allow to better co-locate our proposal within the state of the art.

For our overview we start from languages adopted in software engineering and database design. As we have already pointed out in the introduction, popular diagrammatic formalisms used in these fields, such as the ER model [1] and UML class diagrams [2], have been devised with the primary goal to support design documentation and help communication in the various phases of the development workflow. When used specifically for conceptual modeling, such formalisms are often adopted in a pragmatic way, but a quite-productive line of research has investigated them from a logical perspective with the aim of associating such languages with formal semantics [8–10,30]. In particular, an important effort has been made to exploit DLs to represent and enable automated reasoning in graphical conceptual models used in software development and information systems [31–38]. In these works, the relationship between UML class diagrams or ER models and logical languages is studied mostly at theoretical level only. Two exceptions are [32], where the authors present a tool for translating UML class diagrams into DL ontologies with the aim of verifying their consistency, and [38], where a prototype tool that provides the DL representation of ER models (more precisely, enhanced entity–relationship models) is presented.

Along with ER and UML, other visual languages have also been employed in the software engineering area, such as, for example, object–role modeling [39,40] (ORM and ORM2). ORM provides a graphical notation for modeling and querying business domains in terms of the underlying facts of interest. Unlike ER or UML, ORM treats all facts as relationships, and depicts them through a visual formalism that is meant to be understood by nontechnical users of such domains. In ORM, a model is built around entities, represented through logical predicates, and values, each of which can be described in terms of the types they belong to. Similarly as performed for ER and UML, various research contributions have been made to provide formal semantics to ORM through DLs or even OWL [41–44].

As stated, the above-mentioned works have aimed at reconstructing languages such as ER, UML, or ORM under a logical perspective. Ultimately though, such languages have proven to lack the necessary expressive power to capture current ontology formalisms such as OWL 2 or the more expressive DLs.

Some authors have thus proposed to extend the above languages, in particular UML class diagrams, to achieve the expressiveness needed for ontology specification. In [25,45] the authors define the ontology definition metamodel (ODM), a UML-based metamodel for defining ontologies. It is grounded in the Meta Object Facility of UML 2.0 (MOF2), which is an extensible model-driven integration framework for defining, manipulating, and integrating metadata and data in a platform-independent manner, and allows to visually represent an ontology through a graph. In [26,46], the authors also provide UML profiles which extend ODM with a visual UML syntax for the representation of ontologies in OWL 1 [47]. However, these works were not continued thereafter towards the new version of the standard language [12], and updating them in order to incorporate all the features introduced in OW2 2 could be very complex.

The OntoUML modeling language [27] is also UML-based, but it is tailored towards general conceptual modeling and ontology representation through the ontological guidelines introduced in the unified foundational ontology (UFO), rather than towards providing a visual language for real-world DL ontologies. The principle behind OntoUML is that in order for a modeling language to satisfy the requirements of expressiveness and clarity of a domain, its modeling primitives must be derived from a proper foundational ontology. In other words, a domain-specific ontology must utilize some sort of upper-level ontology as its underlying framework [48] for fundamental ontological structures such as theory of parts, theory of wholes, types and instantiation, identity, etc.

OWLGrEd (http://owlgred.lumii.lv/, accessed on 17 January 2022) [29,49] is a more recent graphical notation for ontologies based on UML class diagrams: concepts are represented as UML classes, attributes as class attributes, and roles as associations between the classes. OWLGrEd's UML classes also allow to specify logical expression in Manchester syntax (http://www.w3.org/TR/owl2-manchester-syntax/, accessed on 17 January 2022) for stating axioms in OWL which are not supported by the graphical notation. OWLGrEd captures OWL 2 completely, and its UML-based notation is quite easy to understand. However, its effectiveness is hindered by the need to use logical formulas in the representation, especially in case of complex ontologies, where the presence of many formulas of this kind can lead to prejudice the intuitive comprehension of the ontology, and by its ambiguous depiction of various kinds of expressions and axioms. Nonetheless, among the related work we discuss, OWLGrEd is the closest in spirit to GRAPHOL, even though our language allows for a completely graphical representation of OWL 2 ontologies. For this reason, we have considered OWLGrEd in a comparative user evaluation study described in Section 6.

Below, we turn our attention to languages and tools for the graphical representation of knowledge bases not specifically based on UML or the other diagrammatic languages we discussed so far. Earlier efforts in this direction have typically focused on preliminary explorations of issues and possible solutions for visual representations of DLs. For instance, in [50], the author discusses general design issues for semantic network formalisms, also providing some details of how such issues may be addressed through an example of a visual language for DLs. Other efforts have focused on investigating the potential of diagrammatic reasoning systems, i.e., visual logics systems which use a graph-based structural form for FOL sentences, as graphical representations of DLs. Examples of such systems are spider and constraint diagrams, as well as conceptual and existential graphs. In [51], the authors investigate which of these systems is compatible with DLs, concluding that existential graphs are best suited for these purposes. Instead, in [33], the authors focus on conceptual graphs, and introduce a conceptual graph-based formalism for the representation of knowledge bases. To the best of our knowledge, there have, however, been no further studies nor practical results in the direction of adopting these systems for the visual representation of real-world ontologies.

Among other proposals, we below focus on GrOWL (http://growl.novasemantics.it/, accessed on 17 January 2022) [52], and Graffoo (http://www.essepuntato.it/graffoo/, accessed on 17 January 2022) [28] and VOWL (http://vowl.visualdataweb.org/, accessed on 17 January 2022) [53], which, similar to ours, are specifically tailored to the representation and/or visualization of OWL ontologies. For a more comprehensive classification and comparison of available languages and tools for ontology editing and visualization, we refer the reader to [54].

GrOWL is a tool for visualizing and editing ontologies, based on the underlying DL semantics of OWL ontologies. GrOWL is able to map both TBox and ABox assertions to a graph-line representation through the use of color, shading, and different shape nodes to encode the properties of the language constructs. Although the core idea behind GrOWL is similar to GRAPHOL's, the project seems to have been discontinued, and the available documentation does not provide an unambiguous indication of the syntax and semantics of the language. Differently to GRAPHOL, OWLGrEd and Graffoo, GrOWL is also quite distant in nature from classical logical languages such as UML or ER, and this poses further difficulties in its understanding in industrial contexts.

Graffoo is a graphical notation for OWL ontologies, developed using the standard library of the graph editor yEd (https://www.yworks.com/products/yed, accessed on 17 January 2022). The graphical elements featured in Graffoo are blocks (or nodes) and arcs. Blocks are used to model classes, datatypes, individuals, ontologies, and rules. Arcs are instead used to model assertions, annotation properties, attributes, and roles. Graffoo has been designed for fully capturing OWL 2, but to this aim, some elements of the language are not completely graphical. Indeed, those OWL 2 constructs that cannot be expressed by means of Graffoo's graphical elements are specified through OWL axioms in Manchester syntax. Therefore, the same arguments given for OWLGrEd about the need of embedding axioms given in a non-graphical way also apply to Graffoo. To the best of our knowledge, there is no editor tailored for Graffoo, but a palette for the yEd editor is available instead.

VOWL (Visual Notation for OWL Ontologies) is a formalism that has been proposed quite recently. It defines a set of graphical primitives and a color scheme, and uses a force-directed graph visualization for the ontology. In VOWL, concepts (i.e., classes in OWL) are represented as circles, and data types are displayed in rectangles. A labeled arrow connecting two circles denotes a role (i.e., an objectProperty in OWL), whereas a labeled arrow connecting a circle to a datatype denotes an attribute (i.e., a dataProperty in OWL). The direction of the arrow establishes the typing of the domain and the range of the property. Cardinality constraints are specified on arrows in the style of UML class diagrams. The mentioned constructs are the basic elements of the representation. A complete list is available at http://vowl.visualdataweb.org/v2/ (accessed on 17 January 2022). VOWL is able to capture visually a good portion of OWL 2, although some constructs are not part of the actual VOWL visualization. The language is not defined through a formalized syntax, and in the documentation it is not clearly specified which fragment of OWL 2 is completely captured in a visual mode by VOWL. The language has two main implementations: WebVOWL [55], which is a web tool for ontology visualization, and ProtégéVOWL, a plug-in for the ontology editor Protégé (which, however, does not implement all visual elements defined in the VOWL specification). In both such environments, essentially only ontology visualization features are provided. Indeed, VOWL has been so far proposed as an ontology visualization language rather than a tool for ontology editing. Apart from all the other differences, this last aspect seems to be the one that mainly distinguishes VOWL from our language GRAPHOL, which is thought for ontology specification.

Besides VOWL and its related visualization environments, there is a number of systems and tools designed for ontology visualization only, which adopt different representation techniques in order to achieve this desired balance. The graphical representation provided by such systems can be either two- or three-dimensional, and adopt visualization strategies as degree of interest [56], space-filling [57], context focus [58], and multiple coordinated views [59].

Among these systems, we can mention OntoGraf (http://protegewiki.stanford.edu/wiki/OntoGraf, accessed on 17 January 2022) and OWLViz (http://protegewiki.stanford.edu/wiki/OntoViz, accessed on 17 January 2022) plug-ins for the popular ontology editor Protégé. The former plug-in uses the layouts library for the Jambalaya plug-in (http://protegewiki.stanford.edu/wiki/Jambalaya, accessed on 17 January 2022) to provide interactive navigation of the relationships in an ontology through an incremental and dynamic graph-like representation. The latter plug-in provides a node-link representation for viewing and navigating class hierarchies, in which the nodes are classes, and the "is-a"-labeled links represent inclusion relationships between them. It is worthwhile mentioning that both such plug-ins, though popular in the past for quick rendering of the main ontology elements and connection thereof, seem to be currently no longer supported by active development or maintenance. Since tools tailored to ontology visualization do not provide any functionalities for ontology editing, they are slightly far from the objectives of this work; hence, we shall not provide further details on them and instead refer the reader to surveys conducted in [54,60,61] for an in-depth discussion.

We conclude this section by mentioning some non-graphical ontology editing environments. These systems typically include features for editing, browsing, visualizing, importing, and exporting ontologies.

Protégé (http://protege.stanford.edu/, accessed on 17 January 2022), which we already mentioned before and which is a popular open-source ontology editor and knowledge base framework [62], is certainly one of the most widely-used non-graphical ontology editors. Protégé supports many languages and formats for ontology development, such as XML schema, RDF(S), and, of course, OWL 2. Moreover, it provides a plug-and-play framework that fosters the development of new functionalities by means of plug-ins (such as the one mentioned above) which can be used to modify both the appearance and the behavior of the system.

The NeOn Ontology Engineering Toolkit (http://neon-toolkit.org/wiki/Main_Page, accessed on 17 January 2022) is an open-source, multi-platform ontology engineering environment [63,64] which is built on the Eclipse platform, and provides a variety of plug-ins for ontology engineering activities such as management, reasoning, and collaboration. In particular, the OntoModel (http://sourceforge.net/projects/ontomodel/, accessed on 17 January 2022) editor plug-in provides ontology visualization and editing functionalities through a UML-based notation.

The commercial TopBraid Composer by TopQuadrant (http://www.topquadrant.com/products/TB_Composer.html, accessed on 17 January 2022) is an ontology and RDF data editing environment, developed as an Eclipse plug-in. It offers support for editing ontologies in OWL 2 or RDF and for running SPARQL (http://www.w3.org/TR/sparql11-query/, accessed on 17 January 2022) queries over them. Furthermore, it provides a visual editor for RDF graphs and for class diagrams, allowing also to generate SPARQL queries directly from the graph view of the ontology.

The OntoStudio Ontology Engineering Environment [65] is a commercial graphical and textual ontology editor. Similar to TopBraid Composer, OntoStudio is developed as an IDE application using the Eclipse platform, and is extendible through various Eclipse plug-ins. OntoStudio supports RDF(S), OWL-2, and other formats for modeling purposes.

While these systems often attempt to offer some visual representation of ontologies, they are seldom successful in achieving a balance between the amount of information that is shown to the user and the complexity and size of the given representation, which is typically provided in terms of a two-dimensional graph. Furthermore, none of the provided visualizations is based on a graphical language with formal syntax and/or that is able to fully render an OWL 2 ontology.

3. Preliminaries

Description logics (DLs) [11] are formalisms used to model a domain of interest in a formal way. They are portions of first-order logic that allow for decidable reasoning. In DLs, the domain of interest is represented in terms of *objects* (i.e., individuals), *concepts* (i.e., abstractions for sets of objects), and *roles* (i.e., binary relationships between concepts). Moreover, some DLs consider also *value-domains*, denoting sets of values, and *attributes*, denoting binary relationships between concepts and value-domains.

We assume to have an alphabet Γ partitioned into Γ_P and Γ_C. The former is in turn partitioned into sets of symbols for atomic concepts, atomic roles, atomic attributes, and atomic value-domains. Γ_C instead contains symbols for constants, and is further partitioned into the sets Γ_O, which is the set of constants denoting objects, and Γ_V, which is the set of values.

We now provide syntax and semantics of the DL language of interest in this work. We notice that the DL we provide in this section captures the DL $\mathcal{SROIQ}(D)$ [66,67], i.e., the DL underlying OWL 2. In Section 4.4, we will discuss which syntactic restrictions to impose to make this language equivalent to $\mathcal{SROIQ}(D)$ (and so to OWL 2). Concepts, roles, attributes, and value-domains expressions in such DL are defined by the following rules:

$$
\begin{aligned}
C \longrightarrow\ & A \mid \neg C \mid C \sqcap \cdots \sqcap C \mid C \sqcup \cdots \sqcup C \mid \exists R \mid \exists R.C \mid \forall R.C \mid \\
& \geq n\,R.C \mid \leq n\,R.C \mid \exists R.Self \mid \exists V \mid \exists V.F \mid \forall V.F \mid \\
& \geq n\,V.F \mid \leq n\,V.F \mid \{c_1,\dots,c_n\} \mid \top_C \mid \bot_C \\
F \longrightarrow\ & T \mid \exists V^- \mid \neg F \mid F \sqcap \cdots \sqcap F \mid F \sqcup \cdots \sqcup F \mid \\
& \top_D \mid \bot_D \mid \{w_1,\dots,w_n\} \\
R \longrightarrow\ & P \mid P^- \mid \neg R \mid R \circ R \mid \top_R \mid \bot_R \\
V \longrightarrow\ & U \mid \neg V \mid \top_A \mid \bot_A
\end{aligned}
$$

where A denotes an atomic concept, P an atomic role, U an atomic attribute, T an atomic value-domain, $\top_C$ (resp., $\top_R, \top_A, \top_D$) the *universal concept* (resp., *role, attribute, value-domain*), and $\bot_C$ (resp., $\bot_R, \bot_A, \bot_D$) the *empty concept* (resp., *role, attribute, value-domain*).

We call C, R, V, and F a *general* concept, role, attribute, and value-domain, respectively. In our treatment, such symbols can be used with subscripts. P^- denotes the *inverse* of an atomic role, while $\neg C$, $\neg R$, $\neg V$, $\neg F$ denote the *negation* of C, R, V, and F, respectively. The expression $\exists R$ (resp. $\exists V$) denotes the domain of a role R (resp. of an attribute V). Instead, the *qualified concept existential restriction* $\exists R.C$ indicates the domain of R restricted to the class C, i.e., it is an abstraction for the set of objects that R relates to some instance of C. Similarly, $\exists V.F$ denotes the qualified domain of V with respect to a value-domain F, i.e., the set of objects that V relates to some value in F. The concept $\forall R.C$, also called *value restriction*, denotes the set of objects that are associated by R only to objects that are instances of C. Similarly, $\forall V.F$ denotes the set of objects that are associated by V only to values in F. The concept $\exists R.Self$ is used to express local reflexivity to a role R. $\exists V^-$ denotes the range of an attribute V. Similarly, $\exists R^-$ denotes the range of a role R, which corresponds to the domain of the inverse of R. The set $\{c_1,\dots,c_n\}$ denotes the concept whose instances are denoted by $c_1,\dots,c_n$, and, similarly, $\{w_1,\dots,w_n\}$ denotes the value-domain whose instances are denoted by $w_1,\dots,w_n$. The symbols $\sqcap$ and $\sqcup$ are the usual *AND* and *OR* logical connectives. $\leq n$ and $\geq n$ indicate *number restrictions*, respectively, *at-most restriction* and *at-least restriction*, where n ranges over the nonnegative integers. Finally, $R \circ R$ denotes a *role chain*.

The semantics of a DL KB is given in terms of interpretations. An *interpretation* $\mathcal{I} = (\Delta^I, \cdot^I)$ consists of:

- A nonempty interpretation domain $\Delta^I = \Delta^I_O \cup \Gamma_V$, where Δ^I_O is the *domain of objects*, and Γ_V is the set of values previously introduced (indeed, in every interpretation each value is intepreted by itself);
- An *interpretation function* $\cdot^I$ that assigns an element of Δ^I_O to each constant in Γ_O, and interprets each DL expression as shown in Table 1.

Table 1. The DL constructs with their semantics.

Construct	Syntax	Semantics
Atomic concept	A	$A^I \subseteq \Delta^I_O$
Atomic role	P	$P^I \subseteq \Delta^I_O \times \Delta^I_O$
Atomic attribute	U	$U^I \subseteq \Delta^I_O \times \Gamma_V$
Atomic value-domain	T	$T^I \subseteq \Gamma_V$
Universal concept	$\top_C$	Δ^I_O
Universal role	$\top_R$	$\Delta^I_O \times \Delta^I_O$
Universal attribute	$\top_A$	$\Delta^I_O \times \Gamma_V$
Universal value-domain	$\top_D$	Γ_V
Empty concept, role attribute, value-domain	$\bot_C, \bot_R, \bot_A, \bot_D$	$\emptyset$
Unqualified role existential restriction	$\exists R$	$\{ o \mid \exists o'. (o, o') \in R^I \}$
Qualified role existential restriction	$\exists R.C$	$\{ o \mid \exists o'. (o, o') \in R^I \wedge o' \in C^I \}$
Qualified role universal restriction	$\forall R.C$	$\{ o \mid \forall o'. (o, o') \in R^I \rightarrow o' \in C^I \}$
Qualified maximum cardinality role restriction	$\leq n\,R.C$	$\{ o \mid \sharp\{o' \mid (o, o') \in R^I \wedge o' \in C^I \} \leq n \}$
Qualified minimum cardinality role restriction	$\geq n\,R.C$	$\{ o \mid \sharp\{o' \mid (o, o') \in R^I \wedge o' \in C^I \} \geq n \}$
Self restriction	$\exists R.Self$	$\{ o \mid (o, o) \in R^I \}$
Unqualified attribute existential restriction	$\exists V$	$\{ o \mid \exists v. (o, v) \in V^I \}$
Qualified attribute existential restriction	$\exists V.F$	$\{ o \mid \exists v. (o, v) \in V^I \wedge v \in F^I \}$
Qualified attribute universal restriction	$\forall V.F$	$\{ o \mid \forall v. (o, v) \in V^I \rightarrow v \in F^I \}$
Qualified maximum cardinality attribute restriction	$\leq n\,V.F$	$\{ o \mid \sharp\{v \mid (o, v) \in V^I \wedge v \in F^I \} \leq n \}$
Qualified minimum cardinality attribute restriction	$\geq n\,V.F$	$\{ o \mid \sharp\{v \mid (o, v) \in V^I \wedge v \in F^I \} \geq n \}$
One-of (concept)	$\{c_1, \ldots, c_n\}$	$\{c_1^I, \ldots, c_n^I\}$
One-of (value-domain)	$\{w_1, \ldots, w_n\}$	$\{w_1, \ldots, w_n\}$
Attribute range	$\exists V^-$	$\{ v \mid \exists o. (o, v) \in V^I \}$
Inverse role	P^-	$\{ (o, o') \mid (o', o) \in P^I \}$
Role chain	$R \circ R$	$\{ (o, o') \mid \exists o''. (o, o'') \in R_1^I \wedge (o'', o') \in R_2^I \}$

Table 1. *Cont.*

Construct	Syntax	Semantics
Concept negation	$\neg C$	$\Delta_O^I \setminus C^I$
Role negation	$\neg R$	$(\Delta_O^I \times \Delta_O^I) \setminus R^I$
Attribute negation	$\neg V$	$(\Delta_O^I \times \Gamma_V) \setminus V^I$
Value-domain negation	$\neg F$	$(\Gamma_V) \setminus F^I$
Concept conjunction	$C_1 \sqcap \cdots \sqcap C_n$	$C_1^I \cap \cdots \cap C_n^I$
Concept disjunction	$C_1 \sqcup \cdots \sqcup C_n$	$C_1^I \cup \cdots \cap C_n^I$

In the table, $c_1^I, \ldots c_n^I$ denote the interpretation of the constants $c_1, \ldots c_n$ from the alphabet Γ_O.

A DL KB $\mathcal{K}$ is a pair $\langle \mathcal{T}, \mathcal{A} \rangle$, where $\mathcal{T}$ is a finite set of intensional assertions, called *TBox*, and $\mathcal{A}$ is a finite set of extensional assertions, called *ABox*. In this paper we focus on the modeling of intensional knowledge, i.e., the TBox, so we will not detail further the form of the ABox (which is the component of the knowledge base maintaining the data).

The TBox assertions we focus on in this work are as follows:

$C_1 \sqsubseteq C_2$ (*concept inclusion*);
$R_1 \sqsubseteq R_1$ (*role inclusion*);
$V_1 \sqsubseteq V_2$ (*attribute inclusion*);
$F_1 \sqsubseteq F_2$ (*value-domain inclusion*).

Concept inclusion assertions state that all instances of one concept are also instances of another concept, analogously for role, attribute, and value-domain inclusion assertions.

An interpretation $\mathcal{I}$ *satisfies* a TBox $\mathcal{T}$ if it satisfies all inclusions in $\mathcal{T}$, where the notion of satisfaction of an inclusion is as follows:

$C_1 \sqsubseteq C_2$ if $C_1^I \subseteq C_2^I$; $R_1 \sqsubseteq R_2$ if $R_1^I \subseteq R_2^I$;
$V_1 \sqsubseteq V_2$ if $V_1^I \subseteq V_1^I$; $F_1 \sqsubseteq F_2$ if $F_1^I \subseteq F_2^I$.

4. The GRAPHOL Language

In this section we introduce the graphical elements and features of the GRAPHOL language for ontologies. We will use the popular Pizza (http://protegewiki.stanford.edu/wiki/Pr4_UG_ex_Pizza, accessed on 17 January 2022) ontology as a running example to illustrate how different expressions and assertions of an ontology are represented in GRAPHOL, and will use the DL syntax for logical symbols presented in Section 3 to define the correspondence between GRAPHOL shapes and their logical meaning.

4.1. Graphol Syntax

The basic principle that guides GRAPHOL in representing ontologies is that a GRAPHOL ontology is a graph whose nodes and edges assume the forms described in Figure 2.

Nodes can be of two kinds: *predicate nodes* and *operator nodes*. Predicate nodes model the terms in the ontology alphabet, i.e., atomic concepts, rendered as rectangles, atomic roles, which are depicted as diamonds, atomic attributes, drawn as circles, atomic value-domains, represented as rounded rectangles, and constants (i.e., individuals and values), denoted through octagons. Each predicate node is associated to a label, which is a name from the ontology alphabet (to distinguish between individual nodes and value nodes, the labels of value nodes are in inverted commas). We note that the shapes used to depict concepts, roles, and attributes are the same as those used in ER diagrams. This choice was made to take advantage of the familiarity that many of the potential users of GRAPHOL may have with this well-known language for conceptual modeling.

The special labels, "Top" and "Bottom", are reserved for representing universal and empty predicates (i.e, concept, role, attribute, or value-domain), respectively. For example, a diamond with label "Top" represents the universal role ($\top_R$), while a diamond with label "Bottom" represents the empty role ($\bot_R$), analogously for concepts, attributes, and value-domains.

Operator nodes are instead used to graphically construct complex expressions. Two shapes for operators are adopted, i.e., the box (which can be either blank or solid), and the hexagon. A blank (resp. solid) box, called *domain (resp. range) restriction node*, is used to represent restrictions on roles or attributes (resp. their inverses). A box is labeled with one of the following keywords: "exists", for existential restriction, "forall", for universal restriction, "self", for self-restriction, and "$(x, -)$" or "$(-, y)$", with x and y positive integers, for min and max cardinality restrictions, respectively. When the label is omitted we intend "exists". The other operator nodes are denoted by a hexagon and can assume one of the following labels: "or" (*union node*), "and" (*intersection node*), "not" (*complement node*), "inv" (*inverse node*), "oneOf" (*one-of node*), and "chain" (*chain node*).

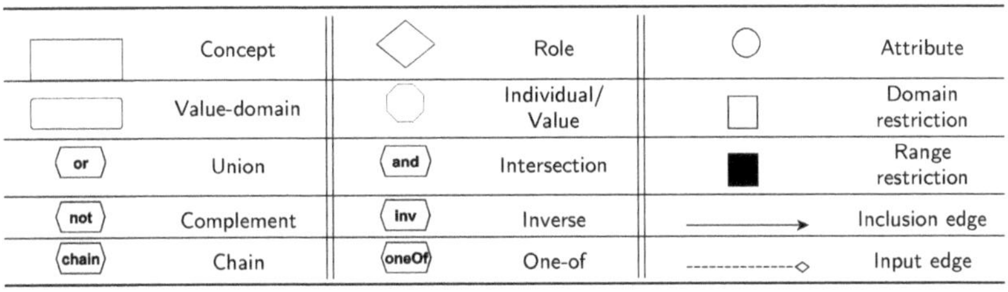

▭	Concept	◇	Role	○	Attribute
▭	Value-domain	⬡	Individual/Value	☐	Domain restriction
or	Union	and	Intersection	■	Range restriction
not	Complement	inv	Inverse	⟶	Inclusion edge
chain	Chain	oneOf	One-of	--------◇	Input edge

Figure 2. Nodes and edges in a GRAPHOL ontology.

We observe that GRAPHOL uses three visual variables [68] to encode the predicate and constructor nodes. These are (i) the *shape* of the nodes, which is used to distinguish between predicate nodes, restriction nodes, and operator nodes, and among the different kinds of predicate nodes; (ii) the *size* of the nodes, which allows to clearly discriminate between the quadrilaterals used for concept nodes, value-domain nodes, and restriction nodes; and (iii) *brightness*, which is used to distinguish the domain restriction node from the range restriction node.

To avoid encumbering the user in learning the GRAPHOL syntax, we have chosen to limit the number of different graphical symbols used to depict GRAPHOL nodes, and to maintain it to around seven, which is the commonly recognized ideal upper bound for software engineering graphical languages [69]. Indeed, experimental studies demonstrate that a high number of different symbols in a language for software engineering increases the learning difficulty by non-expert users [70].

GRAPHOL provides two types of edges: *inclusion edges*, which are solid directed arrow edges (whose target end is denoted by the arrow), used to represent inclusion assertions, and the *input edges*, which are dashed directed diamond edges (whose target end is denoted by the diamond), used to construct ontology expressions.

An *expression* in GRAPHOL is a directed acyclic graph, where the nodes can be both operator and predicate nodes and the edges are input edges only. In every GRAPHOL expression there is a single node without outgoing edges, called *sink*. We give below a formal definition:

Definition 1. *A* GRAPHOL *expression can be of four types: concept, role, attribute, or value-domain, defined inductively as follows:*

1. *A concept expression can be:*
   - *A concept node (in this case the sink is the node itself);*

- A domain or range restriction node, with label "exists", "forall", "$(x,-)$", or "$(-,y)$", taking as input a role expression and a concept expression (in this case the sink is the domain or range restriction node);
    - A domain or range restriction node, with label "self", taking as input a role expression (in this case, the sink is the domain or range restriction node);
    - A domain restriction node, with label "exists", "forall", "$(x,-)$", or "$(-,y)$", taking as input an attribute expression and a value-domain expression (in this case, the sink is the domain restriction node);
    - A union or intersection node taking as input at least two concept expressions (in this case, the sink is the union or intersection node);
    - A complement node taking as input a concept expression (in this case, the sink is the complement node);
    - A one-of node taking as input at least an individual node (in this case, the sink is the one-of node);
2. A role expression can be:
    - A role node (in this case, the sink is the node itself);
    - An inverse node taking as input a role expression (in this case, the sink is the inverse node);
    - A complement node taking as input a role expression (in this case, the sink is the complement node);
    - A chain node taking as input n role expressions, with $n \leq 2$, each associated to a label $1 \leq i \leq n$ and such that there are no two input edges with the same label (in this case, the sink is the chain node).
3. An attribute expression can be:
    - An attribute node (in this case, the sink is the node itself);
    - A complement node taking as input an attribute expression (in this case, the sink is the complement node).
4. A value-domain expression can be:
    - A value-domain node (in this case, the sink is the node itself);
    - A range restriction node with label "exists" taking as input an attribute expression (in this case, the sink is the range restriction node);
    - A union or intersection node taking as input at least two value-domain expressions (in this case, the sink is the union or intersection node);
    - A complement node taking as input a value-domain expression (in this case, the sink is the complement node);
    - A one-off node taking as input at least a value node (in this case, the sink is the one-off node).

Intensional assertions in GRAPHOL, as well as in OWL 2 and DLs, are specified as inclusions. Thus, an *(inclusion) assertion* in GRAPHOL is specified via an inclusion edge from the (sink of the) expression that is included to the (sink of the) expression that it includes. For instance, a concept inclusion assertion between the two concepts C_1 and C_2 is obtained by linking through an inclusion edge the sink of the GRAPHOL expression of C_1 to the sink of the GRAPHOL expression of C_2. Of course, GRAPHOL does not allow to specify inclusion edges between expressions of different types (e.g., a role expression with a concept one).

We finally define a GRAPHOL *ontology* as a set of GRAPHOL inclusion assertions.

To simplify ontology design and to keep the diagram easier to read, we allow in a GRAPHOL ontology to have multiple occurrences of the same predicate, obviously all labeled with the same label (which is the name of the predicate). This is particularly useful in those cases in which a predicate occurs in many assertions of the ontology, and so representing such predicate with a single node would lead to having a plethora of incoming or outgoing edges from that node, likely leading to layout issues. We notice that the tool Eddy [22], which offers an environment for the graphical specification of GRAPHOL ontologies, provides functionalities for the refactoring of the ontology in case a predicate node is modified, e.g., changes on the predicate node label are automatically propagated to all the replicas of such predicate in the ontology.

4.2. Graphol Semantics

An important desiderata of visual modeling languages is to have clear and precise semantics [71,72]. To this aim, here we provide the semantics of GRAPHOL expressions and assertions by giving their one-to-one correspondence with DL expressions and assertions, which in turn have formal semantics, as discussed in Section 3.

We start with GRAPHOL expressions, and define a function Λ which takes as input a GRAPHOL expression E_G and computes a DL expression that encodes it.

To formalize Λ, we use $\text{sk}(E_G)$ to denote the sink of E_G, and $\text{ar}(E_G)$ the set of GRAPHOL expressions linked to $\text{sk}(E_G)$ through input edges (of course, this set can be empty). We formally define Λ as follows:

- If $\text{sk}(E_G)$ is a concept, role, attribute, value-domain, or individual/value node with label S, then $\Lambda(E_G) = S$ (we are considering concept, role, attribute, value-domain, individual, and value alphabets as pairwise disjoint. Moreover, if $S =$"Top", we assume that Λ returns the corresponding DL universal predicate, which depends on the form of $\text{sk}(E_G)$. Analogously if $S =$"Bottom");
- If $\text{sk}(E_G)$ is a domain restriction node with label "exists" (resp., "forall", "$(x, -)$", "$(-, y)$"), and $\text{ar}(E_G) = \{\epsilon_{RA}, \epsilon_{CV}\}$, where either ϵ_{RA} is a GRAPHOL role expression and ϵ_{CV} is a GRAPHOL concept expression or ϵ_{RA} is a GRAPHOL attribute expression and ϵ_{CV} is a GRAPHOL value-domain expression, then $\Lambda(E_G) = \exists \Lambda(\epsilon_{RA}).\Lambda(\epsilon_{CV})$ (resp., $\Lambda(E_G) = \forall \Lambda(\epsilon_{RA}).\Lambda(\epsilon_{CV})$, $\Lambda(E_G) = \geq x\, \Lambda(\epsilon_{RA}).\Lambda(\epsilon_{CV})$, $\Lambda(E_G) = \leq y\, \Lambda(\epsilon_{RA}).\Lambda(\epsilon_{CV})$);
- if $\text{sk}(E_G)$ is a range restriction node with label "exists" (resp. "forall", "$(x, -)$", "$(-, y)$"), and $\text{ar}(E_G) = \{\epsilon_R, \epsilon_C\}$, where ϵ_R is a GRAPHOL role expression and ϵ_C is a GRAPHOL concept expression, then $\Lambda(E_G) = \exists (\Lambda(\epsilon_R))^-.\Lambda(\epsilon_C)$ (resp. $\Lambda(E_G) = \forall (\Lambda(\epsilon_R))^-.\Lambda(\epsilon_C)$, $\Lambda(E_G) = \geq x\, (\Lambda(\epsilon_R))^-.\Lambda(\epsilon_C)$, $\Lambda(E_G) = \leq y\, (\Lambda(\epsilon_R))^-.\Lambda(\epsilon_C)$);
- If $\text{sk}(E_G)$ is a domain (resp., range) restriction node with label "self", and $\text{ar}(E_G) = \{\epsilon_{RA}\}$, where ϵ_{RA} is a GRAPHOL role expression, then $\Lambda(E_G) = \exists \Lambda(\epsilon_{RA}).\text{Self}$ (resp., $\Lambda(E_G) = \exists (\Lambda(\epsilon_{RA}))^-.\text{Self}$);
- If $\text{sk}(E_G)$ is a range restriction node with label "exists" and $\text{ar}(E_G) = \{\epsilon_A\}$, where ϵ_A is a GRAPHOL attribute expression, then $\Lambda(E_G) = \exists (\Lambda(\epsilon_A))^-$;
- If $\text{sk}(E_G)$ is a union (resp. intersection or a one-of) node and $\text{ar}(E_G) = \{\epsilon^1, \ldots, \epsilon^n\}$, then $\Lambda(E_G) = \bigsqcup_{i=1}^{n} \Lambda(\epsilon^i)$ (resp. $\Lambda(E_G) = \bigsqcap_{i=1}^{n} \Lambda(\epsilon^i)$, $\Lambda(E_G) = \{\Lambda(\epsilon^1), \ldots, \Lambda(\epsilon^n)\}$);
- if $\text{sk}(E_G)$ is a complement node and $\text{ar}(E_G) = \{\epsilon\}$, then $\Lambda(E_G) = \neg \Lambda(\epsilon)$;
- If $\text{sk}(E_G)$ is an inverse node and $\text{ar}(E_G) = \{\epsilon_R\}$, then $\Lambda(E_G) = (\Lambda(\epsilon_R))^-$;
- If $\text{sk}(E_G)$ is a chain node and $\text{ar}(E_G) = \{\epsilon_R^1, \ldots \epsilon_R^n\}$, where every ϵ_R^i, where $1 \leq i \leq n$, is a GRAPHOL role expression that is connected to $\text{sk}(E_G)$ through an input edge with label i, then $\Lambda(E_G) = \Lambda(\epsilon_R^1) \circ \Lambda(\epsilon_R^2) \circ \cdots \circ \Lambda(\epsilon_R^n)$.

Analogously, to define the semantics of GRAPHOL inclusion assertions, we use a function Ψ which takes as input one such inclusion α_G and returns its DL encoding. We use source(α_G) to denote the GRAPHOL expression having as sink the node from which the inclusion edge starts in α_G, and target(α_G) to denote the GRAPHOL expression, having as sink the node to which the inclusion edge arrives in α_G. We thus define Ψ as follows: $\Psi(\alpha_G) = \Lambda(\text{source}(\alpha_G)) \sqsubseteq \Lambda(\text{target}(\alpha_G))$. Letting $\mathcal{O}_G$ be a GRAPHOL ontology, we transform $\mathcal{O}_G$ in a DL ontology $\mathcal{O}_{DL}$ by executing Ψ for every assertion in $\mathcal{O}_G$. The semantics of $\mathcal{O}_G$ thus are given by the semantics of $\mathcal{O}_{DL}$, which we have defined in Section 3.

Tables 2 and 3 give examples of application of Λ to GRAPHOL expressions of "depth" 0 or 1, i.e., expressions with either only predicate nodes or a constructor node with only predicate nodes as input.

Table 2. Correspondence between GRAPHOL and DL for concept and role expressions of depth 0 or 1. C, C_1, and C_2 denote atomic concepts, and R, R_1, and R_2 denote atomic roles.

	GRAPHOL	DL
Atomic concept	C	C
Role domain restriction	R —exists/forall/(x,-)/(-,y)— C	$\exists R.C \quad \forall R.C$ $\geq xR.C \quad \leq yR.C$
Role range restriction	R —exists/forall/(x,-)/(-,y)— C	$\exists R^-.C \quad \forall R^-.C$ $\geq xR^-.C \quad \leq yR^-.C$
Attribute domain restriction	V —exists/forall/(x,-)/(-,y)— F	$\exists V.F \quad \forall V.F$ $\geq xV.F \quad \leq yV.F$
Concept intersection	C1 —and— C2	$C_1 \sqcap C_2$
Concept union	C1 —or— C2	$C_1 \sqcup C_2$
Concept complement	not --- C	$\neg C$
One-of (concept)	a, b, c —oneOf	$\{a, b, c\}$
Self restriction	self — R	$\exists R.Self$
Atomic role	R	P
Role inverse	inv --- R	R^-
Role complement	not --- R	$\neg R$
Chain	R1 —1— chain —2— R2	$R_1 \circ R_2$

Table 3. Correspondence between GRAPHOL and DL for attribute and value-domain expressions of depth 0 or 1. V denotes an atomic attribute, and F, F_1, and F_2 denote an atomic value-domain.

	GRAPHOL	DL
Atomic attribute	○ V	U
Attribute complement	not ◇-------○ V	$\neg U$
Atomic value-domain	F	T
Attribute range existential restriction	exists ■◇------○ V	$\exists V^-$
Value-domain intersection	F1 --and-- F2	$F_1 \sqcap F_2$
Value-domain union	F1 --or-- F2	$F_1 \sqcup F_2$
Value-domain complement	not ◇---- F	$\neg F$
One-of (value-domain)	oneOf "1" "2" "3"	{"1", "2", "3"}

4.3. Shortcuts

We have defined some shortcuts to help the designer in specifying a GRAPHOL ontology. Through such shortcuts it is possible to use a more compact representation of some expressions and assertions that often occur in ontologies. Below we describe them, and provide examples of their use.

The *disjoint union node* is a new type of node, having the shape of a black hexagon, used to represent a disjoint union expression, i.e., a union that at the same time states the disjointness between its arguments. Therefore, through a disjoint union node we also represent negative inclusions over its inputs. This shortcut is particularly useful for defining disjoint concept hierarchies. This is inspired by a similar construct used in the ER model and in UML class diagrams. In Figure 3, we give an example of one such hierarchy in the two versions, with and without the use of the shortcut.

The second shortcut we introduce is a compact notation for the definition of the existential domain or range restriction on a role (resp. attribute) taking as input the universal concept (resp. universal value-domain), which is equivalent to an unqualified existential restriction. Since this is among the most recurring restrictions occurring in ontologies, we allow to omit the universal concept (resp. value-domain) (notice also that the OWL 2 syntax includes redundant constructs such as owl:ObjectPropertyDomain and owl:ObjectProperyRange with a similar aim). In other words, to express the unqualified existential restriction on a role or attribute, one can simply link a role or attribute sub-graph to an existential restriction node, as shown in Figure 4.

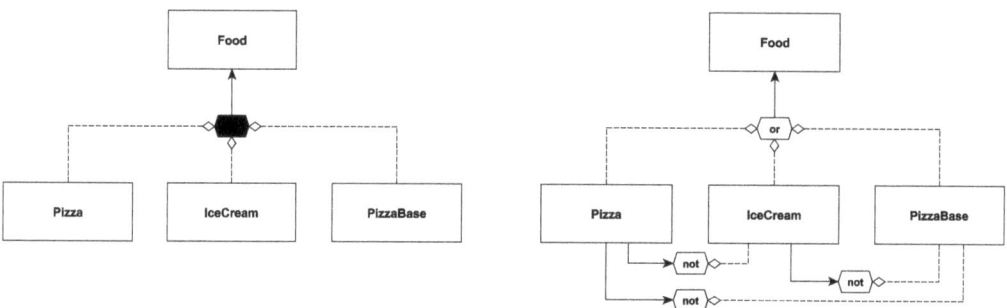

Figure 3. Example of a disjoint concept hierarchy represented in GRAPHOL with (**left-hand side figure**) and without (**right-hand side figure**) the disjoint union node.

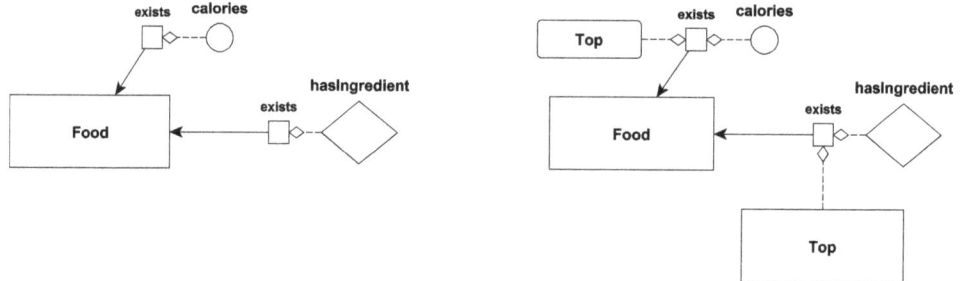

Figure 4. Example of an existential restriction in GRAPHOL with (**left-hand side figure**) and without (**right-hand side figure**) the compact notation.

Another commonly used assertion in ontologies is the one which specifies that a role R (resp., an attribute V) is globally functional, i.e., $\top_C \sqsubseteq\ \leq 1\,R.\top_C$ (resp., $\top_C \sqsubseteq\ \leq 1\,V.\top_D$). Global functionality can be obviously expressed in GRAPHOL through a graphical inclusion assertion. However, in order to provide a more compact representation, we allow to use a blank double-bordered role node (resp., attribute) for a functional role, a solid double-bordered role node for an inverse functional role, and a double-bordered role half blank and half solid for a role that is both functional and inverse functional. Notice that OWL 2 also allows for the use of a compact syntax to specify global functionality (cf. `owl:FunctionalObjectProperty`).

As an example, in the left-hand side of Figure 5 we show the standard GRAPHOL assertion that defines the functionality of a role, and on the right-hand side, the compact notation for a functional role (top left), an inverse functional role (top right), a role that is both functional and inverse functional (bottom left), and, finally, a functional attribute (bottom right).

We further notice that two domain (resp. range) restriction nodes with labels $(x, -)$ and $(-, y)$, respectively, and the same input expressions, can be substituted by a single domain (resp. range) restriction node with label (x, y) and the same inputs. In other terms, *min* and *max* cardinality restrictions can be drawn together. Lastly, if one wishes to define equivalence between two expressions of the same kind, it is possible to use a single inclusion edge with an arrow both on the source end and on the target end instead of two inclusion edges (with the arrow only on the target end) in opposite directions.

Figure 5. Example of globally functional role represented without the compact notation (**left-hand side**), and examples (**right-hand side**) of globally functional role, inverse functional role, functional and inverse functional role, and functional attribute (resp., top left, top right, bottom left, and bottom right) represented with the compact notation.

4.4. Graphol and OWL 2

In this section we study the relationship between GRAPHOL and OWL 2 [73], the W3C standard ontology language. We first study whether GRAPHOL ontologies can be entirely expressed in OWL 2, and then consider the other way around. In fact, for a formal treatment we identify OWL 2 with its underlying DL $\mathcal{SROIQ}(D)$ DL [66,67] (some OWL 2 features not in $\mathcal{SROIQ}(D)$, such as data type restrictions or key axioms, can be modeled in GRAPHOL by using some additional graphical elements, as reported in the Eddy documentation https://github.com/obdasystems/eddy (accessed on 17 January 2022). These aspects are not described here for the sake of simplicity).

According to the GRAPHOL syntax given earlier, GRAPHOL expressiveness goes slightly beyond that of OWL 2. This allowed us to maintain the formal definition of the syntax of our language simple, without burdening it with too many syntactic categories. Of course, due to this choice, reasoning in full GRAPHOL is undecidable [11]. However, by suitably restricting the way in which GRAPHOL expressions can be combined, we easily obtain decidable languages. In particular, we can limit GRAPHOL in such a way that it becomes translatable in OWL 2. To precisely describe this restriction, we need to define *basic role expressions*, which are expressions constituted by either a role node or the inverse node with a role node as input. Below we give a proviso needed to our aims.

Proviso. Role expressions given as input to domain or range restriction nodes, to self nodes, inverse nodes, complement nodes, or chain nodes can be only basic role expressions. Attribute expressions given as input to domain restriction nodes can be only attribute nodes. Role and attribute expressions having the complement node as sink cannot be the source of any inclusion edge. Role expressions having the chain node as sink cannot be the target of any inclusion edge and can be included only in basic role expressions. Attribute expressions in input to range restriction nodes can be only attribute nodes. GRAPHOL inclusion assertions between value-domain expressions must involve at least a value-domain node (i.e., the source or the target of the assertion must be an atomic data type). Finally, value-domains and values are as in OWL 2, and the ontology must obey the same global restrictions imposed on OWL 2 (e.g., only regular role hierarchies are allowed and only simple roles can occur in cardinality restrictions) [66,73].

Theorem 1. *Every* GRAPHOL *ontology constructed under the above proviso is correctly translatable into an OWL 2 TBox in linear time.*

Proof. The function Ψ given in Section 4.2 is obviously applicable to a GRAPHOL ontology restricted according to the above proviso. It is then easy to verify that each DL inclusion assertion returned by Ψ is an OWL 2 axiom. Since Ψ returns one DL inclusion assertion for each GRAPHOL inclusion assertion, the cost of the transformation is linear. □

The following theorem considers instead transformation of OWL 2 TBoxes in GRAPHOL.

Theorem 2. *Every OWL 2 TBox is correctly translatable into a* GRAPHOL *ontology in linear time.*

Proof. We first observe that any OWL 2 ontology can be written as a set of inclusion assertions. Below, we provide some well-known correspondences useful for this aim (Q denotes a role or its inverse, whereas $\top_C$ denotes the universal concept).

(funct Q)	$\equiv$	$\top_C \sqsubseteq\, \leq 1Q.\top_C$	(transitive Q)	$\equiv$	$Q \circ Q \sqsubseteq Q$
(symmetric Q)	$\equiv$	$Q \sqsubseteq Q^-$	(asymmetric Q)	$\equiv$	$Q \sqsubseteq \neg Q^-$
(reflexive Q)	$\equiv$	$\top_C \sqsubseteq \exists Q.Self$	(irreflexive Q)	$\equiv$	$\top_C \sqsubseteq \neg \exists Q.Self$
(disjoint $Q_1\ Q_2$)	$\equiv$	$Q_1 \sqsubseteq \neg Q_2$			

It is then possible to define a function that translates such a *normalized* TBox in GRAPHOL. Intuitively, this function inverts the function Θ introduced in Section 4.2. More precisely, we first define a function Λ^{-1} by induction on the structure of OWL 2 formulas, which can be seen as the inverse of the function Λ introduced in Section 4.2. For the base case, letting S be an atomic concept (resp., role, attribute, or value-domain), $\Lambda^{-1}(S)$ returns a GRAPHOL concept node (resp. role, attribute, or value-domain node) labeled with S. Letting then $\exists P.C$ (resp. $\exists P^-.C$) an OWL 2 expression, with P an atomic role and C a concept, $\Lambda^{-1}(\exists P.C)$ (resp. $\Lambda^{-1}(\exists P^-.C)$) returns the GRAPHOL expression whose sink node is a domain (resp. range) restriction node labeled "exists" taking as input $\Lambda^{-1}(C)$ and $\Lambda^{-1}(P)$. Other inductive cases can be defined analogously. Then, letting $\alpha = \alpha_\ell \sqsubseteq \alpha_r$ be an OWL 2 inclusion assertion, $\Lambda^{-1}(\alpha) = \alpha_G$, where α_G is the GRAPHOL inclusion assertion whose sink node is $\Lambda^{-1}(\alpha_\ell)$ and target node is $\Lambda^{-1}(\alpha_r)$. It is easy to see that the cost of this transformation is linear. □

4.5. Example

In Figure 6, we provide the GRAPHOL specification of a portion of the Pizza ontology we have used in some previous examples. We also present below a logically equivalent representation of such ontology given in terms of DL assertions.

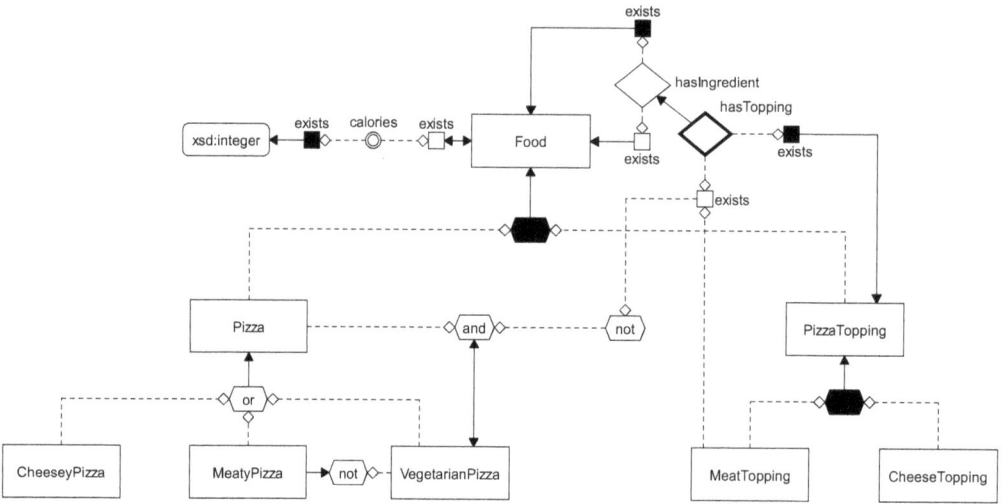

Figure 6. GRAPHOL ontology example: an excerpt of the Pizza ontology.

$$Pizza \sqcup PizzaTopping \sqsubseteq Food \quad Pizza \sqsubseteq \neg PizzaTopping$$
$$MeatTopping \sqsubseteq \neg CheeseTopping \quad MeatyPizza \sqsubseteq \neg VegetarianPizza$$
$$\exists hasIngredient \sqsubseteq Food \quad \exists hasIngredient^- \sqsubseteq Food$$
$$hasTopping \sqsubseteq hasIngredient \quad \exists hasTopping^- \sqsubseteq PizzaTopping$$
$$\exists calories \equiv Food \quad \exists calories^- \sqsubseteq \texttt{xsd:integer}$$
$$(funct\ calories) \quad (funct\ hasTopping^-)$$
$$MeatTopping \sqcup CheeseTopping \sqsubseteq PizzaTopping$$
$$CheeseyPizza \sqcup MeatyPizza \sqcup VegetarianPizza \sqsubseteq Pizza$$
$$Pizza \sqcap \neg \exists hasTopping.MeatTopping \equiv VegetarianPizza$$

5. Comparison with UML Class Diagrams

In this section, we discuss more in depth the relation between GRAPHOL and UML class diagrams. This section is mainly addressed to people knowledgeable with UML and willing to approach ontology modeling. The aim here is to highlight the differences between the two formalisms, so that it can be easier to understand the potential of ontology design and the shift in the modeling tools that is required to move from conceptual models of limited expressiveness to full-fledged powerful ontology languages. The content of this section should also further help understanding the syntax of GRAPHOL starting from that of UML class diagrams. In Figure 7, we show how the main UML constructs are expressible in GRAPHOL and for each construct we specify the corresponding OWL 2 axioms, expressed in DL syntax (UML n-ary relationships are not considered, since they are not directly expressible in OWL 2 and can always be captured using only roles, i.e., binary relationships, through reification, similarly for role attributes. We also note that all domain/range restriction nodes without labels in Figure 7 have to be read as if they were labeled with "exists", as said in Section 4). In the first four rows of the figure we show how to represent in GRAPHOL a UML relationship R between two concepts, with different cardinality restrictions. In the first row, where there are no such restrictions, we simply type R by requiring that its domain belongs to concept C1 and its range to concept C2. This is performed through two GRAPHOL inclusion assertions, corresponding to the DL assertions $\exists R \sqsubseteq C1$ and $\exists R^- \sqsubseteq C2$. In the second row, we add a mandatory participation of C1 to R (indicated in UML with a min cardinality restriction 1..*). In GRAPHOL, this is reflected by adding an inclusion edge from the concept node C1 to the domain of the role node R. In the third row, the UML diagram specifies that the participation of C1 to R is both mandatory and functional (notice the cardinality restriction 1..1). In GRAPHOL this can be easily specified by using the shortcut for global functionality introduced in Section 4.3. Indeed, in UML both the domain and range of a role are always typed on a named concept, and thus every local cardinality restriction is actually global, in the sense that every object participating in the domain or range obeys it. In the next row, the participation of C1 to R is constrained by the cardinality restriction (x,y). This is represented in GRAPHOL through the use of a second domain restriction node labeled with "(x,y)", besides the one used to type the domain of R. The following four rows show the main cases of concept hierarchies. Here, through the union node (the hexagon labeled "or"), we represent the union expression between the two concepts C2 and C3, while we use the black hexagon (a shortcut introduced in Section 4.3) to represent their disjoint union expression. Notice that completeness of a hierarchy is specified through a double-headed arrow. The next two rows describe how attributes and restrictions over them are depicted. Note that in GRAPHOL these are treated analogously as roles (we recall that in UML, in the absence of a cardinality restriction on attributes, they are considered mandatory and functional) Finally, in the last row, we have an example of role hierarchy, depicted in GRAPHOL as two role nodes linked by an inclusion edge.

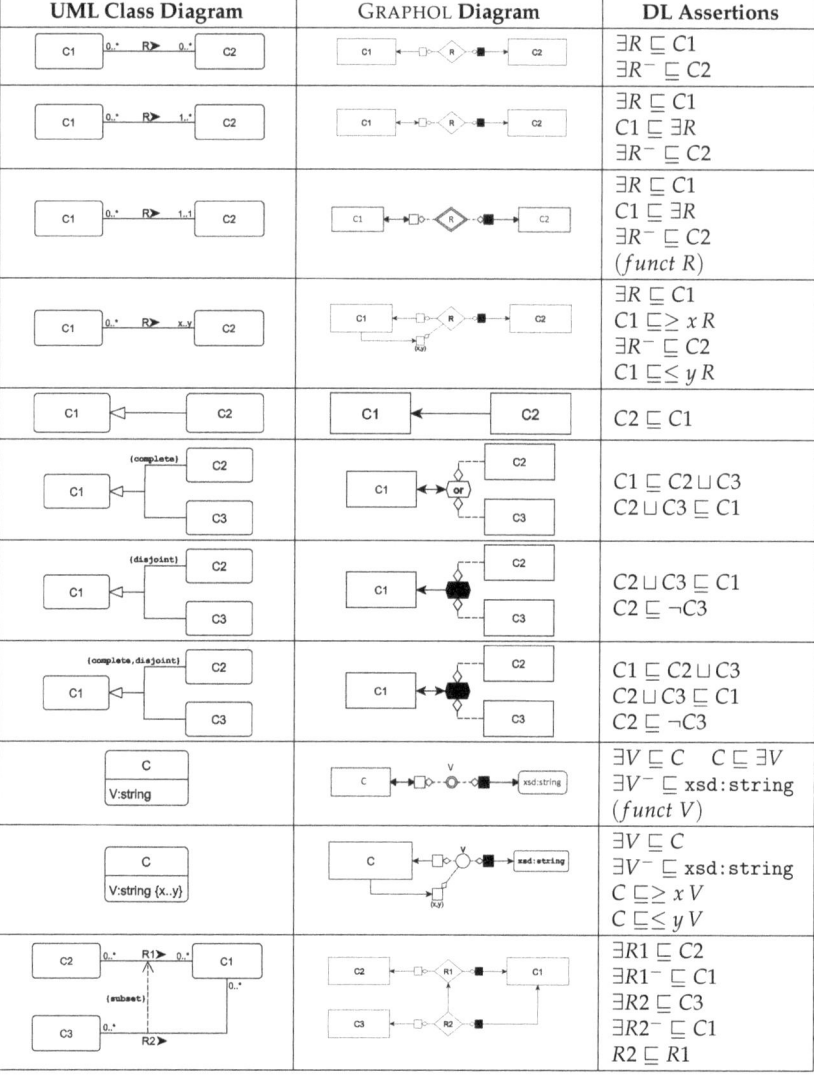

Figure 7. UML constructs, GRAPHOL corresponding diagrams, and related DL assertions.

6. User Evaluation Study

In this section, we present the results and setup of the user evaluation tests we carried out on the GRAPHOL language. The goal of the tests was to evaluate the effectiveness of GRAPHOL for ontology design and understanding. Both these aspects were tested independently and in comparison with other ontology languages similar, in spirit, to GRAPHOL. Users with different backgrounds and levels of experience in ontology and conceptual modeling participated in the tests.

We conducted two different studies on different models and in which users were asked to perform a variety of editing tasks.

6.1. Setup of the Study

Before defining the definitive setup of the user study, we conducted two test runs with ontology and conceptual modeling experts who were already familiar with the GRAPHOL language, which allowed us to iteratively improve the setup of the experiments. Our primary goals for these test runs were to verify that the tasks which we asked to perform were clear, and that their difficulty was adequate for the expertise of the final test participants. Examples of modifications that we made were the removal of overcomplicated tasks, the modification of several questions to avoid ambiguity in what the questions were asking, the refinement of the cheat sheets which were handed out with the questionnaires, and the definition of the time limits for each part of the experiments.

Because we conducted two different studies, with two groups of users and on different dates, we also took advantage of the experience of the first test to refine the second one. For instance, we made some modifications to the tutorial slides which were presented prior to the second test, in light of some doubts that were expressed by the users during the presentation of these slides during the first test.

6.2. Objectives of the Study

The design of our user evaluation study was geared towards the achievement of two main objectives.

1. Evaluate the difficulty of using the GRAPHOL language for ontology comprehension and editing by users very experienced in conceptual modeling and (in some cases) with basic skills in logics and ontologies.
2. Evaluate the difficulty of approaching and learning the GRAPHOL language for users with only basic knowledge of conceptual modeling and little or no experience with ontologies, both in isolation, and in comparison with another graphical ontology language that is heavily based on a formalism that is already familiar to them.

In accordance to these two objectives, we identified two groups of test participants, and defined two different types of tasks for each of these groups. Further details of the test participants, of the required tasks, and of the structure of the two tests are given in the remainder of this section. Here, we give a brief sketch of these two tests: the first one included a series of comprehension tasks and of editing tasks on two ontology models represented in the GRAPHOL language; the second one, involving users with limited knowledge of conceptual modeling and ontologies, instead included two sets of comprehension tasks on two ontologies represented in GRAPHOL and in OWLGrEd [29,49].

The reason for limiting the comparative evaluation of GRAPHOL with OWLGrEd to the comprehension test with less-skilled users is that the purpose of the test was to verify that the GRAPHOL language could be learned and used by these users with no more effort and difficulty than that needed for another language which is, by its very nature, more recognizable, due to its strong relation to UML class diagrams. . Therefore, it was not in our interest to gauge the effectiveness of GRAPHOL against OWLGrEd, or any other similar visual language, among more expert users. Instead, our test with these users was specifically designed towards measuring their perception of GRAPHOL as a viable candidate for future use in the design of ontologies in real life.

Furthermore, we have not carried out a comparative evaluation of our language with ontology editors which do not provide solutions for graphic editing and which are based on formal non-graphic languages, such as Protégé, given that our main goal is to deal with users who are not necessarily experts in formal languages and ontologies.

6.3. Participants

Participants were recruited among computer science master's and Ph.D. students, postdocs, and researchers. Eighteen participants took part in the test: ten with only basic knowledge of conceptual modeling and limited or no experience with ontologies (*beginners*), and eight with advanced skills in conceptual modeling and basic knowledge of ontology design and logic (*experts*). Table 4 recaps some descriptive statistics about the age of the users, their education degree, the number of years of experience with ontologies, and their knowledge in ontologies and conceptual modeling. Note that, as expected, the knowledge of conceptual modeling among experts is in general very high (4.2 out of 5 average, with a low standard deviation of 0.7), and is fairly high among beginners (3.3 out of 5, again with a low standard deviation of 0.7). Furthermore, the average knowledge of ontologies is lower than that of conceptual modeling for both experts and beginners.

Table 4. Statistics of the participants ("Beg." indicates statistics for beginners, "Exp." indicates statistics for experts): for Education, 1 = Bachelor's degree, 2 = Master's degree, 3 = Ph.D; conceptual modeling and ontology knowledge are on a scale from 1 to 5, with 1 indicating no knowledge.

	Age		Education		Conceptual Modeling Knowledge		Ontology Knowledge	
	Beg.	Exp.	Beg.	Exp.	Beg.	Exp.	Beg.	Exp.
Min	22	27	1	2	2	3	1	1
Max	28	47	2	3	4	5	2	3
Median	24.5	31	1	2	3	4	1	2.5
Mean	24.7	34.2	1.1	2.4	3.3	4.2	1.4	2.4
St.dev.	2.3	6.7	0.3	0.5	0.7	0.7	0.5	0.7

6.4. Ontology Models

We chose three different ontologies for the study, the Pizza ontology (http://130.88.198.11/co-ode-files/ontologies/pizza.owl, accessed on 17 January 2022), the Lehigh University Benchmark (LUBM) ontology (http://swat.cse.lehigh.edu/projects/lubm/, accessed on 17 January 2022), and the Family ontology (http://rpc295.cs.man.ac.uk:8080/repository/download?ontology=http://www.mindswap.org/ontologies/family.owl&format=RDF/XML, accessed on 17 January 2022), and modeled excerpts of the Pizza and LUBM ontologies in both GRAPHOL and OWLGrEd, and of the Family ontology in GRAPHOL. These ontologies were chosen for their popularity among the Semantic Web community, and due to the fact that the simple and widely-understood nature of the domain of these ontologies guarantees that the results of the test would not be altered by misinterpretation of the meanings of the terms in the ontologies.

The ontology models can be found in File S1 of the Supplementary Material.

6.5. Language for Comparison

Among the available language candidates for the comparative test, we chose OWL-GrEd [49,74] which allows for designing OWL 2 ontologies through a graphical notation based on UML class diagrams. OWLGrEd was chosen because its goal and its expressive power are akin to GRAPHOL's, while its visual representation and UML-based design principles are rather different from those of GRAPHOL, but are accessible, at least without big efforts, to a user with knowledge in UML class diagrams. As stated earlier, among our goals was to evaluate the difficulty of approaching the GRAPHOL language for a non-expert user, in comparison to that of learning a language based on a formalism with which the user is familiar with, and OWLGrEd is an ideal fit for this task.

The comparative aspect of the study was limited to these two languages in order to avoid encumbering the users with an excessive amount of new information to process during the tests.

Here, we give some further details about OWLGrEd, and in Figures 8 and 9, provide a very simple example of a model represented respectively in GRAPHOL and OWLGrEd. For a complete presentation of OWLGrEd, we refer the reader to [29,49,74].

The OWLGrEd notation is based on UML class diagrams. Specifically,

- OWLGrEd concepts are represented as UML classes, without operations;
- OWLGrEd attributes are represented as UML class attributes, but with different default cardinalities;
- OWLGrEd roles are represented as UML binary associations with the arrow indicating the direction, from the domain to the range. OWLGrEd roles are thus typed in both the domain and the range;
- OWLGrEd cardinalities on roles are represented as UML cardinalities on roles, with the possibility of further refining the cardinality;

- OWLGrEd cardinality restrictions on attributes are represented as UML cardinalities on attributes;
- OWLGrEd inclusions between concepts are represented as UML ISAs between classes;
- OWLGrEd generalizations are represented as UML generalizations, using a special graphical symbol;
- OWLGrEd uses the OWL 2 Manchester syntax to specify expressions which denote complex concepts;
- OWLGrEd role restrictions are represented as red arrows from the concept which is included in the restriction to the concept that qualifies the restriction, labeled with the name of the restricted role.

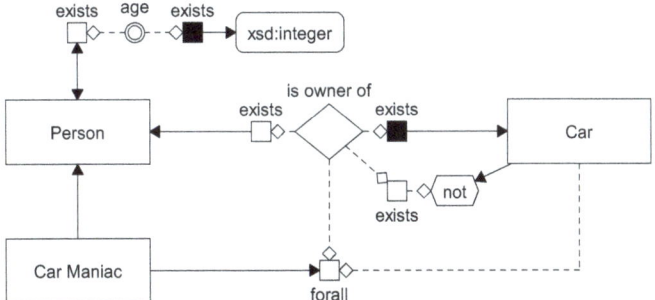

Figure 8. Example of a small ontology in GRAPHOL.

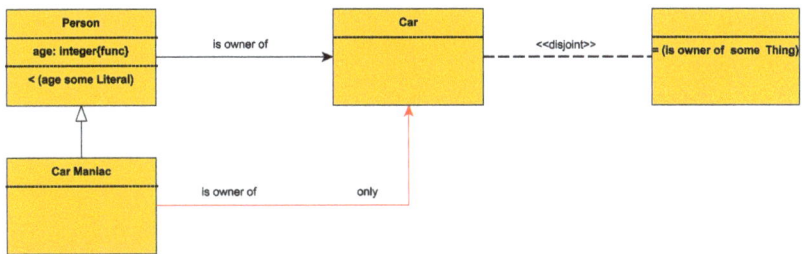

Figure 9. Example of a small ontology in OWLGrEd.

6.6. Tasks

We designed a series of model comprehension tasks for both the Pizza and LUBM ontology models, and of model modification tasks for the Family ontology model. The tasks were designed to present a varying degree of difficulty to the user: those for beginners were limited to more basic aspects of conceptual modeling, while those presented to experts also focused on slightly more advanced aspects.

Each comprehension task consisted of answering a question regarding the domain represented by the given model. Question types vary, from open format questions to closed format (or multiple choice) questions, to yes or no questions. Each modification task instead requested the user to modify the given GRAPHOL model of the Family ontology by modeling one or more assertions, provided in natural language. The complete set of tests is provided in the Supplemental Material.

For each task, the participant was asked to measure the time in minutes in which he completed the task. We also asked each participant to indicate, on a scale from 0 to 4, the clarity and the easiness of each task. To understand the difference between these two response variables, consider that the participant may think he has clearly understood what he must do for a certain task, but may not be able to easily place it into practice, or vice versa. In different words, the first variable is a measure of the quality of the questionnaire, while the second is of the tools the user is provided with to carry out the tasks. Examples of the two question types are provided below.

- Was the question clear?
  Not clear at all ☐ – ☐ – ☐ – ☐ – ☐ Very clear
- Were you able to easily answer this question?
  Not at all ☐ – ☐ – ☐ – ☐ – ☐ Absolutely

6.7. Structure of the Study

Here we provide the details for the evaluation studies of beginners and experts, which were conducted separately, on different dates.

Beginners:
1. *Introduction and brief GRAPHOL tutorial (15 min)*: a general introduction to the purpose of the experiment, and a brief tutorial on ontologies and on the GRAPHOL language.
2. *Brief OWLGrEd tutorial (15 min)*: a brief tutorial on the OWLGrEd language.
3. *Brief user background questionnaire (5 min)*: participants had to answer a brief questionnaire in which they were asked to provide some personal background information, as well as to rate their knowledge of conceptual modeling and ontologies on a scale from 1 to 5 (with 1 indicating extremely low and 5 extremely high expertise), to indicate how many years they had of experience with ontologies (if any), whether they were familiar with some of the more popular ontology editors and knowledge representation and conceptual modeling formalisms, and whether they had any experience with ontologies in real-life scenarios or in manually creating or editing ontologies.
4. *LUBM comprehension tasks (40 min)*: each user was asked to answer ten questions on the LUBM model they were provided. Half of the users were provided a GRAPHOL version of the LUBM model, and half an OWLGrEd version.
5. *Pizza comprehension tasks (40 min)*: each user was asked to answer ten questions on the Pizza model they were provided. Half of the users (those which were provided the OWLGrEd version of the LUBM model) were provided a GRAPHOL version of the Pizza model, and half an OWLGrEd version.
6. *Ex-post survey (10 min)*: after all the comprehension tasks were completed, we asked the participants to compile a short survey regarding their experience. The survey required the users to rate, on a scale from 0 to 4, the general difficulty of the comprehension tasks, the difficulty of learning the GRAPHOL and OWLGrEd symbols, the difficulty of using GRAPHOL and OWLGrEd to read ontologies, and, optionally, to indicate aspects of GRAPHOL and OWLGrEd which they particularly liked, or that they would like to see improved.

Experts:
1. *Introduction and brief GRAPHOL tutorial (30 min)*: participants were given the same introductory tutorial on ontologies and on the GRAPHOL language as the beginners, with the addition of some more complex features on the GRAPHOL language which were featured in the expert questionnaire but not the beginner questionnaire.
2. *Brief user background questionnaire (5 min)*: we asked the participants to fill out the same background questionnaire given to the beginners.
3. *GRAPHOL comprehension tasks (35 min)*: after completing the introductory part on GRAPHOL, each user was asked to answer ten questions on the GRAPHOL model of the Pizza ontology they were provided.
4. *GRAPHOL editing tasks (35 min)*: we asked each participant to perform ten editing tasks on the GRAPHOL model of the Family ontology they were provided.
5. *Ex-post survey (5 min)*: after carrying out both the comprehension and editing tasks, the users were asked to fill out a brief survey, analogous to the one given to the beginners.

We now discuss some more detailed aspects of the study.

- All participants, in support of their tasks, were provided with documentation regarding the languages in play for that specific task. Specifically, the questionnaire included some cheat sheets which recapped the symbols of the GRAPHOL and the OWLGrEd language (the latter only for tests carried out by beginners) and their meaning, along with some examples of the representation of some of the most common ontology expressions and assertions in the two formalisms. Additionally, users were provided with a printout of the slides of the introductory tutorials.
- The order in which the tasks were presented in the questionnaires was intentionally random, i.e., not linked to the expected difficulty of each task. This choice was made in order to compensate for a potential bias given by the learning curve of familiarizing with GRAPHOL or OWLGrEd during the course of the tasks. In other words, we wanted to avoid facilitating the participants by allowing them to face easier questions at the beginning of each task, and more difficult ones at the end, when they would probably have gained familiarity with the language.
- The experimental design method we chose for the comparative study between GRAPHOL and OWLGrEd is the *within-subjects* method, common in HCI [75]. This choice, as opposed to the between-subjects technique, was made mainly due to the limited number of participants to the experiment. Therefore, each user was asked to complete the comprehension tasks both for the GRAPHOL language and for the OWLGrEd language. In order to avoid the transfer of learning effects between tasks, we split the ten users into two groups of five, and asked the first group to first carry out the comprehension tasks on the GRAPHOL version of the LUBM model, and then the comprehension tasks on the OWLGrEd version of the Pizza model, and the second group to do the opposite.

As already stated, all questionnaires we used in our tests can be found in the Supplemental Materials.

6.8. Study Results

Figure 10 summarizes some of the results of the tests. Each box plot shows the full range of variation, from minimum to maximum, indicated by the whiskers, the likely range of variation, indicated by the two boxes, and the median value. The overall correctness results for the comparative test, shown in boxplot (a), indicate a good comprehension level by the novice users of the GRAPHOL language, that can be considered comparable to the one obtained for OWLGrEd, which is based on UML class diagram, which is a formalism which the users were familiar with. Boxplot (b) summarizes the correctness results of the comparative test limited to five questions that deal with complex modeling aspects that go beyond UML, i.e., questions 1, 3, 5, 9, and 10 on the LUBM questionnaires, and questions 2, 4, 5, 7, and 9 on the Pizza questionnaires. These results confirm that users were able to more easily understand the completely graphical representation provided by GRAPHOL than the formulas or non-UML constructs adopted in OWLGrEd. Finally, boxplot (c) shows the correctness results of the non-comparative test by the more expert users. The very high scores indicate that such users quickly learned how to read GRAPHOL diagrams and how to use the language for modeling.

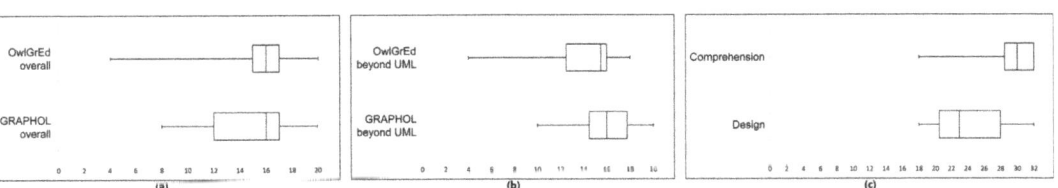

Figure 10. Correctness results for user tests. In boxplots (**a**,**b**) the scale is 0–20 (sum of correctness scores for five students on questions graded from 0 to 4); in boxplot (**c**) the scale is 0–32 (sum of correctness scores for eight students on questions graded from 0 to 4).

6.9. Post-Questionnaire Analysis

Finally, we discuss the results of the post-test questionnaires, which were presented to all participants. We recall that the goal of the post-test questionnaires was to measure the perceived general difficulty of the tasks required, of learning of test language symbols and of using GRAPHOL to read ontologies. The average results of the questionnaires are shown in Figure 11.

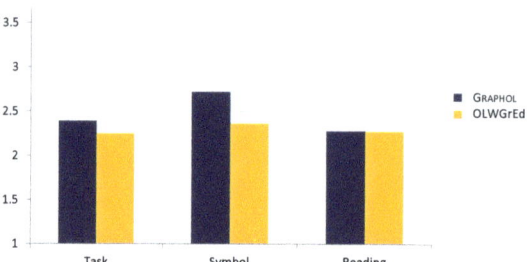

Figure 11. Post-questionnare results (scale: 1–5, with 1 being the best value).

As one can see, the feedback essentially confirms the positive impression gained from the analysis of the test results. Users felt about as comfortable reading ontologies modeled through the novel GRAPHOL language as they were with those in OWLGrEd (almost identical average scores for "Reading Difficulty"), even though, as expected, they felt that learning GRAPHOL's symbols was slightly more difficult than learning OWLGrEd's UML-based ones ("Symbol Difficulty" scores). Indeed, we recall that the participants were knowledgeable in conceptual modeling languages such as UML class diagrams and entity–relationship diagrams (ER). While OWLGrEd strictly adheres to the former (at the cost of recurring to expressions in logical languages when needed), GRAPHOL is rooted in ER, but it adds several graphical elements in order to completely cover OWL 2 without using non-graphical formulas.

The average values in the "Task Difficulty" column are more a reflection of the difficulty of the tests rather than the languages, but in both cases users seem to feel that the tests were not excessively difficult (average difficulty score of 2.4 and 2.2 out of a maximum of 5).

We finally point out that the results of the tests brought to light the need to enhance the usability of the language through a dedicated ontology tool. We used many suggestions we collected during the evaluation study to push forward the development of the Eddy editor tool for GRAPHOL [23], which is also equipped with some specific functionalities to facilitate the specification of GRAPHOL ontologies (e.g., through commands for the automatic construction of some recurrent modeling patterns, such as concept hierarchies or role typing axioms).

7. Conclusions

In this article, we studied the graphical language for ontologies GRAPHOL, which is as expressive as OWL 2. As we have illustrated, the key features of GRAPHOL are its precise semantics, its expressive power, and its completely graphical representation of ontologies, inspired by popular conceptual modeling languages, such as ER. This combination sets GRAPHOL apart from other proposals.

We remark, once again, that an editor, called Eddy [22], specifically tailored to support the specification of GRAPHOL ontologies, is available. This tool provides advanced functionalities for drawing syntactically correct GRAPHOL diagrams, for documenting them, and for translating them into standard OWL 2 syntax. Eddy is currently developed by ODBA Systems (http://obdasystems.com/, accessed on 17 January 2022), a Sapienza startup company, and is available as open-source software (https://github.com/obdasystems/eddy, accessed on 17 January 2022).

Currently, our work is mainly focused on devising GRAPHOL-like mechanisms for the visual specification of SPARQL queries over OWL 2 ontologies. Our idea is to automatically produce a query in SPARQL syntax on the basis of the selections of predicates performed by a user on a GRAPHOL ontology, which naturally allows to trace the basic graph pattern of the query, plus additional conditions imposed on the query variables through user-friendly visual mechanisms [76].

We are also working to add additional features to the language itself, to allow an even broader scope of modeling possibilities. In particular, we are looking into the addition of metamodeling features such as metaconcepts, which are concepts whose instances can be concepts themselves, and metaproperties, which are relationships between metaconcepts. Metaconcept representation could be useful, for instance, for the representation in GRAPHOL of formal ontologies, where specific metaproperties, such as, for instance, rigidity, can be exploited for expressing key aspects of the intended meaning of predicates in ontologies.

Supplementary Materials: The following supporting information can be downloaded at: https://www.mdpi.com/article/10.3390/fi14030078/s1, File S1: GRAPHOL: a graphical ontology language Survey and User Evaluation Study.

Author Contributions: Conceptualization, D.L., D.F.S., V.S. and G.D.G.; Formal analysis, D.L., D.F.S. and V.S.; Methodology, D.L. and D.F.S.; Supervision, D.L.; Validation, D.L., D.F.S. and V.S.; Writing—original draft, D.L., D.F.S., V.S. and G.D.G. All authors have read and agreed to the published version of the manuscript.

Funding: This research received no external funding.

Data Availability Statement: Not applicable.

Acknowledgments: This work was partly supported by the EU within the H2020 Programme under the grant agreement 834228 (ERC Advanced Grant WhiteMec) and the grant agreement 825333 (MOSAICrOWN), by Regione Lombardia within the Call Hub Ricerca e Innovazione under the grant agreement 1175328 (WATCHMAN), and by the Italian MUR (Ministero dell'Università e della Ricerca) through the PRIN project HOPE (prot. 2017MMJJRE), by Sapienza (project CQEinOBDM), and by the J.P.Morgan AI Faculty Research Award 2021 "Resilience-based Generalized Planning and Strategic Reasoning".

Conflicts of Interest: The authors declare no conflict of interest.

References

1. Chen, P.P. The Entity-Relationship Model: Toward a Unified View of Data. *ACM Trans. Database Syst.* **1976**, *1*, 9–36. [CrossRef]
2. Unified Modeling Language (UML) Superstructure, Version 2.0. 2005. Available online: http://www.uml.org/ (accessed on 17 January 2022).
3. Sowa, J.F. *Conceptual Structures: Information Processing in Mind and Machine*; Addison Wesley Publ. Co.: Boston, MA, USA, 1984.
4. Sowa, J.F. (Ed.) *Principles of Semantic Networks: Explorations in the Representation of Knowledge*; Morgan Kaufmann: Burlington, MA, USA, 1991.
5. Woods, W.A. What's in a Link: Foundations for Semantic Networks. In *Representation and Understanding: Studies in Cognitive Science*; Bobrow, D.G., Collins, A.M., Eds.; Academic Press: Cambridge, MA, USA, 1975; pp. 35–82.
6. Woods, W.A.; Schmolze, J.G. The KL-ONE Family. In *Semantic Networks in Artificial Intelligence*; Lehmann, F.W., Ed.; Pergamon Press: Oxford, UK, 1992; pp. 133–178.
7. Brachman, R.J.; Levesque, H.J. The Tractability of Subsumption in Frame-Based Description Languages. In Proceedings of the AAAI-84: Fourth National Conference on Artificial Intelligence, Austin, TX, USA, 6–10 August 1984; pp. 34–37.
8. Borgida, A.; Brachman, R.J. Conceptual Modeling with Description LogicsIn. Chapter 10, pp. 349–372. Available online: http://www.cs.toronto.edu/~jm/2507S/Readings/DLTutorial.pdf (accessed on 17 January 2022).
9. Berardi, D.; Calvanese, D.; De Giacomo, G. Reasoning on UML Class Diagrams. *Artif. Intell.* **2005**, *168*, 70–118. [CrossRef]
10. Catarci, T.; Lenzerini, M. Representing and using Interschema Knowledge in Cooperative Information Systems. *J. Intell. Coop. Inf. Syst.* **1993**, *2*, 375–398. [CrossRef]
11. Baader, F.; Calvanese, D.; McGuinness, D.; Nardi, D.; Patel-Schneider, P.F. (Eds.) *The Description Logic Handbook: Theory, Implementation and Applications*, 2nd ed.; Cambridge University Press: Cambridge, UK, 2007.
12. Bao, J. OWL 2 Web Ontology Language Document Overview (Second Edition). W3C Recommendation, World Wide Web Consortium. 2012. Available online: http://www.w3.org/TR/owl2-overview/ (accessed on 17 January 2022).

13. Amoroso, A.; Esposito, G.; Lembo, D.; Urbano, P.; Vertucci, R. Ontology-based Data Integration with Mastro-i for Configuration and Data Management at SELEX Sistemi Integrati. In Proceedings of the 16th Italian Conference on Database Systems (SEBD), Mondello, Italy, 22–25 June 2008; pp. 81–92.
14. Savo, D.F.; Lembo, D.; Lenzerini, M.; Poggi, A.; Rodríguez-Muro, M.; Romagnoli, V.; Ruzzi, M.; Stella, G. Mastro at Work: Experiences on Ontology-Based Data Access. *Proc. DL* **2010**, *573*, 20–31.
15. Calvanese, D.; De Giacomo, G.; Lembo, D.; Lenzerini, M.; Poggi, A.; Rodriguez-Muro, M.; Rosati, R.; Ruzzi, M.; Savo, D.F. The Mastro System for Ontology-based Data Access. *Semant. Web J.* **2011**, *2*, 43–53. [CrossRef]
16. Civili, C.; Console, M.; De Giacomo, G.; Lembo, D.; Lenzerini, M.; Lepore, L.; Mancini, R.; Poggi, A.; Rosati, R.; Ruzzi, M.; et al. MASTRO STUDIO: Managing Ontology-Based Data Access Applications. *Proc. VLDB Endow.* **2013**, *6*, 1314–1317. [CrossRef]
17. Kharlamov, E.; Giese, M.; Jiménez-Ruiz, E.; Skjaeveland, M.G.; Soylu, A.; Bagosi, T.; Console, M.; Haase, P.; Horrocks, I.; Horrocks, I.; et al. Optique 1.0: Semantic Access to Big Data. The Case of Norwegian Petroleum Directorate's FactPages. In Proceedings of the 12th International Semantic Web Conference (ISWC), Sydney, NSW, Australia, 21–25 October 2013; pp. 65–68.
18. Antonioli, N.; Castanò, F.; Coletta, S.; Grossi, S.; Lembo, D.; Lenzerini, M.; Poggi, A.; Virardi, E.; Castracane, P. Ontology-based Data Management for the Italian Public Debt. In Proceedings of the 8th International Conference on Formal Ontology in Information Systems (FOIS), Rio de Janeiro, Brazil, 22–25 September 2014; pp. 372–385.
19. Aracri, R.M.; Radini, R.; Scannapieco, M.; Tosco, L. Using Ontologies for Official Statistics: The ISTAT Experience. In *Current Trends in Web Engineering*; Springer: Berlin/Heidelberg, Germany, 2018; pp. 166–172.
20. Santarelli, V.; Lembo, D.; Ruzzi, M.; Ronconi, G.; Bouquet, P.; Molinari, A.; Pompermaier, F.; Caltabiano, D.; Catoni, E.; Fabrizi, A.; et al. Semantic Technologies for the Production and Publication of Open Data in ACI-Automobile Club d'Italia. In CEUR Workshop Proceedings, Proceedings of the ISWC 2019 Satellite Tracks (Posters & Demonstrations, Industry, and Outrageous Ideas), Auckland, New Zealand, 26–30 October 2019; Volume 2456, pp. 307–308.
21. Lembo, D.; Li, Y.; Popa, L.; Scafoglieri, F.M. Ontology mediated information extraction in financial domain with Mastro System-T. In Proceedings of the 6th International ACM Workshop on Data Science for Macro-Modeling (DSMM 2020), Portland, OR, USA, 14 June 2020; ACM Press: New York, NY, USA, 2020; pp. 3:1–3:6.
22. Lembo, D.; Pantaleone, D.; Santarelli, V.; Savo, D.F. Drawing OWL 2 ontologies with Eddy the editor. *AI Commun.* **2018**, *31*, 97–113. [CrossRef]
23. Lembo, D.; Pantaleone, D.; Santarelli, V.; Savo, D.F. Easy OWL Drawing with the Grapholl Visual Ontology Language. In Proceedings of the 15th International Conference on the Principles of Knowledge Representation and Reasoning (KR),Cape Town, South Africa, 25–29 April 2016; pp. 573–576.
24. Console, M.; Lembo, D.; Santarelli, V.; Savo, D.F. GRAPHOL: Ontology Representation Through Diagrams. In Proceedings of the 27th International Workshop on Description Logic (DL), Vienna, Austria, 17–20 July 2014; Volume 1193, pp. 483–495.
25. Brockmans, S.; Volz, R.; Eberhart, A.; Löffler, P. Visual modeling of OWL DL ontologies using UML. In Proceedings of the 3rd International Semantic Web Conference (ISWC), Hiroshima, Japan, 7–11 November 2004; Lecture Notes in Computer Science; Springer: Berlin/Heidelberg, Germany, 2004; Volume 3298, pp. 198–213.
26. Djuric, D.; Gasevic, D.; Devedzic, V.; Damjanovic, V. A UML Profile for OWL Ontologies. In Proceedings of the 2003/2004 European Workshop on Model Driven Architecture (MDAFA), Twente, The Netherlands, 26–27 June 2003; Revised Selected Papers; 2004; pp. 204–219.
27. Guizzardi, G. *Ontological Foundations for Structural Conceptual Models*; Centre for Telematics and Information Technology (CTIT): Enschede, The Netherlands, 2005.
28. Falco, R.; Gangemi, A.; Peroni, S.; Shotton, D.M.; Vitali, F. Modelling OWL Ontologies with Graffoo. In *The Semantic Web: ESWC 2014 Satellite Events*; Revised Selected Papers; Lecture Notes in Computer Science; Springer: Berlin/Heidelberg, Germany, 2014; Volume 8798, pp. 320–325.
29. Cerans, K.; Ovcinnikova, J.; Liepins, R.; Grasmanis, M. Extensible Visualizations of Ontologies in OWLGrEd. In *The Semantic Web: ESWC 2019 Satellite Events*; Revised Selected Papers; Lecture Notes in Computer Science; Springer: Berlin/Heidelberg, Germany, 2019; Volume 11762, pp. 191–196.
30. Evans, A.S. Reasoning with UML Class Diagrams. In Proceedings of the 2nd IEEE Workshop on Industrial Strength Formal Specification Techniques (WIFT), Boca Raton, FL, USA, 23 October 1998; IEEE Computer Society Press: Piscataway, NJ, USA,1998.
31. Artale, A.; Franconi, E. Temporal ER Modeling with Description Logics. In Proceedings of the 18th International Conference on Conceptual Modeling (ER), Paris, France, 15–18 November 1999; Lecture Notes in Computer Science; Springer: Berlin/Heidelberg, Germany, 1999; Volume 1728, pp. 81–95.
32. Simmonds, J.; Bastarrica, M.C.; Hitschfeld-Kahler, N.; Rivas, S. A Tool Based on DL for UML Model Consistency Checking. *Int. J. Softw. Eng. Knowl. Eng.* **2008**, *18*, 713–735. [CrossRef]
33. Chein, M.; Mugnier, M.L. *Graph-Based Knowledge Representation: Computational Foundations of Conceptual Graphs*; Springer: Berlin/Heidelberg, Germany, 2008.
34. Kaneiwa, K.; Satoh, K. On the Complexities of Consistency Checking for Restricted UML Class Diagrams. *Theor. Comput. Sci.* **2010**, *411*, 301–323. [CrossRef]
35. Queralt, A.; Artale, A.; Calvanese, D.; Teniente, E. OCL-Lite: Finite Reasoning on UML/OCL Conceptual Schemas. *Data Knowl. Eng.* **2012**, *73*, 1–22. [CrossRef]

36. Franconi, E.; Mosca, A.; Oriol, X.; Rull, G.; Teniente, E. Logic Foundations of the OCL Modelling Language. In Proceedings of the 14th European Conference on Logics in Artificial Intelligence (JELIA), Funchal, Portugal, 24–26 September 2014; pp. 657–664.
37. Oriol, X.; Teniente, E.; Tort, A. Computing repairs for constraint violations in UML/OCL conceptual schemas. *Data Knowl. Eng.* **2015**, *99*, 39–58. [CrossRef]
38. Zhang, F.; Ma, Z.M.; Cheng, J. Enhanced entity-relationship modeling with description logic. *Knowl. Based Syst.* **2016**, *93*, 12–32. [CrossRef]
39. Halpin, T.A. Object-Role Modeling: Principles and Benefits. *Int. J. Inform. Syst. Model. Des. (IJISMD)* **2010**, *1*, 33–57. [CrossRef]
40. Halpin, T.A. Formalization of ORM Revisited. In *OTM Workshops*; Lecture Notes in Computer Science; Springer: Berlin/Heidelberg, Germany, 2012; Volume 7567, pp. 348–357.
41. Franconi, E.; Mosca, A.; Solomakhin, D. ORM2: Formalisation and Encoding in OWL2. In *On the Move to Meaningful Internet Systems: OTM 2012 Workshops*; Springer: Berlin/Heidelberg, Germany, 2012; pp. 368–378.
42. Keet, C.M. Mapping the Object-Role Modeling language ORM2 into description logic language DLRifd. *arXiv* **2007**, arXiv:cs/0702089.
43. Wagih, H.M.; ElZanfaly, D.S.; Kouta, M.M. Mapping object role modeling 2 schemes to OWL2 ontologies. In Proceedings of the 3rd International Conference on Computer Research and Development, Shanghai, China, 11–13 March 2011; Volume 3, pp. 126–132.
44. Sportelli, F.; Franconi, E. A Formalisation and a Computational Characterisation of ORM Derivation Rules. In *On the Move to Meaningful Internet Systems: OTM 2019 Conferences-Confederated International Conferences: CoopIS, ODBASE, C&TC*; Lecture Notes in Computer Science; Springer: Berlin/Heidelberg, Germany, 2019; Volume 11877, pp. 678–694.
45. Brockmans, S.; Haase, P.; Hitzler, P.; Studer, R. A metamodel and UML profile for rule-extended OWL DL ontologies. In *The Semantic Web: Research and Applications*; Springer: Berlin/Heidelberg, Germany, 2006; pp. 303–316.
46. Object Management Group. Ontology Definition Metamodel. Technical Report formal/2009-05-01, OMG. 2009. Available online: http://www.omg.org/spec/ODM/1.0 (accessed on 17 January 2022).
47. Bechhofer, S.; van Harmelen, F.; Hendler, J.; Horrocks, I.; McGuinness, D.L.; Patel-Schneider, P.F.; Stein, L.A. OWL Web Ontology Language Reference. W3C Recommendation, World Wide Web Consortium. 2004. Available online: http://www.w3.org/TR/owl-ref/ (accessed on 17 January 2022).
48. Benevides, A.B.; Guizzardi, G. A model-based tool for conceptual modeling and domain ontology engineering in OntoUML. In *Enterprise Information Systems*; Springer: Berlin/Heidelberg, Germany, 2009; pp. 528–538.
49. Barzdins, J.; Barzdins, G.; Cerans, K.; Liepins, R.; Sprogis, A. *UML Style Graphical Notation and Editor for OWL 2*; BIR, Forbrig, P., Günther, H., Eds.; Lecture Notes in Business Information Processing; Springer: Berlin/Heidelberg, Germany, 2010; Volume 64, pp. 102–114.
50. Gaines, B.R. Designing visual languages for description logics. *J. Logic Lang. Inf.* **2009**, *18*, 217–250. [CrossRef]
51. Dau, F.; Eklund, P. A diagrammatic reasoning system for the description logic ALC. *J. Vis. Lang. Comput.* **2008**, *19*, 539–573. [CrossRef]
52. Krivov, S.; Williams, R.; Villa, F. GrOWL: A tool for visualization and editing of OWL ontologies. *J. Web Sem.* **2007**, *5*, 54–57. [CrossRef]
53. Lohmann, S.; Negru, S.; Haag, F.; Ertl, T. Visualizing ontologies with VOWL. *Semant. Web J.* **2016**, *7*, 399–419. [CrossRef]
54. Dudáš, M.; Lohmann, S.; Svátek, V.; Pavlov, D. Ontology visualization methods and tools: A survey of the state of the art. *Knowl. Eng. Rev.* **2018**, *33*, E10. [CrossRef]
55. Wiens, V.; Lohmann, S.; Auer, S. WebVOWL Editor: Device-Independent Visual Ontology Modeling. In Proceedings of International Semantic Web Conference (ISWC 2018) Posters & Demonstrations, Industry and Blue Sky Ideas Tracks, Monterey, CA, USA, 8–12 August 2018; Volume 2180.
56. da Silva, I.; Santucci, G.; del Sasso Freitas, C. Ontology visualization: One size does not fit all. In Proceedings of theEuroVA 2012: International Workshop on Visual Analytics, Vienna, Austria, 4–5 June 2012; pp. 91–95.
57. Shneiderman, B. Tree visualization with tree-maps: 2-d space-filling approach. *ACM Trans. Graph. (TOG)* **1992**, *11*, 92–99. [CrossRef]
58. de Souza, K.X.; dos Santos, A.D.; Evangelista, S.R. Visualization of ontologies through hypertrees. In Proceedings of the Latin American Conference on Human-Computer Interaction, Rio de Janeiro, Brazil, 17–20 August 2003; ACM Press: New York, NY, USA, 2003; pp. 251–255.
59. Wang Baldonado, M.Q.; Woodruff, A.; Kuchinsky, A. Guidelines for using multiple views in information visualization. In Proceedings of the Working Conference on Advanced Visual Interfaces, Palermo, Italy, 23–26 May 2000; ACM Press: New York, NY, USA, 2000; pp. 110–119.
60. Lanzenberger, M.; Sampson, J.; Rester, M. Visualization in Ontology Tools. In Proceedings of the 2009 International Conference on Complex, Intelligent and Software Intensive Systems, (CISIS), Fukuoka, Japan, 16–19 March 2009; IEEE Computer Society: Washington, DC, USA, 2009; pp. 705–711.
61. Katifori, A.; Halatsis, C.; Lepouras, G.; Vassilakis, C.; Giannopoulou, E.G. Ontology visualization methods—A survey. *ACM Comput. Surv.* **2007**, *39*, 10. [CrossRef]
62. Gennari, J.H.; Musen, M.A.; Fergerson, R.W.; Grosso, W.E.; Crubézy, M.; Eriksson, H.; Noy, N.F.; Tu, S.W. The evolution of Protégé: An environment for knowledge-based systems development. *Int. J. Hum.-Comput. Stud.* **2003**, *58*, 89–123. [CrossRef]

63. Haase, P.; Lewen, H.; Studer, R.; Tran, D.T.; Erdmann, M.; d'Aquin, M.; Motta, E. The NeOn ontology engineering toolkit. In Proceedings of the 17th International World Wide Web Conference (WWW), Beijing, China, 21–25 April 2008.
64. Adamou, A.; Palma, R.; Haase, P.; Montiel-Ponsoda, E.; Aguado de Cea, G.; Gómez-Pérez, A.; Peters, W.; Gangemi, A. The NeOn Ontology Models. In *Ontology Engineering in a Networked World*; Springer: Berlin/Heidelberg, Germany, 2012; pp. 65–90.
65. Weiten, M. OntoSTUDIO® as a Ontology Engineering Environment. In *Semantic Knowledge Management*; Springer: Berlin/Heidelberg, Germany, 2009; pp. 51–60.
66. Horrocks, I.; Kutz, O.; Sattler, U. The Even More Irresistible $\mathcal{SROIQ}$. In Proceedings of the 10th International Conference on the Principles of Knowledge Representation and Reasoning (KR), Lake District, UK, 2–5 June 2006; pp. 57–67.
67. Horrocks, I.; Sattler, U. Ontology Reasoning in the $\mathcal{SHOQ}$(D) Description Logic. In Proceedings of the 17th International Joint Conference on Artificial Intelligence (IJCAI), Seattle, WA, USA, 4–10 August 2001; pp. 199–204.
68. Bertin, J. *Semiology of Graphics: Diagrams, Networks, Maps*; University of Wisconsin Press: Madison, WI, USA, 1983.
69. Miller, G.A. The magical number seven, plus or minus two: Some limits on our capacity for processing information. *Psychol. Rev.* **1956**, *63*, 81. [CrossRef]
70. Nordbotten, J.C.; Crosby, M.E. The effect of graphic style on data model interpretation. *Inf. Syst.* **1999**, *9*, 139–155. [CrossRef]
71. Goodman, N. *Languages of Art: An Approach to a Theory of Symbols*; Hackett Publishing: Indianapolis, IN, USA, 1976.
72. Moody, D.L. The "physics" of notations: Toward a scientific basis for constructing visual notations in software engineering. *Softw. Eng. IEEE Trans.* **2009**, *35*, 756–779. [CrossRef]
73. Motik, B.; Parsia, B.; Patel-Schneider, P.F. OWL 2 Web Ontology Language Structural Specification and Functional-Style Syntax. W3C Recommendation, World Wide Web Consortium. 2012. Available online: http://www.w3.org/TR/owl2-syntax/ (accessed on 17 January 2022).
74. Barzdins, J.; Cerans, K.; Liepins, R.; Sprogis, A. Advanced Ontology Visualization with OWLGrEd. In *CEUR Workshop Proceedings*; Dumontier, M., Courtot, M., Eds.; OWLED. Available online: http://citeseerx.ist.psu.edu/viewdoc/download?doi=10.1.1.365.4375&rep=rep1&type=pdf (accessed on 17 January 2022).
75. Dix, A. *Human-Computer Interaction*; Springer: Berlin/Heidelberg, Germany, 2009.
76. Di Bartolomeo, S.; Pepe, G.; Savo, D.F.; Santarelli, V. Sparqling: Painlessly Drawing SPARQL Queries over Graphol Ontologies. In Proceedings of the CEUR Electronic Workshop Proceedings, Fourth International Workshop on Visualization and Interaction for Ontologies and Linked Data (VOILA@ISWC 2018), Monterey, CA, USA, 8 October 2018; Volume 2187, pp. 64–69.

Article

High-Performance Computing and ABMS for High-Resolution COVID-19 Spreading Simulation

Mattia Pellegrino, Gianfranco Lombardo, Stefano Cagnoni and Agostino Poggi *

Department of Engineering and Architecture, University of Parma, 43124 Parma, Italy; mattia.pellegrino@unipr.it (M.P.); gianfranco.lombardo@unipr.it (G.L.); cagnoni@ce.unipr.it (S.C.)
* Correspondence: agostino.poggi@unipr.it; Tel.: +39-0521-905-728

Citation: Pellegrino, M.; Lombardo, G.; Cagnoni, S.; Poggi, A. High-Performance Computing and ABMS for High-Resolution COVID-19 Spreading Simulation. *Future Internet* 2022, 14, 83. https://doi.org/10.3390/fi14030083

Academic Editor: Joel J. P. C. Rodrigues

Received: 19 February 2022
Accepted: 9 March 2022
Published: 11 March 2022

Publisher's Note: MDPI stays neutral with regard to jurisdictional claims in published maps and institutional affiliations.

Copyright: © 2022 by the authors. Licensee MDPI, Basel, Switzerland. This article is an open access article distributed under the terms and conditions of the Creative Commons Attribution (CC BY) license (https://creativecommons.org/licenses/by/4.0/).

Abstract: This paper presents an approach for the modeling and the simulation of the spreading of COVID-19 based on agent-based modeling and simulation (ABMS). Our goal is not only to support large-scale simulations but also to increase the simulation resolution. Moreover, we do not assume an underlying network of contacts, and the person-to-person contacts responsible for the spreading are modeled as a function of the geographical distance among the individuals. In particular, we defined a commuting mechanism combining radiation-based and gravity-based models and we exploited the commuting properties at different resolution levels (municipalities and provinces). Finally, we exploited the high-performance computing (HPC) facilities to simulate millions of concurrent agents, each mapping the individual's behavior. To do such simulations, we developed a spreading simulator and validated it through the simulation of the spreading in two of the most populated Italian regions: Lombardy and Emilia-Romagna. Our main achievement consists of the effective modeling of 10 million of concurrent agents, each one mapping an individual behavior with a high-resolution in terms of social contacts, mobility and contribution to the virus spreading. Moreover, we analyzed the forecasting ability of our framework to predict the number of infections being initialized with only a few days of real data. We validated our model with the statistical data coming from the serological analysis conducted in Lombardy, and our model makes a smaller error than other state of the art models with a final root mean squared error equal to 56,009 simulating the entire first pandemic wave in spring 2020. On the other hand, for the Emilia-Romagna region, we simulated the second pandemic wave during autumn 2020, and we reached a final RMSE equal to 10,730.11.

Keywords: epidemic modeling; agent-based modeling and simulation; large-scale simulation; actor model

1. Introduction

In the earliest months of 2020, the unexpected COVID-19 spreading put all the world's countries in difficulties because of the lack of countermeasures and knowledge about this novel virus to model its spreading. Moreover, since SARS-CoV-2 is an air-borne disease, it spreads among people due to everyday social interactions that represent themselves as a complex system to be modeled and simulated. Classical methods based on dynamic models like the Susceptible-Exposed-Infectious-Removed (SEIR) model [1,2] can only help with several limitations when high simulation resolution (fine-grained) is desired. Indeed, the class of SEIR models has to be extended to model particular conditions like social distancing, lockdown policies, and mask wearing. Although these extensions are easy to implement with additional equations in the basic model, these models do not still address the primary issue related to the basic reproduction number (R_0), which is not policy-invariant. Indeed, it depends on the average number of contacts among people, assuming that the population distribution is uniformly mixed. Moreover, the contact distribution is mixed heterogeneously in a natural population and shows some complex network characteristics.

Therefore, to avoid the problems of dynamic models, a different modeling and simulation approach should be used. Agent-based modeling and simulation (ABMS) is a better choice because it can model single individuals' characteristics and behaviors with a common trade-off between resolution and population size [3]. This paper proposes a novel case study based on ABMS and on previous experiences to increase the simulation resolution in the same large-scale context of COVID-19 spreading in Italy. Therefore, to avoid the problems of dynamic models, a different modeling and simulation approach should be used. Agent-based modeling and simulation (ABMS) is a better choice because it can model single individuals' characteristics and behaviors with a common trade-off between resolution and population size [3]. This paper proposes a novel case study based on ABMS and on previous experiences to increase the simulation resolution in the same large-scale context of COVID-19 spreading in Italy. The main contributions of our work are the following: (a) a software solution to model and execute millions of concurrent agents using the high-performance computing that maps individuals' behavior to a high simulation resolution; (b) providing a simulator for COVID-19 based on our framework that reaches interesting performances when used to forecast new infections cases using only few days of real data for the initialization; and (c) we propose a commuting model that is suitable for the epidemic context but that can be reused also in different domains.

On the contrary to previous works, we did not assume an underlying network of contacts, modeling social meetings as a function of the geographical distance among the individuals exploiting the commuting properties at different resolution levels (municipalities and provinces). We defined a commuting mechanism combining two distance-based models: the radiation model [4] and the gravity model [5]. To achieve this goal, we implemented a spreading simulator using ActoDemic [6] and validated it on two of the most populated Italian regions: Lombardy and Emilia-Romagna. The next section shows the features of ABMS, and Section 3 introduces the main epidemic models. Section 4 discusses the use of actors in ABMS application. Section 4 introduces the case study and discusses the development. Sections 5 and 6 discuss the features of our simulation model and introduces two simulation use cases. Section 7 discussed the results of the simulations of COVID-19 spreading in the Emilia Romagna and Lombardy regions. Finally, Section 8 concludes the paper by discussing its main features and the directions for future work.

2. Agent Based Modelling and Simulation

Agent-based modeling and simulation (ABMS) is a computational model for simulating phenomena in order to understand their behavior and what governs their results [3] and which exploits multi-agent systems and simulation models [7]. In particular, in an ABMS application, a simulation model is built on a generative and bottom-up process that integrates three types of components: the agents, who can perform one or more different behaviors, the environment in which the agents act by perceiving its state and acting accordingly, and, finally, the mechanisms that guide the interaction between the agents and exploit the direct and indirect exchange of information between system agents [8,9]. In particular, the generative and bottom-up nature of ABMS models offers great potential for addressing phenomena in which conventional modeling and simulation paradigms have difficulty in capturing their fundamental characteristics [10]. In fact, with an ABMS approach, instead of analyzing a phenomenon only in its entirety (as happens in discrete simulation systems), it is possible to analyze it, not only in its entirety but also in its components [11].

Furthermore, since a wide variety of research and application fields uses ABMS models, it follows that ABMS models can have very different characteristics when supporting the simulation of very different phenomena. According to [12], the most suggested ABMS models for complex systems modeling are cellular automata [13], flocking systems [14], and geographic information systems [15].

The success and diffusion of ABMS techniques is also due to the availability of software platforms that facilitate the development of models, the execution of simulations and the analysis of results [16–19]; in particular, among these software platforms, the best known and most used are: ASCAPE [20], MASON [21], Repast [22], AnyLogic [23] and NetLogo [24]. However, such platforms do not provide all the elements necessary to develop real intelligent agents, and so the development of the necessary models for some kinds of ABMS application may require the integration of an AI language (e.g., Prolog) or/and of some machine learning libraries. For example, Chumachenko et al. [25] proposed an intelligent information technology for integrating declarative languages and present an example of application that shows (i) how this technology allows the interoperability between NetLogo and Prolog, and (ii) how this kind of solution allows the resolution of decision-making problems and increases the efficiency of inference in a simulation environment.

Moreover, as introduced above, an important factor that can consolidate ABMS applications' importance is the availability of software platforms that allow the development of highly complex and large-sized applications. A great deal of work has been done in this direction using compute clusters and graphics processing units (GPU)s. Among the main works, we can highlight [26–30]. However, the proposed solutions cannot solve all the problems that must be faced in developing complex ABMS applications with a large number of agents. This is due to many factors [31]; one of the most critical points is that the actions of agents drive the simulation, and each agent decided what to do by interacting with several other agents who, during the simulation, can always be the same or change, bit by bit, with a very high computational cost (n^2) due to the need to identify the new agents at each simulation step. This is a big problem for applications running on a cluster of computers because, like this type of solution, execution is only effective if the processors spend most of their time processing rather than communicating [32]. Furthermore, it is often necessary to maintain the same order of execution of the agents to ensure the repeatability of the results, but in a multi-node system, this involves the use of synchronization protocols that at least increase execution times [33]. Finally, in such applications, the various agent's creations may not be completely simple. In fact, it is possible to have sets of heterogeneous agents which probably require a different method of creation; it may be necessary to configure agents of the same type with different or random data, etc.

3. Agent Based Modeling and Simulation for Epidemic Scenarios

Different ABMS solutions have been proposed to model and solve real and complex epidemic scenarios and, in particular, COVID-19 spreading [34]. Dyke Parunak et al. [35] assert that such scenarios can be modeled both with agents (ABMS) and with equations (EBM), but also that: (i) ABMS is most appropriate for domains characterized by a high degree of localization and distribution and dominated by discrete decisions, and (ii) EBM is most naturally applied to systems that can be modeled centrally, and in which the dynamics are dominated by physical laws rather than information processing. Moreover, they foresee that ABMS will be offered better solutions than EBM if they will provide comparable tools for constructing and analyzing system dynamics models. Rahmandad and Sterman [36] demonstrated that stochastic ABMS can show better performance in respect to differential equation models, when several parameters are unknown and there is the need for capturing heterogeneity across individuals and their network of reciprocal interactions. Ajelli et al. [37] compare ABMS and meta-population strategies for modeling the epidemic in Italy, concluding that a trade-off between the two methods depends on data availability and suggesting the use of hybrid models.

Silva et al. [38] proposed an individual-based simulation model for exploring scenarios for COVID-19 where individuals are modeled as moving particles. In particular, COVID-19 infections take place when two particles come closer than a certain contact radius. Social distancing for COVID-19 is modeled as changes in the contact radius or introducing a momentum term. Hinch et al. [39] modeled COVID-19 spread by replacing the moving particles with contact networks for households, work, and random contacts. Their model should enable scientists and policymakers to quickly compare the effectiveness of non-pharmaceutical interventions like lockdowns, testing, quarantine, and digital and manual contact tracing. In particular, the model is experimented in an environment represented by a city with a default population of 1 million people whose ages and contact patterns are parameterized according to UK demographics. Moreover, the use of contact networks has been proposed by several researchers (see, for example, [40–42]). Truszkowska et al. [43] proposed a high-resolution model using single individuals' features with real data about the COVID-19 outbreak in New Rochelle (NY), where thousands of citizens live. Moreover, they extend the typical simulation by modeling employees, hospitals, schools, and retirement homes and simulating the use of different test strategies, different types of treatment, and the presence of infections that cause similar COVID-19 symptoms. Finally, Chumachenko et al. [44] proposed an ABMS model that divides the individuals on the basis of their epidemic state (susceptible, exposed, infected and recovered); such conditions can be used to model the epidemic spread before the introduction of vaccination of the individuals. Individuals interact with each other and with the modeling environment, and transmission of morbidity and the transitions of individuals between states occur on the basis of probabilistic coefficients. These coefficients are determined experimentally on the basis of official statistics data on the incidence of COVID-19 coming from the Ukraine Health Center. The results of the simulations showed that the most effective measures to reduce epidemic dynamics are self-isolation of patients and tracking of contact individuals of the population, and that the isolation of the entire population is not necessary, but it is enough to isolate 80% of patients in the active phase.

4. Actor Based Modeling and Simulation

Actors are autonomous computational entities that can interact with other actors by exchanging asynchronous messages. When they receive any response, they can concurrently: send other messages, create new actors, and change their behavior to be ready to manage the next messages that they think to receive [45]. Moreover, actors have the suitable characteristics to define and implement the computational agents used in multi-agent systems and ABMS models [46]. Indeed, actors and computational agents share some characteristics: (i) both react to external stimuli (i.e., they are reactive), (ii) both act independently and exhibit control over their internal state (i.e., they are autonomous), and (iii) both interact through the exchange of asynchronous messages and through these messages they are able to coordinate and cooperate with each other (i.e., they are social) [47]. Therefore, the availability of some actor-based software frameworks can simplify the development of computational agents in domains where agents act dynamically, change their behavior, and need to coordinate or cooperate through direct interactions.

4.1. Using Actors for Large Scale ABMS Applications

Several researchers proposed interesting solutions for large scale ABMS applications. For example, Jang and Agha [48] proposed an actor-based software infrastructure, called the actor's adaptive architecture. This infrastructure supports the construction of large-scale agent-based simulations and exploits some distributed computing techniques to optimize the distribution of the agents of the application on a network of computational nodes. Moreover, this software infrastructure uses some optimization techniques to reduce the amount of data exchanged between nodes and support dynamic agents' distribution and search. Scheutz et al. [49] proposed a simulation environment, called SWAGES, that provides an automatic and dynamic distribution of simulations that supports the minimization of the simulation times. In particular, SWAGES allows the use of different programming languages for the definition of the agent models, and provides large data collections and data analysis techniques that can help to simplify the analysis of the results. Moreover, it provides a flexible scheduler offering automatic fault detection and error recovery mechanisms, and so improving the reliability of large-scale simulations. Cicirelli et al. [28] proposed the use of actors for the distribution of simulations on the Repast software platform [22]. In particular, they defined a software infrastructure that: (i) decomposes an application into subsystems (theaters), (ii) each subsystem hosts a set of actors and can be allocated on one of the computational nodes of the application, and (iii) supports agent migration, transparent location naming and efficient communication. Wittek and Rubio-Campillo [50] present an ABMS framework, called Pandora, that is designed for social scientists that uses HPC resources and implemented in the C++ programming language; moreover, Pandora provides a Python interface to the framework that should make possible the development of ABMS to people with minimal programming background. Pandora divides a simulation environment among different computer nodes, and each one of them will own a section of the environment and the agents located in this section. Moreover, data and agents located in the border between adjacent nodes will be copied and sent to neighbors at every time step of simulation, in order to keep data consistent in all the execution. Pandora was used for experimenting the tradeoff of replacing a traditional cluster with a cloud solution. Since the simulation framework requires a high-speed interconnection, this solution should provide low performance, but a cloud cluster should reduce losses and prove that even a cheap cloud cluster can provide interesting computational power for the simulations. However, the experimentation showed that the use of a cloud environment can provide a cost-effective solution. Collier and North [51] proposed an ABMS system, called Repast HPC, that extends the Repast framework (North and Collier, 2006), and is developed in C++ and uses Message Passing Interface (MPI) [52] for supporting large-scale distributed computing. In particular, Repast HPC is an environment where several processes are running in parallel and where a massive number of agents can be distributed across such processes. This is possible because each process has its own scheduler for processing the local events and all the schedulers are synchronized. Finally, Repast HPC allows the definition of a shared context for each process that can host local agents and remote agents copied from another process. This solution should improve simulation performance because the interaction among local and remote agents of the same shared context does not need remote communication. Fan et al. [53] presented an automated HPC system, named DRAS (Deep Reinforcement Agent for Scheduling), that takes advantage of deep reinforcement learning. In particular, DRAS implements a hierarchical neural network that provides some important HPC scheduling features such as resource reservation and backfilling. Each DRAS execution is driven by a specific scheduling objective, and during the execution the system automatically learns to improve its policy through interaction with the scheduling environment and dynamically adjusts its policy as workload changes. The results of its experimentation seem to outperform the existing heuristic and optimization solutions by up to 45%. Finally, Santana et al. [54] proposed a scalable simulator, called InterSCSimulator, to support the simulation of complex and large-scale smart city scenarios. Additionally, in this case, the simulation is based on actors, and each actor models a car or a bus moving in the city from an origin to a destination vertex in the city graph. The experimentation results show that the simulator is scalable and easy to use. Moreover, this simulator supports the analysis of the results of the simulation by generating charts and animated simulations.

4.2. ActoDeS

ActoDeS (Actor Development System) is a framework for the development of distributed systems [55]. This framework is based on the use of concurrent objects (from here named actors) whose main characteristics derive from the actor model [45]. In ActoDeS, an actor is created by another actor; after its creation, the actor can interact with other actors through the exchange of asynchronous messages and, as a consequence, can change its behavior several times; once its work is finished, the actor kills itself. Moreover, an actor keeps messages received and not yet processed in a queue. ActoDeS is implemented using the Java language and allows the development of applications that, depending on the complexity of the application and the availability of hardware, software, and communication resources, can be distributed on one or more computational nodes. Three other main elements are involved in an ActoDeS application: actor spaces, management services, and actor services. In particular, an actor space acts as a "container" for a set of actors and supports their execution through the use of management and actor services. Moreover, in an application involving several actor spaces, each actor space is deployed in a different

Java virtual machine. Therefore, an application involving multiple actor spaces can be distributed over multiple computational nodes. Moreover, the actors of an application can interact through point-to-point, broadcast, multicast and publish-subscribe messaging.

4.3. Using ActoDeS for ABMS Large Scale Applications

As previously introduced, the need to use ABMS in different research and application sectors, makes the availability of ABMS that offer the features necessary in the specific research and application domain. To address this problem, ActoDeS provides several implementations of the actors and components that define an application's runtime. In particular, an actor can have its thread of execution or share it with the other actors of the actor space; moreover, different types of actors can perform simulation steps of different lengths during the execution of an application. Furthermore, as far as the runtime components are concerned, it is necessary to use different scheduling algorithms to guarantee good efficiency to different types of ABMS [56]. In this regard, ActoDeS provides some schedulers which implement the most interesting and well-known scheduling algorithms. These characteristics make ActoDeS a suitable means to build ABMS applications that, depending on the characteristics of the application domain, can be easily realized by choosing the implementations of the actors and runtime components most suitable for that type of application.

ActoDeS supports the development of large-scale ABMS applications by using specialized schedulers for distributed applications and using techniques to simplify and reduce the cost of communication. Among the various types of schedulers provided, a scheduler can remove an idle actor from the execution list, store it in persistent storage, and put it back into the execution list when the actor is ready to restart its execution. This type of scheduler is useful in application domains that involve many actors who, during the simulation, can have long periods of inactivity. In fact, in these conditions, the cost of removing, storing and adding actors can be easily balanced by reducing the number of actors running. In many cases, that solution guarantees a lower use of the hardware and software resources used by the application. Undoubtedly the most critical component to develop and ensure the proper functioning of ABMS applications, and especially of large-scale applications, is communication management. Regarding distributed applications, ActoDeS allows an actor to communicate transparently with actors from other actor spaces (i.e., it needs only to get their remote references). Regarding communication, ActoDeS supports, in addition to point-to-point communication, one-to-many communication via broadcast, multicast, and publish-subscribe protocols, and reduces the cost of one-to-one communication through message aggregation techniques [57,58].

Commonly, in different ABMS applications, each actor must propagate information to all or to a large part of the actors of the application. Naturally, if such messages were disseminated through a point-to-point interaction, the cost of communication would become intolerable even with a limited number of actors. However, ActoDeS provides an actor implementation, called "shared actor", which avoids this type of problem: all the actors of the application share a single mailbox that keeps all the messages sent in the previous and current simulation step and allows the reception of the messages of the previous simulation step. Therefore, this type of actor can receive: (i) the point-to-point messages that are addressed to itself, (ii) all the broadcast messages, and (iii) all the messages from a multicast group to which it has subscribed. Furthermore, separating the messages of two simulation steps avoids the burden of keeping a copy of the current environment when it is necessary to ensure that agents decide their actions with the same information about the environment in which they operate [56]. In some cases, when there is a strong interaction between the application actors, especially when a relevant part of the interaction occurs between the actors of different computation nodes, the cost of communication can cause incorrect behavior or even the failure of the application.

ActoDeS seeks to reduce the cost of communication by adopting a message aggregation technique. This technique is managed by the managers of the different actor spaces and is applied to the messages that are sent to remote actors. In particular, each manager performs the following operations: (i) at the beginning of a simulation step it creates an aggregation message for each remote actor space; (ii) during the execution of the simulation step, inserts the messages addressed to other actor spaces in the appropriate aggregation message; (iii) at the end of the simulation step: (a) sends the appropriate aggregation message to each remote manager, (b) receives an aggregation message from each remote manager and (c) extracts the messages from each aggregation message and sends them to the (local) actors recipients.

A very important feature that an ABMS application development environment should be is the availability of graphical tools to visualize the evolution of simulations, and tools to analyze the data obtained from the simulations. ActoDeS does not provide tools for the visualization of simulations and the analysis of their results, but provides a logging service that allows the saving on a file of the streaming of Java objects that contain the data that describe the relevant actions of an actor (e.g., its initialization, reception, sending and processing messages, creating actors, changing behavior and its arrest). However, the processing of these logging files is quite simple, and therefore, it was not very difficult to create tools that supported these two types of functionality [59,60].

5. The Simulator

Our simulator is built using ActoDemic [6], which is a framework that aims to facilitate the design and development of spreading phenomena in large-scale scenarios. The base unit is represented by actors that, depending on the target application, represent the entities of the system to model and simulate. The actors are implemented using the Java framework ActoDeS as a backbone to support the agents' concurrent execution and distribution over several nodes. Each individual is modeled using a Base Spreader (BS) actor, which has a set of default attributes that can be enabled, configured, and modified to best suit the model. These attributes represent the demographic knowledge we used to model the population, but also the hidden internal state of each individual:

1. Unique identifier
2. Province or municipality of residence
3. Age
4. Number of daily contacts
5. Current infection state
6. If the individual is an essential worker
7. If the individual wears a protective mask during the simulation period.

The last two parameters are necessary to model and simulate different conditions verified in the early stage of the pandemic in Italy between February and May 2020.

In order to model the COVID-19 spread, we adopted the SEIR model, which provides susceptible, exposed, infected, and recovered compartments, and modified it by adding two extra compartments: positive and quarantine. These phases are typical in the COVID-19 infection cycle. At the beginning, all are in the susceptibility state. At this stage, every individual can be infected by another one who is contagious. An individual who gets infected moves from a susceptibility state to an incubation state and remains in this state for a certain amount of time before moving into the next compartment, where it will become infected. An infected subject can spread the virus and infect other individuals. When the infection phase ends, the individual becomes positive. Being positive means that the virus was identified with a COVID-19 test. Due to this result, the individual will be forced into a quarantine state, limiting his/her contacts. After a certain time, a positive could heal or die. There is no death probability, but deaths follow the real death curve of the simulated use case taken into account. In particular, the incubation phase lasts from 7 to 14 days, the infectious phase from 3 to 7 days, and the positive phase from 14 to 30 days [61]. Figure 1 shows a diagram that summarizes the described infection cycle. Moreover, the distinction between positive and negative is necessary to model the use-case in 2020 since real-data refers only to infections found with a delay using the COVID-19 tests several days after the first symptoms [62].

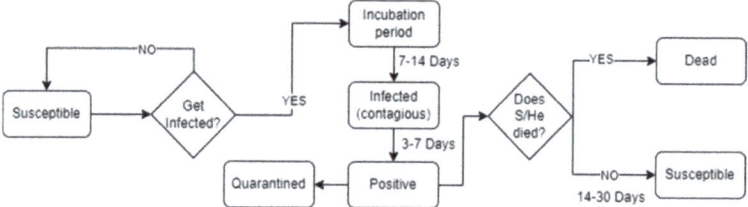

Figure 1. Detailed scheme of our infection cycle.

Contagion is based on a specific transmission probability for each individual. This probability represents the likelihood of being in a condition that supports the virus spread. We use a general COVID-19 transmission probability (CTV) estimated in [6], but this probability is scaled by each individual depending on two other stochastic parameters that are related to the use of protective masks and their efficacy. We used statistics and masks' efficacy presented in [63]. We considered three categories of masks: cloth, surgical, and N95 masks. Efficiency of a mask is evaluated in terms of inward and outward protection. According to [63], a mask's inward efficiency could vary from 20% to 80% for cloth, 70–90% for surgical, and above 95% for N95 masks. On the other hand, outward efficiency could range from 0 to 80% for cloth masks, while surgical and N95 masks are 50–90% and 70–100% outwardly protective, respectively. The effectiveness of a generic mask is assumed to be equal to the average effectiveness of the three previous types. Figure 2 describes the contagion modeling.

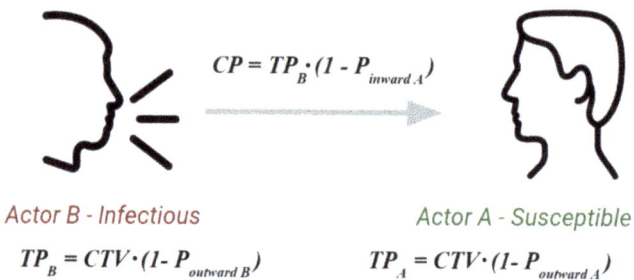

Figure 2. Stochastic contagion modeling.

5.1. Software Architecture with HPC

Since each Base Spreader actor maps exactly one individual, we simulated 10 million agents for the Lombardy region and 5 million agents for the Emilia-Romagna region. Figure 3 shows the logical architecture of the simulator, that is described in the following lines. The simulation process is divided into several "epochs" representing a different day. Moreover, people can change their behavior depending on the current epoch (e.g., normal or lockdown). At the end of each epoch, the simulator provides a synchronization step to update the internal state (infectious state) of each BS depending on their meetings and according to an infectious probability we defined. The simulator involves a set of computational nodes whose execution is driven by a set of ActoDeS schedulers and managers. In particular, each manager has the duty of creating the subset of agents for its computational node and synchronizing the simulation execution on that node with the execution of the other computational nodes. Moreover, one of those managers assumes the role of "master" to partition the agents involved in the simulation, exchanging the information with the other managers to notify the agents under their control. We extensively used the ActoDeS passive actors for the BS implementation in order to allow large-scale development, while managers are active actors. The simulation process is described in Figure 4. The simulated population is divided into N actor spaces, where a manager assumes the duty of managing that portion in terms of execution and communication.

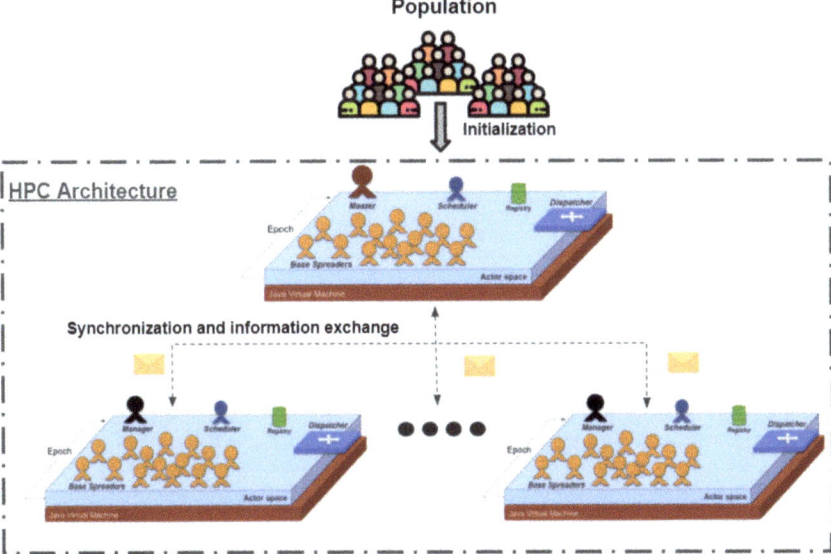

Figure 3. The simulator's architecture on the High Performance Computing (HPC) architecture divides individuals in several actor spaces on different computational nodes.

Finally, in each actor-space, there is an ActoDeS CycleScheduler that effectively manages the passive actors by coordinating their execution by exchanging messages with them until the end.

Every actor-space needs to exchange several pieces of information at the synchronization step. They exchange details about people's meeting, people who must change their infection phase to "Incubated" due an infection, the number of people expected to die in their actor-space, other synchronization messages and finally an end signal. On the other hand, each manager sends to the Master only the currently positive individuals, infected individuals and a report related to the epoch processed. The high-performance computing system of the University of Parma offers various nodes with different characteristics. The one we used, involves two INTEL XEON E5-2683v4 2.1GHz processors (for a total of 32 cores) and 1024 Gb of RAM memory. The actors' population is therefore divided into 32 actor spaces of 137,500 actors each. For Emilia Romagna (5 million agents), the average execution lasts 41 min and uses about 100 Gb of RAM memory. On the other hand, for Lombardy, the average execution lasts 3 h and 30 min and uses about 500 Gb of RAM memory.

We stochastically modeled COVID-19 spreading among two individuals by defining a specific transmission probability (TP) for this virus using the number of infections in the early autumn of 2020 when data were more accurate, rather than the beginning of the pandemic. This TP represents the ability of each BaseSpreader to transmit its state to another actor. Practically, the only actors that can transfer their state are the ones that are in the infectious or positive phases. Since we also modeled protective mask-wearing, the likelihood of infecting someone or being infected is a chain probability of TP, the Poutward (actor's outward mask protection probability) and the Pinward (actor's inward protection probability). Finally, the contagion happens by randomly sampling from a uniform distribution considering the contagion probability and actor's susceptibility.

```
Master ← MasterManager()                        #Creates the master manager
for AS in ActorSpace do
    Managers ← Master.CreateManager()           #Create a manager for each actor space
for M in Managers do
    M.CreateBaseSpreaders()                     #Each Manager instantiates its portion of BSs
Repeat

    For each Manager
        for each BaseSpreader in Manager do
            Manager.gatherBSsMessages()         #Each manager collects all the information from
                                                 the base spreaders and from itself and groups
                                                 them into one aggregation message to avoid
                                                 overhead information
            Manager.sendMessages()              #Each Manager sends its message to the other
                                                 managers
            Manager.sendSynchMessage()          #Each Manager sends a synch message to the other
                                                 managers and wait for the response
            Manager.waitResponses()

    For each Scheduler
        Scheduler.executeStep()
        Scheduler.sendEndStepToAll()            #Each scheduler perform an execution step of all its
                                                 actors and then send and "end step" message to all
Until EndSimulation
```

Figure 4. The simulation process algorithm.

5.2. Commuting Model

To evaluate the robustness of our model and our hyper-parameters, we decided to add further detail to our model exploiting highly detailed data on socio-demographic structure in Italy and the commuting effects between provinces and municipalities. For high school students, university students and workers, there is the possibility that the employment place is located in a different town than that of residence, or even in a different province. Commuting is very common nowadays and plays an important role in the infection spreading even in the most isolated municipalities. Therefore, it is essential to model this phenomenon in a way that is as closely comparable to reality as possible. Commuting models commonly rely on the effectiveness of two parameters:

- The grain: the finer the grain of the model, the more accurate the commuting model is.
- The economic quotient: the most effective models take into account the economic quotient of every zone. Moreover, a municipality with a high number of businesses attracts more workers than another with few job opportunities.

After some analyses, we decided to use the average results between a gravitational model that is presented in [5] and the radial one that is explained in [4]. We chose this approach because the first model has a better commuters' distribution in the various municipalities near the departure one. On the other hand, the second model computes in a more reliable way the correct number of people moving from a given municipality, but tends to distribute the contacts only to the closest town. The gravity model puts in a relationship the inhabitant number of the departure municipality, the inhabitant number of the arrival municipality, and the Euclidean distance between them:

$$c_{i,j} = \theta \frac{N_i^{\tau f} N_j^{\tau t}}{d_{i,j}^{\rho}} \qquad (1)$$

where:

1. $c_{i,j}$ is the probability that an individual living in i works or studies in municipality j
2. N_i, N_j number of individuals living in municipality i (or j)
3. θ proportional constant equal to 0.0005
4. τf inhabitants damping constant of i equal to 0.28
5. τt inhabitants damping constant of j which changes according to the number of people living in j:
    1. 0.65 if the number of inhabitants is greater than 150,000
    2. 0.66 if the number of inhabitants is between 5000 and 150,000
    3. 0.78 if the number of inhabitants is less than 5000
6. $d_{i,j}$ distance between the municipalities i and j
7. ρ constant amplifying the dependence from distance which changes according to the number of people living in j:
    a. 3.05 if the number of inhabitants is greater than 150,000
    b. 2.95 if the number of inhabitants is between 5000 and 150,000
    c. 2.5 0.78 if the number of inhabitants is less than 5000

Due to the lack of data of an economic quotient, we supposed that a municipality with many inhabitants also has a higher economic attraction. For this reason, the constants are set according to the number of people living in the municipality. The radial model, on the other hand, puts in a relationship the inhabitant number of the departure municipality, the inhabitant number of the arrival municipality, and the number of people living in the circle with a radius equal to the distance between the two municipalities. Hence:

$$p_{i,j} = p_i \frac{N_i N_j}{(N_i + S_{i,j})(N_i + N_j + S_{i,j})} \quad (2)$$

where:

1. $p_{i,j}$ is the probability that an individual living in i works or studies in municipality j
2. p_i initial commuting probability of municipality i. This parameter can assume three different values according to the number of people who live in i:
    a. if the number of inhabitants is greater than 150,000
    b. 0.3 if the number of inhabitants is between 5000 and 150,000
    c. 0.4 if the number of inhabitants is less than 5000
3. N_i, N_j number of individuals living in municipality i (or j)
4. $S_{i,j}$ population that lives within the circle with radius equal to the distance between i and j minus the population living in i and j

The values of the constants were identified by applying and comparing the model on the Italian scenario. Moreover, we identified the constants' value using the data available from the Emilia Romagna region [61], and we combined this data with the features extracted from [5,6]. Figure 5 shows the difference between the gravity model and the radial one. In the first one, the Euclidean distance is enough to calculate the commuting probability between Albinea and Reggio nell'Emilia; in the second one, instead, we must also take into account the number of inhabitants contained in the area described by the circumference.

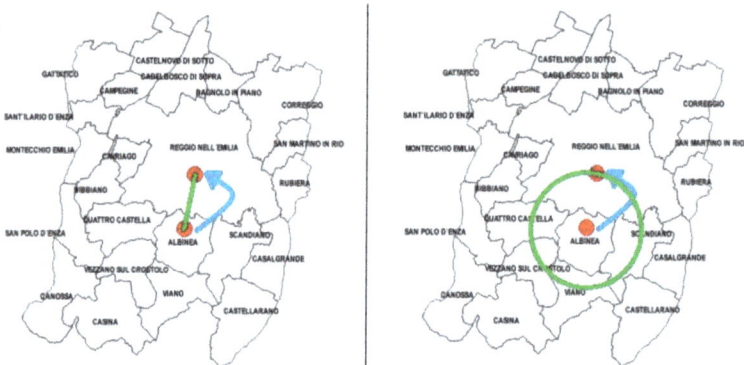

Figure 5. Image representing the difference between the gravity model and the radial one. In this example, we consider the municipality of Albinea (departure) and the municipality of Reggio nell'Emilia (arrival).

6. Use-Cases: Modeling the Emilia-Romagna and Lombardy Regions

To realize a working model for the Reggio Emilia province, we gathered data about contagion at the municipality level [61], and we also collected data about Emilia Romagna [62]. Unfortunately, we were not able to collect contagion data at the municipality level for the whole Emilia-Romagna region; therefore, to determinate our initial condition, we studied the Reggio Emilia province's distribution, dividing the municipalities in different classes according to inhabitants' number, then we extended this class format to the whole region. The geographical coordinates, mandatory for calculating the commuting model distance, was retrieved from [63], and the population size and distribution was provided by ISTAT [64].

To correctly tune the gravitation models and the radial ones, it is necessary to take into account the commuting values provided by the region [65]. The use case considered the second outbreak which affected the entire Italian territory. Therefore, the simulation period concerns the trend of infections between the 1 September 2020 and 15 December 2020. Finally, to validate our model, we compared with the official data provided by the Italian Government (Protezione Civile) and the regional government of Emilia-Romagna.

6.1. Social-Demographic Model

We introduced family groups and occupations (work or student) for the individuals involved in the simulation. In light of that, we can define a new socio-demographic model. The municipalities, with their geographical coordinates and the agents representing the population, are created following the data and probability distributions provided by the census. In our model, there are nine different family types, characterized by a different composition and number of members:

1. Single with children
2. Single without children
3. Single with children plus another adult
4. Couple without children
5. Couple without children plus another adult
6. Couple with children
7. Couple with children plus another adult
8. Adults that live together
9. Family groups (with at least one child)

With "other adult" we intended a person who is not strictly inside the family group but lives in the same habitation. Each type of family has a frequency of appearance, and the number of members may vary depending on a distribution probability shown in the Figure 6.

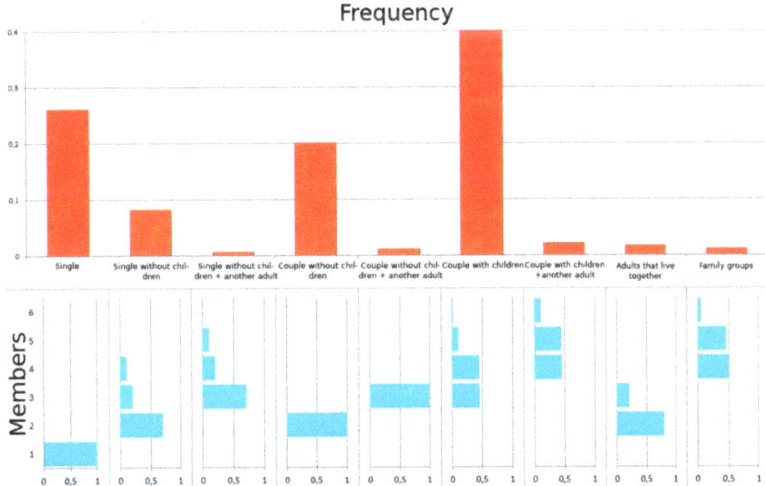

Figure 6. Family type distribution chart with relative number of members.

We introduced three fundamental constraints for building a consistent family group:
1. Any family group must contain at least one adult
2. The age of each child must be between 18 and 43 years less than the younger parent
3. The age difference of a couple is less than or equal to 15 years and they must be adult

We assigned an occupation to each individual based on its age. Moreover, we exploited some probability distributions based on the attendance rate. Finally, we implemented six different school categories, each with a specific attendance rate:
1. Kindergarten, attendance rate: 90%
2. Preschool, attendance rate: 90%
3. Elementary school, attendance rate: 100%
4. Middle school, attendance rate: 100%
5. High school, attendance rate: 92%
6. University, attendance rate: 31%

We have divided the students into classes, with different sizes depending on their category:
1. Kindergarten: 40 children
2. Preschool: 20 children
3. Elementary school: 19 children
4. Middle school: 21 lads
5. High school: 21 lads
6. University: 34 lads

On the other hand, as for workers, we considered different employment rates based on their age:
1. 15–19 years: 8%
2. 20–26 years: 30%
3. 27–34 years: 62.5%
4. 35–54 years: 73.5%
5. 55–70 years: 54.3%

We grouped workers into job groups, which can be of seven different types that differ according to the number of employees:

1. Very small company: up to 5 employees
2. Small company: up to 9 employees
3. Small-medium company: up to 19 employees
4. Medium company: up to 49 employees
5. Medium-large company: up to 99 employees
6. Large company: up to 249 employees
7. Very large company: over 250 employees

Each type of company has a different frequency of appearance, shown in Figure 7.

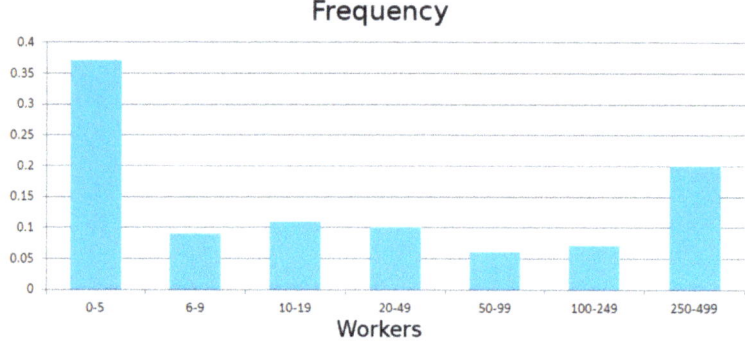

Figure 7. Distribution of work classes.

6.2. Restrictions

In Emilia Romagna's model, there were six different levels of restrictions to represent as precisely as possible the division into bands implemented by the Italian government during the simulation period taken into account:

1. White: no restrictions
2. White from 10/18 to 10/24: represents the restrictions introduced on 18 October 2020: no limitations regarding work, but high schools and universities at 50% in attendance. The number of daily interactions is reduced by 40% to shape the closure of businesses such as bars after 9 pm and restaurants after midnight.
3. White from 10/25 to 11/05: represents the latest restrictions introduced before the zoning: no limitations regarding work, but schools and universities still at 50% in attendance. Closing of activities such as gyms, theaters and cinemas, closing restaurants after 6 pm, also the recommendation not to move. The number of social interactions is reduced by 50% compared to the initial value.
4. Yellow: high schools and universities closed (100% distance learning). Curfew from 22.00. Closure to the public of exhibitions, museums and other places of culture such as archives and libraries. To model these additional restrictions, the number of social interactions is reduced by 60%.
5. Orange: in addition to the limitations of the yellow area, the prohibitions on moving between municipalities except for proven work needs and the closure of catering activities (excluding take-away) are added. The use of smart working is encouraged and recommended even for workers, excluding essentials. In the model, social interactions are reduced by 70% compared to the initial values and cannot take place outside the municipalities (except those related to work activities).
6. Red: in addition to the limitations of the orange zone, the prohibition of movement within the municipality. For this, the daily interactions are reduced by 80% and reduced to zero those regarded as usual ones.

6.3. Spreading Parameters' Selection

To correctly model the contagion evolution, we had to tune the simulator transmission probability, which is a fundamental ActoDemic parameter [6]. We determined it with an empirical procedure: we computed the average of ten simulations for every parameter's value and we searched for the optimal value with a random search across the probability space, trying to chase up the real data curve in Reggio Emilia's province (see Figure 8) and even in Emilia Romagna region (see Figure 9).

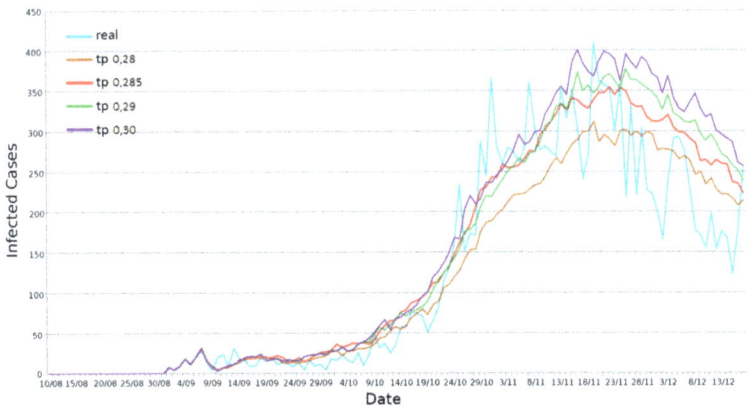

Figure 8. Graph of daily infected persons with different TP values—Reggio Emilia province.

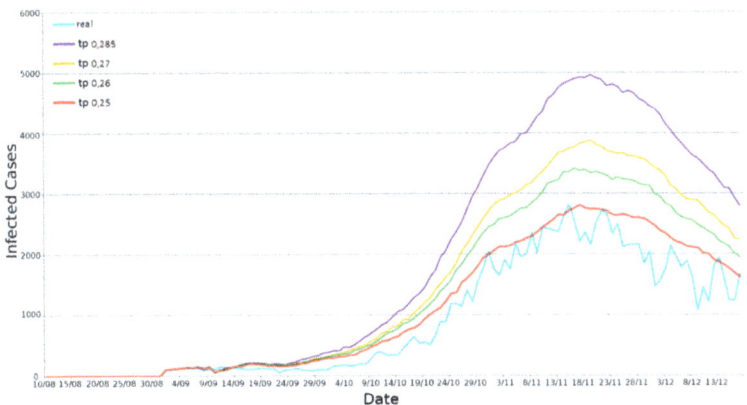

Figure 9. Graph of daily infected persons with different TP values—Emilia Romagna region.

For Reggio Emilia's province, the TP optimal value was 0.285. Moreover, the TP value identified for Reggio Emilia's province was too high when applied to the whole Emilia Romagna scenario. The reason was identified to be due to the commuting mechanism. In fact, each province is also influenced by the contagions of the other provinces. Therefore, we searched for a new TP value which could be suitable for the region scenarios, and then we found 0.25 as the optimal value.

6.4. Results for Emilia-Romagna

After finding an optimal TP for the two considered use cases, we simulated the scenarios again. We highlighted when the restrictions, implemented in the simulator, are enabled. First, we simulated the Reggio Emilia province scenario with a TP equal to 0.285.

We took into consideration the daily infections trend (see Figure 8), obtaining an R2 equal to 0.854, a Pearson correlation equal to 0.941, and an RMSE equal to 48.32 (see Figure 10).

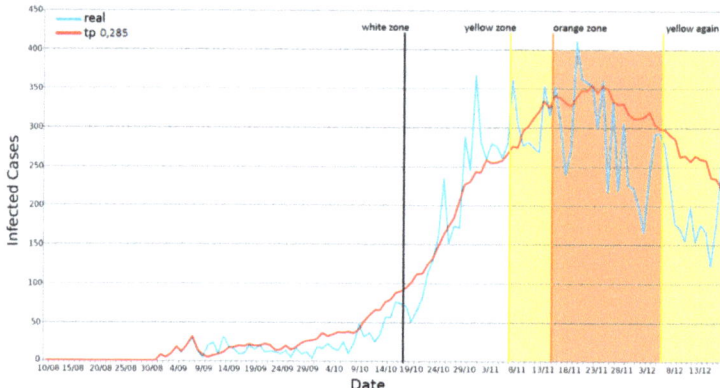

Figure 10. Positives' daily representation—Reggio Emilia province, Emilia Romagna region.

The simulated curve has a very similar trend compared to the real one, which is however very disturbed mainly due to the dissimilarity in the number of daily COVID-19 tests performed in the province. For this reason, we had to create a cumulative curve to better limit data pollution. We got, in this case, an R2 equal to 0.986, a Pearson correlation equal to 0.9988, and an RMSE equal to 608.88 (see Figure 11).

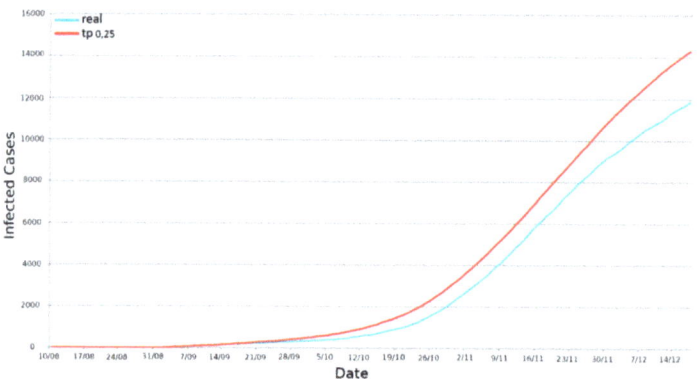

Figure 11. Positives' incremental representation—Reggio Emilia province, Emilia Romagna region.

Secondly, we simulated the use case considering the entire territory of Emilia Romagna. The TP taken into consideration in this case was 0.25. However, we also considered both daily and incremental infections trends. In Figure 12, it is possible to see the curve concerning the daily infections in the region. We obtained an R2 score of 0.881, a Pearson correlation of 0.977, and an RMSE of 319.08. Moreover, for the incremental representation of the infections in Figure 13, we obtained an R2 of 0.922, a Pearson correlation of 0.9993 and an RMSE 10,730.11.

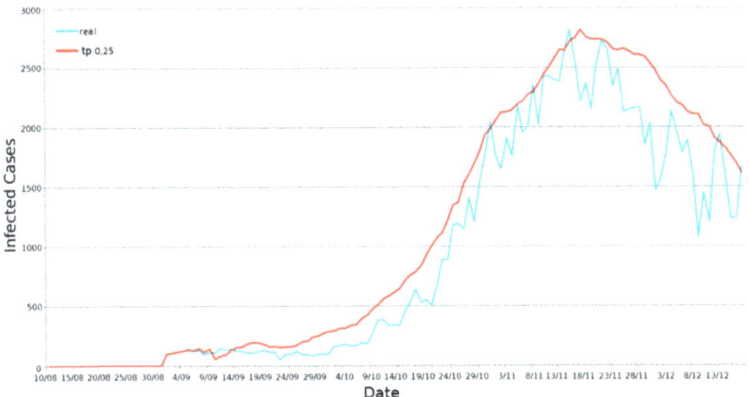

Figure 12. Positives' daily representation—Emilia Romagna region.

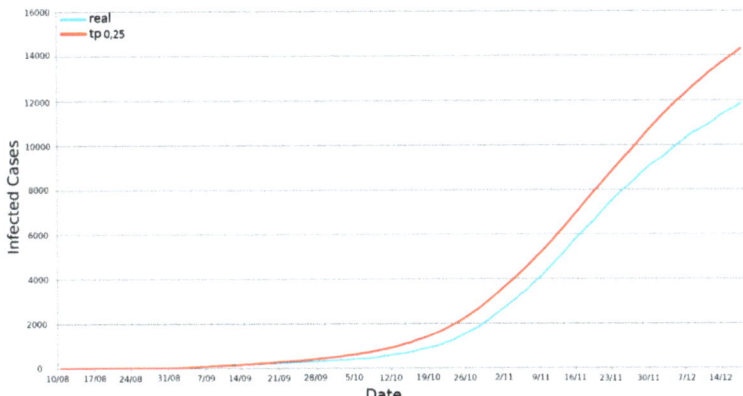

Figure 13. Positives' incremental representation—Emilia Romagna region.

We can infer that the simulator is performing and reliable, and thanks to the achieved result, we can say that our commuting model simulates at best the movement of agents within a bi-dimensional space, whether this space is a province with its municipalities or an entire whole region. Therefore, the simulator can be used to verify the effectiveness of the restriction and predict if they will be effective for lowering the epidemiological curve's trend.

6.5. Results for the Lombardy Region

For the Lombardy region case study, there were no high-resolution data for municipality, rather it was only available at the province level. For this reason, we extended all the features already validated for Emilia-Romagna using the 10 provinces of Lombardy. Moreover, according to [6], we decided to simulate for this case study the first pandemic wave between the 20 February 2020 and the 30 April 2020. We implemented the commuting algorithm considering each province as a large and single urban center. As previously reported, during the first pandemic period, real data about new infections were affected by the small capacity of doing a large number of COVID-19 tests among people. Thus, real data were underestimated and were about eight times higher, as proven by the serological analysis led by Italian institutions in July 2020 [6]. In light of this, we considered the real data contagion incremental curve and a curve representing a serological data projection representing a rough estimate of the neglected and never traced positives from the COVID-19 tracking activity. In Figure 14, it is possible to see how the commuting curve (in black) is very close to our estimation (in green), even though there is no social structure anymore that supports the agents' meeting activity. Moreover, for completeness, we also reported our previous results (in red); this data was obtained using a power-law social network structure. Qualitative data comparison is shown in Table 1. Finally, to validate our model, we compared the simulation data with the official data provided by the Italian Government (Protezione Civile), named "Real Data". Considering that the official data have been recognized as seriously underestimated in the first wave of the pandemic due to the lack of molecular tests, we decided to compare with the results provided by the serological investigation led by the Italian authorities over the Lombardy population in July 2020 to understand the real impact of the spreading in the previous months (serological data).

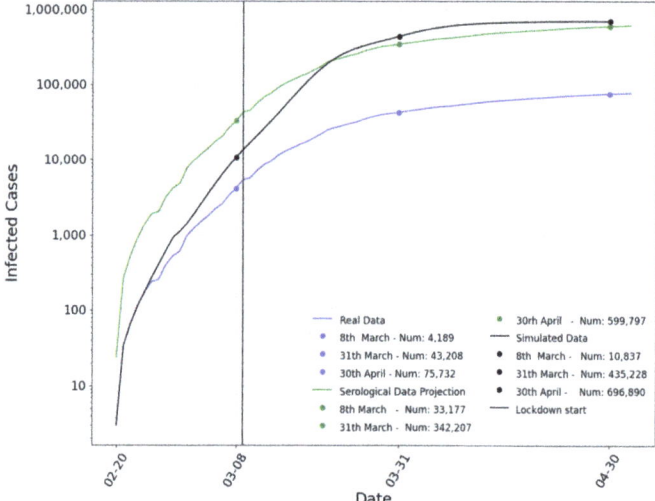

Figure 14. Positives' daily representation—Lombardy region.

Table 1. Pearson correlation and root mean squared error (RMSE) of our model with respect to the serological data projection.

	RMSE	Pearson Correlation
Simulated Data—Real Data	398,042	0.9903

From the data qualitative analysis, it is clear that even the simulation that points the foundations of its social network on commuting mechanisms are plausible and acceptable, proving the robustness of the implemented ABMS model.

7. Discussion

We carried out further tests and simulations in order to validate our model. The realized high-resolution model takes into consideration many factors and parameters to tune up the infection spreading process (see [6] for better understanding how we used it). In particular:

1. The contagion susceptibility by age
2. The protection achieved thanks to wearable protective devices
3. The quarantine mechanism

Moreover, we analyzed how these parameters affect the spreading procedure. Hence, we created a model that does not take these parameters into consideration, but makes the infection process dependent only on transmission probability, without any additional damper. Figure 15 shows different infection trends with different TP values. Considering also the values reported in Table 2, we can assert that the parameters in our model create a sufficient contagion dampening, validating our infection process modeling.

Table 2. Comparison of our model to the null models in terms of root mean squared error (RMSE) and Pearson correlation n.

	RMSE	Pearson Correlation
Simulated Data—Serological	105,343	0.9903
Null model with TP = 0.2–Serological	1,301,649	0.8674
Null model with TP = 0.4–Serological	4,662,723	0.9456
Null model with TP = 0.6–Serological	5,840,197	0.9805
Null model with TP = 0.8–Serological	6,422,819	0.9763
Null model with TP = 1–Serological	6,759,554	0.9616

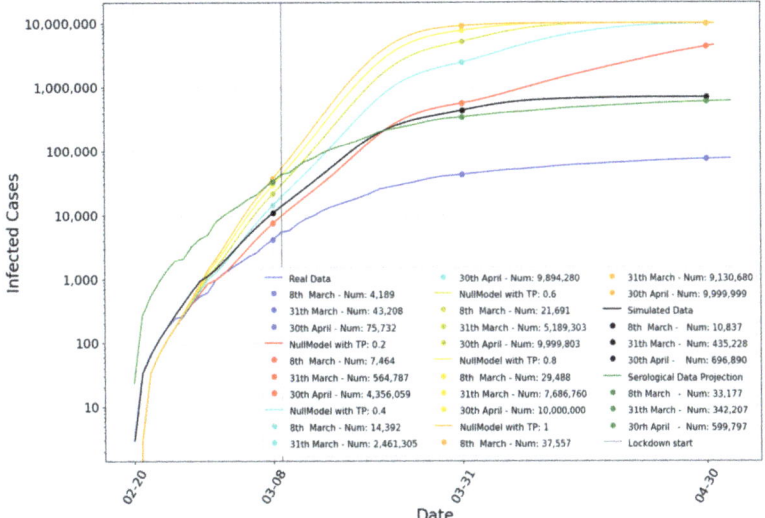

Figure 15. Simulation results without damping parameters with different transmission probability (0.2, 0.4, 0.6, 0.8, 1) (incremental representation—y-axis scale is logarithmic).

We continued our analysis with further studies. For validating our model, we compared our results with other SEIR models. The comparison is shown in Figure 16. We took into account three different SEIR models. The first one (SEIR 1 in Figure 16) is a simple based system dynamics SEIR [2]. The second one [66] (SEIR 2 in Figure 16) takes into account the transmission rate of asymptomatic subjects and a piecewise exponentially-decreasing R_0. The third one [67] (SEIR 3 in Figure 16) optimizes the model's parameters using computational swarm intelligence to model the early stage of the pandemic in Italy. Moreover, we presented in Table 3 a numerical analysis of these models compared with ours. The chart and the analysis showed that our model produces a more accurate prediction of the infection spreading in terms of RMSE and the Pearson correlation.

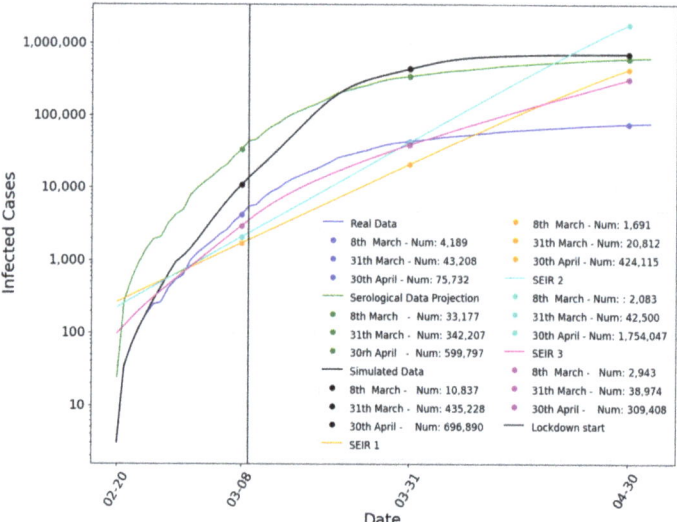

Figure 16. Comparison among our model, the serological data, the real data and the SEIR models (incremental representation—y-axis scale is logarithmic).

Table 3. Comparison of our model to the SEIR models in terms of root mean squared error (RMSE) and the Pearson correlation.

	RMSE	Pearson Correlation
Simulated Data—Serological	105,343	0.990
SEIR 1—Serological	269,197	0.769
SEIR 2—Serological	270,060	0.859
SEIR 3—Serological	318,034	0.713

8. Conclusions

In this paper, we introduced an approach for modeling and simulating large-scale complex systems exploiting an ABMS approach and the high-performance computing with a high-resolution. In particular, we modeled as a use-case the spread of COVID-19 across two Italian regions (Lombardy and Emilia-Romagna). To prove the efficacy of our solutions, we implemented a fine-grained model that takes into account single individuals with a socio-demographic model that also involves a novel commuting model to model for this kind of simulation. The results prove that this kind of solution is be able to solve complex tasks like predicting COVID-19 by exploiting the light-weight actor model and HPC. The results we obtained for both cases Lombardy (RMSE 56,009 during spring 2020) and Emilia-Romagna (RMSE 10,730 simulating autumn 2020) with respect to the real data suggest that the epidemiological domain can really benefit from such kinds of simulations, especially at the beginning of a spreading phenomenon when few reliable data are available. In particular, our ABMS model offers some interesting features which distinguish it from other ABMS: (i) the scheduling of the agents is driven by the messages exchanged from the agents of the application. In particular, at each step of execution an agent can receive more messages, but it can only process the messages received in the previous step; therefore, the behavior of the agents never depends on the order of execution of the agents during a simulation step. (ii) The availability of "remote proxy" reference provided by ActoDeS simplifies the development of agent-based applications because developers do not have to worry if an agent needs to communicate with some local agents or even with some remote agents, (iii) The use of aggregation messages guarantees a strong reduction in the cost of communication and, therefore, allows the development of real large-scale applications. Finally, in our future works, we would like to also stress these large-scale modeling capabilities in other domains and with complex tasks like financial simulation [68], temporal graph-based tasks [69,70] and troll detection [71,72], and also to refine our simulation models [73] and extend ActoDeS, taking advantage of some features offered by the JADE framework [74].

Author Contributions: Conceptualization, A.P.; methodology, M.P. and G.L.; software, M.P.; validation, S.C.; writing—original draft preparation, A.P., M.P. and G.L.; writing—review and editing, S.C.; supervision, A.P. All authors have read and agreed to the published version of the manuscript.

Funding: This research has been partially supported by the Supercomputing Unified Platform Emilia-Romagna—SUPER project.

Data Availability Statement: Not applicable.

Conflicts of Interest: The authors declare no conflict of interest.

References

1. Li, M.Y.; Muldowney, J.S. Global stability for the SEIR model in epidemiology. *Math. Biosci.* **1995**, *125*, 155–164. [CrossRef]
2. He, S.; Peng, Y.; Sun, K. SEIR modeling of the COVID-19 and its dynamics. *Nonlinear Dyn.* **2020**, *101*, 1667–1680. [CrossRef] [PubMed]
3. Macal, C.M.; North, M.J. Tutorial on agent-based modeling and simulation. In Proceedings of the Winter Simulation Conference, Orlando, FL, USA, 4 December 2005.
4. Simini, F.; González, M.C.; Maritan, A.; Barabási, A.L. A universal model for mobility and migration patterns. *Nature* **2012**, *484*, 96–100. [CrossRef] [PubMed]
5. Xia, Y.; Bjørnstad, O.N.; Grenfell, B.T. Measles metapopulation dynamics: A gravity model for epidemiological coupling and dynamics. *Am. Nat.* **2004**, *164*, 267–281. [CrossRef]
6. Pellegrino, M.; Lombardo, G.; Mordonini, M.; Tomaiuolo, M.; Cagnoni, S.; Poggi, A. ActoDemic: A Distributed Framework for Fine-Grained Spreading Modeling and Simulation in Large Scale Scenarios. In Proceedings of the 22nd Workshop "From Objects to Agents" (WOA, 2021), Bologna, Italy, 1–3 September 2021.
7. Niazi, M.; Hussain, A. Agent-based computing from multi-agent systems to agent-based models: A visual survey. *Scientometrics* **2011**, *89*, 479–499. [CrossRef]
8. Bandini, S.; Manzoni, S.; Vizzari, G. Agent based modeling and simulation: An informatics perspective. *J. Artif. Soc. Soc. Simul.* **2009**, *12*, 4.
9. Bandini, S.; Manzoni, S.; Vizzari, G. Agent-based modeling and simulation. In *Complex Social and Behavioral Systems: Game Theory and Agent-Based Models*; Sotomayor, M., Pérez-Castrillo, D., Castiglione, F., Eds.; Springer: Berlin/Heidelberg, Germany, 2020; pp. 667–682.
10. Epstein, J.M. Generative Social Science: Studies in Agent-Based Computational Modeling. In *Princeton Studies in Complexity*; Princeton University Press: Princeton, NJ, USA, 2007.
11. Klügl, F.; Bazzan, A.L. Agent-based modeling and simulation. *AI Mag.* **2012**, *33*, 29. [CrossRef]
12. Grimm, V.; Railsback, S.F. Individual-based modeling and ecology. In *Princeton Series in Theoretical and Computational Biology*; Princeton University Press: Princeton, NJ, USA, 2013.
13. Wolfram, S. Cellular automata as models of complexity. *Nature* **1984**, *311*, 419–424. [CrossRef]
14. Reynolds, C.W. Flocks, Herds and Schools: A Distributed Behavioral Model. Available online: https://dl.acm.org/doi/pdf/10.1145/37401.37406?casa_token=xKKdS6A0HnkAAAAA:Y_z7E8qgBvJFzBVuAJMKujqyHiAfjAj9lQdlIPYYMUaZOhsV_6dmTtx8lV9TU8Uq718OjAp1Wvgslg (accessed on 18 February 2022).
15. Gimblett, H.R. *Integrating Geographic Information Systems and Agent-Based Modeling Techniques for Simulating Social and Ecological Processes*; Oxford University Press: Oxford, UK, 2002.
16. Allan, R.J. *Survey of Agent Based Modelling and Simulation Tools*; Science & Technology Facilities Council: New York, NY, USA, 2010; ISSN 1362-0207.
17. Tobias, R.; Hofmann, C. Evaluation of free Java-libraries for social-scientific agent based simulation. *J. Artif. Soc. Soc. Simul.* **2004**, *7*. Available online: https://www.zora.uzh.ch/id/eprint/115438/1/Robert%20Tobias%20and%20Carole%20Hofmann%20Evaluation%20of%20free%20Java-libraries%20for%20social-scientific%20agent%20based%20simulation.pdf (accessed on 18 February 2022).
18. Nikolai, C.; Madey, G. Tools of the trade: A survey of various agent based modeling platforms. *J. Artif. Soc. Soc. Simul.* **2009**, *12*, 2.
19. Abar, S.; Theodoropoulos, G.K.; Lemarinier, P.; O'Hare, G.M. Agent Based Modelling and Simulation tools: A review of the state-of-art software. *Comput. Sci. Rev.* **2017**, *24*, 13–33. [CrossRef]

20. Parker, M. Ascape: An Agent-Based Modeling Framework in Java. Available online: https://www.osti.gov/servlets/purl/795682-rnZK04/native/#page=158 (accessed on 18 February 2022).
21. Luke, S.; Cioffi-Revilla, C.; Panait, L.; Sullivan, K.; Balan, G. Mason: A multiagent simulation environment. *Simulation* 2005, *81*, 517–527. [CrossRef]
22. North, M.J.; Collier, N.T.; Vos, J.R. Experiences creating three implementations of the repast agent modeling toolkit. *ACM Trans. Model. Comput. Simul.* 2006, *16*, 1–25. [CrossRef]
23. Borshchev, A.; Brailsford, S.; Churilov, L.; Dangerfield, B. Multi-method modelling: AnyLogic. In *Discrete-Event Simulation and System Dynamics for Management Decision Making*; Wiley: Hoboken, NJ, USA, 2014.
24. Wilensky, U.; Rand, W. *An Introduction to Agent-Based Modeling: Modeling Natural, Social, and Engineered Complex Systems with NetLogo*; MIT Press: Cambridge, MA, USA, 2015.
25. Chumachenko, D.; Meniailov, I.; Bazilevych, K.; Chumachenko, T. On intelligent decision making in multiagent systems in conditions of uncertainty. In Proceedings of the 2019 XI International Scientific and Practical Conference on Electronics and Information Technologies (ELIT), Lviv, Ukraine, 16–18 September 2019.
26. Lees, M.; Logan, B.; Oguara, T.; Theodoropoulos, G. Simulating Agent-Based Systems with HLA: The Case of SIM_AGENT-Part II (03E-SIW-076). In Proceedings of the 2003 European Simulation Interoperability Workshop, Stockholm, Sweden, 14–19 September 2003.
27. Massaioli, F.; Castiglione, F.; Bernaschi, M. OpenMP parallelization of agent-based models. *Parallel Comput.* 2005, *31*, 1066–1081. [CrossRef]
28. Erra, U.; Frola, B.; Scarano, V.; Couzin, I. An efficient GPU implementation for large scale individual-based simulation of collective behavior. In Proceedings of the 2009 International Workshop on High Performance Computational Systems Biology, Trento, Italy, 14–16 October 2009.
29. Cicirelli, F.; Furfaro, A.; Giordano, A.; Nigro, L. HLA_ACTOR_REPAST: An approach to distributing RePast models for high-performance simulations. *Simul. Model. Pract. Theory* 2011, *19*, 283–300. [CrossRef]
30. Cordasco, G.; De Chiara, R.; Mancuso, A.; Mazzeo, D.; Scarano, V.; Spagnuolo, C. Bringing together efficiency and effectiveness in distributed simulations: The experience with D-MASON. *Simulation* 2013, *89*, 1236–1253. [CrossRef]
31. Lysenko, M.; D'Souza, R.M. A framework for megascale agent based model simulations on graphics processing units. *J. Artif. Soc. Soc. Simul.* 2008, *11*, 10.
32. Scheutz, M.; Schermerhorn, P. Adaptive algorithms for the dynamic distribution and parallel execution of agent-based models. *J. Parallel Distrib. Comput.* 2006, *66*, 1037–1051. [CrossRef]
33. Som, T.K.; Sargent, R.G. Model structure and load balancing in optimistic parallel discrete event simulation. In Proceedings of the Fourteenth Workshop on Parallel and Distributed Simulation, Bologna, Italy, 28–31 May 2000.
34. Lorig, F.; Johansson, E.; Davidsson, P. Agent-based social simulation of the COVID-19 pandemic: A systematic review. *JASSS J. Artif. Soc. Soc. Simul.* 2021, *24*, 5. [CrossRef]
35. Dyke Parunak, H.V.; Savit, R.; Riolo, R.L. Agent-based modeling vs. equation-based modeling: A case study and users' guide. In *International Workshop on Multi-Agent Systems and Agent-Based Simulation*; Springer: Berlin/Heidelberg, Germany, 1998; pp. 10–25.
36. Rahmandad, H.; Sterman, J. Heterogeneity and network structure in the dynamics of diffusion: Comparing agent-based and differential equation models. *Manag. Sci.* 2008, *54*, 998–1014. [CrossRef]
37. Ajelli, M.; Gonçalves, B.; Balcan, D.; Colizza, V.; Hu, H.; Ramasco, J. Comparing large-scale computational approaches to epidemic modeling: Agent-based versus structured metapopulation models. *BMC Infect. Dis.* 2010, *10*, 190. [CrossRef]
38. Silva, P.C.; Batista, P.V.; Lima, H.S.; Alves, M.A.; Guimarães, F.G.; Silva, R.C. COVID-ABS: An agent-based model of COVID-19 epidemic to simulate health and economic effects of social distancing interventions. *Chaos Solitons Fractals* 2020, *139*, 110088. [CrossRef] [PubMed]
39. Hinch, R.; Probert, W.J.; Nurtay, A.; Kendall, M.; Wymant, C.; Hall, M. OpenABM-COVID19—An agent-based model for non-pharmaceutical interventions against COVID-19 including contact tracing. *PLoS Comput. Biol.* 2021, *17*, e1009146. [CrossRef] [PubMed]
40. Gabler, J.; Raabe, T.; Röhrl, K. People Meet People: A Microlevel Approach to Predicting the Effect of Policies on the Spread of COVID-19. Available online: https://www.econstor.eu/bitstream/10419/232651/1/dp13899.pdf (accessed on 18 February 2022).
41. Wolfram, C. An agent-based model of COVID-19. *Complex Syst.* 2020, *29*, 87–105. [CrossRef]
42. Shamil, M.; Farheen, F.; Ibtehaz, N.; Khan, I.M.; Rahman, M.S. An agent-based modeling of COVID-19: Validation, analysis, and recommendations. *Cogn. Comput.* 2021, 1–12. [CrossRef] [PubMed]
43. Truszkowska, A.; Behring, B.; Hasanyan, J.; Zino, L.; Butail, S.; Caroppo, E.; Jiang, Z.-P.; Rizzo, A.; Porfiri, M. High-Resolution Agent-Based Modeling of COVID-19 Spreading in a Small Town. *Adv. Theory Simul.* 2021, *4*, 2000277. [CrossRef]
44. Chumachenko, D.; Meniailov, I.; Bazilevych, K.; Chumachenko, T.; Yakovlev, S. On intelligent agent-based simulation of COVID-19 epidemic process in Ukraine. *Procedia Comput. Sci.* 2022, *198*, 706–711. [CrossRef]
45. Agha, G.A. *Actors: A Model of Concurrent Computation in Distributed Systems*; MIT, Cambridge Artificial Intelligence Lab: Cambridge, MA, USA, 1985.
46. Kafura, D.; Briot, J.P. Actors and agents. *IEEE Concurr.* 1998, *6*, 24–28. [CrossRef]
47. Wooldridge, M. *An Introduction to Multiagent Systems*; John Wiley & Sons: Hoboken, NJ, USA, 2009.

48. Jang, M.W.; Agha, G. Agent framework services to reduce agent communication overhead in large-scale agent-based simulations. *Simul. Model. Pract. Theory* **2006**, *14*, 679–694. [CrossRef]
49. Scheutz, M.; Schermerhorn, P.; Connaughton, R.; Dingler, A. Swages—An Extendable Distributed Experimentation System for Large-Scale Agent-Based Alife Simulations. Available online: citeseerx.ist.psu.edu/viewdoc/download?doi=10.1.1.86.4219&rep=rep1&type=pdf (accessed on 18 February 2022).
50. Wittek, P.; Rubio-Campillo, X. Scalable agent-based modelling with cloud hpc resources for social simulations. In Proceedings of the 4th IEEE International Conference on Cloud Computing Technology and Science, Taipei, Taiwan, 3–6 December 2012.
51. Collier, N.; North, M. Parallel agent-based simulation with repast for high performance computing. *Simulation* **2013**, *89*, 1215–1235. [CrossRef]
52. Clarke, L.; Glendinning, I.; Hempel, R. The MPI message passing interface standard. In *Programming Environments for Massively Parallel Distributed Systems*; Birkhäuser: Basel, Switzerland, 1994.
53. Fan, Y.; Lan, Z.; Childers, T.; Rich, P.; Allcock, W.; Papka, M.E. Deep reinforcement agent for scheduling in HPC. In Proceedings of the 2021 IEEE International Parallel and Distributed Processing Symposium (IPDPS), Portland, OR, USA, 17–21 May 2021.
54. Santana, E.F.Z.; Lago, N.; Kon, F.; Milojicic, D.S. Interscsimulator: Large-scale traffic simulation in smart cities using erlang. In Proceedings of the International Workshop on Multi-Agent Systems and Agent-Based Simulation, São Paulo, Brazil, 8–12 May 2017.
55. Bergenti, F.; Poggi, A.; Tomaiuolo, M. An actor based software framework for scalable applications. In Proceedings of the International Conference on Internet and Distributed Computing Systems, Calabria, Italy, 22–24 September 2014.
56. Mathieu, P.; Secq, Y. Environment Updating and Agent Scheduling Policies in Agent-based Simulators. In Proceedings of the 4th International Conference on Agents and Artificial Intelligence (ICAART), Algarve, Portugal, 6–8 February 2012.
57. Brisolara, L.; Han, S.I.; Guerin, X.; Carro, L.; Reis, R.; Chae, S.I.; Jerraya, A. Reducing fine-grain communication overhead in multithread code generation for heterogeneous MPSoC. In Proceedings of the 10th International Workshop on Software & Compilers for Embedded Systems Nice France, New York, NY, USA, 20 April 2007.
58. Wesolowski, L.; Venkataraman, R.; Gupta, A.; Yeom, J.S.; Bisset, K.; Sun, Y.; Kale, L.V. Tram: Optimizing fine-grained communication with topological routing and aggregation of messages. In Proceedings of the 43rd International Conference on Parallel Processing, Minneapolis, MN, USA, 9–12 September 2014.
59. Poggi, A. Agent Based Modeling and Simulation with ActoMoS. In Proceedings of the 16th Workshop "From Objects to Agents" (WOA, 2015), Napoli, Italy, 17–19 June 2015.
60. Lombardo, G.; Fornacciari, P.; Mordonini, M.; Tomaiuolo, M.; Poggi, A. A multi-agent architecture for data analysis. *Future Internet* **2019**, *11*, 49. [CrossRef]
61. Riccio, A. Analysis of the SARS-CoV-2 epidemic in Lombardy (Italy) inits early phase. Are we going in the right direction? *medRxiv* **2020**.
62. Godio, A.; Pace, F.; Vergnano, A. Seir modeling of the italian epidemic of SARS-CoV-2 using computational swarm intelligence. *Int. J. Environ. Res. Public Health* **2020**, *17*, 3535. [CrossRef] [PubMed]
63. COVID-19 Aggiornamento Quotidiano dei Dati-Provincia Reggio Nell'Emilia. Available online: https://www.ausl.re.it/covid-19-aggiornamento-quotidiano-dei-dati (accessed on 17 February 2022).
64. Archivio GitHub COVID-19 Dati Regioni. Available online: https://github.com/pcm-dpc/COVID-19/tree/master/dati-regioni (accessed on 17 February 2022).
65. Coordinate Geografiche Comuni Italiani. Available online: https://www.dossier.net/utilities/coordinate-geografiche (accessed on 17 February 2022).
66. Istat. Available online: https://www.istat.it (accessed on 17 February 2022).
67. Analisi Pendolarismo Comune per Comune della Regione Emilia Romagna. Available online: https://statistica.regione.emilia-romagna.it/servizi-online/rappresentazioni-cartografiche/pendolarismo/analisi-comune (accessed on 17 February 2022).
68. Adosoglou, G.; Lombardo, G.; Pardalos, P.M. Neural network embeddings on corporate annual filings for portfolio selection. *Expert Syst. Appl.* **2021**, *164*, 114053. [CrossRef]
69. Lombardo, G.; Poggi, A.; Tomaiuolo, M. Continual representation learning for node classification in power-law graphs. *Future Gener. Comput. Syst.* **2022**, *128*, 420–428. [CrossRef]
70. Lombardo, G.; Poggi, A. A Scalable and Distributed Actor-Based Version of the Node2Vec Algorithm. In Proceedings of the 20th Workshop "from Objects to Agents" (WOA, 2019), Parma, Italy, 26–28 June 2019.
71. Fornacciari, P.; Mordonini, M.; Poggi, A.; Sani, L.; Tomaiuolo, M. A holistic system for troll detection on Twitter. *Comput. Hum. Behav.* **2018**, *89*, 258–268. [CrossRef]
72. Tomaiuolo, M.; Lombardo, G.; Mordonini, M.; Cagnoni, S.; Poggi, A. A survey on troll detection. *Future Internet* **2020**, *12*, 31. [CrossRef]
73. Angiani, G.; Fornacciari, P.; Lombardo, G.; Poggi, A.; Tomaiuolo, M. Actors based agent modelling and simulation. In *International Conference on Practical Applications of Agents and Multi-Agent Systems*; Springer: Cham, Switzerland, 2018; pp. 443–455.
74. Bergenti, F.; Caire, G.; Monica, S.; Poggi, A. The first twenty years of agent-based software development with JADE. *Auton. Agents Multi-Agent Syst.* **2020**, *34*, 36. [CrossRef]

Article

On the Use of the Multi-Agent Environment for Mobility Applications

Mahdi Zargayouna

GRETTIA Laboratory, University Gustave Eiffel, COSYS-GRETTIA, F-77454 Marne-la-Vallée, France; mahdi.zargayouna@univ-eiffel.fr

Abstract: The multi-agent environment is now widely recognised as a key design abstraction for constructing multi-agent systems, equally important as the agents. An explicitly designed environment may have several roles, such as the inter-mediation between agents, the support for interaction, the embodiment of rules and constraints, etc. Mobility applications fit perfectly with a design in the form of a multi-agent system with an explicit environment model. Indeed, in these applications, the components of the system are autonomous and intelligent (drivers, travellers, vehicles, etc.), and the transportation network is a natural environment that they perceive and on which they act. However, the concept of the multi-agent environment may be profitably used beyond this specific geographical context. This paper discusses the relevance of the multi-agent environment in mobility applications and describes different use cases in simulation and optimisation.

Keywords: transportation; mobility; multi-agent systems; environment; modelling; simulation; middleware

Citation: Zargayouna, M. On the Use of the Multi-Agent Environment for Mobility Applications. *Future Internet* **2022**, *14*, 132. https://doi.org/10.3390/fi14050132

Academic Editors: Paolo Bellavista, Agostino Poggi, Ivana Budinská and Ladislav Hluchy

Received: 10 February 2022
Accepted: 22 April 2022
Published: 27 April 2022

Publisher's Note: MDPI stays neutral with regard to jurisdictional claims in published maps and institutional affiliations.

Copyright: © 2022 by the authors. Licensee MDPI, Basel, Switzerland. This article is an open access article distributed under the terms and conditions of the Creative Commons Attribution (CC BY) license (https://creativecommons.org/licenses/by/4.0/).

1. Introduction

Large-scale and complex systems, in different socio-demographic contexts and various land-use configurations, could be analysed by modelling the behaviour and interactions of a large number of self-interested "agents". The multi-agent paradigm provides a high level of detail and allows for the representation of non-linear phenomena and patterns that would be difficult to tackle with analytical approaches [1]. The multi-agent paradigm is a powerful model to design and implement transportation and mobility applications. Indeed, the multi-agent approach deals with systems consisting of many physically or logically distributed interacting components that possess some level of autonomy. These components can perceive their environment and react to changes following their goals. The authors in [2] listed several reasons for the preferred use of multi-agent systems in these applications, such as the natural and intuitive problem solving, the ability of autonomous agents to model heterogeneous systems, the ability to capture complex constraints linking all phases of problem-solving, etc. For Parunak [3], "agent-based modelling is most appropriate for domains characterised by a high degree of localisation and distribution", which is the case for complex and dynamic transportation applications. The agent concept is well suited to represent travellers in transit or road traffic scenarios, for instance [4,5]. They are autonomous entities situated in an environment, adapt their behaviours to the dynamics they perceive, and interact with other agents to achieve specific goals.

There is a growing awareness in the multi-agent community that the multi-agent environment should be considered a primary design abstraction of equal importance to that of the agents. Models and architectures were proposed in the literature for the design of multi-agent environments, validated in a variety of application domains [6]. We believe that one of the domains of choice for modelling multi-agent environments is the transportation domain, especially the mobility applications. Indeed, transportation and mobility applications always have some representation of the environment, typically transportation networks of all modes. The environment in transportation applications has its own dynamics (e.g., traffic conditions, dynamic rules, weather, disruptions, etc.), which argues for its independent and explicit representation. Besides the intuitive representation of the transportation networks as the multi-agent environment, there are several other potential uses of the environment. In this paper, we illustrate different angles of multi-agent environment design in the context of transportation applications. The design of the environment can be considered at several levels of the system construction. It can represent a means of interaction between the agents. It can coordinate and synchronise the activities of the agents. It can also be designed as a mental model for agents to use in their reasoning and planning activities. In Figure 1, we provide three main layers for the design of the multi-agent environment in mobility applications. In the first layer (bottom figure), the environment is a spatial reference on which the agents act. It is also a reference for the resources available to agents, either for sensing or actuation purposes. The second layer (middle figure) is the spatio-temporal environment which extends the spatial environment with the time dimension for planning purposes. It also serves for historical data analysis, learning behaviours, and predicting future events. The third layer (top figure) is the communication environment is not related to the physical environment of the agents and is used for general-purpose communication between the agents. The first level corresponds to the traditional environment understanding and will not be detailed. In the remainder of this paper, we will describe the two other levels, we provide example models to specify them and examples of mobility applications to illustrate them. Note that the proposals for the three layers come from different communities and use cases and were never presented as part of the same model. Here, we try to unify these proposals in the same framework and describe them as different means to represent the multi-agent system's environment.

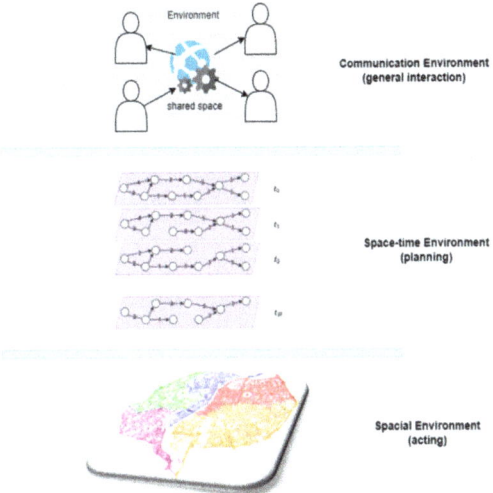

Figure 1. Layers of multi-agent environment.

The remainder of this paper is structured as follows. In Section 2, we present the environment as a spatio-temporal reference to the agents, usually for planing purposes, together with two example applications. In Section 3, we describe a generic design of multi-agent environment to support agents interaction. Section 4 concludes the paper and provides some future works.

2. Environment as a Spatio-Temporal Reference

The environment as a spatial reference is the most straightforward use of the multi-agent environment for mobility applications. A spatial environment provides a reference to the agents on which they can be located, on which they can move, and provides them with metrics to compute a distance between them. This use of the environment is the primary component provided by traffic simulation platforms such as SUMO [7], and general-purpose simulation platforms such as Repast Simphony [8]. The environment provides information about the present situation in the system, such as the positions of all the agents, the states of the entities (e.g., connected or non-connected vehicles), and the current constraints for the agents' actions (e.g., traffic light signals states).

The environment as a spatial reference for the agents reflects the system's present situation. Agents perceive the state of the environment before acting on it. However, cognitive agents usually have some planning activities and have a representation of the time, additionally to the space dimension. This section presents an approach where the multi-agent environment has two linked dimensions: space and time. This representation can either be used by the agents for planning, to reserve certain parts of the network at specific periods, for instance, or to synchronise agents' actions and movements and also as a mental model for the agents, i.e., an internal knowledge representation of the dynamics of the networks through time.

2.1. Space–Time Model of the Environment

Let a transport network $G = (V, E)$, with a set of nodes $V = \{(v_i)\}, i = 0, ..., N$ and a set of arcs $E = \{(v_i, v_j) | v_i \in V, v_j \in V, v_i \neq v_j\}$. Let two matrices $D = \{(d_{ij})\}$ and $T = \{(t_{ij})\}$ of costs, of dimensions $N \times N$ (the arc (v_i, v_j) has a distance of d_{ij} and a travel time of t_{ij}). The representation of the multi-agent environment is made of a duplication of G, H times, with H the maximum allowed time of the considered application: $G(t) = (N(t), E(t))$, with $N(t)$ a set of nodes at time t and $E(t)$ a set of directed links at time t, and $0 \leq t \leq H$. The temporal copies of G are not necessarily identical (cf. Figure 2). Indeed, we can have different travel times between two copies of G to reflect the traffic state. Some nodes may be present in one copy while absent in another, to reflect the expansion of a crisis situation for instance [9]. Arcs may also be absent to reflect vehicle schedules in public transportation as in the application described in the next section. The costs on the edges usually refer to travel times.

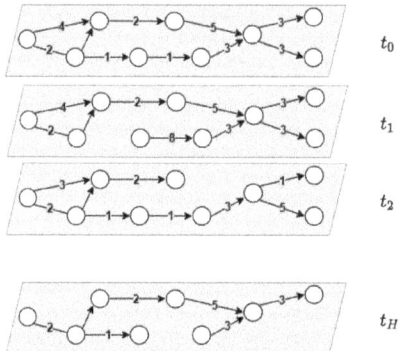

Figure 2. Space–time network.

This representation of the multi-agent environment through time can be either a "passive" knowledge representation used by the agent to plan their future actions or to store historical states of the environment. It can also be used more profitably as an "active" entity, which is materialised as an explicit data structure, may have its dynamics, be accessed by all the agents and have a behaviour that can influence the behaviours of the agents.

So-called time-expanded graphs have long been used in the literature of transportation science, especially for transit networks, to compute shortest paths (e.g., [11,12]). The difference with the model presented in this paper is that the space–time network is active. It can act and react in the system and influence the behaviours of the agents. We describe this concept of active space–time environment with two mobility applications described in the following sections.

2.2. Space–Time Environment in Mobility Simulation

Transportation systems are becoming progressively complex as they are increasingly composed of intelligent and mobile entities. Travellers equipped with mobile devices and vehicles with connection capabilities allow passengers and vehicles to adapt their behaviour with up-to-date information. However, without control, the massive dissemination of information via billboards, radio announcements and individual guidance can have adverse effects and create new traffic concentrations and disruptions. Indeed, with this generalisation of real-time traveller information, the behaviour of modern transportation networks becomes more difficult to analyse and predict. It is then essential to properly observe these effects to consider the adequate methods to face them. To this end, we developed a multi-agent simulation platform that represents travellers, drivers, and public transportation vehicles and makes them move realistically on a multimodal transportation network. To allow travellers to receive only the disruption information relevant to them, the spatio-temporal network model described above is integrated into the simulation platform. In the following, we briefly introduce the multi-agent simulation platform, called SM4T (Simulator for Multi-agent MultiModal Mobility of Travelers) [13], before presenting our method of disseminating information to relevant travellers with spatio-temporal networks.

The multi-agent simulation platform that we designed and implemented allows for the individual representation of travellers moving on a transport network. We enrich it with traveller information capabilities, both at the stops and with personal information directly on the travellers' smartphones. A simulation represents itinerary planners, passengers, public transportation vehicles, and information means in a micro-level and simulate their dynamic movements (cf. Figure 3).

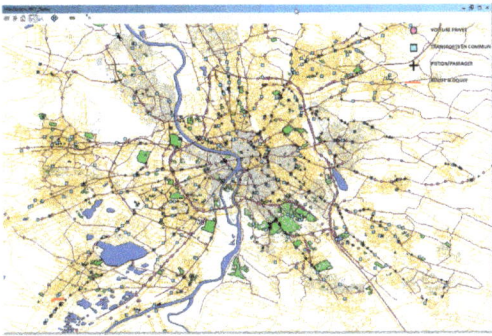

Figure 3. Interface of SM4T.

The multi-agent system of the simulator is composed of the following entities. We define four types of agents: Public transport vehicle agents (representing buses, metros, tramways, etc. in the system), Connected travellers, which represent the passengers that connect to real-time information sources, Non-connected travellers, that represent the travellers that only have a spatial representation of the network, and Local information agents, that provide real-time information locally on the stations of the network. A planning service is defined and is responsible for calculating the best route for the connected travellers only. It bases its calculation on the latest network status, including the ongoing disruptions (cf. Figure 4).

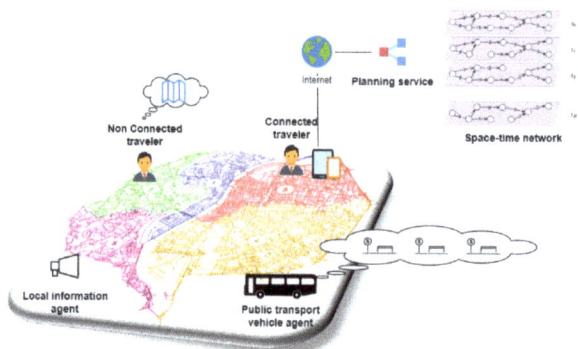

Figure 4. Architecture of the multi-agent system.

Non-connected travellers base their calculations on a static view of the network. They compute their shortest path based on this view. They wait for vehicles at scheduled stops and do not change their route until they either get stuck in an ongoing disruption (delay or line disconnection) or receive local information (from a Local information agent) about an ongoing disruption. When they receive the information, they infer the new network by applying the changes to their mental-and static-view of the transportation network and calculate a new shortest path based on this representation.

On the other hand, Connected travellers have their itineraries monitored by the Planning service. The latter uses the spatio-temporal network model defined earlier, representing the public transportation network, the network topology and the vehicle schedules. Recall that an arc connects two nodes $n_1(t)$ and $n_2(t)$ in $G(t)$ when there is a vehicle departing from n_1 to n_2 at t. Otherwise, the arc is absent. The spatiotemporal network is active in this application: the space–time arcs store listeners for traveller agents and inform them when the departure time or travel time changes or when the vehicle cancels its mission. To be aware of only the events that concern them, the Connected traveller agents subscribe to the only arcs of the multi-agent spatiotemporal environment that form their route. When the travel time of an arc or the departure time of the vehicle changes, the information is broadcast to the subscribed connected travellers. The planning process is then launched with the new network state.

Disruptions are modelled exclusively by modifying the space–time arcs (according to the vehicle schedules). Indeed, a vehicle's delay is injected into the model by dynamically adjusting the space–time arcs representing the corresponding vehicle schedule, setting the destination node time to the delayed arrival times. Breakdowns are also modelled by removing the arcs corresponding to the vehicle's mission from the space–time network. To model the failure of an entire line, the arcs representing the schedules of the remaining vehicles on the line are all deleted. As soon as a schedule is modified, based on the space–time network, the information is immediately detected by the relevant Connected agents, and only to them. Thus, when a timetable is modified, information about the delay or breakdown is sent only to connected travellers interested in these vehicles' missions.

We executed the experiments with the data of the city of Toulouse in France. We chose this French city because we have detailed data about its network and a description of the travel patterns of the region [14]. The data came from Tisséo-SMTC, the public transportation authority of the Greater Toulouse. The public transportation network of Toulouse is composed of 80 lines, 359 itineraries and 3887 edges. Frequencies and edges costs are updated hourly. The multiagent system comprises 18,180 vehicles and from 5000 to 30,000 passengers. We define the number of ticks per simulation to 5000 for a journey from 6 am to 2 am. Every simulated tick corresponds to approximately 14 s. We chose the origins and destinations of passengers coherently with travel patterns of the region (the origins-destinations generation method is in [10]). We executed the simulations on a PC under Windows 7 with a processor Intel Xeon CPU E5-2630 (12 cores at 2 Ghz) with 50 GB of memory.

Previous works have shown that traveller information has little impact in case of minor disturbances. For this reason, we decided to use severe disorders instead in the form of complete disconnection of edges. In every simulation, we generated five random edge disconnections on the network during the whole simulation (one disconnection every 233 real-time minutes approximately). Every disconnection lasts 250 simulated ticks (slightly less than one hour in real-time). Due to edge disconnections, some passengers can no longer find an itinerary to their destination because edge disconnection impacts network connectivity. In the following results, these passengers were not considered (the ratio of passengers without an itinerary is stable, around 5% in all the simulations). Disturbances are random but concern only a certain number of edges that we consider significant to disconnect: the edges through which pass at least five different itineraries. We chose the five randomly disconnected edges between 21 candidate edges that satisfy this requirement.

We considered six different information level scenarios and executed each one 25 times. The first scenario is "the reference configuration" (to which we compared all the others) where no up-to-date information is provided to the passengers, neither local nor personalised. They only have the static description of the network and timetables. In the second scenario, the system provides only local information. The new travel times are available for the only passengers present at the considered stop. We did not consider any connected passengers in this scenario. The system provides local information at the stops in the remaining scenarios (3, 4, 5 and 6), and personal information is only available for the connected passengers. We considered 20%, 50%, 80%, then 100% of connected passengers, respectively, in these scenarios. In the scenarios with local information (all the simulations except the reference configuration), we placed local information agents in all the network stops. We report the average travel times for the passengers. We considered 30,000 passengers (approximately one-quarter of the actual number of passengers).

We executed this system twice: one time with a broadcast of the information about disturbances to all the connected passengers and once using the spatiotemporal network to circumscribe the sending to the only connected passengers. The impact of using the space–time environment on the number of exchanged messages is reported in Table 1. It saves more than 60% of the messages in all the scenarios.

Table 1. Overall number of exchanged messages: broadcast versus space–time environment.

Ratio of Connected Travellers	Broadcast	Space–Time Network	Improvement
20%	634	252	60.25%
50%	1625	575	64.62%
80%	2680	944	64.78%
100%	3413	1105	67.62%

The use of the space–time multi-agent environment in this simulation platform makes the information exchange between agents more efficient and saves communication bandwidth. The impact of travellers' real-time information is reported in [15].

2.3. Space–Time Environment for Planning in Mobility Applications

Vehicle routing problems (VRPs), modelling real-world applications such as dynamic carpooling or online food delivery, are complex optimisation applications that have attracted an enormous research effort for decades. In the online version of these problems, the optimisation of the response time to connected travellers is vital, along with the optimisation of the classical cost criteria (e.g., the size of the fleet of vehicles, the total travelled distance, the total travel times, the total waiting times, etc.). Multi-agent systems, on the one hand, and greedy insertion heuristics, on the other hand, are among the most promising approaches for this purpose. This section describes a multi-agent system coupled with a novel regret insertion heuristic. The heuristic is based on a space–time representation of the multi-agent environment. It serves as a mental model for the agents and as an explicit and active entity, guiding the planning of the agents.

In a VRP, many nodes must be visited once by several capacitated vehicles. These problems are challenging optimisation problems, and solving them has great practical utility. The time-constrained problem is one of the most studied variants of the VRP (Vehicle Routing Problem with Time Windows, VRPTW henceforth). In this variant, the vehicles must visit the nodes within time windows. Vehicle routing problems are divided into two categories: static problems and dynamic problems. In static problems, all the problem data is available before the optimisation process begins. In dynamic problems, the problem data is incomplete before the execution and is discovered progressively during the optimisation. The incomplete data can be any problem element, such as traffic data or available vehicles. However, the dynamic aspect usually refers to the travellers to be transported, which are unknown before execution (as in carpooling and dial a ride systems). Operational problems are never completely static, and it is reasonable to assume that a static system does not meet current operational configurations. Indeed, in real vehicle routing problems, even when all travellers are known in advance (with a reservation system, for example), there is always an element that makes the problem dynamic. These elements can be no-shows, delays, breakdowns, etc.

Online vehicle routing problems could be considered an extreme case of dynamic vehicle routing problems. Indeed, not only is the problem data not completely known before the optimisation starts, but travellers connect to the system in real-time and expect almost immediate responses to their requests. Therefore, the response time of the system in this type of problem is vital. It is more beneficial to immediately provide the current solution to the traveller, rather than waiting a long time for the optimisation system to improve its current solution slightly. Indeed, the traveller is unlikely to wait long for a response to her request.

To meet the requirement of short response times, we relied on the multi-agent paradigm to solve online vehicle routing problems. Multi-agent modelling of online VRPTW is relevant for the following reasons. On the one hand, since it allows the distribution of computations, it should shorten the response time to travellers' requests. On the other hand, nowadays, vehicles are more and more connected and have onboard computing capabilities. In this context, the transportation system is *de facto* distributed and requires appropriate modelling to take advantage of these facilities. The multi-agent system (MAS) we describe in this section comprises vehicle agents, passenger agents, interface agents and planner agents. The multi-agent environment is explicitly modelled as a space–time network and used by the agents to plan their routes. The MAS simulates a distributed version of the so-called "insertion heuristic". Insertion heuristics is a method of inserting individual travellers into vehicle routes. Each traveller is inserted into the route of the vehicle with the minimum marginal cost (the cost can refer to the detour incurred, for example). This method is the fastest known heuristic since there is no reconsideration of previous insertion decisions.

In heuristics and multi-agent methods in the literature, the hierarchical objective of minimizing the number of vehicles mobilised is considered to take priority over the overall costs (including the distance travelled by all vehicles). Most of the heuristics are based on a two-phase approach: minimizing the number of vehicles followed by minimizing the distance travelled [16]. The model we propose in this section aims at minimizing the number of vehicles used in priority while maintaining the use of a "pure" insertion heuristic, i.e., without any additional improvement to meet the response time requirements. To this end, our heuristic encourages vehicle agents to cover a maximum spatio-temporal area of the transportation network, avoiding the mobilisation of a new vehicle if a new traveller appears in an uncovered area.

A space–time pair $<i, t>$—with i a node and t a time—is said to be "covered" by a vehicle agent v if v can be in i at t. The "vehicle action zone" is the set of space–time nodes that the vehicle agent covers. In the context of online VRPTW, maximizing the action zones of the vehicle agents gives them a maximum chance to satisfy the demand of a future (unknown) traveller. By modelling the spatio-temporal action zones of the vehicle agents, we propose a new method to compute the price of inserting the traveller into a vehicle's route. This proposal is a kind of regret insertion heuristic. Regret insertion heuristics, instead of choosing the vehicle with the minimum marginal cost, choose the vehicle and traveller with the greatest "regret". Regret is a measure of the potential price to be paid if a given traveller were not immediately inserted into the route of a given vehicle. There are several methods for calculating regrets, such as the sum of the differences between all available prices and the minimum price [17].

2.3.1. Intuition of Spatio-Temporal Action Zones

Consider a vehicle agent v that has an empty route. Consider also a new traveller c described by: n a node, $[e, l]$ a time window, s a service time, and q a quantity. For v to fit c into its schedule, l must be large enough to allow v to be in n without violating its time constraints (if e is too small, v will have to wait until e). More precisely, the current time t plus the travel time from the depot to n must be less than or equal to l. Based on this observation, we define the action zone of a vehicle agent as the set of pairs $<n, t>$ of the space–time network that remains valid given its current route (n can be visited by the vehicle at t). The conical shadow in Figure 5 illustrates the action zone of a vehicle agent with an empty route.

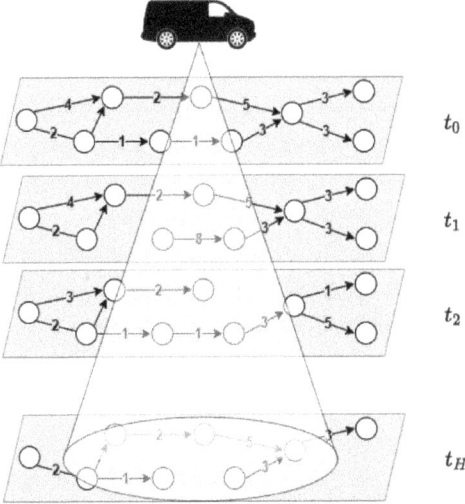

Figure 5. Initial spatio-temporal action zone.

When a vehicle agent inserts a traveller into its route, it has to recalculate its action zone. Indeed, some pairs $<node, time>$ become unfeasible. In Figure 6, a new traveller is inserted into the vehicle route. The vehicle agent's action zone after the traveller's insertion is represented by the inside contour of the bold lines, which represent the space–time nodes that remain feasible after the insertion of the traveller.

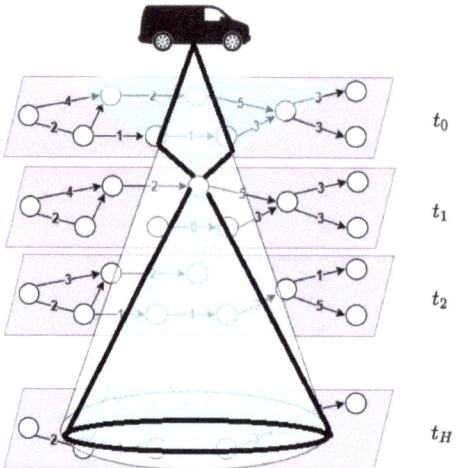

Figure 6. Action zone after insertion of a traveller.

The insertion price sent by a vehicle agent v to a traveller agent c corresponds to the hypothetical decrease in the action zone of v following the insertion of c in its route, i.e., the number of space–time nodes that would no longer be feasible. The idea is that the vehicle chosen for the insertion of a traveller is the one that keeps the maximum chance of being a candidate for the insertion of future travellers. Thus, the maximised criterion by the vehicle agents' fleet is the sum of their action zones, i.e., the capacity of the MAS to react to the appearance of travellers without mobilizing new vehicles.

2.3.2. Coordination of Action Zones

Until now, the space–time model of the environment is used as a mental model of the agents, but it is not explicitly modelled and shared between the agents, and they do not interact with it. This method results in a better space–time coverage of the transportation network, materialised by a minimal mobilisation of vehicles with the appearance of new travellers. Each vehicle agent tries to maximise its action zone independently of the other agents with the mechanism mentioned above. However, it would be more interesting if the agents covered the network in coordination. Specifically, for a vehicle to lose space–time nodes that it alone covers should be more costly than losing nodes that the other agents cover.

To this end, we modelled the environment explicitly and associated with each node in the space–time network the list of vehicles that cover it. Each vehicle notifies the space–time nodes that it is part of its action zone, and each node continuously updates its list. Similarly, when a vehicle agent loses a node in its action zone, the node is notified, updating its list of vehicles.

When the price of inserting a traveller is calculated, each vehicle agent first determines the space–time nodes it would lose if it were to insert the new traveller. Then, it asks each of these nodes about the "price to be paid" if it were no longer covering it. This price is inversely proportional to the number of vehicles covering that node. Specifically, the price to pay is equal to

$$\frac{1}{|v_{<n,t>}|}$$

with $v_{<n,t>}$ designating the vehicle agents covering the space–time node $< n, t >$ and $|v_{<n,t>}|$ the number of these vehicles.

This method, based on an active space–time environment, associates a higher penalty with the decision to stop covering a node less covered by others. Thus, vehicle agents have an incentive to cover the entire network in a coordinated manner.

Marius M. Solomon [18] created a set of different static problems for the VRPTW. It is now admitted that these problems are challenging and diverse enough to compare the different proposed methods with enough confidence. In Solomon's benchmarks, six different sets of problems have been defined: C1, C2, R1, R2, RC1 and RC2. The travellers are geographically uniformly distributed in the problems of type R, clustered in the problems of type C, and a mix of uniformly distributed and clustered travellers is used in the problems of type RC. The problems of type 1 have narrow time windows (very few travellers can coexist in the same vehicle's route) and the problems of type 2 have wide time windows. Finally, a constant service time is associated with each traveller, equal to 10 in the problems of type R and RC, and to 90 in the problems of type C. There are between 8 and 12 files containing 100 travellers in every problem set.

We chose to use Solomon benchmarks while following the modification proposed by [19] to make the problem dynamic. To this end, let $[0, T]$ the simulation time. All the time-related data (time windows, service times and travel times) are multiplied by $\frac{T}{l_0 - e_0}$, with $[e_0, l_0]$ the scheduling horizon of the problem. The authors divide the travellers set into two subsets; the first subset defines the travellers known in advance, and the second is the travellers who reveal during execution. We did not make this distinction since we consider no travellers known in advance. An occurrence time is associated with each traveller, defining the moment when the system knows the traveller. Given a traveller i, the occurrence time that is associated is generated randomly between $[0, \bar{e}_i]$, with:

$$\bar{e}_i = e_i \times \frac{T}{l_0 - e_0} \qquad (1)$$

It is known that the behaviour of insertion heuristics is strongly sensitive to the appearance order of the travellers to the system. For this reason, we do not consider only one appearance order. We launch the process that we just described ten times with every problem file, creating ten different versions of every problem file.

We implemented two MAS with almost the same behaviour; the only difference concerns the measure used by vehicle agents to compute the insertion cost of a traveller. For the first implemented MAS, it relies on the Solomon measure (noted Δ Distance). The second relies on the space–time model (noted Δ Space–Time). We chose to run our experiments with the problems of class R and C, of type 1, which are the instances that are very constrained in time (narrow time windows).

For each problem class and type, we considered different travellers numbers to verify the behaviour of our model with respect to to the problem size. To this end, we considered the 25 first customers, the 50 first customers, and finally, all the 100 customers in each problem file. Table 2 summarises the results. Each cell contains the best-obtained results with each problem class (the sum of all problem files). The results show, with the two classes of problems, that the use of the space–time model mobilises fewer vehicles than the traditional model ($53 < 64, 31 < 34, 92 < 107, 53 < 60, 150 < 181, 108 < 121$). This result validates the intuition of the model, which consists of maximizing the future insertion possibilities for a vehicle agent.

The results show the superiority of this method, in terms of execution times and response times [20], and in terms of number of mobilised vehicles [21], compared to traditional methods.

Table 2. Results summary (criterion: fleet size).

	Δ Distance	Δ Space–Time
Problem	|Fleet|	|Fleet|
R1 25 customers	64	53
C1 25 customers	34	31
R1 50 customers	107	92
C1 50 customers	60	53
R1 100 customers	181	150
C1 100 customers	121	108

3. Environment for Non-Spatial Interaction in Mobility Applications

The third layer in the environment models for multi-agent systems concerns the communication environment. The communication with traffic information or guidance, with a central server or with (non-local) acquaintances, belongs to this layer. This section presents an explicitly modelled multi-agent environment, which we show can have a relevant use in this context.

In dynamic transportation applications such as advanced traveller information systems or dial-a-ride systems, travellers, customers, and vehicles join the system nondeterministically and may also leave at any time. When specifying such open systems, the designer must define an architecture that allows for the integration of unknown agents. Newcomer agents must be able to find agents that have the properties, capabilities, or resources they need. To deal with this problem, known as the connection problem, the authors in [22] propose the concept of middle agents, which are the preferred interlocutors for agents seeking specific capabilities. The author in [23] presents recommendation systems, allowing the connection of distributed agents in open systems. This approach enables agents' gradual and distributed construction of an address book. However, in dynamic transportation systems, the desired capabilities and information sources are usually known: transportation operators, vehicles, real-time traffic information providers, etc. The problem is knowing what information these sources generate is relevant to the new agents, whose context and needs are usually constantly changing. The multi-agent environment is also used for agent matching based on the properties of the agents and the exchanged objects or messages [24].

We adopted an environment-centric approach for agents' interaction in mobility applications for these reasons: (i) it focuses on shared data; (ii) it allows selecting relevant information without having to know or maintain knowledge about the senders of this data. We propose a generic representation of the environment, shared by all agents in the system, allowing associative discovery of other agents and exchanging information between them. Agents do not maintain an address book of others and delegate the mapping of their preferences to the properties of others to the environment. They can also describe the properties of the agents they want to interact with and the messages they want to receive. The presence of a shared environment and the ability to define complex interaction constraints make this model an excellent candidate for the design of open and dynamic transportation systems.

This kind of shared spaces were initiated by Linda [25], which has known several extensions (e.g., Klaim [26], Mars [27] and Lime [28]). Linda-like models are based on the notion of a shared data repository. Agents communicate by exchanging tuples via an abstraction of an associative shared memory called the tuplespace. A tuplespace is a multiset of tuples (tuples duplication is allowed) and is accessed associatively (by contents) rather than by address. Every tuple is a sequence of one or more typed values. Communication in Linda is said to be *generative*: an agent *generates* a tuple and its life cycle is independent of the agent that created it. The model presented in this section is an extension of this model.

3.1. Model

Figure 7 illustrates the architecture of a multi-agent system following our generic model. The modelled MAS executes on a host, where (local) agents add, read and take objects to/from the environment. Every agent is either independent (like agents 1 and 2) or representing a non-modelled external system (traffic information server, for instance) or user (a traveller, for instance) in the MAS (like agents 3 and 4). The system agents interact with the environment via a shared space and don't have to maintain an updated list of the agents and their properties and capacities.

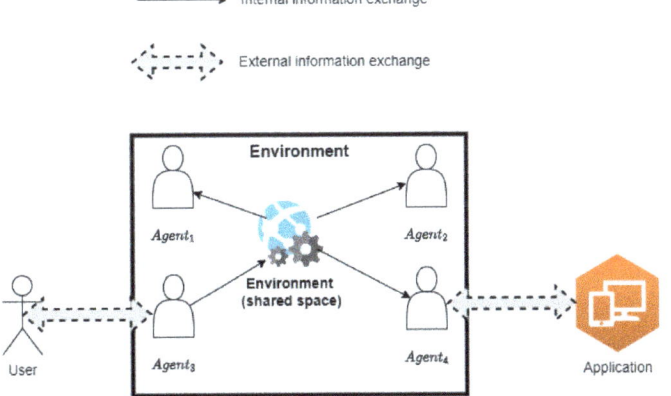

Figure 7. Architecture of a Multi-agent system with general-purpose explicit environment.

For the specification of the system following this architecture, we adopt four primitives inspired by Linda [25] and a set of operators borrowed from Milner's CCS [29]. A MAS adhering to the model is defined by a dynamic set of agents interacting with an environment-denoted Ω_{ENV}, which is composed of a dynamic set of *objects*. Agents can *perceive* (read-only) and/or *receive* (read and take) objects from the environment. Agents are defined by behaviour (a process), a state and local memory in which they store the data they perceive or receive from the environment. The primitives allowing these actions are the following [30]:

$$\mu ::= add(sds) \mid spawn(P, sds) \mid look(sds_p, sds_r, e) \mid update(sds)$$

The primitive $add(sds)$ adds to the environment an object described by sds. For instance, $add(position \leftarrow 1)$ adds the property-value pair $(position \leftarrow 1)$ to Ω_{ENV}. The primitive $spawn(P, sds)$ launches a new agent that behaves like P and which state is described by a description sds. For instance, $spawn(add(position \leftarrow 1), \{id \leftarrow a_1, position \leftarrow 1\})$ creates an agent that has a_1 as id and 1 as $position$ and whose behaviour is $add(position \leftarrow 1)$. The primitive $look(sds_p, sds_r, e)$ allows object perception and reception (perception and removal from the environment). It blocks until a set of objects becomes present in Ω_{ENV} such that the expression e is evaluated to *true*; the objects associated with the variables in sds_p are perceived and those associated with the variables in sds_r are received. For instance, the following instruction:

$$look(\{ticket \leftarrow t\}, \{paper \leftarrow p\}, t.destination = \text{"Berlin"} \wedge t.price \leq budget$$
$$\wedge p.decision = \text{"accepted"})$$

looks for two objects that will be associated with t and p. The object associated with t will be perceived, while the object associated with p will be received. After the execution of this instruction, the two objects will be present in the local memory of the caller agent. The latter will have two additional properties: *ticket*, which refers to the object associated with the variable t and *paper*, which refers to the object associated with p. The perceived *ticket* has "Berlin" as destination and a *price* lower than the budget of the executing agent, while the *received* paper is "accepted" (the property *decision* is equal to "accepted").

The model thus proposes an environment-centric interaction for mobility applications. The advantages compared to point-to-point message exchanges or broadcasting messages to all agents are the following. On the one hand, in point-to-point message exchange, the agents (a traveller and a vehicle, for example) must be synchronised so that the transmission of a message by the first agent corresponds to its reception by the second. On the other hand, the sender must know the physical location of the receiver agent. With our approach, the communication is decoupled in time and space. Decoupling in time allows agents to communicate across time, i.e., their execution times do not have to overlap (the agents do not have to be synchronised by a rendezvous mechanism) to establish communication. The decoupling in space is related to the anonymous generation, and withdrawal of objects and messages from the shared space, i.e., agents do not have to know the location of other agents to communicate, so communication takes place independently of the location of the agents involved. Moreover, the shared space is an associative memory, i.e., data is accessed by content and not by address. In our model, the retrieval of data is not nominative but results from matching with a template, and the first data satisfying the template is returned in a non-deterministic manner.

Compared to the literature, our model provides improvements on two main aspects. On the one hand, we enrich the model with the property-values data structure instead of the tuple data structure. This enrichment results in a more powerful matching mechanism (replacing Linda-like templates). On the other hand, agents in our model have an observable state described by data. Indeed, state-of-the-art models describe what the agents *do*, not what they *are*. With agents' states, agents can condition their interaction with their current context.

3.2. Example Application: Environment-Centred System for Traveller Information

In this section, we describe an application based on our model. We modelled and implemented a traveller information server. The purpose of the server is to inform online travellers about the status of the parts of the transportation network that concern them. Transportation Web services are represented with agents in the server, and their properties are related to the service or the information that they provide. The problem in this kind of application concerns the information flows that are dynamic and asynchronous. Indeed, each information source is hypothetically relevant. An agent cannot know a priori which information will interest him, since this depends on his context, which changes during execution [9].

The objective of this application is to ensure the information of a traveller about his ongoing trip (disturbances, alerts, alternative itinerary). This process is complex because the information sources are distributed, and the management of the follow-up assumes a comparison of all the available information. Using our environment model for this application allows designing an information server parameterised by its users (the travellers). We defined two categories of agents. The first concerns the agents representing the users (that we call PTA for Personal Travel Agent), while the second concerns the agents representing the transportation services (that we call Service Agent).

We implemented a multi-agent system running on a Web server for traveller information. Each Web service has a representation in the multi-agent environment, which is responsible for conveying messages from the server to the transportation Web service conversely. Every user is physically mobile and connects to the server via a transportation assistant app (TAA). During his connection, a PTA agent represents him inside the server, which is his interlocutor during his session. The context of the example is the following: inside the system, an agent represents a trip planning service, and an agent represents a traffic service responsible for the emission of messages related to incidents, traffic jams, etc.

These agents are persistent since they are constantly associated with the service system. On the contrary, PTA agents representing the TAA in the system are volatile, created on a user's connection and erased at the end of his session, i.e., when he/she arrives at destination.

Every stop of the network is described by a line number *line* to which it belongs, and a number *number* reflecting his position on the line. A user u is also described by his current position in the network (the properties *line* and *number*). In a basic execution scenario, u has a path to follow during his trip, i.e. a sequence of tuples $\{(line, number_{source}, number_{destination})_i \mid i \in I\}$, with I the number of transportation means used by the traveller. Every tuple represents a part of the trip, without transfer. The TAA connects to the information server to receive his plan, and the agent u representing him is created. Then, the user is asked to specify his departure and his destination. Once this information is entered, u adds his planning demand in the environment. A demand is an object described by its properties: *emitter, subject*, etc. Afterwards, u keeps on listening to messages that are addressed to him, this way: $look(\emptyset, \{message \leftarrow x\}, x.receiver = id)$. The agent representing the trip planning service is listening to messages asking for a plan: $look(\emptyset, \{request \leftarrow x\}, x.subject = "plan")$. As soon as he/she receives the message, he/she creates a message addressed to the trip planning Web service and awaits the response. When he/she receives the answer, a message is added to the environment addressed to u with the received plan as body: $add(\{emitter \leftarrow id, receiver \leftarrow request.emitter, body \leftarrow plan\})$. The agent u, when he/she receives the message, analyses it and displays the result on the user's TAA. Then, the agent u restrains his interaction to the messages concerning events coming up on his way. To do so, he/she executes the following action:

$$look(\emptyset, \{event \leftarrow x\}, \{x.subject = "alert"\}, x.line = line \land x.number \geq number)$$

The agent u is interested in the alerts concerning his transportation plan, which are expressed by the preceding *look* action. Let us assume that the agent representing the alert service adds an alert message concerning an accident on the way of u, resulting in a serious delay for him. The traveller, via his representing agent u, is notified concerning this alert event. Since the properties *line* and *number* are updated (with an *update* action) at each move of u (each time he/she moves from stop to stop), the segment concerned by the alert messages gets gradually reduced until the end of the trip. The use of the environment, the constant update of the properties of the PTA agents, and the use of *look* actions allowed us to maintain a continuous awareness of the traveller about problems occurring during his trip without relying on continuous requests to the server.

The proposal of an environment-centred system for traveller information shows how our model allows for the design and implementation of a dynamic and open transportation system. Agents join and leave the system freely and have complex interaction constraints. In this application, the interaction constraints concern the current positions and travellers' itineraries.

4. Conclusions

This paper is based on the belief that multi-agent systems are an appropriate paradigm for modelling, simulating, and optimizing dynamic transportation applications [31]. It provides elements advocating that the explicit modelling of the multi-agent environment is a good choice for these applications. We proposed three layers of environment models that are interesting for designing transportation applications. The first layer concerns the spatial environment, which most approaches in the literature adopt. The second layer proposes a spatio-temporal model for interaction and is supported by a spatio-temporal representation of the environment. The third layer concerns shared spaces for general interaction between agents.

The design of the multi-agent environment as an explicit entity is often criticised for introducing centrality into systems that are supposed to be completely distributed. According to these arguments, centrality could lead to communication bottlenecks, low fault tolerance, and low scalability [32]. However, as we can see from the models and applications presented in this paper, this architecture has several advantages, and we believe there is a trade-off between the two visions. In our current work, we developed the idea that we can still benefit from an explicit representation of the multi-agent environment without losing the advantages of distribution, namely fault tolerance and scalability. To do so, we divided the design process into two phases. In the first phase, the system is designed with a conceptually centralised environment. In the second phase, the multi-agent environment is distributed [33]. We worked on environment distributions for each type of environment presented in this paper.

Funding: This research received no external funding.

Institutional Review Board Statement: Not applicable.

Informed Consent Statement: Not applicable.

Data Availability Statement: Data available upon request due to privacy restrictions.

Conflicts of Interest: The authors declare no conflict of interest.

References

1. Bonabeau, E. Agent-based modelling: Methods and techniques for simulating human systems. *Proc. Natl. Acad. Sci. USA* **2002**, *99*, 7280–7287. [CrossRef] [PubMed]
2. Bazzan, A.L.; Klügl, F. A review on agent-based technology for traffic and transportation. *Knowl. Eng. Rev.* **2014**, *29*, 375–403. [CrossRef]
3. Parunak, H.V.D.; Savit, R.; Riolo, R.L. Agent-Based Modelling vs. Equation-Based Modelling: A Case Study and Users' Guide. In Proceedings of Workshop on Modelling Agent Based Systems (MABS98), Paris, France, 4–6 July 1998.
4. Bessghaier, N.; Zargayouna, M.; Balbo, F. Management of urban parking: An agent-based approach. In *Artificial Intelligence: Methodology, Systems, and Applications*; Springer: Berlin/Heidelberg, Germany, 2012; pp. 276–285.
5. Bessghaier, N.; Zargayouna, M.; Balbo, F. An Agent-Based Community to Manage Urban Parking. *Adv. Intell. Soft Comput.* **2012**, *155*, 17–22.
6. Weyns, D.; Michel, F. (Eds.) *Environments for Multi-Agent Systems IV, Fourth International Workshop*; Lecture Notes in Computer Science; Springer: Berlin, Germany, 2015; Volume 9068.
7. Behrisch, M.; Bieker, L.; Erdmann, J.; Krajzewicz, D. SUMO-Simulation of Urban MObility—An Overview. In Proceedings of the Third International Conference on Advances in System Simulation, Barcelona, Spain, 23–29 October 2011; pp. 55–60.
8. Tatara, E.; Ozik, J. How to Build an Agent-Based Model III–Repast Simphony. In Proceedings of the Applied Agent-Based Modeling in Management Research, Academy of Management Annual Meeting, Chicago, IL, USA, 7–11 August 2009.
9. Zargayouna, M. Une repréSentation Spatio-Temporelle de l'Environnement pour le Transport À la Demande. *Workshop Represent. Reason. Time Space* **2005**. Available online: https://basepub.dauphine.psl.eu/bitstream/handle/123456789/5925/plugin-publi288.pdf?sequence=2 (accessed on 9 February 2022).
10. Ksontini, F.; Zargayouna, M.; Scemama, G.; Leroy, B. Building a realistic data environment for multiagent mobility simulation. In Proceedings of the KES International Symposium on Agent and Multi-Agent Systems: Technologies and Applications, Tenerife, Spain, 15–17 June 2016; Springer: Cham, Switzerland, 2016; Volume 58, pp. 57–67.
11. Pyrga, E.; Schulz, F.; Wagner, D.; Zaroliagis, C. Efficient models for timetable information in public transportation systems. *J. Exp. Algorithmics* **2008**, *12*, 1–39. [CrossRef]
12. Schulz, F.; Wagner, D.; Zaroliagis, C. Using multi-level graphs for timetable information in railway systems. In *Workshop on Algorithm Engineering and Experimentation*; Springer: Berlin, Germany, 2002; pp. 43–59.
13. Zargayouna, M.; Othman, A.; Scemama, G.; Zeddini, B. Impact of travellers information level on disturbed transit networks: A multiagent simulation. In Proceedings of the 2015 IEEE 18th International Conference on Intelligent Transportation Systems, Gran Canaria, Spain, 15–18 September 2015; pp. 2889–2894.
14. Zargayouna, M.; Zeddini, B.; Scemama, G.; Othman, A. Simulating the impact of future internet on multimodal mobility. In Proceedings of the 2014 IEEE/ACS 11th International Conference on Computer Systems and Applications (AICCSA), Doha, Qatar, 10–13 November 2014; pp. 230–237.
15. Zargayouna, M. Multiagent simulation of real-time passenger information on transit networks. *IEEE Intell. Transp. Syst. Mag.* **2020**, *12*, 50–63. [CrossRef]
16. Nagata, Y.; Bräysy, O.; Dullaert, W. A penalty-based edge assembly memetic algorithm for the vehicle routing problem with time windows. *Comput. Oper. Res.* **2010**, *37*, 724–737. [CrossRef]
17. Friggstad, Z.; Swamy, C. Approximation algorithms for regret-bounded vehicle routing and applications to distance-constrained vehicle routing. In Proceedings of the Forty-Sixth Annual ACM Symposium on Theory of Computing, New York, NY, USA, 31 May–3 June 2014; pp. 744–753.

18. Solomon, M. Algorithms for the vehicle routing and scheduling with time window constraints. *Oper. Res.* **1987**, *15*, 254–265. [CrossRef]
19. Gendreau, M.; Guertin, F.; Potvin, J.Y.; Taillard, E.D. Parallel tabu search for real-time vehicle routing and dispatching. *Transp. Sci.* **1999**, *33*, 381–390. [CrossRef]
20. Zargayouna, M.; Zeddini, B. Dispatching Requests for Agent-Based Online Vehicle Routing Problems with Time Windows. *J. Comput. Inf. Technol.* **2020**, *28*, 59–72. [CrossRef]
21. Zargayouna, M.; Zeddini, B. Fleet organization models for online vehicle routing problems. In *Transactions on Computational Collective Intelligence VII*; Springer: Berlin/Heidelberg, Germany, 2012; pp. 82–102.
22. Sycara, K.; Wong, H. A Taxonomy of Middle-Agents for the Internet. In Proceedings of the Fourth International Conference on MultiAgent Systems (ICMAS-2000), Washington, DC, USA, 10–12 July 2000; pp. 465–466.
23. Vercouter, L. Conception et Mise en Oeuvre de Systèmes Multi-Agents Ouverts et Distribués. Ph.D. Thesis, Ecole Nationale Supérieure des Mines de Saint-Etienne, Université Jean Monnet-Saint-Etienne, Saint-Étienne, France, 2000.
24. Zargayouna, M.; Trassy, J.S.; Balbo, F. Property Based Coordination. In *Artificial Intelligence: Methodology, Systems, Applications*; Springer: Berlin/Heidelberg, Germany, 2006; Volume 4183, pp. 3–12.
25. Gelernter, D. Generative communication in linda. *ACM Trans. Program. Lang. Syst.* **1985**, *7*, 80–112. [CrossRef]
26. Nicola, R.; Ferrari, G.L.; Pugliese, R. Klaim: A Kernel Language for Agents Interaction and Mobility. *IEEE Trans. Softw. Eng.* **1998**, *24*, 315–330. [CrossRef]
27. Cabri, G.; Leonardi, L.; Zambonelli, F. Reactive tuple spaces for mobile agent coordination. In *MA'98: Proceedings of the Second International Workshop on Mobile Agents*; Springer: Berlin, Germany, London, UK, 1999; pp. 237–248.
28. Picco, G.P.; Murphy, A.L.; Roman, G.-C. LIME: Linda meets mobility. In Proceedings of the International Conference on Software Engineering, Los Angeles, CA, USA, 16–22 May 1999; pp. 368–377.
29. Milner, R. *Communication and Concurrency*; Prentice-Hall: Hoboken, NJ, USA, 1989.
30. Zargayouna, M.; Balbo, F.; Scemama, G. A data-oriented coordination language for distributed transportation applications. In *KES International Symposium on Agent and Multi-Agent Systems: Technologies and Applications*; Springer: Berlin/Heidelberg, Germany, 2009; pp. 283–292.
31. Zargayouna, M. Multiagent Environments for Dynamic Transportation Applications. In *KES International Symposium on Agent and Multi-Agent Systems: Technologies and Applications*; Springer: Berlin/Heidelberg, Germany, 2017; pp. 12–21.
32. Billhardt, H.; Fernández, A.; Lujak, M.; Ossowski, S.; Julián, V.; De Paz, J.F.; Hernández, J.Z. Towards Smart Open Dynamic Fleets. In *Multi-Agent Systems and Agreement Technologies: 13th European Conference, EUMAS 2015, and Third International Conference, AT 2015, Athens, Greece, 17–18 December 2015*; Rovatsos, M., Vouros, G., Julian, V., Eds.; Springer International Publishing: Cham, Switzerland, 2016; pp. 410–424. [CrossRef]
33. Mastio, M.; Zargayouna, M.; Scemama, G.; Rana, O. Distributed agent-based traffic simulations. *IEEE Intell. Transp. Syst. Mag.* **2018**, *10*, 145–156. [CrossRef]

Article
Co-Simulation of Multiple Vehicle Routing Problem Models

Sana Sahar Guia [1], Abdelkader Laouid [1], Mohammad Hammoudeh [2], Ahcène Bounceur [3,*], Mai Alfawair [4] and Amna Eleyan [5]

1. LIAP Laboratory, University of El Oued, El Oued 39000, Algeria; sanasahar-guia@univ-eloued.dz (S.S.G.); abdelkader-laouid@univ-eloued.dz (A.L.)
2. Information & Computer Science Department, King Fahd University of Petroleum & Minerals, Dhahran 31261, Saudi Arabia; m.hammoudeh@kfupm.edu.sa
3. Lab-STICC UMR CNRS, University of Western Brittany UBO, 6285 Brest, France
4. Faculty of Information Technology, AlBalqa Applied University, Amman 11134, Jordan; mai.alfauri@bau.edu.jo
5. School of Computing and Mathematics, Manchester Metropolitan University, Manchester M1 5GD, UK; a.eleyan@mmu.ac.uk
* Correspondence: ahcene.bounceur@univ-brest.fr; Tel.: +33-651122408

Abstract: Complex systems are often designed in a decentralized and open way so that they can operate on heterogeneous entities that communicate with each other. Numerous studies consider the process of components simulation in a complex system as a proven approach to realistically predict the behavior of a complex system or to effectively manage its complexity. The simulation of different complex system components can be coupled via co-simulation to reproduce the behavior emerging from their interaction. On the other hand, multi-agent simulations have been largely implemented in complex system modeling and simulation. Each multi-agent simulator's role is to solve one of the VRP objectives. These simulators interact within a co-simulation platform called MECSYCO, to ensure the integration of the various proposed VRP models. This paper presents the Vehicle Routing Problem (VRP) simulation results in several aspects, where the main goal is to satisfy several client demands. The experiments show the performance of the proposed VRP multi-model and carry out its improvement in terms of computational complexity.

Keywords: complex system; multi-simulation; vehicle routing problem

1. Introduction

Complex systems is a multidisciplinary field and is the subject of active research in several domains such as physics, biology, social sciences and cognitive sciences. The authors of [1–3] define a complex system as a set of heterogeneous entities that interact between them, where each entity is characterized by its cooperative, adaptive and open nature. Simulation is one of the critical tools frequently used to study complex systems [4]. Simulation may reduce experimentation costs by allowing researchers to test various alternatives and scenarios of complex systems [5].

The Vehicle Routing Problem (VRP) presents a complex system [6,7] such that the VRP is considered as a group of dispersed clients that are served by a fleet of vehicles that start and end at one depot [8]. Recently, VRP and its various models attracted the interest of intelligent transport researchers due to the complementary limitations of real-world problems, the potential cost savings and the possibility of service improvement in distributed systems. Due to the intrinsic complexity of determining rigorous models and optimal solutions to a large-scale instance of VRP, the process that involves exact solvers is limited, difficult and time-consuming [9]. Therefore researchers and transportation companies are interested in meta-heuristics such as Ant Colony Optimization (ACO), Genetic Algorithm (GA) and Parctical Swarm Optimization (PSO) to solve real world VRP by producing close to optimal solution. An efficient simulation may offer an opportunity to improve the performance of VRP by modeling different methods for solving various VRP objectives.

Co-simulation is applied in many different multidomain systems [10]. It is proposed to address the issues and challenges of complex systems [11]. In this context, decomposed components of a complex system are modeled by different sub-models, then simulated using a simulator for each sub-model. Co-simulation enables exchanging coupling connections to achieve the behavior of the whole complex system as shown in Figure 1. The co-simulation middleware named Multi-agent Environment for Complex SYstem CO-simulation (MECSYCO) allows the integration of several modeling and simulation software to co-simulate the dynamic behavior of a complex system. MECSYCO makes the possibility to compare simulation results, swap, add, or remove models.

This paper aims to address the challenge of showing the impact of simulating a VRP multi-model as several interacting simulators by reducing the traveled distance and the obtained time during vehicles routing with the aim to satisfy clients demands. In this context, we will design and implement multiple VRP models as complex systems with several perspectives of multi agent simulators. Each simulator in the proposed solution solves different objectives of the VRP and then makes them interact into the co-simulation platform. Multi agent simulators that represent the VRP models are developed using Netlogo and the whole system is reproduced based on the MECSYCO co-simulator. We observed that the interacting VRP models provide high quality solutions by minimizing significantly the cost of services offered to the clients, in terms of computational time and travel distance.

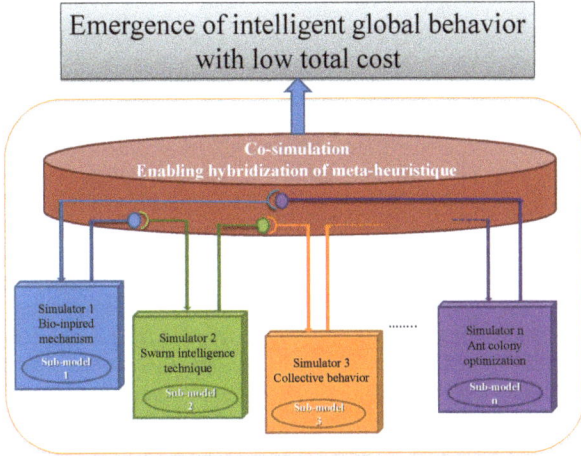

Figure 1. Co-simulation of coupled system.

The rest of this work is organized as follows: In Section 2, we present the summary of the related multi-simulation of complex system research and introduce an overview of the used platform in the co-simulation and we describe the problem formulation of the VRP. The proposed solution is presented in Section 3. Section 4 provides the implementation details and the experiments results. Section 5 concludes the work and give some future work avenues.

2. Related Work

To better simulate the behavior of the whole complex and dynamic system, multi-modeling and co-simulation are used to provide a strategy that collects a set of models from different discipline [12]. The modular architecture in the multi-agent environment of complex system co-simulation middleware offers the integration of heterogeneous simulators and models. In the literature, several works such as [5,13], have been proposed for the simulation of the complex system as interacting models for reproducing the behavior of the entire system. The work of [14] captures the improvement of decomposing and integrating continuous systems using MECSYCO as discrete environment. In [15], the authors designed the co-simulation of complex system with integral multi-agent simulators, while MECSYCO was used in [16] to integrate the modeling and the simulation tools to co-simulate the complete cyber-physical system.

The hybridization of meta-heuristics in the multi-agent system is used to facilitate the development of meta-heuristic frameworks' optimization. In addition, the development of hybrid meta-heuristics is flexible in multi-agent systems and it offers simultaneous exploration of various areas of the research space [17].

Several studies have been performed to solve different variations of VRP by using multi-agent systems [18]. The work of [19] uses the reinforcement learning and pattern matching to provide a multi-agent distributed framework where each agent adapts itself. In [20], the authors solve the VRP with Time Windows (VRPTW) by exploiting the principle of reinforcement learning to improve the agent actions based on the solutions generated by other agents and the environment interactions.

To improve the result of VRP, this paper aims to create an interacting VRP model by combining the multi-agent simulators to reproduce the entire VRP multi-model. From the literature, we observe that there is no proposal in multi agent systems that integrates simulators into a co-simulation platform to reproduce the entire VRP multi-model.

2.1. Co-Simulation of a Complex System

MECSYCO has been used as a middle-ware to simulate and model complex systems which allows the utilization of existing simulators for the implementation of heterogeneous and numerical simulations. MECSYCO focuses on both, the DEVS common formalism proposed by [21] that uses a discrete-event abstraction for the design of dynamic system [22], and on the Agent and artifact architecture using a multi-agent concepts [13] to perform the heterogeneous co-simulation of complex system. In this case, each model or simulator has been considered as an agent and the interaction between simulators corresponds to the indirect cooperation between agents using the defined concept of artifact in [23]. Coupling artifact aims to determine the input output connections between two models and to create the model agent (m-agent) which uses the artifact for leading their model and interchanging input/output data. MECSYCO manipulates a model as various composed models in interactions without a global coordinator using a simulator for each model [24]. This step occupies the management of decentralized multi model simulation in order to integrate several aspects of the same system into a coherent one and to deal with the main challenges of modeling and simulation of a complex system. On the other hand, MECSYCO already includes integrated simulators such as multi agent platform Netlogo, which is frequently used for simulating complex systems and modeling natural and social phenomena.

2.2. Mathematical Formulation of the Problem

This section deals with the mathematical formulation of the problem. In the combinatorial optimization field, VRP is one of the most challenging research problems. The issue was studied more than 40 years ago. It involves defining the best sequence of routes for a fleet of vehicles to provide the service to a specific set of clients. The fleet of vehicles is situated at a central depot, every vehicle has certain capacity and each client has a given demand. The aim is to optimize the total traveled distance to serve a geographically dispersed group of clients [25]. First, we have the following data:

1. One depot;
2. A set of commands;
3. A fleet of vehicles.

The objective is to reduce the total traveled distance from a depot to serve clients, using a similar fleet of vehicles. The issue of solving the VRP faces several design challenges and focuses on the assignment of clients to the routes. This process involves the determination of several routes for each depot by (1) assigning each client to a unique route without exceeding the capacity of the vehicle, and (2) determining a series of clients on every vehicle route. Hence, the mathematical formulation of the vehicle routing problem can be described as follows:

- R denotes the set of nodes, $R = \{r_0, r_1, r_2, \ldots, r_n\}$, with r_0 is the depot and $r_i, i \neq 0$ is the client;
- V denotes the sets of vehicles;
- N is the number of all clients;
- M is the number of vehicles;
- $Q(k)$ is the capacity of vehicle k;
- E is the edge set between nodes defined as: $E = \{(r_i, r_j) | i \neq j \land r_i, r_j \in R\}$;
- b_i is the demand of client i;
- c_{ij} is the cost of transporting one unit from node i to node j;
- x_{ij}^k is 1, if vehicle k travels from node i to node j; 0, otherwise;
- y_{ik} is 1, if vehicle k offers service for client i; 0, otherwise.

From these definitions the objective function problem can be formulated as follows:

$$\min \sum_{i \in R} \sum_{j \in R} c_{ij} \sum_{k \in V} x_{ij}^k \tag{1}$$

where Equation (1) represents the objective function that aims to reduce the total travel cost and the constraints formulations are:

$$\sum_{j \in R} x_{0j}^k = 1, \forall k \in V \tag{2}$$

$$\sum_{j \in R, j \neq i} \sum_{k \in V} x_{ij}^k = 1, \forall i \in R \tag{3}$$

$$\sum_{i \in R} b_i y_{ik} \leq Q(k), \forall k \in V \tag{4}$$

$$\sum_{i \in R} x_{il}^k = \sum_{j \in R} x_{lj}^k, \forall l \in R, \forall k \in V \tag{5}$$

where Equation (2) aims to ensure that every client is allocated in the single route and Equation (3) is the capacity constraint set for vehicles. Whereas Equation (4) is defined to assure that each client can be served only once and Equation (5) ensures that all delivery vehicles must return to the original depot after finishing their task.

3. The Designed Model

The goal of this paper is to solve the VRP by building a complex simulation using a society of interacting co-evolving VRP models. The proposed approach provides a solution based on the agent and artifact concept [23,26,27]. The simulation is performed by m-agents that manage their model and data exchange using artifacts.

The first task to do is to define a solution for solving each VRP model using an atomic VRP simulator. Then, the second task is to determine the input output connections between these simulators. The final task is to construct coupled interacting co-evolving VRP models.

3.1. Description of Atomic VRP Models

The routing and scheduling of a service correspond to the creation of vehicle routes for the depot. By assigning each client to a unique route and respecting the capacity of the vehicle the order of the clients on every vehicle route will be determined. To this end, we develop two models to solve VRP such that each model is to satisfy a different objective.

The first is to try to minimize the total traveling distance and the second is to minimize the number of vehicles.

3.1.1. First VRP Model

We use ant colony optimization for the VRP, where the colony of ants is created from the depot. Each Ant constructs a route for vehicles that will serve the clients starting from the depot and returning to the same depot. The principle of the routing algorithm is described below, see Algorithm 1.

Algorithm 1 Routing and sequencing of the first model

Require: $R, ant\_colony, Q(k)$;
Ensure: $route\_map$;
1: **for** $(a \in ant\_colony)$ **do**
2:     $route\_map \leftarrow r_0$;
3:     $R \leftarrow R - r_0$;
4:     $k \leftarrow 0$;
5:     $Q(k) \leftarrow 0$;
6:     $i \leftarrow r_0$;
7:     **while** $R \neq \emptyset$ **do**
8:         **for** $(r_j \in R)$ **do**
9:             $p_{ij} \leftarrow probability\_of\_point_i\_to\_choose\_point_j$;
10:         **end for**
11:         $r_s \leftarrow r_j\_with\_highest\_p_{ij}$;
12:         $Q(k) \leftarrow Q(k) + demand(r_s)$;
13:         **if** $Q(k) > capacity\_of\_vehicle$ **then**
14:             $k \leftarrow k + 1$;
15:             $Q(k) \leftarrow 0$;
16:             $route\_map \leftarrow route\_map + r_0$;
17:             $i \leftarrow r_0$;
18:         **else**
19:             $route\_map \leftarrow route\_map + r_s$
20:             $i \leftarrow r_s$
21:             $R \leftarrow R - r_s$;
22:         **end if**
23:     **end while**
24: **end for**
25: **return** $route\_map\_of\_the\_best\_ant\_solution$;

The improvements of the solution shown in Algorithm 1 reached in successive iterations. In each iteration all ants in the colony travel between a pair of clients. The probability of an ant to visit an unvisited client is calculated based on the pheromone and the distance and a client will be chosen according to this probability. Then the ant checks if it can visit the given client, i.e., if its current load allows it to add the demand of the client and verify the vehicle's capacity violation. If yes, the ant visits the specified client (adding client's demand and indicating it as selected). Otherwise, the ant ends the current trip with empty load (returning to its colony) and the algorithm restarts a new trip. We apply the following equations for a client i to choose the next client j

$$p_{ij} = \frac{(\tau_{ij})^\alpha \times (\eta_{ij})^\beta}{\sum_{l \in R}(\tau_{il})^\alpha \times (\eta_{il})^\beta} \qquad (6)$$

$$\eta_{ij} = \frac{1}{cost_{ij}} \qquad (7)$$

where p_{ij} is the probability of the point i to choose point j, τ_{ij} is the strength of pheromone trail between point i and j, α is the coefficient that controls the influence of the pheromone trail τ_{ij}, β is the coefficient that controls the influence of the visibility η_{ij}, and R is a set of clients.

At the end of each iteration, the pheromone trail evaporates according to the following equation:

$$\tau_{ij} = (1 - \rho) \times \tau_{ij} \tag{8}$$

where ρ is the coefficient of the pheromone evaporation and the update state is calculated by applying the next equation:

$$\tau_{ij} = \tau_{ij} + \Delta\tau_{ij} \tag{9}$$

where

$$\Delta\tau_{ij} = \frac{best\_known\_solution}{best\_global\_cost} \tag{10}$$

3.1.2. Second VRP Model

VRP of the second model uses a similar algorithm routing and sequencing of the first model. The difference is that each ant in this model tries to reduce the number of vehicles to visit all clients and to add all possible ones whose demand does not exceed the capacity of the current vehicle. The algorithm of the second model is formulated as follows, see Algorithm 2.

Algorithm 2 Routing and sequencing of the second model

Require: R, ant_colony, $Q(k)$;
Ensure: $route\_map$;
1: **for** ($a \in ant\_colony$) **do**
2:    $route\_map \leftarrow r_0$;
3:    $R \leftarrow R - r_0$;
4:    $C \leftarrow R - r_0$;
5:    $k \leftarrow 0$;
6:    $Q(k) \leftarrow 0$;
7:    $i \leftarrow r_0$;
8:    **while** $R \neq \emptyset$ **do**
9:      **while** $C \neq \emptyset$ **do**
10:        **for** ($r_j \in C$) **do**
11:           $p_{ij} \leftarrow probability\_of\_point_i\_to\_choose\_point_j$;
12:        **end for**
13:        $r_s \leftarrow r_j\_with\_highest\_p_{ij}$;
14:        $C \leftarrow C - r_s$;
15:        $Q(k) \leftarrow Q(k) + demand(r_s)$;
16:        **if** $Q(k) < capacity\_of\_vehicle$ **then**
17:           $route\_map \leftarrow route\_map + r_s$
18:           $i \leftarrow r_s$
19:           $R \leftarrow R - r_s$;
20:        **end if**
21:      **end while**
22:      $k \leftarrow k + 1$;
23:      $Q(k) \leftarrow 0$;
24:      $route\_map \leftarrow route\_map + r_0$;
25:      $i \leftarrow r_0$;
26:    **end while**
27: **end for**
28: **return** $route\_map\_of\_the\_best\_ant\_solution$;

In Algorithm 2, the ant checks if its current load allows it to add the demand of the chosen client and verifies the vehicle's capacity violation. If yes, the ant visits the specified client (adding client's demand and indicating it as selected). Otherwise, the ant selects another unvisited node according to the calculated probability. When all clients have been visited, the ant ends the current trip with empty load (returning to its colony) and the algorithm begins a new trip. We improve the solution by local search and we use a two-opt local search algorithm in the end of both Algorithms 1 and 2.

3.2. Structuring VRP Multi-Model

In order to co-simulate the multi-model of VRP, we use MECSYCO, which allows to lunch of several VRP models. In this approach, we focus on the reuse of atomic VRP models defined in Section 3.1 and making them interact. Figure 2 shows an overview on the model coupling of M_1 and M_2.

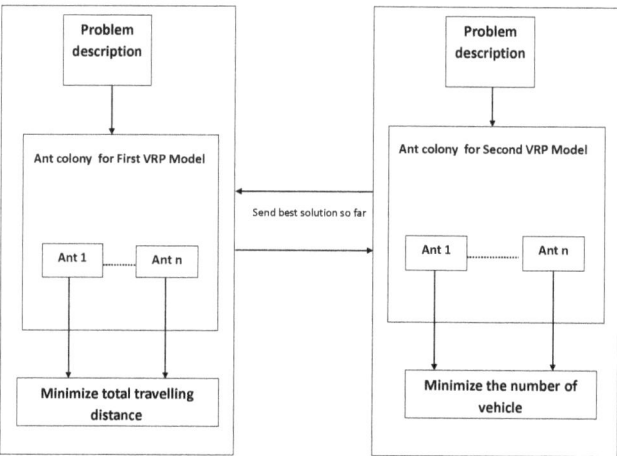

Figure 2. Model dependency overview.

As VRP models are created separately, each model has its own description and proceeds its own execution. It should couple these VRP models to reconstruct the entire multi-model using the co-simulation of MECSYCO. To this end, we define the connections between both models by specifying the input and output ports.

3.2.1. Exchanging Data between Simulators: Input and Output Connections

To predict the impact of co-simulation of VRP multi-model, we show the first model M_1 which represents the solution of VRP using Algorithm 1, where the objective is to minimize the total traveled distance. The second model M_2 implements Algorithm 2 that tries to minimize the total number of vehicles used to solve the same VRP. The aim in this case is to reproduce the VRP multi-model as a society of interacting and co-evolving models. We have to couple the two aforesaid models M_1 and M_2 using the concepts of Agent and Artifacts that are presented in Section 1. To couple M_1 and M_2 we need to define the input and output ports of each model and the connections between them.

The solution is improved by successive iterations where every model, i.e., M_1 or M_2, shares the improved solution with the other. M_1 and M_2 read the input and try to improve their solution as illustrated in Figure 3.

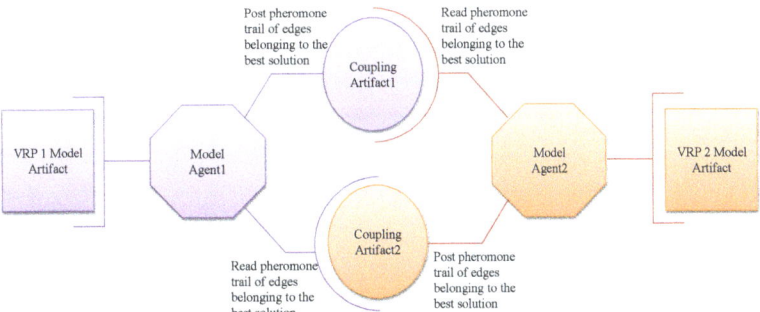

Figure 3. Coupling VRP models.

Specifically, when the model M_1 finds new best solution in a given iteration, it sends the following inputs to the model M_2

1. Ed: Set of edges belonging to the best solution (for each one of these edges the model M_1 sends a pair of nodes delimiting this edge).
2. P: Set of pheromones trail of each edge belonging to the best solution and the model M_2 retrieves these values of pheromone and modify its own values to have the new ones sent by M_1.

These sent pheromones trail to the model M_2 will modify the pheromone trail of the same edges in M_2 for improving the best solution finding. According to the ant colony system, in Algorithms 1 and 2 the ant chooses the next node to be added to the solution according to

- The cost of the best solution represented by the total traveled distance;
- The edge with minimum distance to be traveled;
- The edge with high value of pheromone trail.

The edge with high value of pheromone trail have a high probability to be added to the solution. Here, the model M_2 have edges with elevated values of pheromone trail from:

- Those of its own best solution;
- Those of M_1's best solution.

In the same way, when model M_2 finds a new best solution, it sends its best solution to model M_1 and replaces the current value of pheromone trail in this model by those of the new best solution in model M_2. Figure 4 show more details on the behavior of models in interaction.

3.2.2. Interchanging Models

When executing two similar models of VRP, they give two different solutions in each iteration. Instead of coupling two different VRP models, we can simply integrate two similar models M_1 or two similar models M_2. Here, we keep the same input and output connections as defined in the previous section. So, if one model has a good solution, it sends it to the second model and reciprocally. Specifically, when we couple two same models M_1, they will have different solutions in each iteration, and the first one have better solution, send the following inputs to the second model M_1:

1. Ed: Set of edges belonging to the best solution.
2. P: Set of pheromones trail of each edge belonging to the best solution and the second model M_1 retrieves these values of pheromone and modify its own values to have the new ones sent by the first model M_1.

This may impact on the solution of each model and redirect it to the best solution by reinforcing the pheromone of edges that have a good solution in each model. Moreover, we can study the evolution of the computational time when proceeding the co-simulation of VRP models, thereby the co-simulation of VRP models for finding a good solution.

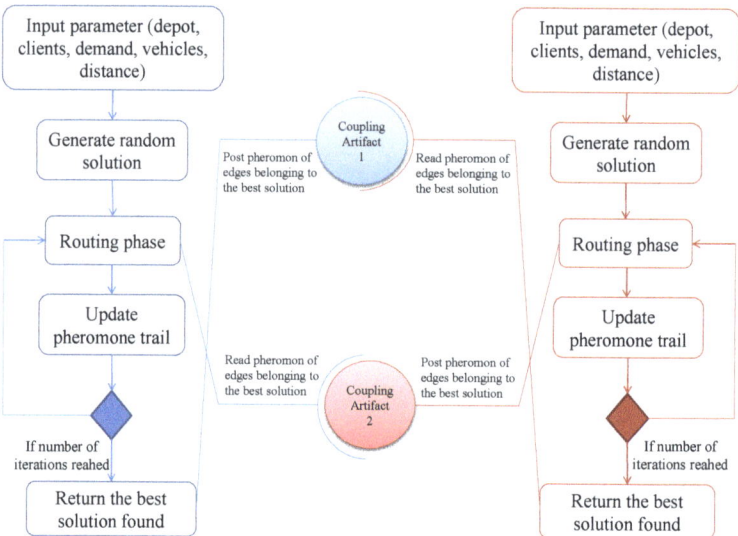

Figure 4. Behavior of two models in interaction.

Thus, we interchange models to compare different executions and study the accuracy of the best multi model. Figure 5 shows the VRP models' interaction graph.

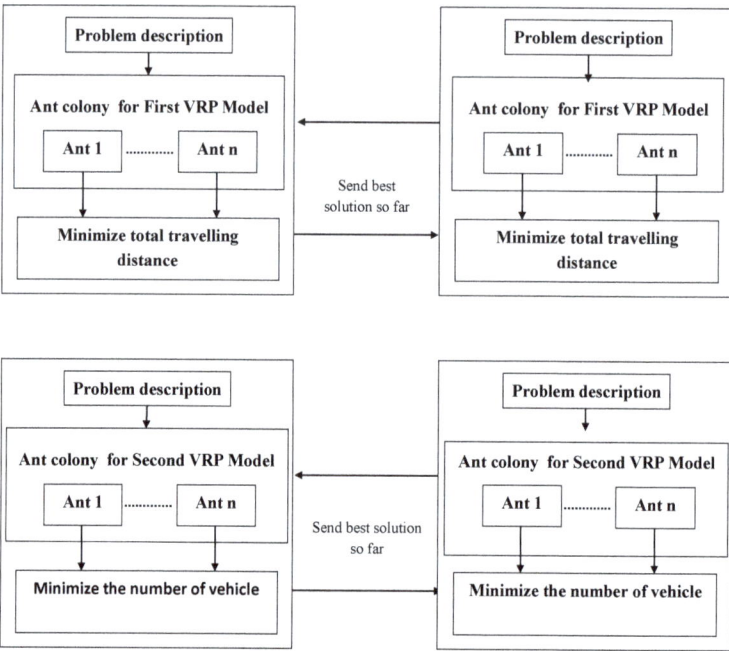

Figure 5. Graph of VRP interaction models.

By using MECSYCO we may launch more than one model of VRP at the same time following the routing algorithm defined in Section 2. The execution gives two different solutions that are improved in each iteration. The whole architecture of the multi-model is modular, transparent and parallel so the simulation can be viewed as a set of distributed and reusable components such that:

- The modeling is performed by model artifact.
- Conducting the models is accomplished by the model-agents.
- The coordination process is carried out by the coupling-artifacts.

As a result, we easily can add, remove or interchange models without being interested with coupling and coordination issues.

4. Implementation and Results

The VRP models are implemented using Netlogo [28] which is an environment designed for modeling and simulating the natural and social experiences. We use MECSYCO to perform the co-simulation of the VRP models based on the following parameters of hardware:

- Memory: 7.7 GB;
- CPU: Intel® Core™ i5-8250U CPU @ 1.60GHz × 8;
- Graphic Card: Intel® UHD Graphics 620 (Kabylake GT2);
- Operating System: ubunto 16.04 LTS 64 bits;
- Disk: 964 GB.

In the analysis, we study the behavior and the experiment results of VRP models on several VRP instances from [29] and then we evaluate the improvement carried out by the co-simulation of the VRP multi-model in term of quality of obtained results and computational time.

4.1. Implementing VRP Models

In the definition and implementation of the VRP graphs using Netlogo, we use the turtles agent to represent nodes with their turtle variables. The coordinate of each client and the links agent are used to define the edge between two nodes. We use the link variables for determining for each edge the link cost of these two nodes and the value of pheromone trail.

Table 1 represents the result obtained by executing single model VRP: model M_1 with BKS is the best-known solutions which were given by [29], Perc-Dev is the percentage deviation of the result reached by the model M_1 and Processing time (s) is the processing time for the execution of the model M_1.

Table 1. VRP results of M_1.

Inst.	BKS	Model 1	Per-Dev %	Processing Time (s)
A-n32-k5	784	794	1.25	16.261
A-n33-k5	661	661	0	26.46
A-n33-k6	742	759	2.23	11.98
A-n60-k9	1408	1442	2.35	91.18
B-n78-k10	1266	1332	4.95	112.18

Table 2 represents the result obtained by executing single model VRP, i.e., model M_2. Both models M_1 and M_2 are based on an ant colony system in their implementation, and they can interchange the following data: the cost of solution is calculated by the total traveled distance, edges belonging in the best solution found and the values of pheromone trail of these edges.

Other data can be exchanged between these models such as the route of the best solution or the route of each vehicle, etc. However, we skip these exchanged data to avoid more machine resources occupation because we must reserve more memory space to store the solution (routes) which takes a considerable time during the exchange.

Table 2. VRP result of M_2.

Inst.	BKS	Model 2	Per-Dev %	Processing Time (s)
A-n32-k5	784	807	2.85	19.241
A-n33-k5	661	661	0	38.84
A-n33-k6	742	757	1.98	16.82
A-n60-k9	1408	1491	5.56	90.83
B-n78-k10	1266	1318	3.94	1043.46

4.2. Co-Simulation of VRP Multi-Model

In this section, we run different forms of combined models and perceive the improvement provided by their co-simulation. In order to develop interactive VRP multi-models, we use MECSYCO which offers multiple integrating VRP models by defining the input and output port of coupling artefact. VRP instances [29] are a set of 100 instances created to offer a more universal and stable experimental setting.

Experiments were carried out in order to analyze the performance of the proposed VRP multi-model. The main objective is to assess whether the co-simulation has a direct impact on the qualitative performance of the obtained results. In this context, three composition are proposed for the interaction between the VRP multi-model used in the experiments:

- Coupling two different VRP models: M_1 with M_2.
- Coupling two same VRP models: M_1 with M_1.
- Coupling two same VRP models: M_2 with M_2.

Tables 3–5 show the result of VRP co-simulation where:

- Symbol A means: after co-simulation;
- Symbol B means: before co-simulation;
- Perc-Dev B is the percentage deviation of single model before co-simulation;
- Perc-Dev A is the percentage deviation after co-simulation for two models in interaction;
- Processing time B (s) is the processing time in second for just one model before co-simulation;
- Processing time A (ms) is the processing time in milliseconds after co-simulation for two models in interaction.

Table 3 presents the co-simulation results of model M_1 with M_1 which demonstrate enhanced performance of the found solution in terms of percentage deviation and processing time compared with the execution of single model M_1.

Table 3. The obtained co-simulation result of models M_1 with M_1.

Inst.	Per-Dev B %	Per-Dev A %	Processing Time B (s)	Processing Time A (ms)
A-n32-k5	1.25	0.63	16.26	381
A-n33-k5	0	0	26.46	377
A-n33-k6	2.23	1.32	11.98	160
A-n60-k9	2.35	1.53	91.18	162
B-n78-k10	4.95	2.98	112.18	739

Table 4 shows the result of the combination of the two same models M_2 with M_2. We perceive that there is an improvement in the found solution compared with one model M_2 in both the solution cost and the time of processing.

Table 4. The obtained co-simulation result of models M_2 with M_2.

Inst.	Per-Dev B %	Per-Dev A %	Processing Time B (s)	Processing Time A (ms)
A-n32-k5	2.85	0.63	19.24	959
A-n33-k5	0	0	38.84	774
A-n33-k6	1.98	2.11	16.82	310
A-n60-k9	5.56	2.89	90.83	2242
B-n78-k10	3.94	0.62	1043.46	2633

Table 5 shows the obtained results of integrating two different models M_1 with M_2. We observe that there is an improvement in the found solution compared with the result of a single model M_1 or M_2 in terms of solution and time of processing.

Table 5. The obtained co-simulation result of models M_1 with M_2.

Inst.	Per-Dev B %	Per-Dev A %	Processing Time B (s)	Processing Time A (ms)
A-n32-k5	2.85	1.63	16.26	152
A-n33-k5	0	0	26.46	525
A-n33-k6	2.23	1.46	11.98	413
A-n60-k9	2.35	1.88	91.18	2877
B-n78-k10	4.95	3.28	112.18	12,022

Figures 6 and 7 show the co-simulation processing time when coupling the same or different models. We conclude that the co-simulation of models is faster than the unique model M_1 or M_2. On the other hand, during data exchange between models we proceed to post and read best solutions for each interacting model. Instead of sending the best solution as a sequence of routes, we choose to send it as separate edges with their pheromone trail. After the execution, we observe that this action has a significant impact on the behavior of the model in constructing its solution and the model builds better solutions quickly. In addition, it does not spend a lot of time interchanging data and occupies a reasonable memory size to store the best solution.

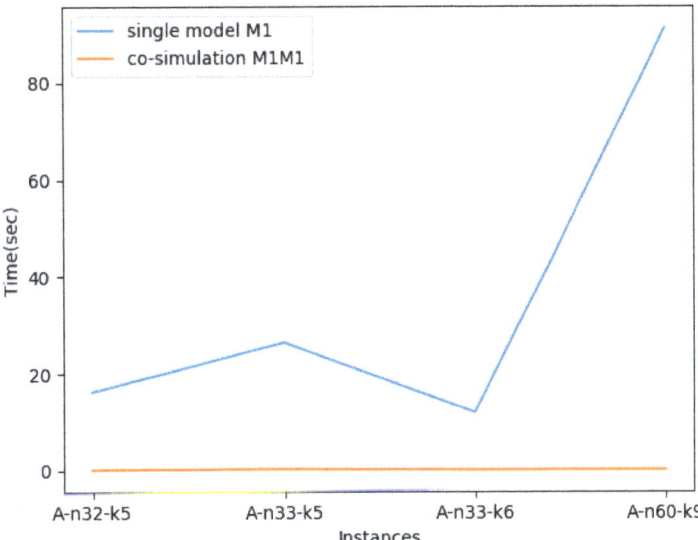

Figure 6. *Cont.*

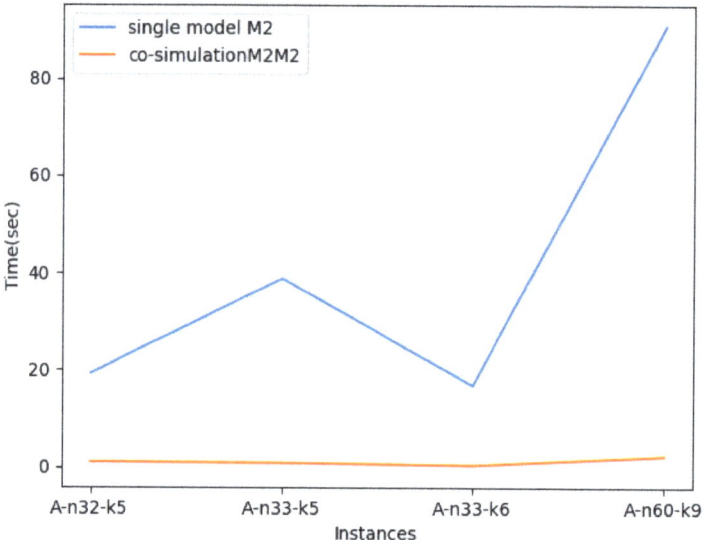

Figure 6. The execution time of co-simulation models compared with single model M_1 or M_2.

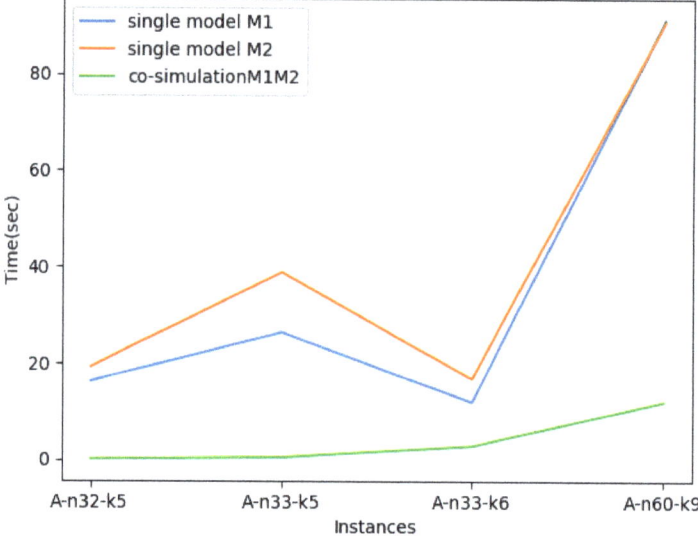

Figure 7. The execution time of co-simulation models M_1 with M_2.

4.3. Discussion

We conducted several experiments in a single VRP model and multiple VRP models in interaction, Single VRP models implementing different algorithms of ACO metaheuristics gave close to optimal solutions; the VRP multi-model improved these results compared with single ones. We coupled

- Two different models M1 and M2;
- Two same models M1 with M1;
- Two same M2 with M2.

Always the result of coupled models was the best according to single model M1 or single model M2. It was especially time consuming.

Figure 8 displays the co-simulation processing time of the three coupled systems and shows that the coupled system using two same models M_1 has the best result.

Co-simulation enables the integration of heterogeneous models/simulators homogeneously, in the future we can implement other types of metaheuristic and define the appropriate interchanging data between them, in order to study the amelioration of results in each different case.

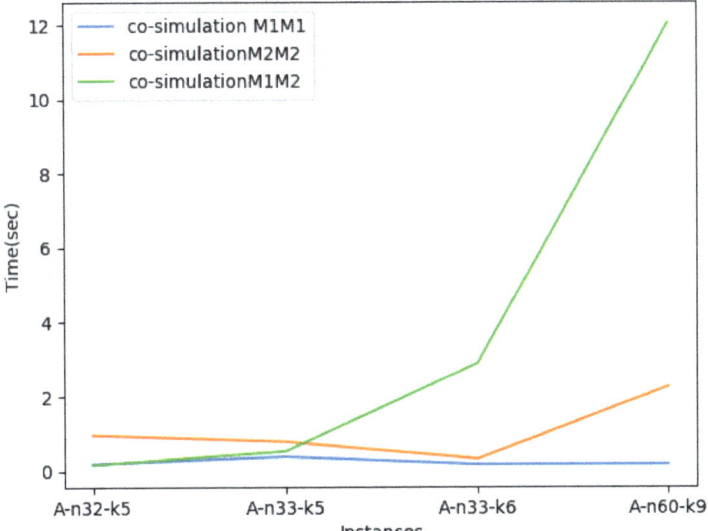

Figure 8. The execution time of co-simulation models.

5. Conclusions

This paper discusses the integration of VRP simulators created in Netlogo platform into MECSYCO co-simulation middleware. The proposed VRP multi-models in interaction implement ant colony meta-heuristic for solving two different objectives. The obtained results show the efficiency of better solution finding of VRP multi-models compared with single VRP models in terms of processing time and travel distance. We conclude that the type of data exchanged between models gives more qualitative performance to the solution short execution time to solve the problem.

In the future, we will evaluate the proposed approach by introducing other variants of VRP such as the Multi Depot Vehicle Routing Problem (MDVRP) and the Vehicle Routing Problem with Time Window (VRPTW). Moreover, the atomic VRP models can be implemented using other types of meta-heuristics and the combination of these models can be performed by defining other input and output connections.

Author Contributions: Conceptualization, S.S.G.; methodology, A.L.; software, M.H. and A.L.; validation, S.S.G. and A.L.; formal analysis, A.B.; investigation, A.E.; resources, M.A.; data curation, M.H.; writing—original draft preparation, S.S.G.; writing—review and editing, A.L. and M.H.; visualization, A.B. and A.E.; supervision, A.L.; project administration, A.L. and M.H.; funding acquisition, M.A. All authors have read and agreed to the published version of the manuscript.

Funding: This research received no external funding.

Institutional Review Board Statement: Not applicable.

Informed Consent Statement: Not applicable.

Data Availability Statement: Not applicable.

Acknowledgments: We would like to express our gratitude to Yagoub Mohammed Amine for their meaningful support of this work.

Conflicts of Interest: The authors declare no conflict of interest.

References

1. Pokrovskii, V.N. *Thermodynamics of Complex Systems*; IOP Publishing: Bristol, UK, 2020; pp. 2053–2563. [CrossRef]
2. Comin, C.H.; Peron, T.; Silva, F.N.; Amancio, D.R.; Rodrigues, F.A.; da F. Costa, L. Complex systems: Features, similarity and connectivity. *Phys. Rep.* **2020**, *861*, 1–41. [CrossRef]
3. Dorigo, M.; Floreano, D.; Gambardella, L.M.; Mondada, F.; Nolfi, S.; Baaboura, T.; Birattari, M.; Bonani, M.; Brambilla, M.; Brutschy, A.; et al. Swarmanoid: A novel concept for the study of heterogeneous robotic swarms. *IEEE Robot. Autom. Mag.* **2013**, *20*, 60–71. [CrossRef]
4. Liboni, G. Complex Systems Co-Simulation with the CoSim20 Framework: For Efficient and Accurate Distributed Co-Simulations. Ph.D. Thesis, Université Côte d'Azur, Nice, France, 2021.
5. Camus, B.; Bourjot, C.; Chevrier, V. Considering a multi-level model as a society of interacting models: Application to a collective motion example. *J. Artif. Soc. Soc. Simul.* **2015**, *18*, 7. [CrossRef]
6. Nazari, M.; Oroojlooy, A.; Snyder, L.; Takác, M. Reinforcement learning for solving the vehicle routing problem. *Adv. Neural Inf. Process. Syst.* **2018**, *31*, 9861–9871.
7. Vidal, T.; Laporte, G.; Matl, P. A concise guide to existing and emerging vehicle routing problem variants. *Eur. J. Oper. Res.* **2020**, *286*, 401–416. [CrossRef]
8. Wang, Z.; Sheu, J.B. Vehicle routing problem with drones. *Transp. Res. Part B Methodol.* **2019**, *122*, 350–364. [CrossRef]
9. Li, Y.; Soleimani, H.; Zohal, M. An improved ant colony optimization algorithm for the multi-depot green vehicle routing problem with multiple objectives. *J. Clean. Prod.* **2019**, *227*, 1161–1172. [CrossRef]
10. Chen, W.; Ran, S.; Wu, C.; Jacobson, B. Explicit parallel co-simulation approach: Analysis and improved coupling method based on H-infinity synthesis. *Multibody Syst. Dyn.* **2021**, *52*, 255–279. [CrossRef]
11. Gomes, C.; Thule, C.; Broman, D.; Larsen, P.G.; Vangheluwe, H. Co-simulation: State of the art. *arXiv* **2017**, arXiv:1702.00686.
12. Pierce, K.; Gamble, C.; Golightly, D.; Palacin, R. Exploring Human Behaviour in Cyber-Physical Systems with Multi-modelling and Co-simulation. In Proceedings of the International Symposium on Formal Methods, Pasadena, CA, USA, 24–27 May 2019; pp. 237–253.
13. Siebert, J.; Ciarletta, L.; Chevrier, V. Agents and artefacts for multiple models co-evolution. Building complex system simulation as a set of interacting models. In Proceedings of the Autonomous Agents and Multiagent Systems-AAMAS 2010, Toronto, ON, Canada, 10–14 May 2010; pp. 509–516.
14. Paris, T.; Tan, A.; Chevrier, V.; Ciarletta, L. Study about decomposition and integration of continuous systems in discrete environment. In Proceedings of the 49th Annual Simulation Symposium (ANSS 2016): 2016 Spring Simulation Multi-Conference (SpringSim'16), Pasadena, CA, USA, 3–6 April 2016.
15. Paris, T.; Ciarletta, L.; Chevrier, V. Designing co-simulation with multi-agent tools: A case study with NetLogo. In *Multi-Agent Systems and Agreement Technologies*; Springer: Berlin/Heidelberg, Germany, 2017; pp. 253–267.
16. Camus, B.; Paris, T.; Vaubourg, J.; Presse, Y.; Bourjot, C.; Ciarletta, L.; Chevrier, V. Co-simulation of cyber-physical systems using a DEVS wrapping strategy in the MECSYCO middleware. *Simulation* **2018**, *94*, 1099–1127. [CrossRef]
17. Silva, M.A.L.; de Souza, S.R.; Souza, M.J.F.; de Franca Filho, M.F. Hybrid metaheuristics and multi-agent systems for solving optimization problems: A review of frameworks and a comparative analysis. *Appl. Soft Comput.* **2018**, *71*, 433–459. [CrossRef]
18. Mguis, F.; Zidi, K.; Ghedira, K.; Borne, P. Distributed approach for vehicle routing problem in disaster case. *Ifac Proc. Vol.* **2012**, *45*, 353–359. [CrossRef]
19. Martin, S.; Ouelhadj, D.; Beullens, P.; Ozcan, E.; Juan, A.A.; Burke, E.K. A multi-agent based cooperative approach to scheduling and routing. *Eur. J. Oper. Res.* **2016**, *254*, 169–178. [CrossRef]
20. Silva, M.A.L.; de Souza, S.R.; Souza, M.J.F.; Bazzan, A.L.C. A reinforcement learning-based multi-agent framework applied for solving routing and scheduling problems. *Expert Syst. Appl.* **2019**, *131*, 148–171. [CrossRef]
21. Kim, T.G.; Praehofer, H.; Zeigler, B. Theory of Modeling and Simulation: Integrating Discrete Event and Continuous Complex. Dynamic Systems. 2000. Available online: https://www.semanticscholar.org/paper/Theory-of-Modeling-and-Simulation%3A-Integrating-and-Zeigler-Praehofer/92131a3aed0d72ccfe92364eee87e228c9c773e6 (accessed on 29 March 2022).
22. Van Tendeloo, Y.; Vangheluwe, H. Discrete event system specification modeling and simulation. In Proceedings of the 2018 Winter Simulation Conference (WSC), Gothenburg, Sweden, 9–12 December 2018; pp. 162–176.
23. Ricci, A.; Viroli, M.; Omicini, A. Give agents their artifacts: The A&A approach for engineering working environments in MAS. In Proceedings of the 6th international joint conference on Autonomous Agents and Multiagent Systems, Honolulu, HI, USA, 14–18 May 2007; pp. 1–3.
24. Camus, B.; Vaubourg, J.; Presse, Y.; Elvinger, V.; Paris, T.; Tan, A.; Chevrier, V.; Ciarletta, L.; Bourjot, C. Multi-Agent Environment for Complex Systems Cosimulation (Mecsyco)-Architecture Documentation. 2016. Available online: http://mecsyco.com/dev/doc/User%20Guide.pdf (accessed on 29 March 2022).

25. Savelsbergh, M. *Vehicle Routing and Scheduling*; Technical Report; Georgia Tech Supply Chain and Logistics Institute: Atlanta, GA, USA, 2002.
26. Omicini, A.; Ricci, A.; Viroli, M. Artifacts in the A&A meta-model for multi-agent systems. *Auton. Agents Multi-Agent Syst.* **2008**, *17*, 432–456.
27. Ricci, A.; Piunti, M.; Viroli, M. Environment programming in multi-agent systems: An artifact-based perspective. *Auton. Agents Multi-Agent Syst.* **2011**, *23*, 158–192. [CrossRef]
28. Gooding, T. Netlogo. In *Economics for a Fairer Society*; Springer: Berlin/Heidelberg, Germany, 2019; pp. 37–43.
29. Uchoa, E.; Pecin, D.; Pessoa, A.; Poggi, M.; Vidal, T.; Subramanian, A. New benchmark instances for the Capacitated Vehicle Routing Problem. *Eur. J. Oper. Res.* **2017**, *257*, 845–858. [CrossRef]

Article

Pedestrian Simulation with Reinforcement Learning: A Curriculum-Based Approach

Giuseppe Vizzari *,† and Thomas Cecconello †

Department of Informatics, Systems and Communication, University of Milano-Bicocca, Viale Sarca 336/14, 20126 Milano, Italy
* Correspondence: giuseppe.vizzari@unimib.it
† These authors contributed equally to this work.

Abstract: Pedestrian simulation is a consolidated but still lively area of research. State of the art models mostly take an agent-based perspective, in which pedestrian decisions are made according to a manually defined model. Reinforcement learning (RL), on the other hand, is used to train an agent situated in an environment how to act so as to maximize an accumulated numerical reward signal (a feedback provided by the environment to every chosen action). We explored the possibility of applying RL to pedestrian simulation. We carefully defined a reward function combining elements related to goal orientation, basic proxemics, and basic way-finding considerations. The proposed approach employs a particular training *curriculum*, a set of scenarios growing in difficulty supporting an incremental acquisition of general movement competences such as orientation, walking, and pedestrian interaction. The learned pedestrian behavioral model is applicable to situations not presented to the agents in the training phase, and seems therefore reasonably general. This paper describes the basic elements of the approach, the training procedure, and an experimentation within a software framework employing Unity and ML-Agents.

Keywords: pedestrian simulation; multiagent systems; reinforcement learning

Citation: Vizzari, G.; Cecconello, T. Pedestrian Simulation with Reinforcement Learning: A Curriculum-Based Approach. *Future Internet* 2023, 15, 12. https://doi.org/10.3390/fi15010012

Academic Editors: Agostino Poggi, Martin Kenyeres, Ivana Budinská and Ladislav Hluchy

Received: 12 November 2022
Revised: 18 December 2022
Accepted: 21 December 2022
Published: 27 December 2022

Copyright: © 2022 by the authors. Licensee MDPI, Basel, Switzerland. This article is an open access article distributed under the terms and conditions of the Creative Commons Attribution (CC BY) license (https://creativecommons.org/licenses/by/4.0/).

1. Introduction

Architects, designers, and planners dealing with decisions about the structuring of environments subject to potential crowding employ commercial, off-the-shelf tools for the simulation of pedestrian and crowd dynamics on an everyday basis, especially in collective transportation facilities and in the urban context in general. Decisions related to the spatial arrangement, dimensioning, and even maintenance of specific facilities in which congested situations can arise call for the elaboration of what-if scenarios, indicating what would plausibly happen within a given geometry subject to certain levels of demand. Crowd managers (a relatively new kind of role) are called to plan situations in which existing facilities must be used for hosting large numbers of pedestrians for abnormal functions (e.g., concerts and fairs). With growing frequency, they use these tools to evaluate the crowd management procedures before they are enacted. The results of research on pedestrian and crowd simulation have thus lead to successful technology transfer, but the overall scenario still presents open challenges for researchers in different fields and disciplines to improve model expressiveness (i.e., simplifying the modeling activity or introducing the possibility of representing phenomena that have not yet been considered), the adequacy of the instruments in properly supporting the activity of modelers, and the efficiency of the simulators based on those approaches.

Despite the substantial effort and significant results achieved, the need to properly hand-craft simulation models for a given situation still represents a serious issue: on one hand, the modeler needs to have both serious competence on the topic of pedestrian and crowd dynamics (in addition to other more technical abilities, such as the ability to manage computer-aided design (CAD) files representing the planned or analyzed environment); on the other hand, their activities often involve arbitrary decisions (e.g., about the extent of the influence of a structural element of the environment over pedestrians). Therefore, the scenarios produced by two different modelers might present differences that, in some cases, might even be potentially relevant. Generally, expert modelers would reach a consensus on most (if not all) modeling decisions; however, what they would call a "modeling mistake" could instead suggest a limit of or a problem with the underlying modeling approach.

Abstracting away from the specific case at hand, this kind of pattern can be found in different areas of application of informatics to computer-supported analysis, control, and expert decision support in even moderately complex sociotechnical systems: while pedestrians and crowd studies can be considered as a specific case of very current traffic and transportation [1], the same paradigm can be suitably applied to the investigation of future scenarios in the areas of the Internet of Things [2], digital twins [3], and smart cities [4]. Once again, we are facing a "knowledge bottleneck": in this particular case, it is about guiding the decisions on how to act in a given situation, but generally within a complex systems perspective, making it very difficult to effectively tackle the problem through optimization techniques.

In the last years, we have also witnessed an evolution in machine learning (ML) approaches, which are being employed with ever growing frequency, even for supporting scientific research in almost every context. The growing availability of data describing pedestrian and crowd behavior (see in particular https://ped.fz-juelich.de/da/doku.php, accessed on 11 November 2022) is motivating researchers to evaluate if this area of application can also see a proper application of these approaches, under which assumptions and conditions, and with what kind of performance, especially compared with existing approaches.

This study represents a contribution in this direction: in particular, we adopted a reinforcement learning (RL) (see the foundational book [5]) approach to the definition of a model for pedestrian locomotion in a built environment. RL represents a type of machine learning technique that is increasingly bing investigated for the implementation of autonomous agents, in particular when the acceptance of the term "autonomous" is strong and closer to the definition provided by [6] ("A system is autonomous to the extent that its behavior is determined by its own experience".) than the most widely adopted definitions in agent computing. RL describes how to train an agent situated in an environment in order to maximize an accumulated numerical reward signal (received by the environment as a feedback to every chosen action). The goal of a simulation should therefore be expressed in terms of a reward function, for which a higher accumulated value should be associated with a higher quality in the simulation dynamics. An RL agent is provided with a model of perception and action, but in addition to these modeling elements and the reward function, the approach can autonomously explore the space of potential agent behaviors and converge to a policy (i.e., a function mapping the state and perception to an appropriate action to be carried out in that context). Although the approach can exploit a certain amount of initial knowledge (analogous to reflexes in animals and humans, or internalized norms, rules, and shared ways to evaluate the acceptability of a given state of affairs), the overall goal is to grant the agent the ability to learn so it can adjust its behavior to improve its performance.

RL approaches, as with most areas of the ML landscape, has been strongly reinvigorated by the energy, efforts, promises, and results brought by the deep learning revolution, and it seems one of the most promising ways to investigate how to provide an agent higher levels of autonomy. On a more pragmatic level, recent developments and results in the RL area suggest that this approach may be an alternative to current agent-based approaches to the modeling of complex systems (see, for instance, the introduction by [7]) Currently, behavioral models for agents require human modelers to manually define agents' behavioral rules, often requiring a complicated interdisciplinary effort, as well as validation processes based on the acquisition and analysis of data describing the studied phenomenon. RL can partly automate this kind of process, focusing on the definition of an environment representation, the definition of a model for agent perception and action, and defining a reward function and training procedure. The learning process is, in theory, able to explore the potential space of the policies (i.e., agent behavioral specifications) and converge to the desired decision-making model. While defining a model of the environment, as well as agent perception and action, the definition of a reward function and overall training procedure are tasks requiring substantial knowledge about the studied domain and phenomenon, the learning process may significantly simplifythe modeler's work, while solving issues related to model calibration. Although a few examples of applications of this approach can be found in the literature (a relevant selection is discussed in Section 2), the results achieved so far highlight significant limitations, especially in the capability of the generalization of the training phase. Learned behavioral models are sometimes very specific to the types of environments adopted within the training procedure, and this represents a serious problem because (i) it is inconvenient to pay computational costs for performing training in every scenario to be analyzed; (ii) the results of each training process are essentially different behavioral models, trained in different situations, and they are thus not comparable.

This paper presents an experimentation of this approach to pedestrian modeling, trying to start from the last considerations. Whereas RL agents learn how to behave to optimize their expected cumulative reward, pedestrians generally do not exhibit optimal behavior. Therefore, we carefully defined a reward function (combining contributions related to proxemics, goal orientation, and basic way-finding considerations). The most important aspect of this study, however, is the adopted learning process: we defined a particular training curriculum (a concept introduced by [8]), a set of scenarios growing in difficulty supporting the incremental acquisition of proper orientation, walking, and pedestrian interaction competences. Curriculum learning is a general approach not specifically related to RL, but it has been considered as a promising transfer learning approach for RL (as discussed, for instance, by [9]). We considered it particularly well suited for adoption in the RL context: the necessary reflection on the shaping of a reward function seems compatible with the formulation of a *structure* to be given to the overall learning process, leading to a general pedestrian decision model that can be employed in a wide variety of situations (hopefully most of the plausible ones considered in this line of work). The goal of this study was not to systematically investigate all the different alternatives in every single modeling choice (the RL approach is potentially powerful but it is also quite complicated, with a many choices for the different involved concepts and tasks, and several alternative for each of them), but rather to perform a first investigation, trying to achieve results that can be analyzed, especially considering experimental situations in which some data about pedestrian movements are available at least to perform the first steps toward a validation, to evaluate if the overall approach can be really promising, and possibly identifying some criticalities, benefits, and limitations.

After setting the present study within the relevant research landscape, we describe the fundamental elements of the approach, its implementation within a software framework (we are in the process of preparation of a software repository in which the framework will be made available for download) employing Unity (https://unity.com) and ML-Agents (https://github.com/Unity-Technologies/ml-agents, accessed on 11 November 2022), describing the achieved simulation results: in particular, we compare the achieved pedestrian model with both the basic pedestrian agents made available by Unity and with results from the literature in simple benchmark scenarios. We finally discuss the current limits of the approach and our current implementation, as well as ongoing future developments.

2. Related Literature

Pedestrian and crowd dynamics, as suggested in the Introduction, represents an area in which scientific research has produced valuable results, which are now being practically employed by off-the-shelf tools: PTV Viswalk (https://www.ptvgroup.com/en/solutions/products/ptv-viswalk/, accessed on 11 November 2022) officially states that it employs mechanisms based on the *social force model* introduced by [10]. An interesting and compact discussion of the field from a research oriented standpoint was presented by [11], although it is difficult to provide a compact and yet substantial and comprehensive introduction to the field. This is particularly due to the fact that human decisions related to locomotion can refer to several aspects and areas of knowledge (ranging from environmental and social psychology, to geography, and even anthropology, to mention some of the most apparent) and, despite the fact that technology transfer was successfully carried out, there are still decision-making tasks that are actively being investigated. Way-finding and path-planning activities, for instance, are objects of recent intense research, and researchers have tried to consider factors such as partial or imprecise knowledge of an environment (as discussed by [12]), its dynamic level of congestion, and human factors such as imitation (as proposed by [13]), which can influence overall observed system dynamics.

Machine learning approaches have not yet delivered results able to substitute the traditional hand-crafted models adopted in commercial simulators, and they are still in the stage of active research. One of the first approaches was designed by [14], who investigated both RL techniques (Q learning) and a classification approach to basically choose an action among a small set of available alternatives, based on a description of the current situation and employing a decision tree.

More recently, different authors tried to frame the problem so that *regression* techniques could be employed, either to predict the scalar value of the pedestrian's velocity vector (see, in particular, the study by [15]) or to predict the both the walking speed and direction to be employed (as presented by [16]) considering the current perceived situation. The basic idea is that, owing to the growing availability of raw data describing pedestrian experiments (see the above mentioned website gathering and making available videos and tracking data about pedestrian and crowd experiments (https://ped.fz-juelich.de/da/doku.php, accessed on 11 November 2022)), we could simply devise a deep neural network to be trained according to the contextual situation perceived by a pedestrian and the velocity actually adopted in the next frame of the video. While this approach is relatively straightforward, it is quite limited in terms of the actual possibility to produce a *general model* of pedestrian behavior: even when the whole process should lead to the successful training of the network and to achieving very good results in the specific situations documented in the dataset, there is no guarantee that the network would produce plausible movement predictions in different situations not covered by the experiments.

There is also a trend of research not really working toward the achievement of fully-fledged pedestrian models, but rather focusing on *trajectory forecasting*. Quoting [17], this task can be defined as: "given the past trajectories of all humans in a scene, forecast the future trajectories which conform to the social norms". The temporal window associated with the prediction is understandably leaned toward the *short term*: generally, these studies focused on a *scene*, representing a relatively small area, in which relatively few pedestrians move, and the horizon of the prediction is limited to few seconds. Most recent studies employed deep learning techniques that are to a certain extent related to the above-mentioned approaches with regression.

The RL approach has recently been applied again to the problem of pedestrian behavioral modeling and simulation [18]: the authors clearly and honestly discussed the limits of the achieved model. In particular, although trained agents achieve encouraging quantitative results, from the perspective of the capability of the model to generalize and face potentially complicated environments, social interaction situations, and movement patterns, in some situations, they actually cannot complete the movement they wanted to perform. We emphasize that this is completely understandable when applying an approach that basically explores the space of potential policies for identifying reasonable behavioral specifications in a complicated situation, but this testifies that there is still a need to perform further investigations to fully evaluate the adequacy of the RL approach to the problem of pedestrians and crowd simulation.

A general consideration of RL compared with other ML approaches is that, on the one hand, RL requires the modelers to provide a set of assumptions, not just about the model of perception and action of the agent. This is a cost, but it also means that the model can embed (i) concepts about how the environment is actually conceived and interpreted by the agent in relation to its goal oriented behavior, and (ii) an idea of what should be considered desirable behavior (and what should be considered bad choices), and this can represent a way of guiding the learning process in a large space of potential policies. From this perspective, the presented approach is in tune with recent methods on heuristics-guided RL [19] (although we did not technically employ the techniques and framework proposed by the authors), not just for accelerating the training process, but also to achieve a more generally applicable behavioral model.

3. Proposed RL Approach

3.1. Representation of the Environment

For sake of simplicity, in this experimental study, we considered square environments of 20×20 m surrounded by walls, as depicted in Figure 1. We anticipated that the framework and especially the learned policies work in larger areas, but the reference overall scenario for this work is represented by indoor movements in everyday buildings and facilities or outdoor environments with structures (e.g., barriers) constraining pedestrian movements. Environments that we employed for both training and testing the model respected this size constraint.

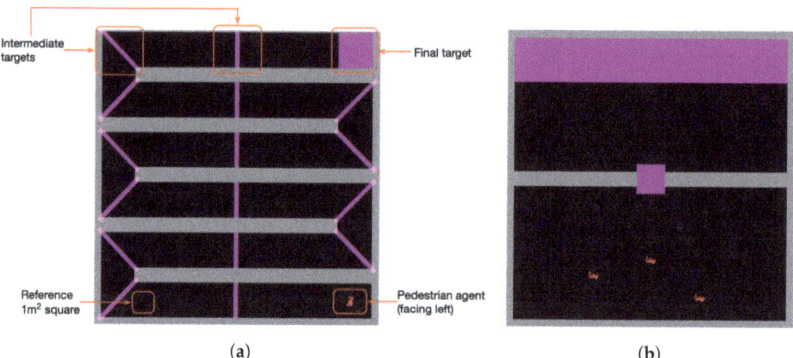

Figure 1. Example environments and annotations: (**a**) 'turns' environment and annotations; (**b**) 'unidirectional door' environment and annotations.

The smaller squares (of 1×1 m) in Figure 1 are depicted to allow a simpler appraisal of distances. Gray objects are walls, obstacles, and anything that agents perceive as a 'wall'. Violet rectangles are intermediate and final goals. These markers (in the vein of what was proposed by [20]) do not hinder the possibility of moving through them, and they are essentially a modeling tool to support agent's navigation in the environment. One of our goals in the study was to provide an alternative to Unity's path finding and (more generally) pedestrian agent control mechanisms. The agent perception model is introduced below, but we anticipated that they were able to perceive these markers and to select intermediate or final movement targets; we also show that reaching intermediate or final targets influences the agent's reward.

Environments must therefore undergo a preparation phase before being used in the proposed approach: while this kind of activity is difficult to automate and it requires manual effort, all commercial simulation platforms that we are aware of have an analogous requirement. An example of an environment annotated with this rationale is shown in Figure 1a: in this case, the targets in the middle of the horizontal corridors create an affordance: the incentive for agents to move toward that direction although the actual bend at the end of the corridor is still fairly distant. Moreover, oblique intermediate targets in the bends guide agents in the change of direction, also helping them to achieve a plausible trajectory, avoiding taking trajectories excessively biased toward the internal part of the bend (see, e.g., the considerations proposed by [21] or [22]). Figure 1b shows an environment in which a door (an open one) is present: in this case, the target is used to guide agents in passing through the opening, because the final target is obstructed and not perceivable from positions inside a large portion of the southern room.

3.2. Agent Perception Model

Agents are provided with a limited set of *projectors* of rays, each extending up to a certain distance (10 m in these experiments) and providing specific information about what is "hit" by the ray and the associated distance from the agent.

Projectors (and therefore rays) are not uniformly distributed around the agent; they are more densely present in front of the pedestrian to loosely resemble real human visual perception.

The angle between the rays and the direction an agent is facing (both positive and negative) follows the rule described in Equation (1):

$$\alpha_i = Min(\alpha_{i-1} + \delta * i,\ max\_vision) \quad (1)$$

where δ was set to 1.5, *max_vision* to 90 and α_0 to 0. As a consequence, projectors emit rays at 0°, ±1.5°, ±4.5°, ±9°, ±15°, ±22.5°, ±31.5°, ±42°, ±54°, ±67.5°, ±82.5°, and ±90°. Figure 2 graphically depicts this distribution.

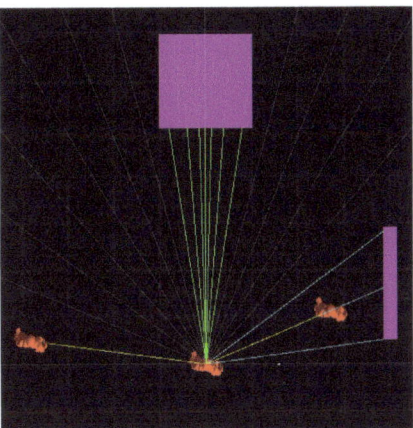

Figure 2. Rays and provided information: yellow = agent, cyan = intermediate target, green = final target, and transparent = wall or none of the others. Pedestrian agents are depicted in red.

The overall number of projectors and rays is therefore 23, but the information associated with and conveyed by rays is different for different objects:

- *Walls and targets* are associated with four observations that are intended to support basic navigation of the environment (i.e., choice of the direction to be followed): (i) a distance (a numeric value normalized employing a ReLU-inspired function to be between 0 and 1, with distances above 10 m capped at 1), and a one hot encoding indicating if the perceived entity is a wall (ii), a target still not visited (iii), or an already visited one (iv); as shown in Figure 2 this type of ray is not blocked by agents.
- *Agents and walls* are associated with additional information, whose intended meaning is instead to support the regulation of distance between the agent and nearby heterogeneous entities that may generate an impact (which should be avoided): rays bringing this kind of information about agents and walls are therefore associated with a distance (i) (analogous to the one in the previous type of ray), a Boolean type (agent or wall) (ii), and optional information about direction of movement (iii) and walking

speed (only relevant for agents) (iv); unlike the previous type of ray, this one is blocked by the first entity that would cause a collision.

Some of the acquired information is therefore potentially doubled: in case a wall is hit by the ray, its presence and distance are highlighted by the two different ray types. In the future, we can attempt to remove references to walls in the second type of ray, but the present results show that this redundancy does not seem to cause training convergence issues.

Other relevant information for the agent observation is its own current walking speed. To improve the performance of the neural networks typically employed in recent RL algorithms all observations, in addition to those for which normalization has already been introduced, current walking speed was normalized in the interval [0,1]. For the normalization of walking speed, we set the maximum velocity for agents to be 1.7 m/s. The overall agent's observation is summarized in Table 1. Essentially, the overall number of observations for each RL pedestrian agent was 185 (1 due to its own previous walking speed, 23 rays each associated with 4 observations for walls and targets, and 23 rays associated with 4 observations for agents and walls).

Table 1. Summary of agent observations.

Type of Observation	Observation	Value
Intrinsic	Own speed	Number
Walls and Targets	Distance	Number
	Type/Tag	One Hot Encoding
Agents and Walls	Distance	Number
	Type/Tag	Boolean
	Direction	Number
	Speed	Number

The overall agent perception model is therefore a simplification of real human perceptive capabilities: the discrete nature of the projected rays makes it possible that, in some situations, objects (obstacles or other agents) might be not immediately perceived, especially when they are not in the center of the field of view. Nonetheless, this definition represents a good balance between plausibility and performance, limiting the computational cost of agent perception as well as the structure of agent observation for the RL algorithm.

3.3. Agent Action Model

The agent action in this model is essentially a change in its speed vector; this translates into two potential changes, for each decision, essentially related to the magnitude of the vector, i.e., *walking velocity* and *direction*.

Each agent is triggered by the overall execution engine to take a decision about if and how to change its own actual speed vector three times per second, in line with [23], in an attempt to consider cognitive plausibility, quality of the achieved results, and computational cost.

The agent's action space was therefore modeled as the choice of two (conceptually) continuous values in the $[-1,1]$ interval that were used to determine a change in velocity vector for magnitude and direction.

The first element, a_0, causes a change in the walking speed defined by Equation (2):

$$speed_t = Max\left(speed_{min}, Min\left(speed_{t-1} + \frac{speed_{max} * a_0}{2}, speed_{max}\right)\right) \quad (2)$$

where $speed_{min}$ was set to 0, and $speed_{max}$ was set to 1.7 m/s. According to this equation, the agent is able to reach a complete stop, or the maximum velocity is two actions (i.e., about 0.66 s). To account for the heterogeneity within the simulated pedestrian population, each agent is provided with an individual desired walking velocity that is drawn from a normal distribution with average of 1.5 m/s and a standard deviation of 0.2 m/s; so, for each agent, the actual $speed_{max}$ does differ.

The second element of the decision, a_1, determines the change in the agent's direction according to Equation (3):

$$\alpha_t = \alpha_{t-1} + a_1 * 20 \tag{3}$$

The walking direction can therefore change 20° each 0.33 s, which is plausible for normal pedestrian walking, but would be probably not be reasonable for modeling running and/or sport related movements.

For the perception model, the model associated with the agent's action presents limits: for instance, it is not suited to situations in which an agent can choose to jog or run or to perform sudden and significant changes in the walking direction (such as basketball players trying to dribble around opponents). Normal walking scenarios, not emergency evacuation situations, seem compatible with this setting.

3.4. Reward Function

As briefly discussed in the Introduction, RL employs a feedback signal from the environment to the trained agents to guide their learning process as a form of weaker substitute for labels in supervised learning approaches. This feedback signal is defined as a *reward function*, which represents a central element of an RL approach, because agents are trained to maximize the accumulated instantaneous rewards associated with their actions. Pedestrian decision-making activities are fairly complex: conflicting tendencies are evaluated and sometimes reconciled quickly, almost unconsciously, while we walk. Sometimes, individual and collective actions are reasonable or at least explainable in retrospective, in a combination of individual and collective intelligence, that however leads to suboptimal overall performance (see, for instance, the above-cited studies by [13,24]).

Given the above considerations and exploiting the available knowledge on this topic, we hand-crafted a reward function. Initially, we defined basic components, i.e., factors that are generally agreed upon as elements influencing pedestrian behavior. In a second phase, we performed a sort of initial tuning of the related weights, defining the relative importance of the different factors. A fully fledged sensitivity analysis was not performed, whichwill be object of future studies.

The overall reward function is defined in Equation (4)

$$Reward : \begin{cases} +6 & \text{Final target reached} \\ +0.5 & \text{Intermediate target reached} \\ -1 & \text{Reached a previously reached intermediate target} \\ -0.5 & \text{No target in sights} \\ -0.5 & \text{Agent in very close proximity} < 0.6 \text{ m} \\ -0.005 & \text{Agent in close proximity} < 1 \text{ m} \\ -0.001 & \text{Agent in proximity} < 1.4 \text{ m} \\ -0.5 & \text{Wall in proximity} < 0.6 \text{ m} \\ -0.0001 & \text{Each step complete} \\ -6 & \text{Reached the end of steps per episode} \end{cases} \tag{4}$$

The only way to increase the cumulative reward is therefore the reaching of intermediate or final targets. It is not uncommon in RL settings to have a *single* source of a positive reward, i.e., the achievement of the final goal. Let us remind the reader that our goal was to achieve a *generally and directly applicable, yet plausible*, pedestrian behavioral model. In most situations, pedestrians move within an environment structured in several interconnected rooms, whose overall structure is known (e.g., the building hosting their office or workplace, a school or university they attend, or transport stations they use every day). Using just a single positive reward associated with the achievement of the final goal would require the agent to explore the environment through a training process at the end of which the model would have internalized the environment. By instead allowing the annotation of the environment, there are passages and waypoints that are intermediate targets to be pursued, and this allows agents, through training a macro behavioral specification basically guiding them, to reach intermediate targets until the final one is in sight, and then it should be pursued.

However, reaching targets that have been previously visited has a negative reward, because it implies moving back away from the final goal, and it makes it much less reasonable to try to "exploit" the reward to reach a formally reasonable but totally implausible policy (i.e., reach as many intermediate targets before reaching the final one before the end of the episode). Negative rewards thus are used to suggest that some actions should not be chosen unless they eventually lead to the final goal (and unless better alternatives do the same): a small negative reward granted due to the simple passage of time is usual, which pushes agents to avoid standing still and to actively look for solutions, but we also have negative rewards due to proxemics (as introduced in the foundational work [25]), and to penalize walking too close to walls (again, unless necessary). Finally, the penalization of actions leading to a position from which no target (either intermediate or final) can be seen stimulates agents to pursue the goals.

It must be stressed that the definition of this function is both crucial and hard to complete; moreover, the definition of the reward function is related to the adopted training process, in our case, a curriculum-based approach, so we needed to anticipate some elements in these considerations that we more thoroughly introduce shortly. Let us consider, for instance, the last point, where the penalization to actions bring an agent to a position from which no target can be perceived. We can wonder if having a small bonus for actually seeing a target instead would work analogously: all positive rewards, however, should be defined carefully, because they can lead to pathological behaviors. In this case, in complex scenarios, the training process can converge to a local stationary point in the policy space associated with a behavior for which an agent finds an intermediate target and stands still, achieving a relatively small bonus for each subsequent decision of the episode, rather than trying to reach the final target. This would imply receiving a long sequence of negative rewards. In turn, the small bonus for actually having a target in sight is used in one of the scenarios included in the curriculum (in particular, observe), whose goal is to lead agents to learn that, in certain situations, they should simply stand still, for instance while queuing and waiting for a bottleneck to become reachable, instead of performing overly frequent and essentially useless small turns at very low velocity (or while standing still).

We decided to set the duration of an episode to a very high number of turns. Having adopted a curriculum-based approach, episodes are strongly related to the steps of the curriculum (each episode belongs to a step of the curriculum), and they are generally to be solved (termination conditions are given in Section 4.1) before moving forward to the next stage of the curriculum. As shown in Section 4.5, the overall approach has good convergence properties.

3.5. Adopted RL Algorithm

For this study and experimentation. we adopted the state-of-the-art deep RL algorithm provided by ML-Agents and, in particular, Proximal Policy Optimization (PPO), initially introduced by [26]). PPO is a policy gradient algorithm whose goal is directly learning the policy function π by calculating the gradient of the return achieved as a result of the action choice. Methods of this kind have better convergence properties than dynamic programming methods, but they need a more abundant set of training samples.

Policy gradients function by learning the policy's parameters through a policy score function, $J(\Theta)$, through which it is possible to apply gradient ascent to maximize the score of the policy with respect to the policy's parameters, Θ. A common way to define the policy score function is through a loss function:

$$L^{PG}(\Theta) = E_t[log\pi_\Theta(a_t|s_t)]A_t \quad (5)$$

which is the expected value of the log probability of taking action a_t at state s_t times the advantage function A_t, representing an estimate of the relative value of the taken action. As such, when the advantage estimate is positive, the gradient is positive as well. By means of gradient ascent, the probability of taking the correct action increases, while the probabilities of the actions associated with negative advantage instead decrease in the other case.

The goal of this study was essentially to evaluate the adequacy of the overall approach to the problem of achieving a proper pedestrian simulation model, without introducing novel RL algorithms. We did not compare the performance of different RL algorithms on the same problem, which will be the object of future studies.

4. Curriculum Learning

4.1. Rationale of the Approach

Curriculum learning, introduced by [8], represents a strategy within machine learning initially devised with the aim of reducing the training times by presenting examples in a specific order of increasing difficulty during training, illustrating gradually more concepts and more complications to the overall decision. Curriculum learning was later employed more specifically as a *transfer* learning technique in RL and multiagent RL, as discussed by [9]. The agent can exploit experiences acquired by carrying out simpler tasks while training to solve more complex ones, in an *intra-agent* transfer learning scheme. In some situation, it was also reported to support a better generalization of the overall training process (see, for instance, [27]). The capability of an agent to generalize the experience and be able to face situations not already experienced during training by leveraging elements of similarity with past experiences is also extremely important for our problem. Pedestrian simulation generally implies analyzing the implications of different, alternative designs on the same crowding condition, without having to perform training for every specific design (which would lead to incomparable results, because they would be achieved by means of different pedestrian models). Within our specific context, in particular, we verified that agents can be trained to "solve" individual scenarios that are present in our curriculum, and, in some cases, the training would even be shorter than the overall curriculum based training process. However, the achieved pedestrian model was not able to produce plausible results in all of the scenarios included in the curriculum, which were assembled as a reasonable representation of a wide class of indoor environments.

A naive application of a curriculum approach, however, initially led to issues somewhat resembling the *vanishing gradient* problem (as discussed by [28]). Technically, here we do not have a recurrent neural network (or an extremely deep one such as those employed for classification of images trained on huge annotated datasets) but, as we show, the overall training process is relatively long and the "oldest experiences" are overridden by the more recent ones.

Within each step of the curriculum execution, a number of parallel executions (for the proposed results 16) of scenarios associated with the specific curriculum steps is carried out. Each execution (representing an episode) can be completed by the agents (every agent reaches the goal) or when a specified duration is reached (some agents have not yet reached the goal); then, it is repeated, unless a successful termination condition for the curriculum step is verified. A step of the curriculum is considered successfully completed whenever two conditions are met: (i) a sufficiently high number of agents have been trained in the scenario (a fixed number, manually established considering the level of crowding in the scenario), and (ii) the average cumulative reward for trained agents in the last episode, excluding the top and bottom 10% (for avoiding being excessively influenced by a small number of outliers), exceeds a given threshold (specifically configured for every step of the curriculum, being dependent on the configuration of the environment). These termination conditions are important, and they can probably be improved and generalized, but, for the time being, we accepted the limit of a manual- and expert-based definition.

The finally adopted approach, therefore, proceeds training agents in a set of scenarios in growing complexity, one at a time, and provides a final retraining in a selected number of earlier scenarios before the end of the overall training to refresh previously acquired competences.

4.2. Details of the Curriculum

Starting from the above considerations, we defined a specific curriculum for RL pedestrian agents based on this sequence of tasks of increasing complexity that were subgoals of the overall training:

- Steer and walk toward a target;
- Steer to face target;
- Reach the target in narrow corridors;
- Walk through bends avoiding walking too close to walls;
- Avoid collisions with agents walking in the same direction;
- Avoid collisions with agents walking in conflicting directions;
- Combine all behaviors.

We defined this sequence through our expertise in the context of pedestrian simulation, as well as according to a preliminary experimental phase in which we identified issues and difficulties in achieving the desired behavior. For instance, the second step—steering to face a target—was introduced after initial experiments in which we realized that as a consequence of training in more geometrically complex scenarios, agents sometimes had difficulties in finding their targets when the environment was not essentially "guiding them" toward the final target.

It would be interesting to evaluate to what extent this sequence is robust, if it can be improved, or if it is close to the optimum, but such an analysis was not performed at this stage of the research, because we were interested in evaluating the adequacy of the approach and the possibility of achieving promising results in the domain of pedestrian simulation. This kind of analysis (also of ablative nature: is this curriculum minimal or can some steps be safely removed?) on the structure and content of the curriculum will be the object of future studies.

We also included specific test scenarios, that is, environments that were not included in the training curriculum but that were used to evaluate the ability of agents to exhibit plausible behaviors in scenarios that were not experienced in the training phase, rather than just showing that they memorized the environments they had seen.

4.3. Training Environments

Table 2 reports the different environments that were defined for each of the subgoals of the overall training. It also shows which environment was included in the final retraining phase that had to be carried out before using the trained agents for simulation in new environments.

Ti save space, we do not describe every environment and scenario included in the curriculum; instead, we provide a selection of these training environments in Figure 3. Several of these scenarios replicate experiments that were carried out with real pedestrians to study specific behaviors, such as the analyses by [29] or by [30], although we currently did not investigate high-density situations that seem difficult to simulate with a tool such as Unity (which includes 3D models for pedestrians and components for the management of physics that should be overridden for managing significant levels of density, e.g., higher than 1 pedestrian per square meter).

Table 2. Training environment curriculum.

Behavior	Environment	Retraining
Steer and walk toward a target	StartEz	✗
	Start	✓
Steer to face target	Observe	✓
Reach the target in narrow corridors	Easy corridor	✗
Walk through bends avoiding walking too close to walls	Turns	✗
	Turns with obstacles	✓
Avoid collisions with agents walking in the same direction	Unidirectional door	✓
Avoid collisions with agents walking in conflicting directions	Corridor	✓
	Intersection	✓
	T Junction	✓
Combine all behaviors	Crowded Bidirectional Door	✓

We also do not have the space for commenting on the training in all of these scenarios; however, we can highlight some stylized findings that we did observe:

- Within the corridor environment, agents learn to walk in lanes that, due to the low density, are quite stable.
- The turns and turns with obstacles environments produce plausible results in terms of trajectories, but this is mostly due to the placement of intermediate target helping agents in having smooth and plausible paths (as suggested in Section 3.1); once again, similar issues with the management of pedestrian trajectories in bends is present are model-based simulation approaches, as discussed by [21], and in more general situations, as discussed by [31].
- All the environments in which agents had to face narrow passages were crucial in leading them to accept the trade off between choosing some actions leading to an immediate negative reward (i.e., passing close to a wall) and achieving a longer-term positive reward (i.e., reaching the final target).
- All the environments in which agents had to interact with others were analogously decisive, but with a different role: they helped agents understand how to balance the need to slow down, and sometimes even stopping and waiting (when steering is simply not possible or not sufficient) to avoid collisions, with the overall necessary intermediate and final goal orientation. In some situations, at least within our training process, something similar to the "faster is slower" effect [32] was present, because without proper motivations, agents would have inevitably ended up pushing others, and they would not have learned some respectful and collaborative behavior, which is essential to queuing processes.

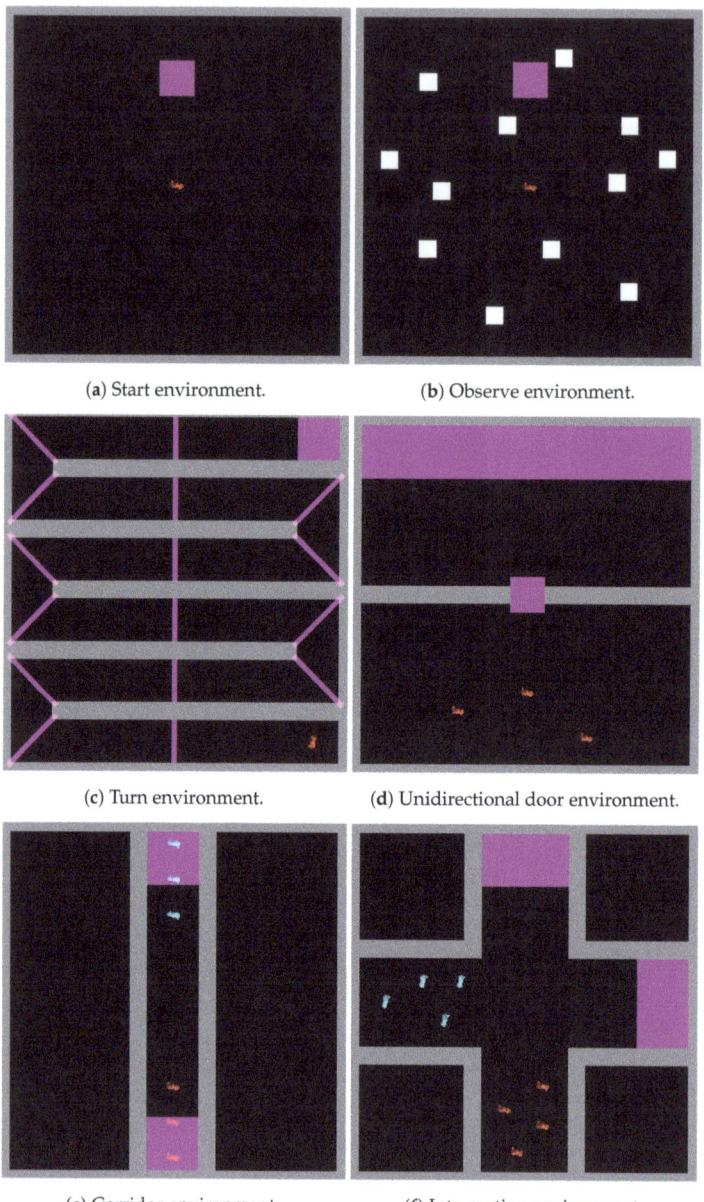

(a) Start environment. (b) Observe environment.

(c) Turn environment. (d) Unidirectional door environment.

(e) Corridor environment. (f) Intersection environment.

Figure 3. A selection of training environments: white blocks are obstacles, and agents can be red or blue to indicate that they belong to groups having different goals in the environment (e.g., the eastern or northern exits in the intersection environment).

4.4. Training Configuration

Listing 1 reports the defined training configuration file (detailed descriptions of different fields are reported at https://github.com/Unity-Technologies/ml-agents/blob/release_16_docs/docs/Training-Configuration-File.md, accessed on 11 November 2022). The employed ML-Agents version we adopted was 0.25.1 for Python and 1.0.7 for Unity.

Listing 1. Training configuration file.

```
ehaviors:
 edestrian:
  rainer_type: ppo
  yperparameters:
   atch_size: 512
   uffer_size: 5120
   earning_rate: 0.003
   eta: 0.01
   earning_rate_schedule: constant
  etwork_settings:
   idden_units: 256
   um_layers: 2
  eward_signals:
   xtrinsic:
    amma: 0.99
    trength: 1.0
  ax_steps: 100000000000000000
  ime_horizon: 64
```

Once again, we were interested in evaluating the adequacy of the approach, so we did not perform a systematic analysis of the effect of changing the different hyperparameters. This task will be object of future studies. We just comment here on some of the adopted choices:

- The neural network employed within the PPO algorithm is a fully connected network with 2 hidden layers of 256 nodes each (remember that the agent has 185 observation input signals, associated with inputs to this neural network); a bigger network leads to (sometimes much) longer training times, but it does not improve the quality of the achieved results, whereas a smaller network does not converge to a reasonable policy.
- We employed a basic PPO without curiosity mechanisms, as presented by [33]; therefore, we had essentially just extrinsic reward signals.
- We adopted a very high number for max_steps to let the curriculum guide the actual training, rather than predefined parameters. We also maintained the default value of `time_horizon`.

4.5. Reward Trend During Training

The preliminary tests that we conducted before reaching this configuration for the curriculum, which were based on a single scenario or were based on curricula significantly more compact than the one described above, were unsuccessful, or, at least, they did not produce good results within the same time frame associated with training with this configuration for the curriculum.

The overall training time with the defined curriculum varied according to different factors, but on a Windows-based PC with an Intel Core i7-6820HL @ 2.70 GHz, employing only the CPU (the adopted version of ML-Agents suggests doing so, becuase it would not properly exploit a GPU), would require around 37 min to reach the final retraining phase (which is significantly shorter). Technically, agents were trained in 9 equal environments at the same time, with a Unity velocity set to 100 (i.e., one second of simulation execution corresponded to 100 simulated seconds). The available hardware would not allow further compression of simulated time, but future developments in the ML-Agents framework could produce significant improvements (especially if they would fully exploit GPUs). On the other hand, such a possibility would call for some changes in the training phase workflow.

Figure 4 shows the trend in the cumulative reward. The Tensorboard average reward is the raw measure provided by Tensorboard, while the *average reward* is computed averaging out the cumulative reward achieved by agents in 36 episodes within an environment. The *Trimmed average reward* actually removes the 10% top- and 10% bottom-performing episodes.

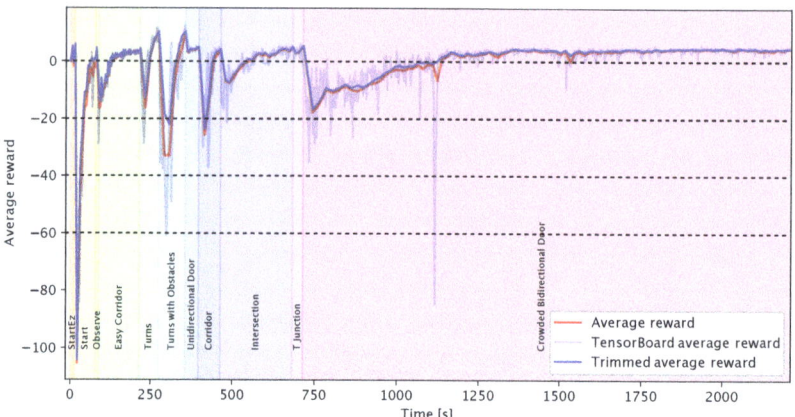

Figure 4. Trend in the reward throughout the training phase.

The different colors highlight the duration of the different scenarios of the curriculum. As expected, the reward dropped (sometimes dramatically) when agents changed the environment, but over time, the training converged. It also clearly shows that environments in which agents have more significant interactions are tougher for training the algorithm. A vanilla PPO was able to successfully converge in such situations, which are much closer to situations that call for specific multiagent RL algorithms. In these situations, the basic approaches often fail due instability in the reward trend that depends on more factors outside the scope of control of the trained agent; specific reward functions that balance individual and aggregated level evaluation of the situation and new algorithms are typically employed. We also conducted an analogous experimentation considering groups of pedestrians, a situation that makes pedestrian-to-pedestrian interaction both more complex and much more frequent (essentially uniformly present in each step of the training) than the type described in the present study, and PPO was not able to converge. The description of this additional experimentation was beyond the scope of the present study.

5. Analysis of Achieved Results

5.1. Qualitative Analysis of Generalization in Test Scenarios

After the training phase, we evaluated the ability of the trained agents to perform smooth and plausible movements in some specific environments that were not presented within the training phase. The goal was basically to understand if the approach was able to grant pedestrian agents, through the above-described training process, a general capability to produce realistic behaviors even in newly encountered situations.

In particular, we evaluated agents' behaviors in the environment depicted in Figure 5 (*"anchor"* environment), in which agents enter from the NE and NW corners make a sharp bend and move north (a movement pattern with a junction between two flows that is not that different from the T-junction environment). Trained agents do not have particular problems, although they might have a hesitation close to the point in which the flows merge due to the sudden necessity to interact and coordinate with other pedestrians coming from the two entrances (something that is also plausible and that can be qualitatively observed in real-world experiments).

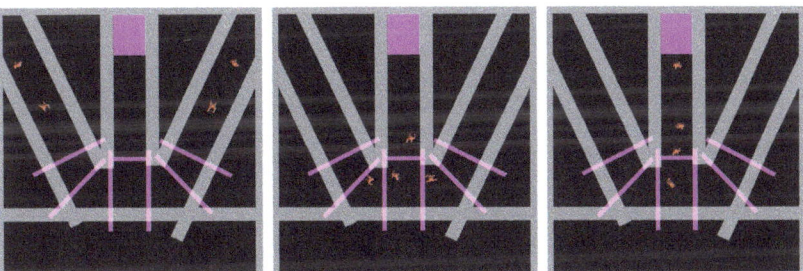

Figure 5. Anchor environment execution.

Figure 6 shows the *"omega"* environment, a maze-like structure in which 90° and U-turns to the right and left are present without choices among different passages (the flow is unique, and there are basically no choices for agents, which need to regulate the distances from other agents and obstacles). We emphasize that the training environments did not include all of these configurations for bends. Trained agents exhibited a reasonable behavior, slowing down before the bends to avoid collisions with walls.

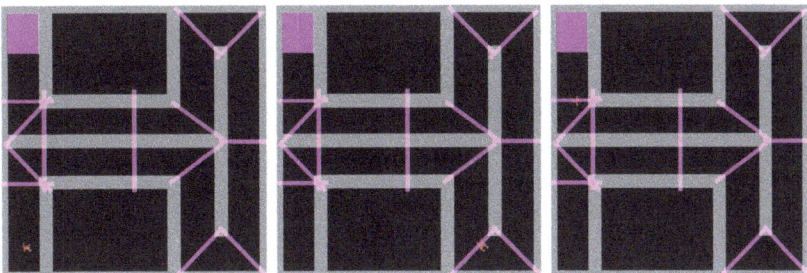

Figure 6. Omega environment execution.

The environment shown in Figure 7 (*"door choice"*) is a relatively simple situation that includes the choice of a passage between two alternatives leading from the southern to the central region, in addition to a single passage to the northern region that includes the final target. Within the training environments, agents never face a situation in which they have to choose among two or more intermediate targets, and we wanted to understand if instead it would be necessary to include this kind of situation in a proper curriculum for training pedestrian dynamics.

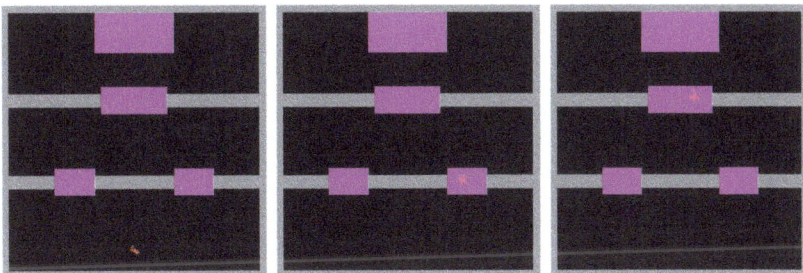

Figure 7. "Door choice" environment execution.

Trained agents did not have a problem in performing a plausible movement pattern in this scenario. They did not always choose the closest passage, but (i) real-world experiments showed that real pedestrians are not necessarily optimizing the expected travel time (although this generally happens when additional factors to distance, such as congestion, influence their decisions); (ii) additional modifications to the model and to the training curriculum would be necessary to achieve a complete capability to perform way-finding in more complicated situations, especially to be competitive with hand-written and calibrated models.

Figure 8 finally depicts the *"bidirectional door"* environment, a variant of the "crowded bidirectional door" employed in the training. The situation in which the agent is trained includes a number of pedestrians trying to move from the northern to the southern room and vice versa. The lower number of pedestrians present in this situation, coupled with their random initial position, paradoxically can represent a problem for the agents, because they cannot perceive the potential conflict until the very last moments. This scenario was therefore aimed at finding out if the trained agents were able to move at free-flow speed and then slow down when they perceive a conflicting pedestrian, avoiding it while avoiding a complete disruption of the overall trajectory.

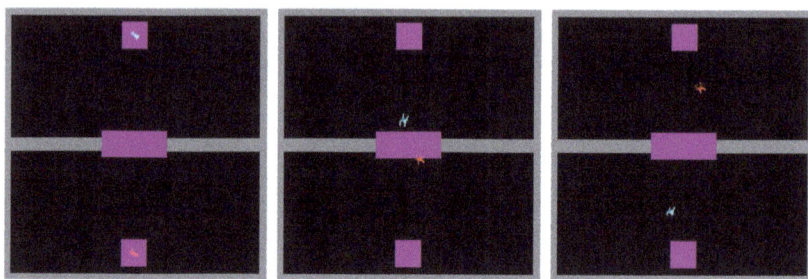

Figure 8. "Bidirectional door" environment execution.

When agents had initial positions granting them immediate mutual perception, they would start moving cautiously, and they crossed the door keeping their right, then moved to the final target. Otherwise, agents started moving at full velocity until they perceived each other, slowing down, and again changing position to avoid each other when passing through the door, generally keeping their right. Sometimes agents did not follow the most direct path to the final target after passing through the door, but the overall behavior was acceptable.

We did not test if the side preference changed or in what proportion, something that could be due to the randomness in the training process or to some systematic bias (maybe due to the spatial structure of the training environments) that leads to an uneven distribution of this preference.

5.2. Quantitative Analyses of Achieved Pedestrian Dynamics

While we mostly talked about the results from an RL perspective (training convergence and trend in the reward during training), and we qualitatively described the overall pedestrian behavior in test environments, we now show some quantitative results in one of the most complicated and challenging environments, the "crowded bidirectional door".

First, Figure 9 shows the distribution of the desired and actual (average) walking speed of pedestrians during a single execution, showing that pedestrian interactions coupled with the environmental structure played a significant role in shaping the overall system dynamics. Agents needed to negotiate who will pass first through the door, and this happened without direct forms of interaction, just through the mutual perception and the learned behavioral policy, which has embedded a sort of emergent norm (e.g., "cautiously approach a passage and pass without bumping other people, stopping and waiting if necessary"). We also appreciate the finding that basically all agents smoothly performed their movement. Some agents were very fast, but the slowest ones (due to the initial position, they were bound to wait for the others to pass through the door) still moved at about 0.5 m/s.

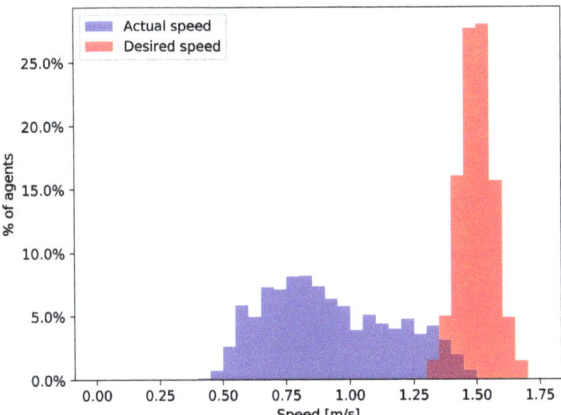

Figure 9. Desired and actual walking speeds in the "crowded bidirectional door" environment.

Figure 10a,b show agents' trajectories in the whole "crowded bidirectional door" environment and in a focused area centered on the door, respectively, to better highlight the movement patterns and some observable systematic implications of the model definition. Red trajectories are associated with pedestrians starting in the southern region, whereas the blue ones are associated with those starting from the northern part of the environment. Some relevant comments about this overall resulting dynamics can be provided:

- For the qualitative analysis of the "bidirectional door" environment, we observed a preference, because agents systematically used the right side of the passage, forming stable lanes, that were instrumental to the overall smoothness of the flow; the door was actually wide enough to accommodate the passage of two pedestrians, and in the presence of a narrower passage, the result would likely be different. This kind of phenomenon is observed in the real world, but it is not necessarily stable (especially at higher densities [34]). Our primary target, compatibly with the limits of the Unity framework and adopted 3D pedestrian models, was not to model high-density situations, and narrow passages essentially implied a locally high density, so we think that, for this model, this level of density is probably the limit.
- Although agents used most of the passage distributing relatively well, they systematically avoided points close to the walls. This was partly due to the physics of the Unity framework, which would not allow a collision between a pedestrian and a wall. However, the sharp and especially straight borders (in [35], real world trajectories have "sharp" borders, but they are "jagged") of the blue and red point clouds on the side of the walls (but not on the border between pedestrian flows) seem to suggest that the proxemic threshold for wall distance indicated in the reward function was perfectly (and maybe too systematically) internalized by the trained agents.

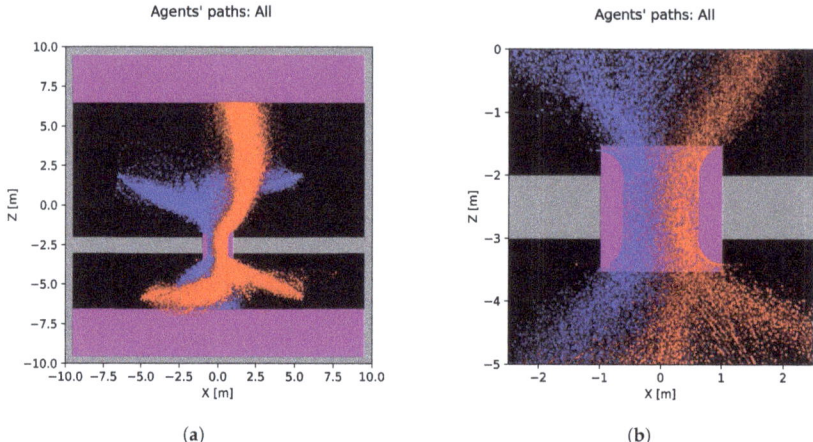

Figure 10. Agent trajectories in the "crowded bidirectional door" environment. (**a**) Agent positions in the overall environment. (**b**) Agent positions in the door area.

Figure 11 shows a fundamental diagram, in particular the relationship between walking speed and density in a given area (a 5 m × 5 m square centered on the door connecting the northern and southern regions.) Velocity dropped, as expected, with the increase in the density (as extensively discussed, for instance, in [35]). A quantitative comparison with real-world data was however not reasonable at this stage of the research, because the measurement mechanism is quite basic and might need improvements (measuring density is still object of discussion and research, as discussed by [36]). However, the velocity levels are plausible, and the drop in velocity with the growth in the density was expected, although it was maybe a bit larger than what is observed in reality. The achieved movement pattern is explainable but probably not the one that was expected. Agents cautiously approached the passage, because the initial distribution and density were such that they almost immediately could perceive another pedestrian potentially causing a collision, plus several other pedestrians competing for using the door. When they finally moved through the door, they actually sped up and reach maximum velocity in the door area (also because the reward function tells them that being close to walls is unpleasant, so they try to minimize the time spent in this condition). However, they have to slow down to coordinate with agents after the door that let them pass. While this movement pattern seems to be not in conflict with available observations [30], additional comparisons are necessary for more serious validation. We also have to consider the fact that learning to balance goal-driven tendencies and collision avoidance within an RL approach to pedestrian simulation is not simple, and past attempts generally ended in failures to complete some movement patterns, as discussed by [18].

A systematic validation of the model is still probably not that important because the model is still the object of study and improvement; we provide some additional results that can be used as a form of comparison with data about real-world pedestrian dynamics. In particular, the T-junction environment was used for observing the pedestrian dynamics that were analyzed by [30]. Figure 12 shows where the pedestrians' positions, focused in the area where the flows originated from the right and left sides of the area, actually merge, and a heatmap shows pedestrians' average velocity in the different points of the environment, with a metric scale supporting interpretation and comparison with experimentally observed data. The results are interesting and promising: the density of our simulations was actually lower than that experienced by pedestrians in real-world experiments, but the movement patterns showed some stylized movements that are in good agreement with real-world data. (i) The lower part of the square in which the left and right corridors meet is not used much by pedestrians, who tend to have a smooth and more round trajectory within the bend, (ii) pedestrians tend to keep to their side but some mixing between pedestrians coming from the left and right sides of the environment could be observed after the bend, when the pedestrians move toward the upper part of the environment. The level of density within this simulation was still too low to have a reasonable comparison with real-world experiments, and this represents one of the limits of the current simulation framework. However, the observed velocities also showed that interaction among agents, within the merge area and at the beginning of the north corridor, led to conflicts and a reduction in walking speed, in agreement with expectations and empirical evidence.

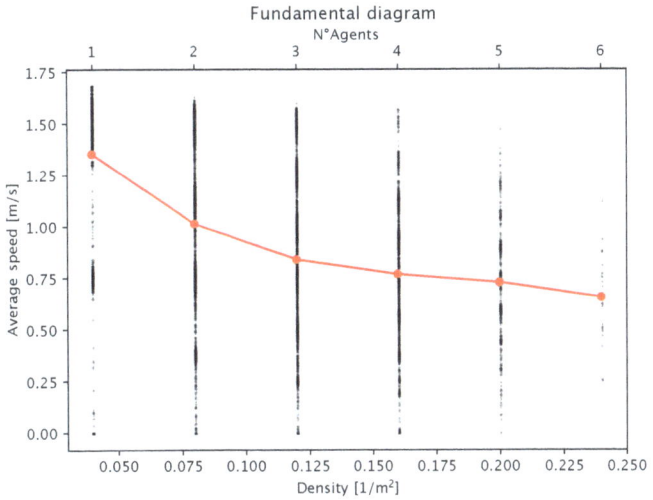

Figure 11. Fundamental diagram (speed vs. density) in a 25 m^2 (5 × 5 m) area around the door.

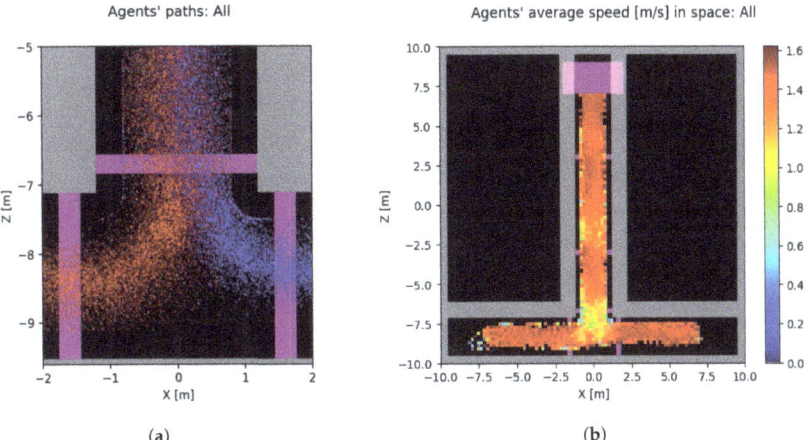

Figure 12. Quantitative results describing pedestrians' dynamics in the T-junction environment. (a) Agents' positions in the merge area. (b) Agents' velocities in the whole environment.

In terms of the scalability of the approach, we were able to perform experiments with over two hundred agents employing the decision-making model trained through the described method. The overall *inference* scalability was therefore quite reasonable. On the other hand, the *training* scalability was much more limited (it would currently be impossible to perform the proposed training workflow with hundreds of agents), although, as suggested above, the adoption of GPU support in the training phase would significantly improve the situation.

5.3. Limitations in Large Environments

While the achieved results are generally encouraging, and they suggest that the overall goals of the research are plausibly within reach, there are a number of limitations, some of which have already been considered in defining the approach and for which we have some analyses and considerations.

First, although the proposed approach was set on a microscopic scale, the considered environments, despite being reasonably representative of human indoor environments, do not present relatively large halls, so one might wonder if the model achieved through the above-described RL procedure would be able to generate plausible behaviors.

We defined a few additional environments in which we could perform experiments to acquire some insight into the above query. Figure 13 shows two environments lager than the ones in which the training took place (50 m by 50 m squares), structured into lecture-hall-like rooms in which a relatively large number of agents (60 per room) was initially positioned. Agents must exit these rooms, enter a common corridor, and move toward the northern exit. The two environments differed in the position of doors in the lecture halls, which were positioned in the corner of the room for the environment in Figure 13a and at a midwall position for the environment in Figure 13b.

We performed several experiments with agents whose behavior was based on the above-defined training procedure. While most of them were able to successfully vacate the room, some of them (in particular due to the fact that the single exits from the rooms represented bottleneck) took some time to vacate them); in almost every situation, a small number of agents was unable to complete the task within reasonable time. While most of the other agents were able to queue nearby the room exit and then move toward the final target and exit the environment, the failing agents remained in the room, effectively unable to locate the intermediate target, traveling around in circles. Our interpretation of this behavior is that the room size was large enough to make the combination of the defined perception mechanism and curriculum experience insufficient for robust environment navigation.

Therefore, and only with the aim of determining the possibility of adding experiences to agents' training by presenting them additional environments in the curriculum, we introduced two additional scenarios at the end of the above defined curriculum. In particular, we created two large environments, depicted in Figure 13c,d, to propose situations in which the agent needed to turn around to find an intermediate target that was both relatively far and not immediately in sight, and to further experience situations in which agents must find a way to coordinate actions, for instance, by queueing and waiting for other agents having a better initial position to vacate an area of shared interest (i.e., the bottleneck). These environments were similar, both in terms of structure and intended effects on training, to other ones that were already present in the curriculum, which could probably be substituted by these new ones, or we could consider randomizing not just the position of doors, but also the size of the environment (at least within a predefined range). For the sake of simplicity, however, we simply initially added these two steps to the curriculum and considered the effects on training and the final capability of agents to successfully perform the tasks. The achieved results were encouraging: situations of agents that lost track in the large environment with lecture halls were avoided, and agents were, in general less, inclined to move quickly toward the lecture hall exit, forming a jam; they were more respectful of personal distances. A more quantitative discussion of the results in this scenario would require a more thorough analysis, but the present results show that the overall curriculum approach represents a plausible step toward achieving if not an acceptable general model for pedestrian movement, at least a useful starting point for a short fine-tuning phase to be carried out in the specific studied situation.

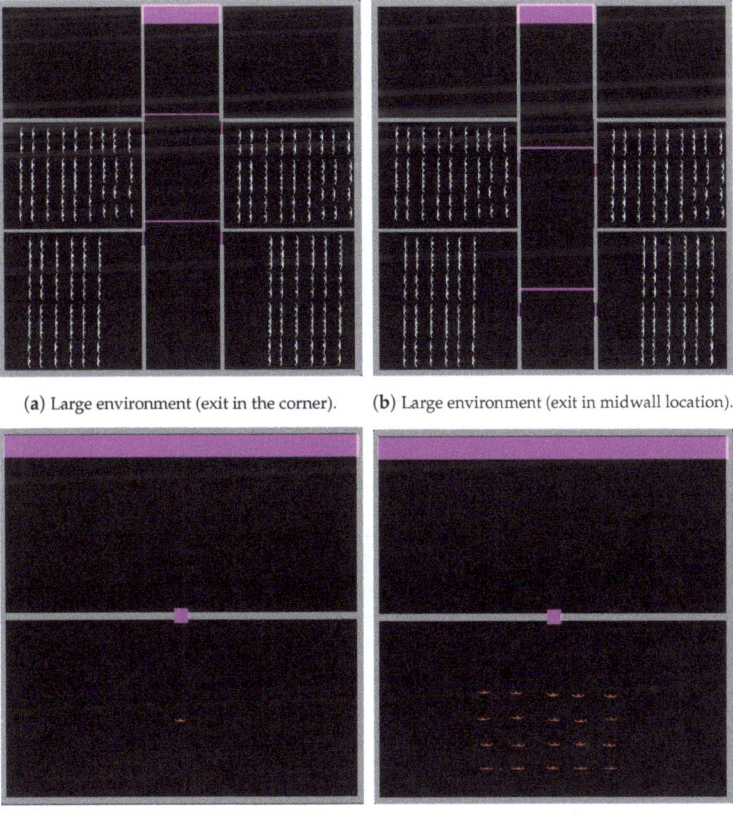

(**a**) Large environment (exit in the corner). (**b**) Large environment (exit in midwall location).

(**c**) Additional bottleneck environment. (**d**) Analogous crowded environment.

Figure 13. Additional large environments in which the model was tested (**a**,**b**), and those finally included in the curriculum (**c**,**d**).

6. Conclusions and Future Developments

This paper presented a study exploring the adequacy of applying RL techniques to pedestrian simulation, not just focusing on the possibility to train agents through RL techniques to move within a specific environment, but also considering the need to achieve general models, which are applicable to a wide range of situations. The results we achieved and described in the paper are promising and encouraging, and they show that developing pedestrians and crowd simulation with RL is feasible.

The present study has several limitations that essentially define different lines for future research in different contexts:

- Analysis is needed of the effects of changes in the RL algorithm, hyperparameters, configuration of the curriculum (in this last element, an ablation study in an attempt to identify a minimal curriculum). We reached the presented solution performing some comparisons with alternative settings, but a systematic analysis of each of these aspect would require a focused specific study.
- Validation and expressiveness: Additional quantitative experiments are necessary to improve the evaluation of the achieved results on the side of pedestrian simulation, toward a validation of the model or the acquisition of new objectives for model improvement. Moreover, there might be different situations (especially environmental geometries). For instance, none of the environments we described proposed round

walls; we just employed straight ones. Here, the agents trained through the approach described in this paper might not be able to produce realistic behaviors.
- Overcoming some current behavioral limits: (i) Modeling groups within the simulated pedestrian population is not possible, and preliminary work in this direction suggests that a change in the adopted RL algorithm will be necessary due to the more systematic presence of agent-to-agent interaction, and a multiagent reinforcement learning perspective is necessary [37]; (ii) dealing with high-density situations, which will also imply more fine tuning Unity-specific parameters for the management of the interaction of 3D articulated models such as those associated with pedestrians; (iii) further exploring the capability of the model to perform way-finding, possibly achieving the capability to adapt to the perceived level of congestion, as discussed by [13].

Beyond the specific results in the proposed application context, we think that the overall approach can be of wider interest and applicability, at least within a number of situations in which agent-based and multiagent models and technologies have already been applied. Whenever the analyzed system is intrinsically distributed in nature, when it comprises a number of autonomously deciding but interacting entities, the presented approach can represent at least a starting point to the definition of an effective simulation model. As a general comment to the approach, it must be clear that it represents a useful instrument in the management of what we intuitively called the "knowledge bottleneck" about how to define the actions of agents acting and interacting within the simulated environment, Nonetheless, this approach still requires substantial knowledge about the studied domain. In our example, knowledge and experience in the pedestrian and crowd behavior, and in how to measure, evaluate, and analyze it, were instrumental in the definition of a perception and action model, in the definition of the reward function, and in the configuration of the curriculum-based training process.

Author Contributions: Conceptualization, G.V.; methodology, G.V.; software, T.C.; validation, G.V.; formal analysis, G.V. and T.C.; investigation, G.V. and T.C.; resources, G.V. and T.C.; data curation, G.V. and T.C.; writing—original draft preparation, G.V.; writing—review and editing, G.V. and T.C.; visualization, G.V. and T.C.; supervision, G.V. and T.C.; project administration, G.V. and T.C.; funding acquisition, G.V. All authors have read and agreed to the published version of the manuscript.

Funding: This research received no external funding.

Data Availability Statement: Authors are in the process of preparation of a software repository in which the framework will be made available for download and for sake of reproducibility.

Acknowledgments: The authors would like to thank Thomas Albericci and Alberto Gibertini for their support in the development of the experimental framework and execution of the simulation campaign. The authors also want to express gratitude to the anonymous reviewers for their support in improving the manuscript.

Conflicts of Interest: The authors declare no conflicts of interest.

References

1. Bazzan, A.L.C.; Klügl, F. A review on agent-based technology for traffic and transportation. *Knowl. Eng. Rev.* **2014**, *29*, 375–403. [CrossRef]
2. Savaglio, C.; Ganzha, M.; Paprzycki, M.; Bădică, C.; Ivanović, M.; Fortino, G. Agent-based Internet of Things: State-of-the-art and research challenges. *Future Gener. Comput. Syst.* **2020**, *102*, 1038–1053. [CrossRef]
3. Croatti, A.; Gabellini, M.; Montagna, S.; Ricci, A. On the Integration of Agents and Digital Twins in Healthcare. *J. Med. Syst.* **2020**, *44*, 161. [CrossRef]
4. Mualla, Y.; Najjar, A.; Daoud, A.; Galland, S.; Nicolle, C.; Yasar, A.U.H.; Shakshuki, E. Agent-based simulation of unmanned aerial vehicles in civilian applications: A systematic literature review and research directions. *Future Gener. Comput. Syst.* **2019**, *100*, 344–364. [CrossRef]
5. Sutton, R.S.; Barto, A.G. *Reinforcement Learning, an Introduction*, 2nd ed.; MIT Press: Cambridge, MA, USA, 2018.
6. Russell, S.J.; Norvig, P. *Artificial Intelligence: A Modern Approach*, 4th ed.; Pearson: London, UK, 2020.
7. Bandini, S.; Manzoni, S.; Vizzari, G. Agent Based Modeling and Simulation: An Informatics Perspective. *J. Artif. Soc. Soc. Simul.* **2009**, *12*, 4.

8. Bengio, Y.; Louradour, J.; Collobert, R.; Weston, J. Curriculum Learning. In Proceedings of the Proceedings of the 26th Annual International Conference on Machine Learning, Montreal, QC, Canada, 14–18 June 2009; Association for Computing Machinery: New York, NY, USA, 2009; pp. 41–48. [CrossRef]
9. Silva, F.L.D.; Costa, A.H.R. A survey on transfer learning for multiagent reinforcement learning systems. *J. Artif. Intell. Res.* **2019**, *64*, 645–703. [CrossRef]
10. Helbing, D.; Molnár, P. Social force model for pedestrian dynamics. *Phys. Rev. E* **1995**, *51*, 4282–4286. [CrossRef]
11. Schadschneider, A.; Klingsch, W.; Klüpfel, H.; Kretz, T.; Rogsch, C.; Seyfried, A. Evacuation Dynamics: Empirical Results, Modeling and Applications. In *Encyclopedia of Complexity and Systems Science*; Meyers, R.A., Ed.; Springer: Berlin/Heidelberg, Germany, 2009; pp. 3142–3176.
12. Andresen, E.; Chraibi, M.; Seyfried, A. A representation of partial spatial knowledge: A cognitive map approach for evacuation simulations. *Transp. A Transp. Sci.* **2018**, *14*, 433–467. [CrossRef]
13. Vizzari, G.; Crociani, L.; Bandini, S. An agent-based model for plausible wayfinding in pedestrian simulation. *Eng. Appl. Artif. Intell.* **2020**, *87*, 103241. [CrossRef]
14. Junges, R.; Klügl, F. Programming Agent Behavior by Learning is Simulation Models. *Appl. Artif. Intell.* **2012**, *26*, 349–375. [CrossRef]
15. Tordeux, A.; Chraibi, M.; Seyfried, A.; Schadschneider, A. Prediction of pedestrian dynamics in complex architectures with artificial neural networks. *J. Intell. Transp. Syst.* **2020**, *24*, 556–568. [CrossRef]
16. Zhao, X.; Xia, L.; Zhang, J.; Song, W. Artificial neural network based modeling on unidirectional and bidirectional pedestrian flow at straight corridors. *Phys. A Stat. Mech. Its Appl.* **2020**, *547*, 123825. [CrossRef]
17. Kothari, P.; Kreiss, S.; Alahi, A. Human Trajectory Forecasting in Crowds: A Deep Learning Perspective. *IEEE Trans. Intell. Transp. Syst.* **2021**, *23*, 7386–7400. [CrossRef]
18. Martinez-Gil, F.; Lozano, M.; Fernández, F. Emergent behaviors and scalability for multi-agent reinforcement learning-based pedestrian models. *Simul. Model. Pract. Theory* **2017**, *74*, 117–133. [CrossRef]
19. Cheng, C.; Kolobov, A.; Swaminathan, A. Heuristic-Guided Reinforcement Learning. In Proceedings of the Advances in Neural Information Processing Systems 34: Annual Conference on Neural Information Processing Systems 2021, NeurIPS 2021, Virtual, 6–14 December 2021; Ranzato, M., Beygelzimer, A., Dauphin, Y.N., Liang, P., Vaughan, J.W., Eds.; NeurIPS Foundation: San Diego, CA, USA, 2021; pp. 13550–13563.
20. Crociani, L.; Vizzari, G.; Bandini, S. Modeling Environmental Operative Elements in Agent-Based Pedestrian Simulation. *Collect. Dyn.* **2020**, *5*, 508–511. [CrossRef]
21. Crociani, L.; Shimura, K.; Vizzari, G.; Bandini, S. Simulating Pedestrian Dynamics in Corners and Bends: A Floor Field Approach. In *Proceedings of the Cellular Automata*; Mauri, G., El Yacoubi, S., Dennunzio, A., Nishinari, K., Manzoni, L., Eds.; Springer International Publishing: Cham, Switzerland, 2018; pp. 460–469.
22. Dias, C.; Lovreglio, R. Calibrating cellular automaton models for pedestrians walking through corners. *Phys. Lett. A* **2018**, *382*, 1255–1261. [CrossRef]
23. Paris, S.; Donikian, S. Activity-Driven Populace: A Cognitive Approach to Crowd Simulation. *IEEE Comput. Graph. Appl.* **2009**, *29*, 34–43. [CrossRef]
24. Haghani, M.; Sarvi, M. Imitative (herd) behaviour in direction decision-making hinders efficiency of crowd evacuation processes. *Saf. Sci.* **2019**, *114*, 49–60. [CrossRef]
25. Hall, E.T. *The Hidden Dimension*; Doubleday: New York, NY, USA, 1966.
26. Schulman, J.; Wolski, F.; Dhariwal, P.; Radford, A.; Klimov, O. Proximal Policy Optimization Algorithms. *arXiv* **2017**, arXiv:1707.06347.
27. Baker, B.; Kanitscheider, I.; Markov, T.M.; Wu, Y.; Powell, G.; McGrew, B.; Mordatch, I. Emergent Tool Use From Multi-Agent Autocurricula. In Proceedings of the 8th International Conference on Learning Representations, ICLR 2020, Addis Ababa, Ethiopia, 26–30 April 2020.
28. Hochreiter, S. The Vanishing Gradient Problem During Learning Recurrent Neural Nets and Problem Solutions. *Int. J. Uncertain. Fuzziness Knowl.-Based Syst.* **1998**, *6*, 107–116. [CrossRef]
29. Zhang, J.; Seyfried, A. Comparison of intersecting pedestrian flows based on experiments. *Phys. A Stat. Mech. Its Appl.* **2014**, *405*, 316–325. [CrossRef]
30. Zhang, J.; Klingsch, W.; Schadschneider, A.; Seyfried, A. Transitions in pedestrian fundamental diagrams of straight corridors and T-junctions. *J. Stat. Mech. Theory Exp.* **2011**, *2011*, P06004. [CrossRef]
31. Chraibi, M.; Steffen, B. The Automatic Generation of an Efficient Floor Field for CA Simulations in Crowd Management. In *Cellular Automata—Proceedings of the 13th International Conference on Cellular Automata for Research and Industry, ACRI 2018, Como, Italy, 17–21 September 2018*; Lecture Notes in Computer Science; Mauri, G., Yacoubi, S.E., Dennunzio, A., Nishinari, K., Manzoni, L., Eds.; Springer: Berlin/Heidelberg, Germany, 2018; Volume 11115, pp. 185–195. [CrossRef]
32. Haghani, M.; Sarvi, M.; Shahhoseini, Z. When 'push' does not come to 'shove': Revisiting 'faster is slower' in collective egress of human crowds. *Transp. Res. Part Policy Pract.* **2019**, *122*, 51–69. [CrossRef]
33. Pathak, D.; Agrawal, P.; Efros, A.A.; Darrell, T. Curiosity-driven Exploration by Self-supervised Prediction. In Proceedings of the 34th International Conference on Machine Learning, ICML 2017, Sydney, NSW, Australia, 6–11 August 2017; Volume 70, pp. 2778–2787.

34. Kretz, T.; Wölki, M.; Schreckenberg, M. Characterizing correlations of flow oscillations at bottlenecks. *J. Stat. Mech. Theory Exp.* **2006**, *2006*, P02005. [CrossRef]
35. Zhang, J.; Klingsch, W.; Schadschneider, A.; Seyfried, A. Ordering in bidirectional pedestrian flows and its influence on the fundamental diagram. *J. Stat. Mech. Theory Exp.* **2012**, *2012*, P02002. [CrossRef]
36. Steffen, B.; Seyfried, A. Methods for measuring pedestrian density, flow, speed and direction with minimal scatter. *Phys. A Stat. Mech. Its Appl.* **2010**, *389*, 1902–1910. [CrossRef]
37. Zhang, K.; Yang, Z.; Başar, T., Multi-Agent Reinforcement Learning: A Selective Overview of Theories and Algorithms. In *Handbook of Reinforcement Learning and Control*; Vamvoudakis, K.G., Wan, Y., Lewis, F.L., Cansever, D., Eds.; Springer International Publishing: Cham, Switzerland, 2021; pp. 321–384. [CrossRef]

Disclaimer/Publisher's Note: The statements, opinions and data contained in all publications are solely those of the individual author(s) and contributor(s) and not of MDPI and/or the editor(s). MDPI and/or the editor(s) disclaim responsibility for any injury to people or property resulting from any ideas, methods, instructions or products referred to in the content.

Article

A Multi-Agent Approach to Binary Classification Using Swarm Intelligence

Sean Grimes * and David E. Breen

Department of Computer Science, Drexel University, Philadelphia, PA 19104, USA
* Correspondence: spg63@drexel.edu

Abstract: Wisdom-of-Crowds-Bots (WoC-Bots) are simple, modular agents working together in a multi-agent environment to collectively make binary predictions. The agents represent a knowledge-diverse crowd, with each agent trained on a subset of available information. A honey-bee-derived swarm aggregation mechanism is used to elicit a collective prediction with an associated confidence value from the agents. Due to their multi-agent design, WoC-Bots can be distributed across multiple hardware nodes, include new features without re-training existing agents, and the aggregation mechanism can be used to incorporate predictions from other sources, thus improving overall predictive accuracy of the system. In addition to these advantages, we demonstrate that WoC-Bots are competitive with other top classification methods on three datasets and apply our system to a real-world sports betting problem, producing a consistent return on investment from 1 January 2021 through 15 November 2022 on most major sports.

Keywords: prediction; swarm; multi-agent; Wisdom-of-Crowds; sports-betting; collective-intelligence

1. Introduction

We present extensions to a multi-agent-based system for binary classification, capable of being distributed across multiple compute nodes, using agents each with partial knowledge of the information space. The system is based on Wisdom of Crowds (WoC), and uses a honey-bee-derived swarm mechanism for opinion aggregation, that provides a prediction and associated confidence value. The multi-agent design allows new features to be incorporated into classification problems without re-training the existing agents, reducing the computational costs and training time of adding new feature to an existing model.

Artificial neural networks (ANNs), specifically deep neural networks (DNNs), and ensemble learning methods are the current 'state-of-the-art' approaches to classification problems [1]. Both families of methods, however, require a computationally expensive re-training operation to incorporate additional features, i.e., if the number of inputs to the network changes [2]. Some specialized types of convolutional (CNN) and recurrent (RNN) neural networks allow for variable length input for image and time-series data (respectively), but add significant complexity over typical DNNs and do not generalize to binary classification problems well [3,4]. Transfer learning allows a classification model developed for one task to be used for a different, but related, task and can incorporate an additional intermediate input layer to process additional input features [5]. Transfer learning adds complexity to a network and does not guarantee that an existing model will perform well on the new problem [6]; the features used to train the original model may not be predictive for the new dataset [7].

A multi-agent-based classification system has been previously reported in Grimes et al. [8], and is based on prediction markets (PMs), WoC, and swarm intelligence—the collective intelligence or behavior of simple, decentralized agents. PMs are built to determine the probability of a future event taking place by collecting truthful input from participants, aggregating the input and forming a collective knowledge [9]. In order to accomplish this,

PMs expect all participants to be well-informed agents, a very difficult requirement to implement with computer-based agents in any non-trivial system. Expert computer-based agents are difficult to develop, both from a programming and information availability standpoint; how can you program an 'expert' agent without having significant subject matter knowledge yourself? Othman said on computer-based agents "agent-based modeling of the real world is necessarily dubious. Attempting to model the rich tapestry of human behavior within economic structures—both the outstandingly bad and the terrifically complex—is a futile task" [10].

Wisdom of Crowds is an alternative prediction method which performs better with an information-diverse pool of participants and does not require expert participation. Predictive error decreases as information diversity increases [11]. WoC achieves this behavior by requiring a competent opinion aggregation mechanism that takes input from all participating agents and outputs an overall prediction. Previous work in this area has investigated the Unweighted Mean Model (UWM), Weighted Voter Model (WVM) and other aggregation mechanisms [12–14]. The classification method used in our work employs a more complex, honey-bee-derived swarm optimization algorithm as the WoC aggregation mechanism, which has previously shown to improve classification performance compared with other methods and allows for a confidence score to be associated with each prediction [8].

In this paper, we show how this method compares with other common classification methods using three datasets, predicting the metastasis status of breast cancer patients, the success of Hollywood movies, and the satisfaction of airline passengers. We demonstrate that additional features can be included without re-training existing agents, which improves overall classification performance. Additionally, we show this algorithm can be distributed across multiple compute nodes, and describe the challenges with distributed opinion aggregation and our approach to solving those challenges. We also include real-world results when applying this method to sports betting across multiple sports and bet types.

Section 2 describes the overall system design, how additional features are added to the classification problem, a 'meta-swarm' method, and how the system is distributed across hardware nodes. Section 2 also describes the datasets used in testing and how our system was applied to a sports betting problem. Section 3 presents comparisons with our WoC-Bots and 'meta-swarm' methods with results from AdaBoost, XGBoost, Random Forest, a Deep Neural Network, and Logistic Regression for three datasets. Also presented are results for including additional features, distributing our agents across hardware nodes, and multi-year testing on sports betting. Section 4 discusses the presented results and reviews the benefits to a multi-agent design. Section 5 reiterates our approach using WoC-Bots and swarm intelligence in addition to presenting possible ideas for future work.

2. Materials and Methods

2.1. System Design

The classification method uses simple agents (WoC-Bots) without expert knowledge. At the core of each agent is a simple multi-layer perceptron (MLP) classifier with 1 to 4 hidden layers—depending on input size—generally rounded to the nearest integer value of $input\_size * 0.3$. The goal is for the MLP to be as shallow as possible while still extracting features from the input. For the datasets we have tested, using the formula above has proven successful given each agent only receives a small subset of the available input. The rest of the agent is designed as a modular system for efficiently modifying agent behavior. Each agent's MLP classifier is trained with a different, small, subset of features. This initially gives the group of agents a diverse set of knowledge. All agents with relevant knowledge for the classification task then interact with one another, share knowledge, determine the trust they have in other agents and the confidence in their own opinion, and change their opinion given enough evidence.

As with work described in [8,14], we use the DeepLearning4j (DL4J) [15] implementations of the Adam updater [16], softmax activation function [17], and standard stochastic gradient descent for the MLP implementation and deep neural network. DL4J is "an open-source, distributed deep-learning project in Java and Scala spearheaded by the people at Skymind, a San Francisco-based business intelligence and enterprise software firm". All code was written in Kotlin (versions 1.3.20–1.3.41), running on the Java Virtual Machine (version 11). All features, agent history data, and trained agents were stored in SQLite3 databases. IntelliJ IDE was used for our development environment.

Prior to the interaction and opinion aggregation steps, each agent receives 1 to 4 highly correlated features in common between all agents. Feature correlation was determined using principal component analysis, run externally to the system being described here. Other available features were distributed across multiple agents randomly, with duplicate features and multiple agents with the same feature set neither limited nor encouraged. Agents that show poor MLP classification performance during the initial training step are not included in the remainder of the classification steps. Poor performance was defined as less than 50% accuracy on the test set.

2.1.1. Interaction Period

Table 1 presents the attributes which describe the internal state of an agent during the interaction period. Many of these values are available to other agents during interactions within the social interaction arena. The `confidence` attribute can be biased to favor accuracy, precision, or recall metrics depending on which metric is the most important for the given classification problem. For example, a classification task such as the breast cancer dataset we present in the results section may benefit from biasing towards recall to better avoid false negative predictions

$$confidence = accuracy * 0.25 + precision * 0.25 + recall * 0.50. \qquad (1)$$

Table 1. Internal scoring variables.

Variable	Description
current_prediction	Binary, class 0 or class 1.
trust_score	Updated during interaction based on agreement and performance.
features	A list of features used by the agent's classifier.
prior_performance	Long-term history of agent performance, varied between 0.7 and 1.3 where 1.0 is average performance.
certainty	Initialized to MLP classifier performance, updated during interaction period. Represents how strongly the agent believes in the current prediction.
eval_accuracy	Initial classification accuracy.
eval_precision	Initial classification precision.
eval_recall	Initial classification recall.
confidence	Biased value based on accuracy, precision, and recall.

The interaction arena can take any 2D shape comprised of square faces. In this work, the arena is a square with the number of available discrete spaces available to the agents equal to 2 times the number of participating agents. Agents are initialized randomly inside the arena and agents are not allowed to share spaces with other agents at initialization. After initialization, up to two agents can share the same space, which starts an interaction between those two agents. Following the interaction, agents are moved within the arena in a "Manhattan-like" fashion, moving either one space north, south, east, or west within the bounds of the arena. The direction is randomly selected and agents cannot interact with each other two times in a row or more than twice within five separate movements. Agents who cannot move because of these restrictions are 'teleported' to a randomly selected empty space within the arena. Agents are also 'teleported' to a random empty space every 10–15 iterations to further facilitate information dispersal.

The interaction period is operated in discrete iterations; each agent is moved during each iteration and all interactions between agents must complete before the next iteration can begin. The number of iterations is based on the number of participating agents where

$$interaction_{iters} = num\_agents * 0.10 \tag{2}$$

to balance run time with information dispersal. Any agent with missing data for the current classification task does not participate; all agents in the interaction arena and subsequent steps have complete information for the features they were assigned for the current classification question.

During the interaction period, two agents, agent a and agent b, interact when sharing a space within the arena. The following equations govern the updates to the internal state of agents during the interaction and determine if and when an agent's prediction will change, and what confidence the agent has in its current prediction. The equations assume agent a is receiving information from agent b, however during an interaction the inverse will also occur.

Once two agents meet, agent a first determines how willing it is to accept information from agent b, a function of a's current certainty, where $a_{certainty}$ represents a's current certainty and $a_{acceptance}$ represents a's willingness to accept information from agent b

$$a_{acceptance} = 1.0 - a_{certainty}. \tag{3}$$

Agent a determines how much influence to allow agent b, $b_{influence}$, a function of agent b's confidence, trust_score, and certainty, and agent a's acceptance, $a_{acceptance}$,

$$b_{influence} = b_{confidence} * a_{acceptance} * b_{trustCertainty}, \tag{4}$$

where $b_{trustCertainty}$ represents trust_score * certainty,

$$b_{trustCertainty} = b_{trustScore} * b_{certainty}. \tag{5}$$

Agent b's influence is further modified based on agent b's prior_performance, represented by $b_{priorPerf}$, such that the corrected influence can be represented by $b_{correctedInfluence}$,

$$b_{correctedInfluence} = b_{priorPerf} * b_{influence}. \tag{6}$$

If agent a and agent b have different predictions, $b_{correctInfluence}$ will be multiplied by -1 to act against agent a's current predictive belief. Agent a's updated certainty, $a_{certainty}$, can be calculated by Equation (7), where a's certainty increases if both agents a and b have the same prediction and decreases if the predictions are different,

$$a_{certainty} = a_{certainty} + b_{correctedInfluence}. \tag{7}$$

If agent a's certainty value falls below 0.50, agent a will change its prediction. If the prediction is changed, agent a's certainty is updated by Equation (8),

$$a_{certainty} = 1.0 - a_{certainty}. \tag{8}$$

2.1.2. Swarm Aggregation

Opinion aggregation in WoC systems is an open problem [18]. Previous work has shown promise in aggregating human opinions [19,20], and the work presented here continues with the honey-bee-derived "swarm intelligence" aggregation mechanism published in [8]. Bees and other simple organisms are able to forage large areas, finding near optimal food sources and new nesting locations by sending a subset of bees, the scouts, to search the environment around the colony [21]. Returning scout bees will advertise the location of their find using a "waggle dance", with the movements indicating direction relative to the sun and the length of dance thought to be proportional to the quality of the discovery. Scouts which dance for longer periods of time generally recruit more bees to their discovery [22]. As long as a discovered food source remains high quality, the bees will continue to advertise it, allowing it to remain productive. Advertisement of the food source will naturally decline as it becomes depleted and fewer scouts advertise the location [23].

The computer-based version of the honey-bee foraging algorithm operates similarly. The swarm aggregation step is designed for all agents to support a single binary opinion, either 1 or 0. All of the agents which participated in the social interaction step must also participate in the swarming step. Initially, 20% of agents are randomly selected to be "presenters", similar to the "scout" bees in nature. The remaining agents are assigned as "watchers", which are assigned to the presenting agents. Initial assignment of "watchers" is accomplished using 'fitness proportionate selection' [24]. Each of the presenting agents has an assigned probability, a_{prop}, between 0 and 1, where the sum of all probabilities of all presenting agents is 1 after normalization. The probability for each agent is calculated by Equation (9), an equally weighted combination of the presenting agent's prior_performance, $a_{priorPerf}$, confidence, $a_{confidence}$, and trust_score, a_{trust}.

$$a_{prob} = (a_{priorPerf} + a_{confidence} + a_{trust})/3 \qquad (9)$$

The 'fitness proportionate selection' algorithm uses the computed probabilities for each of the presenting agents to assign "watchers" to be supporters of each of the presenting agents using a_{prob}, such that presenting agents with a higher a_{prob} will more frequently be assigned "watchers" than those with a lower a_{prob} value. "Watchers" can only be assigned to a single presenting agent at any given time and 'support' that presenting agent simply by being assigned to it. However, each "watcher" can request re-assignment two times if its prediction is different from that of the presenting agent it was assigned and if its $a_{priorPerf}$ value is higher than the presenting agent's, allowing a high performing agent the opportunity to move to an agent it thinks better represents its prediction. However, this process uses the same fitness proportionate selection algorithm, which offers no guarantee that a move will be seen as beneficial to the watching agent. The limit of two moves accomplishes three things, reducing compute time, preventing a potential infinite loop of constant movement, and introducing further diversity of opinion where agents may be assigned to support an agent they disagree with. Once assignment and agent movement is complete the presenting agent represents itself and the watchers it was assigned; e.g., if a presenting agent is assigned 10 watchers that presenting agent's opinion is now worth 11 'votes' during the final aggregation process.

The "presenters" and "watchers" now represent a swarm of agents which goes through iterative steps to arrive at a collective binary prediction with an associated confidence value by repeating the process of assigning watchers to presenters and taking a vote of all presenting agents. While this process is running, the decision threshold is iteratively lowered if a higher threshold has not been met. The initial threshold is 100% agreement directly following the initial process of assigning watchers to presenters and taking a vote of all presenting agents. If this threshold is met, the prediction is considered "Very High Confidence", the prediction and confidence are returned and the swarming period ends. When there is no immediate agreement, agents perform an interaction period with all of the "watchers" assigned to the "presenter" and with the "presenting" agent. This interaction step follows the same protocols outlined in Section 2.1.1. This step facilitates additional information dispersal between agents. Following the interaction step, a new group of presenting agents is randomly selected and the agents go through the same steps as previously outlined. This process can run for an additional 100 iterations with the threshold for agreement lowered to 90%; if the 90% threshold is met at any point the prediction is considered "High Confidence" and the swarming period ends.

When neither of the above thresholds are met, the decision threshold is further reduced to 75% for an additional 50 iterations of selection, voting, and interaction. If the

75% threshold is met the prediction is "Medium Confidence". However, if the threshold has still not been met, a weighted vote is taken from all presenters and watchers, and the prediction is "Low Confidence". The weighting is based on the agent's `certainty` score, with agents more certain in their opinion given more weight than those who are less certain. The confidence thresholds were initially selected using the breast cancer dataset described in Section 2.2.1 based on experimentation with the goal of 100% accuracy for the "Very High Confidence" interval. The number of iterations for each threshold was selected to balance classification performance with runtime. A future goal is to automate the selection of threshold values for each dataset and classification constraints. For example, some usage scenarios may prefer more samples captured in the "Very High Confidence" interval while having a lower average accuracy for that category.

The confidence categories can be summarized as:

- Very High Confidence: All presenting agents agree on a prediction class immediately following fitness proportionate selection,
- High Confidence: 90% of presenting agents agree on a prediction class within 100 iterations of the swarming process,
- Medium Confidence: 75% of presenting agents agree on a prediction class after 100–150 additional iterations of the swarming process,
- Low Confidence: Weighted vote of presenters and watchers if above thresholds are not met.

2.1.3. Additional Features

Another benefit of the multi-agent approach to classification versus a traditional monolithic neural network is the ease at which new input features can be added to the computation. While some convolutional networks can accept variable length inputs, most traditional networks can only be expanded vertically with new layers while holding existing weights stable. They cannot expand horizontally, i.e., to include previously unknown input feature(s), at the input layer without re-training the network [25]. While each of our agents has a fixed number of inputs at creation, an internal MLP network restriction, the interactive and swarm steps of the overall system do not have restrictions on the number of participating agents. As noted in Section 2.1.1, agents with missing data simply do not participate. A natural extension to the variable number of participating agents is the ability to include newly generated agents representing the new data, a feature that does not require the re-training of the existing agents.

When new features become available, we generate new agents using a combination of the new features and the existing features. Combining the new and existing features in the newly generated agents solves two problems; (1) new agents need to know about the features that the existing agents are trained on, and (2), the existing agents need a way to determine `trust_score` and `prior_performance` metrics for the newly generated agents. Both the social interaction arena and swarm components of the system rely on social variables built around agent prior performance, trust, and existing knowledge of features. Newly generated agents derive estimated `prior_performance` and `trust_scores` values from the existing features they receive. The estimates come from averaging these values from existing agents that have similar features. The averaging step does have some shortcomings, particularly when agents with similar, but not identical, features are used to generate the estimates; the estimated values may not accurately reflect the correct `trust_score` and `prior_performance` of the newly generated agents. However, the new agents have shorter interaction and prior performance histories compared with existing agents, which allows for larger initial modifications to these metrics during the interaction step, typically correcting any poor estimates within a few interaction periods.

Incremental features addition was tested using two datasets, one attempting to predict breast cancer metastasis status by including additional measurements of cellular morphology data derived from whole-slide images of a representative hematoxylin and eosin (H&E) stained slide of the primary tumor. These data are in addition to the primary dataset as described in Section 2.2.1. The second dataset that was used for testing attempted to predict the success of Hollywood movies. The initial predictions were made with a combined dataset from The Movie Database (TMDb) and MovieLens using only data available in both datasets. Additional features were included from MovieLens, which included cast information beyond the leading cast member, as well as information about the production company and producers. More information about these data are available in Section 2.2.2.

2.1.4. Meta-Swarm

An additional use of the multi-agent design and aggregation mechanism was developed to incorporate predictions from other sources. Sources can be other classification methods or direct predictions. This is conceptually similar to stacking in ensemble learning, where multiple weak learners predictions' are used as input to a 'meta-learner' and a regression method is used to combined the predictions from the weak learners [26]. However, in the system presented here, the original prediction from WoC-Bots and predictions from other sources are encapsulated into agents, replacing the MLP step as originally described in Section 2.1. As previously described, the agents are initialized in the interaction arena, interact socially to share information and develop trust, and an aggregate prediction with a confidence value is made following the swarm step.

This method has been applied to the breast cancer, Hollywood success, and airline satisfaction datasets using input from WoC-Bots, XGBoost, AdaBoost, RandomForest, Logistic Regression, and a Deep Neural Network. Our method was also used in a real-world application of the system for sports betting, using WoC-Bots and independent prediction sources as input. Previous testing has indicated that additional information sharing during the interaction phase improves overall predictive accuracy, precision, and recall [14]. Therefore, while applying this method, each input prediction was represented by five identical agents to facilitate additional information sharing within the interaction arena. Testing indicated no additional predictive benefit to representing each prediction with more than five agents. Agents which represented the same input prediction were allowed to interact with each other. Detailed results using the meta-swarm approach can be seen in Section 3 for the three datasets tested and the sports betting application.

2.1.5. System Distributability

The multi-agent nature of this system lends itself well to being distributed across multiple computational nodes using a cluster of otherwise independent machines. There are three main phases of this work to consider for distributability, the per-agent training phase where each small MLP network is trained, the social interaction phase, and the swarming phase where agents interact and vote before a system-wide prediction is made.

The training phase relies on a small amount of data which can be made available on a node-by-node basis or transferred across the network without significant delay. During this phase each agent is independent and distribution is straightforward. Agents can be placed on each node randomly, or using an initialization algorithm to optimally pick a node for each agent based on computational load or network limitations. The MLP network for each agent can be trained independently from any other agent and the small size and depth of the network do not limit training to powerful hardware.

The social interaction phase initializes all participating agents in the interaction arena. The flexible design of the arena allows each compute node to represent some subdivision of the full arena, e.g., an arena with 4 nodes and 120 possible spaces will be subdivided so that each node is responsible for a block of 30 spaces. An agent moving between each subdivision is moved between nodes. The movement algorithm governing each agent can encourage or discourage movement between nodes to balance information dispersal with network transit times. Figure 1 shows a possible configuration with a single interaction arena split across 16 nodes. The dark outline represents the bounds of the arena and the lighter internal lines represent boundaries between nodes. Agents can move between nodes freely during the interaction period, which requires network transfers, either explicitly from some node to another node, or implicitly through shared storage.

The work presented here takes advantage of a disk-based database and a networked Ceph storage cluster that is shared by each node to implicitly share data on each node without explicit network transfer; no agent is serialized for transfer across the network stack. After each iteration in the interaction arena, the state of each agent is flushed to an SQLite database, which is updated and accessible to all nodes using the networked Ceph storage cluster. As each agent crosses a boundary between nodes, a per-agent flag is set indicating on which node the agent is present. Each node checks a table to determine which agents are present on that node prior to the start of every interaction iteration.

Figure 1. Representation of the full interaction arena split across 16 nodes.

The swarming phase of the system can require frequent movement of agents between nodes due to the frequent re-selection process for "presenters" and "watchers" while the swarm is iterating. The selection process randomly selects "presenters" and then distributes agents to available nodes. This can reduce the benefit of distributing this method across multiple compute nodes, due to the additional run time cost from network transfers.

The swarming phase of the system can work in two distinct modes of operation. The first option requires a simple command and control node, which is responsible for selecting the "presenters" and "watchers", as described in Section 2.1.2, and uniformly distributes the agents to available nodes. Each additional iteration of the swarming process does, however, require global knowledge and control to re-distribute agents to each node. This method does produce results identical to swarming on a single node, but is the slower of the two options.

The second option allows localized swarming on each node with aggregation at the end of the swarming process. Following the interaction phase, the agents can either stay on their current node, or agents can be randomly distributed to nodes. There is no additional movement of agents between nodes throughout the swarming process. In order to accomplish this, a method of representing each node's prediction was developed. Initial methods attempted to assigned a weight to each node based on multiple factors, such as confidence category for the node's prediction, the average prior performance of agents on the node, the average prior performance of the top 15% of agents on the node, and the average confidence of all agents on the node and the top 15% of agents on the node. Of these methods, assigning a node weight based on average performance of the top 15% of agents produced the best results, however the accuracy of this method did not match the the previous option or single-node swarming.

Another method to represent each node was implemented and tested based on the meta-swarm that was described in Section 2.1.4. As with the above option, each node receives a random distribution of agents and the swarming process happens locally on each node. When the swarming process is complete each node's prediction is encapsulated into an agent and these agents are moved to a single node to interact and swarm before a final prediction is made. While this does require a single node capable of running the swarming process, the maximum number of agents is equal to the number of nodes and each agent is computationally simple, this should not present computational limitations for any node that is also capable of participating in the swarming process. This method has shown similar performance to the first, network-intensive option, on two of the three datasets presented in this paper.

2.2. Datasets

The following breast cancer metastasis status, Hollywood movie success, and airline satisfaction datasets were used to test our method against existing 'state-of-the-art' classification methods, including XGBoost [27], AdaBoost [28], RandomForest [29], Logistic Regression [30], and a DL4J DNN implementation. These methods were selected for comparison based on their state-of-the-art status and common use in binary classification tasks [1]. Logistic Regression was also considered for comparison to show performance against a pure statistical probability model. These datasets were also used to demonstrate the incremental feature addition component of our agent-based system. The sports betting data were used to demonstrate the flexibility of the agent-based design, making an initial classification prediction using data as described in Section 2.2.4, then including that prediction as a series of agents in a meta-swarm that utilizes predictions from other sources, aggregates the agent opinions, and renders a final prediction.

2.2.1. Breast Cancer Metastasis Status

We applied our agent-based method to predict lymph node metastasis status, node-positive or node-negative, in 483 de-identified breast cancer patients using all features which were available for at least 50% of patients. Previous work in this area considered only the most highly correlated features and required feature completeness [31,32]. The confidence attribute for all agents was biased to prefer high recall scores to better avoid false negatives, specifically $(0.25 * accuracy, 0.25 * precision, 0.50 * recall)$. Table 2 describes the clinical features available for use in the classification task. The additional cellular morphology features available for classification are:

- Cellular mean area
- Cellular mean circularity
- Cellular mean eccentricity
- Cellular mean intensity
- Standard area
- Standard circularity
- Standard eccentricity
- Standard intensity

Table 2. Characteristics of patient populations.

Feature	n = 483	%
Age		
≤45	103	21.3
>45	380	78.7
PT Max size (mm)		
≥200	5	1.0
100–199	15	3.1
50–99	51	10.6
25–49	125	25.9
0–24	271	56.1
unknown	16	3.3
Angio Lymphatic Invasion		
Absent	127	26.3
Present	200	41.4
Unknown	156	32.3
pT Stage		
Unknown	36	7.5
pT1	210	43.5
pT2	173	35.9
pT3/pT4	64	13.3
Histologic Grade		
Unknown	33	6.8
1	53	11.0
2	164	34.0
3	233	48.2
Tubule Formation		
Unknown	30	6.2
1 (>75%)	13	2.7
2 (10–75%)	98	20.3
3 (<10%)	342	70.8
Nuclear Grade		
Unknown	29	6.0
1	20	4.1
2	151	31.3
3	283	58.6
Lobular Extension		
Unknown	202	41.8
Absent	147	30.4
Present	134	27.7
Pagetoid Spread		
Unknown	213	44.1
Absent	177	36.6
Present	93	19.3
Perineureal Invasion		
Unknown	267	55.3
Absent	186	38.5
Present	30	6.2
Calcifications		
Unknown	115	23.8
Absent	126	26.1
Present	176	36.4
Present w/ DCIS	66	13.7
ER Status		
Unknown	51	10.6
Negative	155	32.1
Positive (>10%)	277	57.3

Table 2. *Cont.*

Feature	$n = 483$	%
PR Status		
Unknown	54	11.2
Negative	201	41.6
Positive (>10%)	228	47.2
P53 Status		
Unknown	81	16.8
Negative	255	52.8
Positive (>5%)	147	30.4
Ki67 Status		
Unknown	56	11.6
Negative	114	23.6
Positive (>14%)	313	64.8
Her2 Score		
Unknown	83	17.2
0	119	24.6
1	169	35.0
2	54	11.2
3	58	12.0

2.2.2. Hollywood Movie

Success of a movie was defined as its revenue being greater than 2× the reported budget for the movie, accounting for advertising and promotion budgets which are generally less than the production budget. This dataset came from combining TMDb and MovieLens datasets, accounting for movies included in both sources, gives 3699 movies available for testing and training. The `confidence` attribute for all agents was equally biased between accuracy, precision, and recall. The features found in Table 3 were used in the initial classification comparison testing and were originally selected based on principal component analysis, showing high correlation with predicting movie success. The following features were used for incremental feature addition testing:

- Cast, top 5 listed
- Crew, top 5 listed
- Production company
- Director

2.2.3. Airline Satisfaction

We used a publicly available airline passenger satisfaction dataset to test our method on a dataset with a large number of samples, roughly 120,000. Both the breast cancer and Hollywood movie dataset are small, with 483 and 3699 samples, respectively. The airline satisfaction dataset allowed us to verify that our agents are not over-fitting on specific input that may appear frequently and continues to perform in line with other popular classification methods. The `confidence` attribute for all agents was equally biased between accuracy, precision, and recall.

The dataset has 22 input features, seen in Table 4. Passengers reported being either satisfied, neutral, or not satisfied. We considered neutral passengers to be dissatisfied for binary classification purposes. This more evenly split the dataset (48% satisfied and 52% not satisfied) compared with considering neutral passengers satisfied. Features with a possible value of 0 were considered not applicable (N/A). For example, a 0 value for "In-flight WiFi satisfaction" indicates this feature was not present on the airplane, and not an applicable feature for classification for that customer.

Table 3. Features available for classification.

Features	Description
budget	given to all agents, reported budget for movie
tmdb_popularity	dynamic variable from TMDb API attempting to represent interest in movie
revenue	used for sanity checks, reported revenue
runtime	unreliable metric for success without including genre information
tmdb_vote_average	average score from TMDb, can be combined with ML average
tmdb_vote_count	total votes for a movie from TMDb, can be combined with ML count
ml_vote_average	average score from ML, can be combined with TMDb average
ml_vote_count	total votes for a movie from ML, can be combined with TMDb count
ml_tmdb_genres	combined genre information from TMDb and ML; first 2 listed genres used
vote_average	combined tmdb_vote_average and ml_vote_average
vote_count	combined tmdb_vote_count and ml_vote_count

Table 4. Airline features available for classification.

Features	Description
Gender	Passenger gender: male, female, other
Customer type	Loyal or disloyal
Age	Customer age
Type of travel	Personal or business
Seat class	First, business, eco+, eco
Flight distance	Distance of journey
In-flight WiFi satisfaction	0 (N/A) 1–5
Flight time convenience	Satisfied with departure/arrival time
Ease of online booking	0 (N/A) 1–5
Gate location satisfaction	1–5
Food/drink satisfaction	1–5
Online boarding satisfaction	0 (N/A) 1–5
Seat comfort	1–5
In-flight entertainment	0 (N/A) 1-5
On-board service satisfaction	0 (N/A) 1–5
Leg room satisfaction	0 (N/A) 1-5
Baggage handling satisfaction	0 (N/A) 1–5
Check-in service satisfaction	1–5
Cleanliness	1–5
Departure delay	in minutes
Arrival delay	in minutes

2.2.4. Sports Betting

The system was tested on sports betting data from January 2021 through November 2022 on college football, National Collegiate Athletic Association (NCAA) Football Bowl Subdivision (FBA), professional football, National Football League (NFL), college basketball (NCAA Division 1), professional basketball, National Basketball Association (NBA), professional hockey, National Hockey League (NHL), professional baseball, Major League Baseball (MLB), and professional soccer (multiple leagues). The system was tested primarily on "spread" bets, where the favorite needs to win by some pre-defined margin, or the losing team needs to lose by less than some pre-defined margin. It was also tested on "moneyline" bets, where the team that wins the game also wins the bet, with no "spread" taken into account. This is a more common bet type for lower scoring sports like baseball, hockey, and soccer. Moneyline bets are also common in basketball and football when teams are evenly matched and the spread would be very small, less than 2.5–3.5 points. Some testing was done on predicting the total score of a game, but this was not successful for any of the major sports. Professional soccer moneyline bets were tested with three possible outcomes: win, loss, and draw. The moneyline bets for all other tested sports were binary: win or lose. In total, roughly 10,500 bets were tested and the value of each bet was typically around 0.5–1% of 'units' available for betting. For example, if there were 1000 units available, each bet would typically represent 5 to 10 'units'.

Sports betting data were sourced from numerous independent data sources. The data used include historical betting odds data for the NHL, NBA, MLB, NFL, and NCAA basketball and football. Historical odds were also available for the five major European soccer leagues. Historical data for the US MLS soccer league were found to be inaccurate and were not used. Odds data for second-tier European soccer leagues were also found to be inaccurate for certain years and accurate for others. Only years with verified accurate data were included in the training set.

Play-by-play data were available for the NBA, NFL, and MLB. However, these play-by-play data were only used to build season-long statistical data for players and teams when those data were otherwise unavailable through free sources. Some preliminary testing has shown the granularity of play-by-play data increases the noise, which then decreases predictive performance. Roster data, injury information, and game-by-game stats were found on ESPN.com https://www.espn.com/ (accessed on 1 January 2021 through 15 November 2022), Yahoo! Sports https://sports.yahoo.com/ (accessed on 1 January 2021 through 15 November 2022), and The Action Network https://www.actionnetwork.com/ (accessed on 1 January 2021 through 15 November 2022).

ESPN.com was used to determine upcoming games. The Action Network publishes odds from major US-based sports books and was used to determine the best betting odds for upcoming games. For each game, agents were given information about the competing teams. Statistical information for each team was pulled from ESPN or Yahoo! Sports, looking at the past 3, 5, and 10 games, as well as season-long trends and associated stats, e.g., points scored vs. points allowed for NBA teams over the same 3, 5, and 10 games. Roster information for each team was gathered from ESPN and stats for the listed players are populated from both ESPN and Yahoo! Sports. Players season stats, as well as previous 3, 5, and 10 games stats are included. In some sports, match-up specific stats were also available, this included the NBA, NHL, and MLB. MLB stats also included pitcher vs. expected batter lineups from Yahoo! Sports. The current betting line is then pulled from The Action Network and the agents are asked, "will team a win by 5 points" if the spread betting line is "−5". Due to the limitations of making binary predictions, the agents will also be asked the same question on either side of the line until the prediction changes. Both the associated confidence from the swarm step and the distance from the published line when the opinion changes influence the overall confidence in the prediction, with greater distance from the published line giving more confidence in the prediction. For example, if the agents predict team a does not win by 6 points, there is less confidence in the published −5 betting line than when the agents predict team a will win by 9 points.

Predictions from other sources were also gathered and included in the 'meta-swarm' step, as described in Section 2.1.4. Predictions came from ESPN.com (BPI rankings), ESPN.com (fan rankings), Yahoo! Sports (fan rankings), The Action Network ('public' betting, 'expert' picks, 'sharp' action), SportsChatPlace https://scpbetting.com/ (accessed

on 1 January 2021 through 15 November 2022), CollegeFootballNews https://collegefootb
allnews.com/ (accessed on 1 January 2021 through 15 November 2022), Winners and Whiners https://winnersandwhiners.com/ (accessed on 1 January 2021 through 15 November 2022) and FiveThirtyEight https://fivethirtyeight.com/sports/ (accessed on 1 January 2021 through 15 November 2022).

3. Results

3.1. Classification Method Comparison

The following sections show comparisons on three datasets with our WoC-Bots method, the meta-swarm method described in Section 2.1.4 and five popular classification methods: AdaBoost, XGBoost, Random Forest, Deep Neural Network, and Logistic Regression.

3.1.1. Breast Cancer Metastasis

Figure 2 shows the comparison for accuracy, recall, and precision of WoC-Bots with the other classification methods for a breast cancer dataset, predicting node-positive or node-negative disease in breast cancer patients. The results presented here were generated using the clinical features identified in Table 2, but not the additional cellular morphology features described in Section 2.2.1. The leftmost set of columns shows results for the WoC-Bots method, the rightmost set of columns shows results for the "meta-swarm" method described in Section 2.1.4, taking all of the methods listed on Figure 2 as input. The other sets of columns represent popular classification methods. Random Forest produced the best accuracy at 86.9% and the best precision results at 84.0%. The DNN implementation produced the best recall at 92.5%. WoC-Bots outperformed AdaBoost and Logistic Regression in accuracy and recall, but had the second lowest precision results at 72.0% (tied with AdaBoost). The meta-swarm implementation, while not producing the best results for any of the three metrics, improved consistency between the three metrics, produced the second highest accuracy at 84.8%, and the second highest precision at 82.0%.

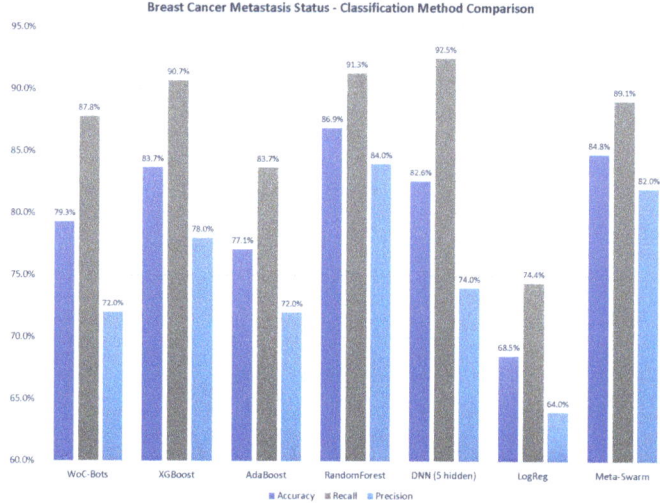

Figure 2. Comparison of five classification methods with two versions of the swarm (first and last columns) for the breast cancer dataset.

While WoC-Bots were outperformed by the XGBoost, Random Forest, and DNN methods, WoC-Bots can provide associated confidence values with each prediction. Table 5 shows how many predictions fall into each confidence interval and the intervals associated accuracy. The combined "Very High", "High", and "Medium" confidence interval captured 78.9% of patients with a combined accuracy of 86.8%. The "High" confidence interval captured 31.9% of patients with an accuracy of 93.1%. WoC-Bots are able to stratify patients into confidence intervals, allowing for improved accuracy within a subset of samples.

Table 5. Confidence Interval Distribution and Accuracy—WoC-Bots for Breast Cancer Metastasis Status.

Interval	$n = 483$	% of n	Accuracy (%)
Very High Confidence	3	0.62	100
High Confidence	154	31.9	93.1
Medium Confidence	224	46.4	82.3
Low Confidence	102	21.1	64.7
Very High + High + Medium	381	78.9	86.8

Figure 3 presents computation times, in milliseconds, needed to perform a single classification for this dataset using WoC-Bots and other methods. The timing results for all methods were run on the same hardware—AMD Threadripper 1950x CPU, 64 GB of RAM, and 2x Nvidia 2070 GPUs. WoC-Bots and the deep neural network were implemented in Java. The other methods were implemented in Python. As expected, methods which require additional iterative steps take longer to complete, with the WoC-Bots system having the most steps, and taking the most time.

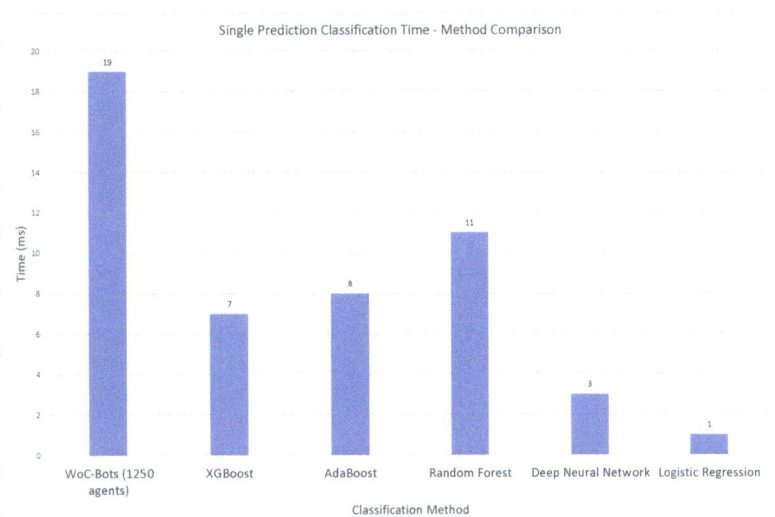

Figure 3. Runtime Comparison for a Single Prediction for All Methods.

3.1.2. Hollywood Movie Success

Figure 4 presents the same information as Figure 2 for the Hollywood movie success dataset. A movie was considered successful if the revenue was greater than two times the initial budget for the movie. The results presented here use the features listed in Table 3 only, not including the additional cast, crew, production, and director information. WoC-Bots performed very similarly to a DNN implementation, with 81.1% accuracy compared to 81.3% for the DNN. WoC-Bots outperformed the DNN with a precision of 84.0% compared with 82.9% and were outperformed on recall with 79.7% for WoC-Bots and 80.8% for the DNN. The XGBoost and Random Forest methods again outperformed the other classification methods on the accuracy and precision metrics.

The meta-swarm was again tested, outperforming all other methods with an accuracy of 83.7%. Additionally, only the XGBoost method had a better recall value at 82.9% compared with the meta-swarm's recall of 82.6%. Confidence intervals were tested with this dataset, but applied to the output of the meta-swarm instead of directly to WoC-Bots. Table 6 shows the results of this analysis, with 61.4% of samples captured in the "Very High", "High", and "Medium" confidence intervals with a combined accuracy of 87.8%. Additionally, the "Very High" interval was more useful for this dataset, capturing 1.4% of samples with an accuracy of 96.1% and the "High" interval captured over 25% of samples with an accuracy of 91.6%.

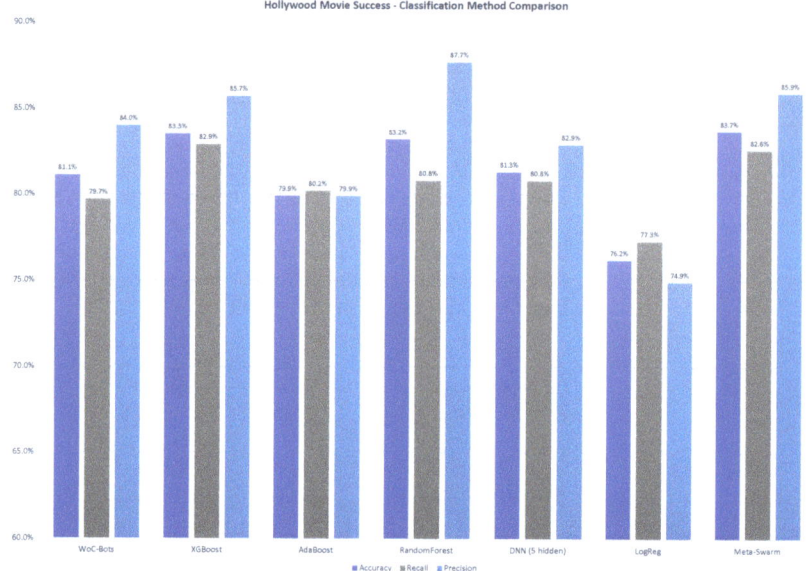

Figure 4. Comparison of five classification methods with two versions of the swarm (first and last columns) for the Hollywood movies dataset.

Table 6. Confidence Interval Distribution and Accuracy—Meta-Swarm for Hollywood Success.

Interval	$n = 3699$	% of n	Accuracy (%)
Very High Confidence	51	1.4	96.1
High Confidence	958	25.9	91.6
Medium Confidence	1261	34.1	84.5
Low Confidence	1428	38.6	77.3
Very High + High + Medium	2271	61.4	87.8

3.1.3. Airline Passenger Satisfaction

Figure 5 presents the same classifications methods as Figures 2 and 4. This dataset, however, was far more predictive than the previous datasets, with accuracies over 95% for all methods except logistic regression. Additionally, all methods were consistent with a slighter higher precision than accuracy, and a slightly lower recall than accuracy. WoC-Bots performed similarly to XGBoost, AdaBoost, and Random Forest, better than logistic regression, and slightly worse than the deep neural network. With most methods already performing well, the meta-swarm did not improve over any of them, though, did reduce variability between accuracy, precision, and recall. Table 7 shows the confidence intervals for the meta-swarm for this dataset. Over 15% of samples fell in the "Very High" interval, over 70% in the "High" interval with the remaining 15% split almost evenly between "Medium" and "Low" confidence. The accuracy values for each interval were very similar, with the "Very High Confidence" interval being outperformed by the "High" and "Medium" intervals. We did not find the confidence intervals to be useful for this dataset; the airline data are highly predictive which made it difficult to stratify samples into confidence intervals.

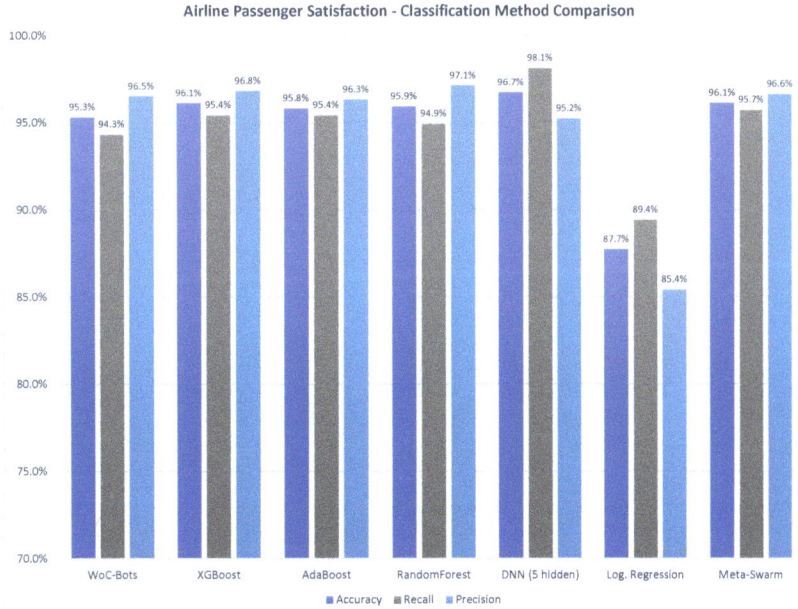

Figure 5. Comparison of five classification methods with two versions of the swarm (first and last columns) for the airline passenger satisfaction dataset.

Table 7. Confidence Interval Distribution and Accuracy—Meta-Swarm for Airline Passenger Satisfaction.

Interval	$n = 129{,}882$	% of n	Accuracy (%)
Very High Confidence	19,797	15.24	95.7
High Confidence	92,125	70.93	96.2
Medium Confidence	9109	7.01	95.9
Low Confidence	8851	6.81	95.7

3.2. Additional Features

The following sections show the predictive performance improvements produced when including additional features for the breast cancer and Hollywood movies datasets. The goal is to show our method can incorporate new features as they become available without requiring a costly re-training of the full system of agents, and without significant loss of predictive performance compared with a full re-training. This process requires generating new agents, which increases the total number of participating agents. In both datasets, we show results that control for additional predictive performance when including more agents in the simulation.

3.2.1. Breast Cancer Metastasis

Figure 6 shows the original accuracy of our WoC-Bots method for predicting lymph node metastasis status in breast cancer patients. The leftmost column shows the original results from Figure 2 with 750 agents. The second–from–left column shows the results when using the same clinical features only, but with 1250 agents. The accuracy improved by 0.13%, indicating that increasing the number of agents may minimally improve the accuracy.

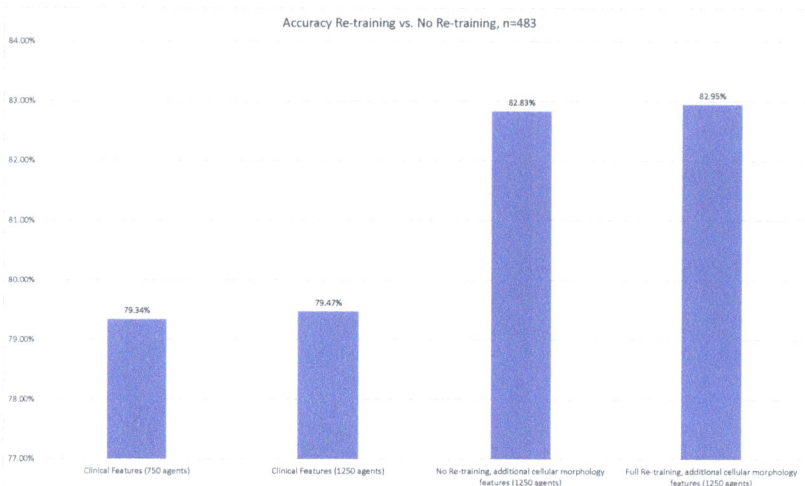

Figure 6. Cellular Morphology Features—System Accuracy.

The second-from-right column shows the prediction accuracy after adding the cellular morphology features to the original clinical features. We use the same number of agents (1250) as the previous test and generate additional agents as outlined in Section 2.1.3. In this case, the accuracy increased 3.49% from the original test (left column), and 3.36% as compared with the original clinical features and same number of agents (1250), indicating the accuracy increase largely comes from incorporating the new cellular morphology data rather than from simply generating additional agents. The rightmost column shows the accuracy results after fully re-training the agents with the original clinical features and additional cellular morphology data, with 1250 agents trained on all of the available data. This test shows a small increase in accuracy, 0.13%, compared with the prior method, but requires an expensive re-training of all participating agents. The time and computation cost of re-training depends on the number of agents and available hardware. Using 4x Nvidia GTX 1070 GPUs, an AMD Threadripper 1950x CPU, and an M.2 SSD for storage it takes 2 h, 25 min to generate and train 1250 new agents compared with 35 min to generate and train 500 new agents, a speedup of 4.1×. In testing, available GPU memory will have a large impact on total run time.

3.2.2. Hollywood Movie Success

Figure 7 shows similar results when adding new features to the Hollywood movie success test. For this dataset we started with 600 agents and an accuracy of 81.14%. The accuracy did increase more in this test by simply adding more agents, to 81.38%, an increase of 0.25% when moving from 600 to 1000 agents, shown in the second–from–left column. The second–from–right column shows the accuracy after including the additional cast, crew, production, and director information, an increase to 86.77% using the same number of agents, 1000. The rightmost column again shows the accuracy after fully re-training all 1000 agents with all features. We see a slightly larger increase compared with the breast cancer dataset, increasing to 87.81% from 86.77%, an increase of 1.04%.

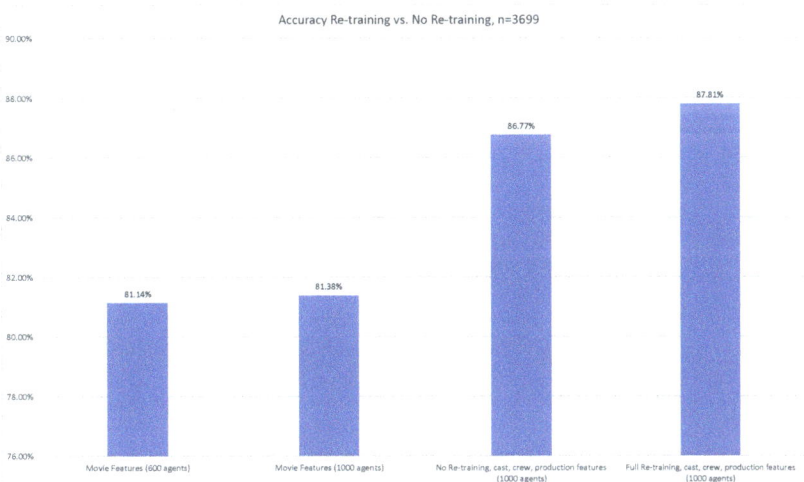

Figure 7. Cast, Crew, Production Features—System Accuracy.

It is currently unclear why there was a larger increase when fully re-training agents for this dataset. One possibility is that the additional features were more correlated with the output than in the breast cancer dataset, but this has not been confirmed using principal component analysis. Using the same hardware as described above, it took 12 min to generate and train 400 new agents, and 43 min to fully re-train 1000 agents.

3.3. System Distributability

Section 2.1.5 describes the distributed design of the system, with agents allowed to freely move between nodes during the interaction phase and two different methods used during the swarm phase, one that is less compute-efficient, but produces results identical to swarming on a single node, and a second method which is more compute-efficient, but may not produce the same predictive performance as swarming on a single node. WoC-Bots, and the meta-swarm (depending on number of inputs) both can have a large number of participating agents with many decisions directed by a random number generator (which way to move, which node to be distributed to, etc.). Additionally, large multi-agent systems will have variances in their outcomes based on agent-to-agent interactions and agents interacting within their environment [33]. The results presented in this section set a seed to the main random number generator used by the system to guarantee that each run of the system produces the same ordering of interactions and to hold predictive results consistent across multiple runs.

The following tests were conducted using virtual machines with the following hardware:

- CPU: AMD Opteron 6376 (Released November 2012); four virtual CPU (vCPU) cores per virtual machine
- RAM: 12 GB DDR3 per virtual machine
- Ceph-based network storage,

This was with all virtual machines configured with identical virtualized hardware, and with no control over how physical hardware was divided by the virtualization software. For example, when running with four virtualized nodes, those four nodes could be powered by a single hardware CPU, or with each node on a dedicated hardware CPU, or some other possible combination. We found that 12 GB of RAM was enough to allow all agents to maintain themselves in memory without swapping to disk during all phases of this system. Running on more modern, single-node hardware, the interaction step takes an average of 19 ms for 1250 agents and 96 ms for 5000 agents (Threadripper 1950x CPU and 64GB RAM).

3.3.1. Runtime Performance

Figure 8 shows interaction run times for 1250 agents on multiple node configurations. Runtime initially increases when using both two and four nodes, with testing showing this is largely due to network transfer penalties associated with frequent writes to the networked storage, as agents traverse nodes. However, nine nodes outperform a single node, with continued runtime improvements when moving to 16 nodes. Figure 9 shows the same node configuration but with 5000 agents participating. There is an increase in overall runtime, with runtime analysis indicating that CPU-bound tasks are the primary cause. The network transfer time takes a similar amount of absolute time in both the 1250 and 5000 agent configurations, indicating there is some initial time penalty. However, we do see a decrease in runtime moving from one node to two nodes, with further decreases in runtime as more nodes are included. Without additional hardware it is difficult to determine how many additional nodes will continue to improve runtime performance.

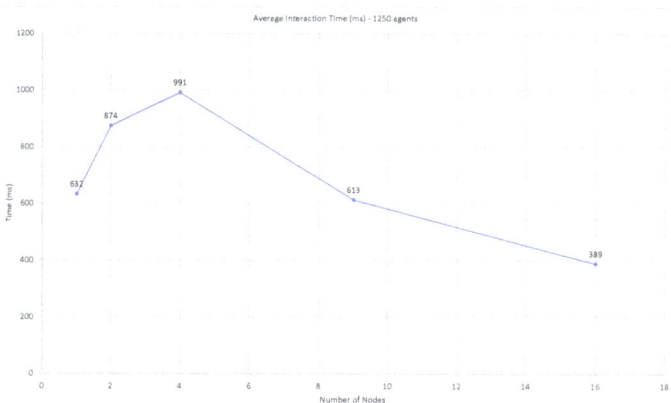

Figure 8. Interaction time (ms) for 1250 agents on 1, 4, 9, and 16 nodes, using data from Section 2.2.1 with cellular morphology features.

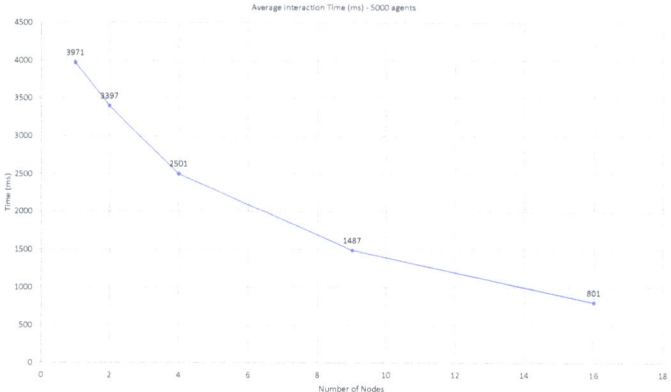

Figure 9. Interaction time (ms) for 5000 agents on 1, 4, 9, and 16 nodes, using data from Section 2.2.1 with cellular morphology features.

3.3.2. Swarm Performance—Timing and Accuracy

Figure 10 shows the average time the swarm phase takes when allowing agents to move freely between available nodes. Using this method, the swarming phase operates exactly as it would when a single node is used; however, it is distributed across multiple nodes, with agents frequently moving between nodes. Runtime initially decreases with two nodes, dropping from 9128 ms to 6788 ms, and continues to drop to 5421 ms with four nodes and 4918 ms with nine nodes. However, runtime increases with 16 nodes, to 5301 ms. The swarming phase is not compute-intensive, but when free movement is allowed between nodes it is very network transfer-intensive, which is demonstrated with the increase in runtime when moving from 9 nodes to 16 nodes.

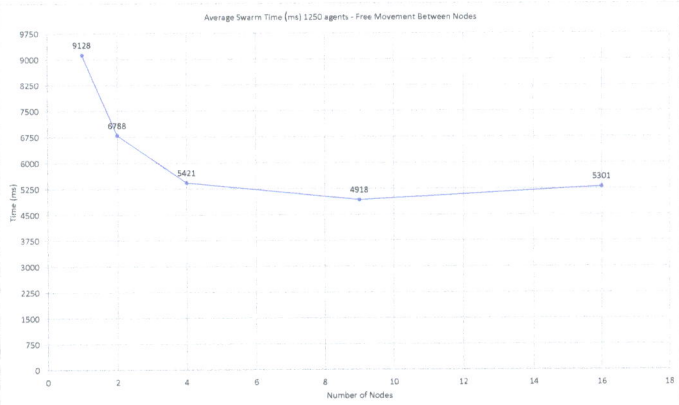

Figure 10. Swarm timing (ms) for 1250 agents on 1, 2, 4, 9, and 16 nodes, using data from Section 2.2.1 with cellular morphology features, with agents moving freely between nodes.

Figure 11 shows the average runtime for the swarm phase when disallowing agent movement between nodes. Agents must remain on the node they are initialized on, all swarming processes happen locally on each node, with each node represented in a meta-swarm phase once localized swarming is complete. Using this method we see runtime continue to decrease with additional nodes, indicating the increase in runtime using the previous method was from network transfers between nodes.

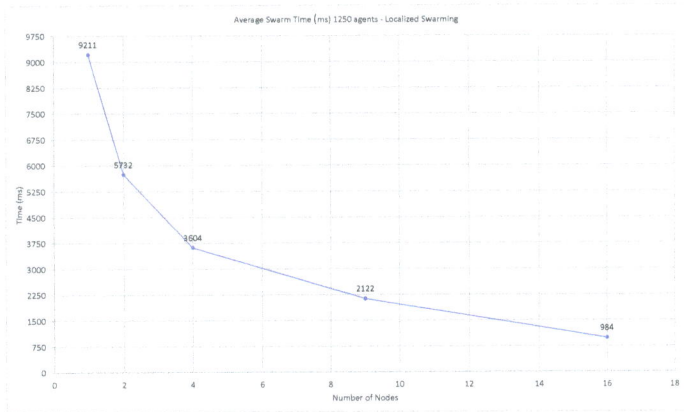

Figure 11. Swarm timing (ms) for 1250 agents on 1, 2, 4, 9, and 16 nodes, using data from Section 2.2.1 with cellular morphology features, with node-localized swarming.

Figure 12 shows the prediction accuracy using both of the above methods. In all cases, the predictive performance is decreased when swarming is node-local. The accuracy drops minimally in two of the three examples; dropping from 82.95% to 82.51%, a decrease of

0.44% in the breast cancer dataset and from 95.30% to 94.27%, a decrease of 1.03%, in the airline passenger satisfaction dataset. However, the accuracy drops substantially when predicting Hollywood movie success, going from 81.0% to 74.97%, a decrease of 6.03%. It is currently unclear why this dataset has a larger decrease in predictive performance using the node-local swarming method, a phenomenon that can be studied in future work.

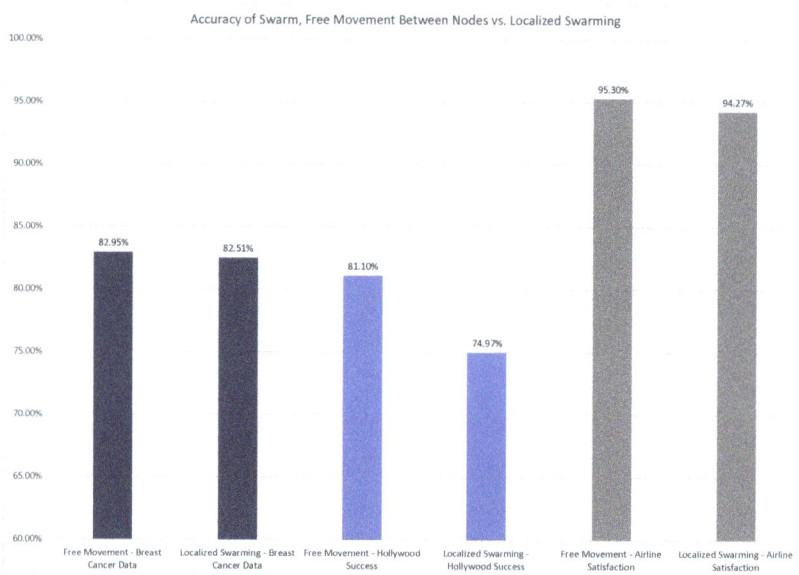

Figure 12. Comparison of prediction accuracy for breast cancer, Hollywood success, and airline passenger satisfaction when allowing free movement between nodes vs. node-local swarming.

3.4. Sports Betting

Our classification method has been applied to sports betting with some success over a 20-month period and most major sports. The primary focus has been on spread and moneyline bets, with no success in predicting the total score in any major sports. In total, there have been 10,500+ bets tested with the value of each bet being between 0.5% and 1.0% of available units. The system started with 150 units and has accumulated over 11,300 units in the past 20 months. As expected in a highly volatile, real-world use case, there is variability in the results over shorter periods of time, but over any 60+ day period of time the results are strictly increasing.

On 1 October 2021, the system switched to the 'meta-swarm' mode instead of relying only on predictions made by WoC-Bots. Other sources of information included in the calculation are described in Section 2.2.4. At all times the predictions from the system were allowed to be ignored in extraordinary cases, such as late-breaking injury news or unexpected local events, e.g., city-wide protests in some event location. Less than 3% of predictions from the system were ignored. When predictions were ignored, no action was taken on the event. Other news and information was assumed to be accounted for in the betting line offered, injury reports, and team roster information for the event.

Figure 13 shows the total units returned by the system over this time period. Note that around 1 June 2021 the system did briefly go negative. Over this period of the year the only major sports being played are MLB and soccer, both sports that have proven to be more volatile and more difficult for this system to predict. Additional volatility was suspected to come from data inconsistencies. All major sports in the preceding year disallowed fans, had shortened seasons, or were playing condensed seasons to account for lost time due to the COVID-19 pandemic. This impacted sports and teams differently, with a larger impact seen in cardio-intensive sports such as soccer, and on teams with older players as compared with the league average. In all sports, except the NHL, the home field advantage enjoyed prior to the COVID-19 pandemic was reduced.

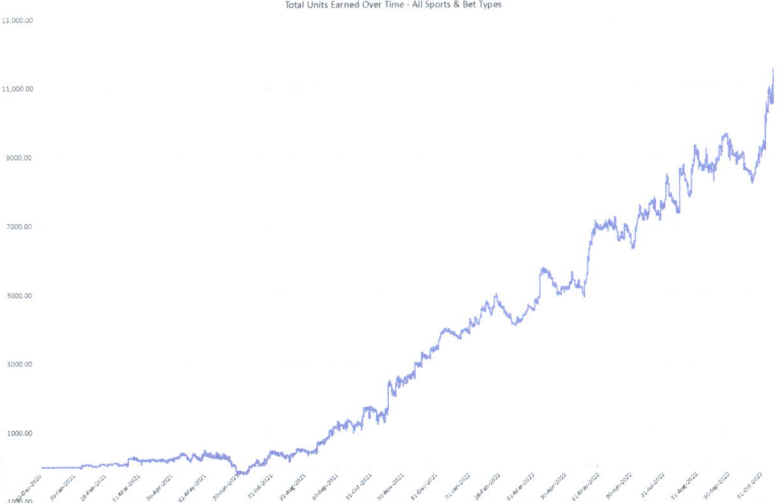

Figure 13. Total units earned over time for all sports tested on, moneyline and spread bets, 1 January 2021 through 15 November 2022.

Tables 8 and 9 show the total units risked, units returned beyond the units risked, the return on investment (ROI), the total bets, total winning bets, and the win rate for WoC-Bots (1 January 2021 through 30 September 2021) and the meta-swarm (1 October 2021 through 15 November 2022). In sports betting, the ROI is dictated not just by a win or loss, but also by the odds offered by the sports book. Both WoC-Bots and the meta-swarm have tended to prefer underdog bets with better odds. Bets on underdogs have positive odds; this means if the bet wins you receive more units back than were risked. For example, if 10 units are risked on odds of +220 and the bet wins you will receive 32 units, the original 10 risked units, and 22 additional units for the win. Spread bets are typically set with odds at −110, meaning if 10 units are risked and the bet wins you receive 19.09 units back, the original 10 risked units and 9.09 additional units for the win.

Table 8. WoC Bets: Risk, Return and Win Rate (Accuracy) for Spread and Moneyline Bets.

Values	Spread Bets	Moneyline Bets
Units Risked	8212	18,532
Units Returned	628.5	668
ROI	9.5%	3.6%
Total Bets	1161	3282
Winning Bets	572	1481
Win Rate	49.06%	45.12%

The win rate in both tables can be thought of as the accuracy of the predictions. Notice that the win rate is below 50% for spread and moneyline bets using both WoC-Bots and the meta-swarm. The default spread line offered by a sports book will be set to −110 odds, but most sports books allow betters to pick their own spread line with different odds. For example, a default line could be `team-xyz` (−5.5) for −110 odds, meaning that `team-xyz` needs to win by six points to win the bet. The sports books will also offer options such as (−6.5) for +105 odds or (−7.5) for +115 odds. When the prediction has a high associated confidence value we can take a custom line with positive odds on a spread bet, allowing for a win rate below 50% to still be profitable. This can also be seen for moneyline bets; the win rate for moneyline bets using the meta-swarm actually drops, from 45.15% using WoC-Bots only, to 40.19%. However, the ROI increases from 3.6% using WoC-Bots to 6.7% using the meta-swarm. The system became better at selecting underdog winners, increasing the ROI despite the decrease in win rate.

Table 9. Meta-Swarm: Risk, Return and Win Rate (Accuracy) for Spread and Moneyline Bets.

Values	Spread Bets	Moneyline Bets
Units Risked	48,159	80,408
Units Returned	4863.5	5364.5
ROI	10.1%	6.7%
Total Bets	2376	3225
Winning Bets	1174	1296
Win Rate	49.33%	40.19%

Some testing has been done to improve win rate by biasing the agents to prefer favorites. This testing has shown poor results, with negative ROI despite an increase in win rate. The only exception to this is the last 15–20% of both the NBA and MLB seasons, where many teams know their playoff positions and the favorites tend to win more frequently than during the early and middle parts of the seasons. This is, however, reflected with worse odds on favorites, which requires a significantly higher win rate to maintain a positive ROI.

4. Discussion

Our classification system has demonstrated competitive performance with other state-of-the-art classification methods for multiple different datasets with a varied number of samples and input features. While Random Forest and a Deep Neural Network implementation outperformed WoC-Bots in maximum accuracy on the tested datasets, WoC-Bots outperformed AdaBoost and Logistic Regression methods in two of the three tested datasets and performed similarly to all of the top methods in the third dataset. WoC-Bots' accuracy, precision, and recall metrics tracked similarly with the other classification methods; XG-Boost, AdaBoost, Random Forest, DNN, and WoC-Bots all showed higher recall scores and lower precision scores on the breast cancer dataset. Similarly, the same methods showed higher precision and lower recall scores for the Hollywood dataset, indicating WoC-Bots are learning similar information as the other classification methods. While WoC-Bots prediction runtime is the slowest of the methods shown in this paper, runtime optimization has not yet been a focus. This is something that can and should be improved in future work; for example, the interaction arena interactions can be optimized to a series of matrix multiplication operations for each pair of interacting agents. Further, this optimization step would also reduce the runtime during the swarming phase. The current system allows for easy behavioral modification while testing a new method, but this is an intended future optimization.

The multi-agent design allows for new, previously unknown features to be included in any existing classification problem without re-training the full network (or set of existing agents). We demonstrated significant accuracy improvements when adding new features, while also demonstrating similar overall performance when compared with re-training the agents with all of the available features. This method is useful when the final set of features is unknown or constantly expanding. The real-world results we have shown with sports betting made use of this feature frequently to incorporate new data from recent games, as new data sources were discovered or new metrics were developed to track player and team performance. Individual WoC-Bots were quickly updated to include results from the most recent games and new bots were generated to represent novel data sources or statistical metrics.

WoC-Bots can be distributed across multiple hardware nodes, with no requirement for a single powerful machine to train a very deep and wide monolithic neural network. We demonstrated improved runtime performance when adding compute nodes for both the interaction and swarming steps of the system. The 'meta-swarm' system developed to represent the prediction of each of the nodes has greatly reduced the runtime of the distributed swarm step by allowing each agent to stay on a single node throughout the process. This system has shown similar accuracy to a single-node swarm in two of the three tested datasets.

A by-product of developing the distributed 'meta-swarm' was the ability to include additional prediction sources into the overall prediction, after the WoC-Bots have made their initial prediction. We have shown this reduces the overall variance in accuracy, precision, and recall in all of the datasets tested, while also producing the best accuracy of all methods tested on the Hollywood dataset. This system, primarily using the 'meta-swarm' extension, has been applied to a real-world problem, making predictions about the outcomes of sporting events.

5. Conclusions

We have demonstrated a multi-agent, binary classification system based on Wisdom-of-Crowds which uses a honey-bee-derived swarm mechanism for opinion aggregation. Our system is competitive with other, state-of-the-art, classification methods when tested on three different datasets. The multi-agent design allows for multiple, significant, advantages over the other classification methods; WoC-Bots can be distributed across multiple hardware nodes, incrementally include new features without re-training existing agents, and the aggregation mechanism is flexible enough to incorporate predictions from other sources. Further, the aggregation mechanism can provide confidence values for each prediction, which allow us to stratify samples into confidence categories, significantly improving the average accuracy, precision, and recall for a subset of samples in two of the three tested datasets. The meta-swarm, where we incorporate predictions from other classification methods and sources, improved the variance between the three metrics (accuracy, recall, precision), and had the best overall accuracy when predicting the success of Hollywood movies.

We applied our method to a real-world sports betting problem, producing consistent return on investment using both WoC-Bots directly as well as the meta-swarm, incorporating the predictions from WoC-Bots and other freely available prediction sources. Over a period of nine months, we saw an ROI of 9.5% on spread bets and 3.6% on moneyline bets using WoC-Bots alone, and an ROI of 10.1% on spread bets and 6.7% on moneyline bets over a year of using the meta-swarm.

Future work should focus on improving the performance when distributing the interaction and swarm steps by optimizing the network transfers. Additional investigation should also focus on why the meta-swarm step did not perform well on the Hollywood dataset, aimed at determining why the distributed performance was significantly worse than single-node swarming when a similar performance drop was not present in the breast cancer or airline passenger satisfaction datasets. It is unclear if this is a fundamental issue with some types of data or if this was a limitation of a specific dataset.

Author Contributions: Conceptualization, S.G.; methodology, S.G. and D.E.B.; software, S.G.; investigation, S.G. and D.E.B.; resources, S.G. and D.E.B.; data curation, S.G.; writing—original draft preparation, S.G.; writing—review and editing, S.G. and D.E.B.; supervision, D.E.B. All authors have read and agreed to the published version of the manuscript.

Funding: This research received no external funding.

Institutional Review Board Statement: The study to gather the breast cancer dataset was conducted in accordance with the Declaration of Helsinki, and approved by the Institutional Review Board of Drexel University College of Medicine for studies involving humans. Protocol code: 1411003203A001. Approval date: 2014-11-03. Investigator: David Edward Breen. Title: Online Digital Storage Array for Archived Histology Slide Imaging. IRB approval is not applicable for the Hollywood, airline passenger satisfaction, or sports betting data.

Informed Consent Statement: Informed consent was obtained from all subjects involved in the study to gather the breast cancer dataset.

Data Availability Statement: Some, but not all, of the data used in this publication are made available. The breast cancer dataset is being withheld due to patient privacy concerns. The sports betting data, while available from public sources, are also being withheld due to discrepancies in various jurisdictions on the legality of sports betting. The transformed dataset used for Hollywood success prediction can be found at https://data.mendeley.com/datasets/gj66mt4s4j/2 (accessed on 21 October 2019) and the dataset used for airline passenger satisfaction can be found at https://data.mendeley.com/datasets/8ppmphw235 (accessed on 20 December 2022). The code will be made available upon reasonable request Sean Grimes, spg63@drexel.edu.

Acknowledgments: The authors would like to thank Mark D. Zarella, and Fernando U. Garcia, for their support and guidance in refining this approach for use with breast cancer patients and for help in understanding how to best use the available patient features. The authors would also like to thank ESPN, Yahoo Sports!, The Action Network, SportsChatPlace, CollegeFootballNews, Winners and Whiners, and FiveThirtyEight for making sports data available and their analysis of the sporting world.

Conflicts of Interest: The authors declare no conflict of interest.

Abbreviations

The following abbreviations are used in this manuscript:

MDPI	Multidisciplinary Digital Publishing Institute
DOAJ	Directory of open access journals
WoC	Wisdom of Crowd
MLP	Multi-layer Perceptron
ANN	Artificial Neural Network
DNN	Deep Neural Network
CNN	Convolutional Neural Network
RNN	Recurrent Neural Network
PM	Prediction Market
API	Application Programming Interface
DL4J	DeepLearning4j
JVM	Java Virtual Machine
UWM	Unweighted Mean Model
WVM	Weighted Voter Model
TMDb	The Movie Database
NCAA	National Collegiate Athletic Association
FBS	Football Bowl Subdivision
NFL	National Football League
NBA	National Basketball Association
NHL	National Hockey League
MLB	Major League Baseball
MLS	Major League Soccer
ROI	Return on Investment

References

1. Zhang, C.; Liu, C.; Zhang, X.; Almpanidis, G. An up-to-date comparison of state-of-the-art classification algorithms. *Expert Syst. Appl.* **2017**, *82*, 128–150. [CrossRef]
2. Hashemi, M. Enlarging smaller images before inputting into convolutional neural network: Zero-padding vs. interpolation. *J. Big Data* **2019**, *6*, 1–13. [CrossRef]
3. Kim, E.; Cho, S.; Lee, B.; Cho, M. Fault detection and diagnosis using self-attentive convolutional neural networks for variable-length sensor data in semiconductor manufacturing. *IEEE Trans. Semicond. Manuf.* **2019**, *32*, 302–309. [CrossRef]
4. Naul, B.; Bloom, J.S.; Pérez, F.; van der Walt, S. A recurrent neural network for classification of unevenly sampled variable stars. *Nat. Astron.* **2018**, *2*, 151–155. [CrossRef]

5. Torrey, L.; Shavlik, J. Transfer learning. In *Handbook of Research on Machine Learning Applications and Trends: Algorithms, Methods, and Techniques*; IGI Global: Hershey, PA, USA, 2010; pp. 242–264.
6. Olivas, E.S.; Guerrero, J.D.M.; Martinez-Sober, M.; Magdalena-Benedito, J.R.; Serrano, L. *Handbook of Research on Machine Learning Applications and Trends: Algorithms, Methods, and Techniques: Algorithms, Methods, and Techniques*; IGI Global: Hershey, PA, USA, 2009.
7. Yosinski, J.; Clune, J.; Bengio, Y.; Lipson, H. How transferable are features in deep neural networks? *arXiv* **2014**, arXiv:1411.1792.
8. Grimes, S.; Zarella, M.D.; Garcia, F.U.; Breen, D.E. An agent-based approach to predicting lymph node metastasis status in breast cancer. In Proceedings of the 2021 IEEE International Conference on Bioinformatics and Biomedicine (BIBM), Houston, TX, USA, 9–12 December 2021; pp. 1315–1319.
9. Yi, S.K.M.; Steyvers, M.; Lee, M.D.; Dry, M.J. The wisdom of the crowd in combinatorial problems. *Cogn. Sci.* **2012**, *36*, 452–470. [CrossRef]
10. Othman, A. Zero-intelligence agents in prediction markets. In Proceedings of the 7th International Joint Conference on Autonomous Agents and Multiagent Systems: Volume 2, Estoril, Portugal, 12–16 May 2008; pp. 879–886.
11. Ostrom, E. The Difference: How the Power of Diversity Creates Better Groups, Firms, Schools, and Societies. By Scott E. Page. Princeton: Princeton University Press, 2007. 448p. 19.95 paper. *Perspect. Politics* **2008**, *6*, 828–829. [CrossRef]
12. Hastie, R.; Kameda, T. The robust beauty of majority rules in group decisions. *Psychol. Rev.* **2005**, *112*, 494. [CrossRef]
13. Valentini, G.; Hamann, H.; Dorigo, M. Self-organized collective decision making: The weighted voter model. In Proceedings of the International Conference on Autonomous Agents and Multi-Agent Systems, Paris, France, 5–9 May 2014; pp. 45–52.
14. Grimes, S.; Breen, D.E. Woc-Bots: An Agent-Based Approach to Decision-Making. *Appl. Sci.* **2019**, *9*, 4653. [CrossRef]
15. Team, D. Deeplearning4j: Open-source distributed deep learning for the JVM. *Apache Softw. Found. Licens.* **2018**, *2*. Available online: http://deeplearning4j.org/ (accessed on 27 June 2022).
16. Kingma, D.P.; Ba, J. Adam: A method for stochastic optimization. *arXiv* **2014**, arXiv:1412.6980.
17. Goodfellow, I.; Bengio, Y.; Courville, A. *Deep Learning*; MIT Press: Cambridge, MA, USA, 2016. Available online: http://www.deeplearningbook.org (accessed on 10 October 2022).
18. Du, Q.; Hong, H.; Wang, G.A.; Wang, P.; Fan, W. CrowdIQ: A New Opinion Aggregation Model. In Proceedings of the 50th Hawaii International Conference on System Sciences, Hilton Waikoloa Village, HI, USA, 4–7 January 2017.
19. Rosenberg, L.; Pescetelli, N.; Willcox, G. Artificial Swarm Intelligence amplifies accuracy when predicting financial markets. In Proceedings of the IEEE 8th Annual Conference on Ubiquitous Computing, Electronics and Mobile Communication, New York City, NY, USA, 19–21 October 2017; pp. 58–62.
20. Rosenberg, L. Artificial Swarm Intelligence, a Human-in-the-loop approach to AI. In Proceedings of the 13th AAAI Conference on Artificial Intelligence, Phoenix, AZ, USA, 12–17 February 2016.
21. Tereshko, V.; Loengarov, A. Collective decision making in honey-bee foraging dynamics. *Comput. Inf. Syst.* **2005**, *9*, 1.
22. Von Frisch, K. *The Dance Language and Orientation of Bees*; Harvard University Press: Cambridge, MA, USA, 2013.
23. Beekman, M.; Ratnieks, F. Long-range foraging by the honey-bee, Apis mellifera L. *Funct. Ecol.* **2000**, *14*, 490–496. [CrossRef]
24. Lipowski, A.; Lipowska, D. Roulette-wheel selection via stochastic acceptance. *Phys. A Stat. Mech. Its Appl.* **2012**, *391*, 2193–2196. [CrossRef]
25. Zhang, Y.; Zhao, D.; Sun, J.; Zou, G.; Li, W. Adaptive convolutional neural network and its application in face recognition. *Neural Process. Lett.* **2016**, *43*, 389–399. [CrossRef]
26. Wolpert, D.H. Stacked generalization. *Neural Netw.* **1992**, *5*, 241–259. [CrossRef]
27. Chen, T.; He, T.; Benesty, M.; Khotilovich, V.; Tang, Y.; Cho, H.; Chen, K. Xgboost: Extreme gradient boosting. *R Package Version 0.4-2* **2015**, *1*, 1–4.
28. Schapire, R.E. Explaining adaboost. In *Empirical Inference*; Springer: Berlin/Heidelberg, Germany, 2013; pp. 37–52.
29. Biau, G.; Scornet, E. A random forest guided tour. *Test* **2016**, *25*, 197–227. [CrossRef]
30. Wright, R.E. Logistic regression. In *Reading and Understanding Multivariate Statistics*; APA Publishing: Washington, DC, USA, 1995; pp. 217–244.
31. Van Zee, K.J.; Manasseh, D.M.E.; Bevilacqua, J.L.; Boolbol, S.K.; Fey, J.V.; Tan, L.K.; Borgen, P.I.; Cody, H.S.; Kattan, M.W. A nomogram for predicting the likelihood of additional nodal metastases in breast cancer patients with a positive sentinel node biopsy. *Ann. Surg. Oncol.* **2003**, *10*, 1140–1151. [CrossRef]
32. Kohrt, H.E.; Olshen, R.A.; Bermas, H.R.; Goodson, W.H.; Wood, D.J.; Henry, S.; Rouse, R.V.; Bailey, L.; Philben, V.J.; Dirbas, F.M.; et al. New models and online calculator for predicting non-sentinel lymph node status in sentinel lymph node positive breast cancer patients. *BMC Cancer* **2008**, *8*, 66. [CrossRef]
33. Lowe, R.; Wu, Y.; Tamar, A.; Harb, J.; Abbeel, P.; Mordatch, I. Multi-agent actor-critic for mixed cooperative-competitive environments. *arXiv* **2017**, arXiv:1706.02275.

Disclaimer/Publisher's Note: The statements, opinions and data contained in all publications are solely those of the individual author(s) and contributor(s) and not of MDPI and/or the editor(s). MDPI and/or the editor(s) disclaim responsibility for any injury to people or property resulting from any ideas, methods, instructions or products referred to in the content.

Article

Dealing with Deadlocks in Industrial Multi Agent Systems

František Čapkovič

Institute of Informatics, Slovak Academy of Sciences, 845 07 Bratislava, Slovakia; frantisek.capkovic@savba.sk

Abstract: Automated Manufacturing Systems (AMS) consisting of many cooperating devices incorporated into multiple cooperating production lines, sharing common resources, represent industrial Multi-Agent Systems (MAS). Deadlocks may occur during operation of such MAS. It is necessary to deal with deadlocks (more precisely said, to prevent them) to ensure the correct behavior of AMS. For this purpose, among other methods, methods based on Petri nets (PN) are used too. Because AMS are very often described by PN models, two PN-based methods will be presented here, namely based on (i) PN place invariants (P-invariants); and (ii) PN siphons and traps. Intended final results of usage these methods is finding a supervisor allowing a deadlock-free activity of the global MAS. While the former method yields results in analytical terms, latter one need computation of siphons and traps.

Keywords: automated manufacturing systems; multi-agent systems; Petri nets; P-invariants; siphons and traps; supervisor

Citation: Čapkovič, F. Dealing with Deadlocks in Industrial Multi Agent Systems. *Future Internet* **2023**, *15*, 107. https://doi.org/10.3390/fi15030107

Academic Editors: Agostino Poggi, Martin Kenyeres, Ivana Budinská and Ladislav Hluchy

Received: 14 February 2023
Revised: 2 March 2023
Accepted: 3 March 2023
Published: 9 March 2023

Copyright: © 2023 by the authors. Licensee MDPI, Basel, Switzerland. This article is an open access article distributed under the terms and conditions of the Creative Commons Attribution (CC BY) license (https://creativecommons.org/licenses/by/4.0/).

1. Introduction

Recent decades represent a huge evolution of Automated Manufacturing Systems (AMS), previously named Flexible Manufacturing Systems (FMS). We can even talk about the new industrial revolution. According to [1], this evolution is realized mainly by the development in four axes, namely products, technology, business strategies, and production paradigms. The edited book [2] offers a wide perspective on modern design and operation of production networks. The evolution of the manufacturing system in the future is presented in [3].

The operation of AMS often has a similar character to Discrete-Event Systems (DES), where the next state depends only on both the current state and the occurrence of discrete events. Petri nets (PN) [4,5] are frequently used for modeling and control of DES. The family of AMS is a typical representative of DES where many devices cooperate together—robots, machine tools, transport belts, automatically guided vehicles (AGV), etc. They are frequently called to be resources. They are shared by multiple production lines, robotized working cells, etc. These devices and their aggregates, in the form of lines and cells, can also be considered industrial agents and the whole AMS as a multi-agent system. The adequate resource allocation is very important in AMS in order to avoid deadlocks. A deadlock in general is a state in which two or more processes are each waiting for the other one to execute, but neither can go on. Hence, deadlock is undesirable and bad phenomenon. Due to deadlocks, either the entire plant or some of its parts remain stagnate. Thus, the primal intention of the production cannot be achieved. For a design of deadlock-free AMS discrete mathematics is necessary. PN-based discrete mathematical models of AMS yield a suitable background for this.

There exists a large number of publications interested in this topic. From the older ones, the following works should be mentioned in particular [6–10], as well as the UML (Unified Modeling Language)-based work [11] applied in software engineering. While in [6,9] foundations of the P-invariant-based method were laid, in [7,8] the method based on siphons and traps was elaborated. A generalized view on deadlocks in multi-agent systems is presented in [10]. Among the more recent works should be mentioned [12–15], as well as the author's survey article [16]. While in [12] a comprehensive survey of Petri net siphons were presented, in [13,15] unreliable resources are investigated and the robust control for AMS containing such resources is designed. In [14], deadlocks in mobile agent systems are detected and resolved.

In relation to the elimination of deadlocks, in [16–21] three categories of strategies are distinguished: (i) deadlock detection and recovery—which is used in cases where deadlocks are infrequent and their consequences are not too serious; (ii) deadlock prevention—it imposes restrictions on the interactions among resources and their users to prevent resource requests that may lead to deadlocks; and (iii) deadlock avoidance—it grants a resource to a user only if the resulting state is not a deadlock.

Consequently, it is impossible to address to such a broad issue in one paper. In this paper, only two methods of deadlock prevention in AMS by means of PN-based models are introduced and compared. Both methods add monitors (additional places) into the original PN model of AMS in order to remove deadlocks. One method enumerates monitors and their interconnections with the original PN model using P-invariants and the other using siphons and traps.

1.1. Formal Methods in AMS

Formal methods for modeling, simulation, supervisory control, performance evaluation and fault diagnosis of AMS are very important part of global understanding of AMS. They yield an efficient help and knowledge at constructing and real implementation of AMS. A suitable review of such methods is presented in the e-book [22]. As to modeling AMS there are presented also models based on place/transition Petri nets (P/T PN), timed Petri nets (TPN), and hybrid Petri nets (HPN).

The supervisory control of AMS determined for the deadlock prevention and avoidance are presented by means of: (i) finite state automata (FSA); (ii) the Petri net view on AMS which are perceived as resource allocation systems (RAS); (iii) HPN-based inventory control systems; (iv) stochastic flow models (SFM); (v) the infinitesimal perturbation analysis (IPA); and (vi) the max-plus algebra.

The performance evaluation is watched by colored TPN, by continuous PN (CPN), by the timed process algebra, and by the Petri net-based complex system scheduling.

The fault diagnosis of AMS is analyzed by means of FSA, by the fault diagnosis of PN and by the control reconfiguration of discrete-event manufacturing systems modeled by non-deterministic input/output (I/O) automata.

Along with the development of information technologies, such as cloud computing, mobile Internet, information acquisition technology, and big data technology, traditional engineering knowledge and formal methods for knowledge-based software engineering undergo fundamental changes. Hence, networks also play an increasingly important role.

Within this context, it is necessary to develop new methodologies as well as technical tools for network-based approaches. The term "network" may have different meanings in different contexts. To resolve bottleneck problems in AMS, deadlock prevention and avoidance by means of Petri nets is crucial.

Although introduced topics cover a large set of formal methods in AMS it cannot be said that this set is complete. New methods are under development.

1.2. Agents Cooperation, Negotiation and Reentering in AMS

Important strategies in MAS (multi-agent systems) are cooperation and negotiation. A structural and Petri net-based approach to modeling of these strategies was elaborated in author's older work [23] and in the chapter [24] where also the perspectives of learning in this area were analyzed.

In [25], a connection of the structural model of reenterable AMS on a computer-based supervisory controller for monitoring the status of jobs and regulating the part routing as well as the machine job selection by means of siphons of Petri nets as to resolving deadlocks was explored. Namely, there are many approaches to modeling and analysis of manufacturing systems. In addition to those ones mentioned above in the previous Subsection (i.e., automata,

Petri nets, perturbation methods) there exist methods based on digraphs, alphabet-based approaches, control theoretic techniques, expert systems design, etc.

The so-called *complex networks* are an interdisciplinary area. Numerous natural and artificial systems are composed of a large number of individuals that interact with each other in various ways, and then perform surprising useful functions. Examples of such networks include, e.g., neural networks, social networks, and many others, but also MAS in general, including industrial MAS where AMS and RAS belong, and doubtlessly also PN that successfully model and analyze them.

1.3. The Paper Organization

In the following Section 2, preliminaries concerning theory of PN and the PN-based modeling of AMS will be concisely introduced. Then, Section 3 will be devoted to the presentation and illustration of the method of deadlock prevention, based on P-invariants. In Section 4, the method of deadlock prevention, based on PN siphons and traps, will be presented and illustrated. Section 5 will discuss and illustrate three PN models of AMS being more complicated from the computation point of view, namely problematic because of very long-lasting even impossible computations. In Section 6, the comparison of both methods will be introduced. Then, Section 7 contains a concise conclusions of this paper.

2. Preliminaries

Firstly, it is necessary to introduce several basic definitions. First, one is the author own definition extracted from knowledge published in [7,16], next three are the standard elementary definitions of P-invariants, siphons, and traps from the classical literature about Petri nets [4,5]. Last two definitions are taken over from [7].

Definition 1. *A Petri net is a bipartite directed graph (BDG). It may be formally described by the quadruplet $N = (P, T, F, W)$. Here, P and T are finite nonempty sets, namely P is a set of places ($|P| = n$), representing the first kind of BDG nodes, and T is a set of transitions ($|T| = m$), representing the second kind of BDG nodes. It is valid that $P \cup T \neq \emptyset$ and $P \cap T = \emptyset$. The set $F = (P \times T) \cup (T \times P)$ is the flow relation of the net N. It is expressed by directed arcs from places to transitions and vice versa. The mapping $W : (P \times T) \cup (T \times P) \to \mathbb{N}$ assigns weights to directed arcs. The weight of an arc $f : W(f) > 0$ if $f \in F$ and $W(f) = 0$ otherwise. Here $\mathbb{N} = \{0, 1, 2, ...\}$, i.e., it contains natural numbers plus zero. The Petri net $N = (P, T, F, W)$ is named ordinary and denoted as $N = (P, T, F)$ if $\forall f \in F, W(f) = 1$. N is called generalized if $\exists f \in F, W(f) > 1$. Petri net is called a state machine if, and only if, (iff) $\forall t \in T, |{}^{\bullet}t| = |t^{\bullet}| = 1$, i.e., when each transition has only one input place and only one output place.*

A mapping from P to $\mathbb{N}$ is a marking M of N. The marking $M(p)$ means the number of tokens located in the place p. Thus, we may say that the place p is marked by a marking M iff $M(p) > 0$. In case of a subset $S \subseteq P$ we say that it is marked by M iff at least one place in S is marked by M. The sum of tokens located in all places of S is $M(S) = \sum_{p \in S} M(p)$. S is empty at M iff $M(S) = 0$. The pair (N, M_0) is called the marked net or a net system. Here, M_0 is an initial marking of N.

PN marking is evolved as follows

$$\mathbf{M}_{k+1} = \mathbf{M}_k + \mathbf{N}.\vec{\sigma}_k, \ k \in \mathbb{N}, \tag{1}$$

with $\mathbf{M}_0 = (M_0(p_1), M_0(p_1), \ldots, M_0(p_n))^T$ being the $(n \times 1)$ initial marking. Here, $\mathbf{N}$ is the $(n \times m)$-dimensional incidence matrix based on the set F and $\vec{\sigma}_k$ is a $(m \times 1)$-dimensional firing vector (the binary vector, where its entry with the value 1 denotes the corresponding transition $t \in T$ able to be fired). $M(p)$ denotes (as it was already mentioned above) the number of tokens in place p. $(n \times 1)$ marking vectors $\mathbf{M}$ are sometimes named also as *state vectors*. $\mathbf{N} = \mathbf{N}^+ - \mathbf{N}^-$, where $\mathbf{N}^+ = \mathbf{Post}$ and $\mathbf{N}^- = \mathbf{Pre}$ are, respectively, the output flow matrix and the input flow matrix. In other words, the matrix representing the output of transitions to places and the matrix representing the input of places to transitions.

For economy of space, in general, markings and vectors can be described by the formal sum notation. Thus, $\sum_{p \in P} M(p)p$ denotes the vector **M**. For example, in a net with $P = \{p_1, \ldots, p_5\}$ a marking where in p_2 are 3 tokens and in p_3 are 2 tokens may be written as $3p_2 + 2p_3$ instead of the vector notation $(0, 3, 2, 0, 0)^T$.

Definition 2. *A vector **I** is a place invariant P (shortly, P-invariant) of PN iff* $\mathbf{I} \neq \mathbf{0}$ *and* $\mathbf{I}^T.\mathbf{N} = \mathbf{0}^T$. *Here, **N** is the incidence matrix of N.*

Definition 3. *Any set $S \subseteq P$, $S \neq \emptyset$ with $^\bullet S \subseteq S^\bullet$ is said to be a siphon. Verbally said, if every transition having an output place in S has an input place in S. If a siphon does not contain another siphon, being its proper subset, it is said to be a minimal siphon. A proper subset is any subset of the set except itself. A minimal siphon S is called a strict minimal siphon (SMS) if $^\bullet S \subsetneq S^\bullet$. In other words, if there is no siphon contained in it as a proper subset. A SMS does not contain a trap (the trap is defined below by Definition 4). When at the initial marking $\mathbf{M_0}$ $M_0(S) = \sum_{p \in S} M_0(p) = 0$, S is called an empty siphon.*

Definition 4. *Any set $Q \subseteq P$, $Q \neq \emptyset$ with $Q^\bullet \subseteq {}^\bullet Q$ is called a trap. In other words, if every transition having an input place in Q has an output place in Q.*

Definition 5. *A siphon S is said to be controlled in a net (N, M_0) iff $\forall M \in R(N, M_0), M(S) > 0$. Here, $R(N, M_0)$ expresses the reachability of markings from the initial marking. Consequently, any siphon containing a marked trap is controlled, since the marked trap can newer be emptied. Thus, in ordinary PN a controlled siphon does not cause any deadlock.*

Definition 6. *A siphon S in an ordinary PN (N, M_0) is [7] invariant controlled by P-invariant **I** under the initial marking $\mathbf{M_0}$ iff $\mathbf{I}^T.\mathbf{M_0} > 0$ and $\forall p \in P\backslash S, I(p) \leq 0$, or equivalently, $\mathbf{I}^T.\mathbf{M_0} > 0$ and $||\mathbf{I}||^+ \subseteq S$. Here, $||\mathbf{I}||^+ = p \in P|I(p) > 0$ is the positive support of **I**.*

Here, it is necessary to notify and emphasize that both methods examined in this paper require a rather wide mathematical background that cannot be either simplified nor abbreviated. Otherwise, the integrity of the interpretation of the methods would be violated. The mathematics used in examples should contribute to an accurate understanding of the application of both methods to particular cases of AMS.

2.1. Petri Nets and Resource Allocation Systems

Resource allocation systems (RAS) are a special class of concurrent systems, especially AMS. There, the attention is focused above all on resources. The set of Petri net-based models of RAS represent, in general, a subset of complete set of PN. Finite set of resources is shared in a competitive way by a finite set of processes. Such a competition induces (or may induce) existence of deadlocks. PN-based models of RAS are useful at synthesizing policies of deadlock prevention and/or deadlock avoiding. They make possible to design beforehand deadlock-free AMS, what is very useful especially preliminary to the creation of the final design of the structure of real AMS determined for application in production.

There are several standard paradigms of RAS [26–29]. Specific nomenclatures have been established for them—see, e.g., a survey made in [16], where also their mutual relations and their relations to PN as a whole, are displayed. Most frequently used paradigms of them are the following two: (i) S^{3}PR (Systems of Simple Sequential Processes with Resources) suitable for AMS with flexible routing and the acquisition of the single-unit of the resource and (ii) S^{4}PR (System of Sequential Systems with Shared Process Resources) which enables the modeling AMS with flexible routing and the acquisition of more units of the resource. The relation S^{3}PR $\prec$ S^{4}PR in this case expresses that systems S^{4}PR model more complicated AMS than systems S^{3}PR are able to model. In future, there may be S*PR (S^{3}PR $\prec$ S^{4}PR $\prec$ S*PR) paradigms suitable to model of yet more complicated AMS, where yet more copies of resources will be allowed. However, the asterix needs not always be just a greater integer than it was in previous two paradigms.

Some of the amount of paradigms, especially S^3PR and S^4PR, can be modeled and simulated in Matlab by means of the tool [30].

2.2. Methods for the Deadlock Prevention and Avoiding

As already mentioned, two main streams of methods are represented by methods based on: (i) reachability trees and P-invariants of PN and (ii) PN siphons and traps.

In the former case, it is necessary to mention the most principal contributions [6,8,9,31–33] important for the evolution of the P-invariants-based methods. The origin of this method consists in the effort to deal with the problem of the forbidden state in DES. Namely, it was shown in the literature that if a set $\mathcal{L}$ of legal PN markings is expressed by a set of s linear inequality constraints (so called General Mutual Exclusion Constraints (GMEC)) and if $\mathcal{L}$ is controllable, then the PN-based solution exists and it is maximally permissive. The controllability of $\mathcal{L}$ means that from any marking $M \in \mathcal{L}$ no forbidden marking is reachable by firing a sequence containing only uncontrollable transitions. In the opposite case, a general forbidden marking constraint may be enforced by PN-based controller only if the Petri net model of the system is safe. Hence, PN P-invariants are used in order to compute the feedback controller that enforces GMEC. They perform transformations on the system's specifications to obtain constraints in the desired form. The controller is a set of control Petri net places. When the controller is added to the PN model of the plant, control places ensure a live and maximally permissive behavior of the closed loop system with respect to the forbidden states or markings. The controller design has a linear complexity in the number of system states. However, there are cases where such PN controller does not exist. Especially, when the set of legal markings $\mathcal{L}$ *is not convex*, there does not exist any PN place that can forbid the reachability of bad markings when allowing all legal ones. The concept of PN P-invariants was extended also to PN with uncontrollable and unobservable transitions. However, in this case maximally permissiveness cannot be guaranteed.

In the latter case, there are lots more such basal publications—[6,7,10,28,34–57]. Siphons are tied to dead transitions whose existence leads to the loss of liveness of PN-based models of AMS. Siphon control is an effective way to prevent the occurrence of deadlocks. In a general case, particularly for models of AMS based on generalized PN, a siphon-based deadlock prevention policy cannot find an optimal (i.e., maximally permissive) supervisor. However, for PN models of AMS based on ordinary PN it is possible. Siphons in the PN model of a plant are divided into elementary and dependent ones. A monitor is added to the plant model for each elementary siphon, in such a way that the siphon will be *invariant-controlled*. The method guarantees that no further emptiable control-induced siphon is generated due to the addition of the monitors. When all elementary siphons are controlled, the controllability of a dependent siphon is ensured by properly setting the *control depth variables* of its related elementary siphons.

The explanation of the term invariant-controlled siphon, as well as the term control depth variable, will be explained and illustrated below in the Section 4.2. However, this is applicable only for S^3PR paradigm of RAS. In case of S^4PR paradigm (modeled by generalized PN), which uses multiple resource requirements and information about the weight of arcs, the concept of extended elementary siphons have to be used. Namely, due to the complicated utilization of resources, it is insufficient to represent the relationship between elementary and dependent siphons in generalized PN in such way as it is in case of ordinary PN. Extended elementary siphons are find by an iterative process—see, e.g., [58].

A methodology for modeling and analyzing fault-tolerant manufacturing systems that not only optimizes normal productive processes, but also performs detection and treatment of faults is presented in [59]. The coordination of cooperative multirobot system by means of PN is elucidated in [60].

The methodological framework yielded by the S^4PR paradigm of RAS has raised considerable interest [61] on the grounds of a well-balanced compromise between modeling flexibility and the provision of sound and effective correction techniques.

In [62], a very general class of Petri nets are defined. This class has been called Petri nets of resource allocation (PNRA) to model as many kinds of RAS as possible. It not only focuses on the resources shared by processes, but also pays attention to the interaction/collaboration among processes.

At the solving of deadlock problems in AMS modeled with PN in [63], the attention is focused on adding a set of recovery transitions.

Here, in this paper, devoted to deadlock prevention and avoiding, it is not a sufficient space to analyze all introduced literature sources in details item by item. Namely, this area has many isolated particulars which are analyzed in detail in the above literature [6–10,28,31–57].

Methods based on P-invariants are divided into many subclasses interested in deterministic and/or unreliable resources, methods suitable for ordinary and/or generalized PN, methods using linear and/or non-linear restrictions, methods applying optimization based on the linear programming (usually mixed integer linear programming (MILP)), etc.

Methods based on siphons and traps have still lots more such subclasses. The very good literature review of methods concerning the deadlock prevention is made in [26]. Likewise, in [53] a crucial literature review concerning the deadlock control is presented. A variety of deadlock-control policies is mentioned there. The optimization based on MILP is one of them. Such optimization can eliminate the need to compute completely all elementary siphons, which shorten the computational time for finding indispensably needed siphons.

In the following two sections, principles of both methods of the prevention of deadlocks will be introduced and mathematically described. Illustrative examples explaining the application of both methods in details will be introduced there as well.

3. P-Invariant-Based Method of Prevention Deadlocks

P-invariants are vectors $\mathbf{I}$ with the important property. The multiplication of such vectors with any marking (state) vector $\mathbf{M}$ reachable from a given initial marking $\mathbf{M}_0$ yields the same result. It is the relation of the state conservation, as follows

$$\mathbf{I}^T.\mathbf{M} = \mathbf{I}^T.\mathbf{M}_0 \tag{2}$$

Taking into account the consecutive states obtained by firing of only one transition, we have for each transition t

$$\mathbf{I}^T.\vec{col}_t(\mathbf{N}) = 0, \tag{3}$$

where, $\vec{col}_t(\mathbf{N})$ is the column of the incidence matrix $\mathbf{N}$ corresponding to the transition t. These vectors are solutions of the following equation

$$\mathbf{I}^T.\mathbf{N} = \mathbf{0}^T \tag{4}$$

what corresponds with the original Definition 2 of P-invariants introduced in the Section 2.

Consider the inequality representing linear combinations restricting behavior of marking $\mathbf{M}$

$$\mathbf{L}.\mathbf{M} \leq \mathbf{b} \tag{5}$$

Here, $\mathbf{L}$ is a matrix of integers, $\mathbf{b}$ is an integer vector. An efficient help at creating $\mathbf{L}$ yields the reachability tree (RT) of the net N. After removing inequality by adding slack variables, we have

$$\mathbf{L}.\mathbf{M} + \mathbf{s} = \mathbf{b}, \tag{6}$$

where entries of the $(n_s \times 1)$ vector $\mathbf{s}$ represents slack variables.

Just the Equation (4) represents the base of the method for the supervisor synthesis. Namely, when we force there $[\mathbf{L}|\mathbf{I}_s]$ instead of $\mathbf{I}^T$, we obtain (7) and some additional PN places (slacks) can be added to N. Thus, the extended (augmented) PN $N_1 = N \circ N_s$ (where the symbol $\circ$ expresses a composition) will arise. N_s is the PN which will (after finding its interconnections with N) ultimately create the supervisor. Then, slacks will create the places of the supervisor, frequently called monitors. In N_1 we have the following structure of (4) in the form

$$[\mathbf{L}|\mathbf{I}_s] \cdot \begin{bmatrix} \mathbf{N} \\ \mathbf{N}_s \end{bmatrix} = \mathbf{0}, \qquad (7)$$

where $\mathbf{I}_s$ is $(n_s \times n_s)$-dimensional *identity matrix*; n_s is the number of slacks; $\mathbf{L}$ is a $(n_s \times n)$-dimensional matrix which in a suitable form expresses the conditions imposed on marking (state) vectors of the original PN N, and $\mathbf{N}_s$ is the $(n_s \times m)$-dimensional matrix. After finding $\mathbf{N}_s$ from (7) by computing, we have the structure of the PN-based model of the supervisor—i.e., interconnecting arcs between N and N_s. Consequently, in general,

$$\mathbf{L}.\mathbf{N} + \mathbf{N}_s = \mathbf{0} \qquad (8)$$
$$\mathbf{N}_s = -\mathbf{L}.\mathbf{N} \qquad (9)$$
$$\mathbf{N}_s = \mathbf{N}_s^+ - \mathbf{N}_s^-, \qquad (10)$$

where $\mathbf{N}_s^+$ is $\mathbf{Post}_s$ and $\mathbf{N}_s^-$ is $\mathbf{Pre}_s$ of $\mathbf{N}_s$.

The marking $\mathbf{M}_a$ of the supervised system N_1 consists of the state vector $\mathbf{M}$ of the N augmented with the state vector $\mathbf{M}_s$ of the supervisor N_s. Analogically, the incidence matrix $\mathbf{N}_a$ of the net N_1 consists of the incidence matrix $\mathbf{N}$ of N augmented with the incidence matrix $\mathbf{N}_s$ of the net N_s. The marking and the incidence matrix of the net N_1 are as follows

$$\mathbf{M}_a = \begin{pmatrix} \mathbf{M} \\ \mathbf{M}_s \end{pmatrix} \qquad (11)$$

$$\mathbf{N}_a^- = \begin{pmatrix} \mathbf{N}^- \\ \mathbf{N}_s^- \end{pmatrix} \qquad (12)$$

$$\mathbf{N}_a^+ = \begin{pmatrix} \mathbf{N}^+ \\ \mathbf{N}_s^+ \end{pmatrix}, \qquad (13)$$

Here, $\mathbf{N}_a$, $\mathbf{N}$ and $\mathbf{N}_s$ are expressed by sub-matrices $\mathbf{N}_a^+$ and $\mathbf{N}_a^-$, $\mathbf{N}^+$ and $\mathbf{N}^-$, and $\mathbf{N}_s^+$ and $\mathbf{N}_s^-$.

Because of the prescribed conditions we have

$$[\mathbf{L}|\mathbf{I}_s] \cdot \begin{bmatrix} \mathbf{M}_0 \\ {}^s\mathbf{M}_0 \end{bmatrix} = \mathbf{b}, \qquad (14)$$

where $\mathbf{b}$ is the $(n_s \times 1))$-dimensional vector (see (5) and (6)). Its integer entries represent the limits for number of tokens in (5). Sometimes $\mathbf{b} = \mathbf{1}$ where $\mathbf{1}$ is the vector with all its entries equal to 1. Because

$$\mathbf{L}.\mathbf{M}_0 + {}^s\mathbf{M}_0 = \mathbf{b} \qquad (15)$$

the initial state vector of the supervisor can be simply computed as follows

$${}^s\mathbf{M}_0 = \mathbf{b} - \mathbf{L}.\mathbf{M}_0 \qquad (16)$$

Example 1

Consider the simple example of N modeling an AMS with two production lines $\{p_7, t_1, p_1, t_2, p_2, t_3\}$ and $\{p_8, t_4, p_3, t_5, p_4, t_6\}$ with two common resources p_5 and p_6, introduced in Figure 1. Places p_7 and p_8 are idle process places, p_1, p_2, p_3, and p_4 are active process places, and p_5 and p_6 are resource places. A token in an active process place models, e.g., a part being processed. In Figure 1, active process places are empty till firing t_1 and/or t_4. Tokens located in a resource place model, e.g., the available capacity of buffers. Tokens located in an idle place indicate the maximal number of concurrent activities that can occur in a process represented by the corresponding production line.

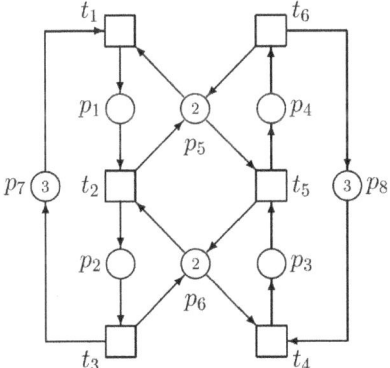

Figure 1. The PN model of an AMS.

Parameters of N are as follows

$$\mathbf{N}^- = \begin{pmatrix} 0 & 1 & 0 & 0 & 0 & 0 \\ 0 & 0 & 1 & 0 & 0 & 0 \\ 0 & 0 & 0 & 0 & 1 & 0 \\ 0 & 0 & 0 & 0 & 0 & 1 \\ 1 & 0 & 0 & 0 & 1 & 0 \\ 0 & 1 & 0 & 1 & 0 & 0 \\ 1 & 0 & 0 & 0 & 0 & 0 \\ 0 & 0 & 0 & 1 & 0 & 0 \end{pmatrix} \quad \mathbf{N}^+ = \begin{pmatrix} 1 & 0 & 0 & 0 & 0 & 0 \\ 0 & 1 & 0 & 0 & 0 & 0 \\ 0 & 0 & 0 & 1 & 0 & 0 \\ 0 & 0 & 0 & 0 & 1 & 0 \\ 0 & 1 & 0 & 0 & 0 & 1 \\ 0 & 0 & 1 & 0 & 1 & 0 \\ 0 & 0 & 1 & 0 & 0 & 0 \\ 0 & 0 & 0 & 0 & 0 & 1 \end{pmatrix} \quad (17)$$

This N has, at the given initial state $M_0 = (0, 0, 0, 0, 2, 2, 3, 3)^T$, the fairly branched (patulous) reachability tree (RT) with 33 nodes (including M_0). All RT nodes, being the reachable markings $M_0, \ldots, M_{32}$ are the columns of the following matrix (in the ascending order):

$$\mathbf{X}_r = \begin{pmatrix} 0 & 1 & 0 & 2 & 0 & 1 & 0 & 0 & 1 & 2 & 0 & 1 & 1 & 0 & 2 & 0 & 1 & |2| & 0 & 1 & 0 & 0 & 1 & 2 & 1 & 0 & 1 & 0 & 0 & 1 & 0 & 1 & 0 \\ 0 & 0 & 0 & 0 & 1 & 0 & 0 & 0 & 1 & 0 & 1 & 0 & 0 & 0 & 1 & 2 & 1 & |0| & 1 & 0 & 0 & 0 & 2 & 1 & 1 & 1 & 0 & 0 & 2 & 1 & 1 & 2 & 1 \\ 0 & 0 & 1 & 0 & 0 & 1 & 2 & 0 & 0 & 1 & 1 & 2 & 0 & 1 & 0 & 0 & 1 & |2| & 0 & 1 & 2 & 0 & 0 & 1 & 0 & 1 & 2 & 1 & 0 & 1 & 0 & 0 & 1 \\ 0 & 0 & 0 & 0 & 0 & 0 & 0 & 1 & 0 & 0 & 0 & 0 & 1 & 1 & 0 & 0 & 0 & |0| & 1 & 1 & 1 & 2 & 0 & 0 & 1 & 1 & 1 & 2 & 1 & 1 & 2 & 1 & 2 \\ 2 & 1 & 2 & 0 & 2 & 1 & 2 & 1 & 1 & 0 & 2 & 1 & 0 & 1 & 0 & 2 & 1 & |0| & 1 & 0 & 1 & 0 & 1 & 0 & 0 & 1 & 0 & 0 & 1 & 0 & 0 & 0 & 0 \\ 2 & 2 & 1 & 2 & 1 & 1 & 0 & 2 & 1 & 1 & 0 & 0 & 2 & 1 & 1 & 0 & 0 & |0| & 1 & 1 & 0 & 2 & 0 & 0 & 1 & 0 & 0 & 1 & 0 & 0 & 1 & 0 & 0 \\ 3 & 2 & 3 & 1 & 2 & 2 & 3 & 3 & 1 & 1 & 2 & 2 & 2 & 3 & 0 & 1 & 1 & |1| & 2 & 2 & 3 & 3 & 0 & 0 & 1 & 2 & 2 & 3 & 1 & 1 & 1 & 2 & 0 & 2 \\ 3 & 3 & 2 & 3 & 3 & 2 & 1 & 2 & 3 & 2 & 2 & 1 & 2 & 1 & 3 & 3 & 2 & |1| & 2 & 1 & 0 & 1 & 3 & 2 & 2 & 1 & 0 & 0 & 2 & 1 & 1 & 2 & 0 \end{pmatrix} \quad (18)$$

Because RT is too big, it cannot be introduced here full. In Figure 2, at least its principal fragment is introduced.

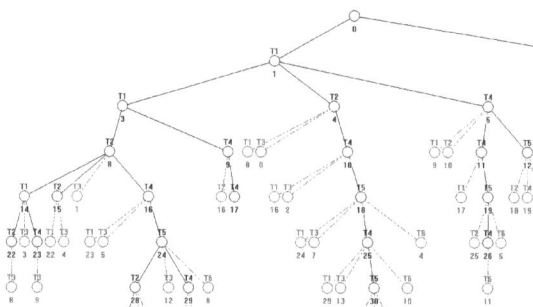

Figure 2. The principal fragment of the RT.

From the RT fragment we can find the solitary deadlock $M_{17} = (2, 0, 2, 0, 0, 0, 1, 1)^T$—see (18), where it is separated. This deadlock can be reached by following paths:

$$\mathbf{M}_0 \xrightarrow{t_1} \mathbf{M}_1 \xrightarrow{t_1} \mathbf{M}_3 \xrightarrow{t_4} \mathbf{M}_9 \xrightarrow{t_4} \mathbf{M}_{17} \tag{19}$$

$$\mathbf{M}_0 \xrightarrow{t_1} \mathbf{M}_1 \xrightarrow{t_4} \mathbf{M}_5 \xrightarrow{t_1} \mathbf{M}_9 \xrightarrow{t_4} \mathbf{M}_{17} \tag{20}$$

$$\mathbf{M}_0 \xrightarrow{t_1} \mathbf{M}_1 \xrightarrow{t_1} \mathbf{M}_3 \xrightarrow{t_2} \mathbf{M}_8 \xrightarrow{t_1} \mathbf{M}_{14} \xrightarrow{t_4} \mathbf{M}_{23} \xrightarrow{t_3} \mathbf{M}_9 \xrightarrow{t_4} \mathbf{M}_{17} \tag{21}$$

$$\mathbf{M}_0 \xrightarrow{t_1} \mathbf{M}_1 \xrightarrow{t_1} \mathbf{M}_3 \xrightarrow{t_2} \mathbf{M}_8 \xrightarrow{t_4} \mathbf{M}_{16} \xrightarrow{t_1} \mathbf{M}_{23} \xrightarrow{t_3} \mathbf{M}_9 \xrightarrow{t_4} \mathbf{M}_{17} \tag{22}$$

Hence, we can see that in RT the node M_9 immediately precedes the node M_{17} representing the deadlock. These nodes are marking vectors $\mathbf{M}_9 = (2, 0, 1, 0, 0, 1, 1, 2)^T$ (the 10th column of $\mathbf{X}_r$ because the first column is $\mathbf{M}_0$) and $\mathbf{M}_{17} = (2, 0, 2, 0, 0, 0, 1, 1)^T$ (the 18th column of $\mathbf{X}_r$). After comparing entries of these vectors, from (19) follows the restriction $M(p_1) + M(p_3) < 2$ (i.e., only one of them can be marked), i.e., $\mathbf{L} = (1, 0, 1, 0, 0, 0, 0, 0)^T$ and $\mathbf{b} = (2)$. Consequently, $\mathbf{N}_s = (-1, 1, 0, -1, 1, 0)$ and $^s\mathbf{M}_0 = (2)$ because in (16) $\mathbf{L}.\mathbf{M}_0 = 0$. Hence, with respect to (11)–(13) we have the augmented PN N_a (i.e., the original uncontrolled net N together with the net N_s representing the supervisor) and the augmented vector $^a\mathbf{M}_0$ of the initial marking as follows

$$\mathbf{N}_a = \begin{pmatrix} 1 & -1 & 0 & 0 & 0 & 0 \\ 0 & 1 & -1 & 0 & 0 & 0 \\ 0 & 0 & 0 & 1 & -1 & 0 \\ 0 & 0 & 0 & 0 & 1 & -1 \\ -1 & 1 & 0 & 0 & -1 & 1 \\ 0 & -1 & 1 & -1 & 1 & 0 \\ -1 & 0 & 1 & 0 & 0 & 0 \\ 0 & 0 & 0 & -1 & 0 & 1 \\ - & - & - & - & - & - \\ -1 & 1 & 0 & -1 & 1 & 0 \end{pmatrix} \quad {}^a\mathbf{M}_0 = (\mathbf{M}_0^T | {}^s\mathbf{M}_0^T)^T = \begin{pmatrix} 0 \\ 0 \\ 0 \\ 0 \\ 2 \\ 2 \\ 3 \\ 3 \\ - \\ 2 \end{pmatrix} \tag{23}$$

Thus, we have the supervisor represented by the single PN place p_9 (monitor) interconnected with the original PN model as it can be seen in Figure 3.

After computing RT of the augmented net, we can find that it contains 28 nodes and no deadlock exists there. It means that the augmented net works correctly.

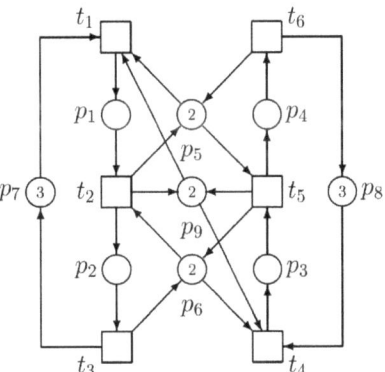

Figure 3. The controlled PN model of the AMS.

4. Siphon and Trap-Based Method of Prevention Deadlocks

Such approaches are much more widespread than approaches based on P-invariants. There are many sources in literature. Let us mention at least some of them [7,8,12,13,16,29].

Invariants, siphons, and traps are structural entities of PN. All of them can be computed, e.g., by the Matlab-based tool presented in [30]. The problem of deadlock prevention in a concurrent system represented by N is equivalent to the problem of avoidance of empty siphons in the ordinary PN model of N. When at least one empty siphon occurs in ordinary PN N, the net is totally deadlocked [5].

At the supervisor synthesis it is sufficient to consider only minimal siphons. It is necessary to ensure that the sum of the number of tokens in each minimal siphon S is never less than one, namely in any reachable marking M. In such a case, the general condition $\mathbf{S}_i.\mathbf{M} \geq b$ for ith siphon can be replaced by the condition in the form $\mathbf{S}_i.\mathbf{M} \geq 1$. This can be derived as follows.

Consider the following formal specification in N

$$1^T.\mathbf{M} \geq b \qquad (24)$$

where $\mathbf{l}$ is a $(n \times 1)$-dimensional vector, $\mathbf{M}$ is a marking and b is a scalar; b and the entries of $\mathbf{l}$ are integers. The relation (24) says that the weighted sum of the number of tokens in each place should be greater than or equal to a constant.

In [6], it was proved that if a Petri net $N = (P, T, F, W)$ with incidence matrix $\mathbf{N}$ and initial state $\mathbf{M}_0$ satisfies the following relation

$$b - 1^T.\mathbf{M}_0 \leq 0 \qquad (25)$$

then a control place p_c can be added, that enforces (24). Let $\mathbf{N}_c : T \rightarrow \mathbb{Z}$ ($\mathbb{Z}$ is the set of integers) denotes the weight vector of arcs connecting p_c with the transitions in the net N; $\mathbf{N}_c$ is obtained by $\mathbf{N}_c = 1^T.\mathbf{N}$. In general, when there are more p_c than one, $\mathbf{N}_c = \mathbf{L}^T.\mathbf{N}$ with $\mathbf{L}$ being the matrix were rows represent particular 1^T appertaining to particular p_c. The initial number of tokens in p_c is $M_0(p_c) = 1^T.\mathbf{M}_0 - b \geq 0$ or, in general, $\mathbf{M}_c^0 = \mathbf{L}.\mathbf{M}_0 - \mathbf{b} \geq \mathbf{0}$.

The controlled Petri net is maximally permissive. The control process enforces *just enough control* to avoid all illegal markings. This is the basis for deadlock prevention, i.e., for the synthesis of the control algorithm based on siphons. Thus, the place invariant guarantees that for any marking $\mathbf{M}$ in the set of reachable markings of N

$$1^T.\mathbf{M} - M(p_c) = b \qquad (26)$$

Here, as it was defined above, $M(p_c)$ is the number of tokens in the control place p_c. Due to the fact that $M(p_c)$ is non-negative, the inequality in (24) is satisfied. Equation (25) expresses the demand that (24) must be satisfied for $\mathbf{M}_0$, otherwise no solution exists there. $\mathbf{b}_c$ represents the row which extends the incidence matrix $\mathbf{N}$ of the uncontrolled net N with respect to the control place p_c. In general, for more additive places $p_1, \ldots, p_s$, it can be written

$$\mathbf{L}.\mathbf{M} \geq \mathbf{b}, \quad \text{or} \quad \mathbf{L}.\mathbf{M} - \mathbf{M}_c = \mathbf{b} \tag{27}$$

where $\mathbf{L}$ is $(n_s \times n)$ matrix of positive integers greater than or equal to 0. $\mathbf{L}$ has the weighted vectors $\mathbf{l}_i^T$, $i = 1, \ldots, s$, as its rows. The vector $\mathbf{b}$ is $(n_s \times 1)$ vector of restrictions with entries being positive integers greater than or equal to 0; $\mathbf{M}_c$ is $(n_s \times 1)$ vector of slacks with entries being positive integers greater than or equal to 0. Thus, we obtain the controlled PN model (with the incidence matrix $\mathbf{N}_{ex}$) consisting of original uncontrolled model (with the incidence matrix $\mathbf{N}$) and the siphon-based controller (with the incidence matrix $\mathbf{N}_c$) as follows

$$\mathbf{N}_c = \mathbf{L}.\mathbf{N} \tag{28}$$
$$\mathbf{M}_c^0 = \mathbf{L}.\mathbf{M}_0 - \mathbf{b} \geq 0 \tag{29}$$
$$\mathbf{N}_{ex} = \begin{pmatrix} \mathbf{N} \\ \mathbf{N}_c \end{pmatrix}; \quad \mathbf{M}_{ex}^0 = \begin{pmatrix} \mathbf{M}_0 \\ \mathbf{M}_c^0 \end{pmatrix} \tag{30}$$

The controller consists of monitors and their interconnections with the original PN model.

Replacing $\mathbf{l}_i^T$ by the siphon $\mathbf{S}_i$, or, in general, replacing $\mathbf{L}$ by the matrix of siphons $\mathbf{S}_m$ (where particular siphons are its rows) we obtain

$$\mathbf{N}_c = \mathbf{S}_m.\mathbf{N} \tag{31}$$

4.1. Example 2

Minimal siphons and traps of the PN model in Figure 1 are the following

$$\begin{aligned}
&\cancel{S_1 = \{p_1, p_2, p_7\}} & &\cancel{Tr_1 = \{p_1, p_2, p_7\}} \\
&\cancel{S_2 = \{p_2, p_3, p_6\}} & &\cancel{Tr_2 = \{p_2, p_3, p_6\}} \\
&\cancel{S_3 = \{p_1, p_4, p_5\}} & &\cancel{Tr_3 = \{p_1, p_4, p_5\}} \\
&\cancel{S_4 = \{p_3, p_4, p_8\}} & &\cancel{Tr_4 = \{p_3, p_4, p_8\}} \\
&S_5 = \{p_2, p_4, p_5, p_6\} & &Tr_5 = \{p_1, p_3, p_5, p_6\}
\end{aligned}$$

Denote $S = S_5$ and $T = Tr_5$. In this simple example, the siphon and trap can be illustrated by Figure 4. Above introduced crossed siphons are equaled to traps. Such a siphon cannot be emptied once it is initially marked (this is ensured by the corresponding marked trap). Residual siphons are strict minimal siphons (SMS). Consequently, there is only one SMS, namely S_5. In a vector form it is denoted as $\mathbf{S}$ as follows

$$\mathbf{S} = \begin{pmatrix} 0 & 1 & 0 & 1 & 1 & 1 & 0 & 0 \end{pmatrix}^T \tag{32}$$

The siphon corresponds with the Figure 4 as well as the trap Tr_5. With respect to (31)

$$\mathbf{N}_c = \mathbf{S}.\mathbf{N} = \begin{pmatrix} -1 & 1 & 0 & -1 & 1 & 0 & 0 & 0 \end{pmatrix} \tag{33}$$

what is the same structure of the supervisor like in the previous approach based on P-invariants. Thus, the PN model of the controlled (supervised) AMS is in Figure 3. However, it must be said that such a coincidence of the results achieved by both methods occurs only rarely, not in general.

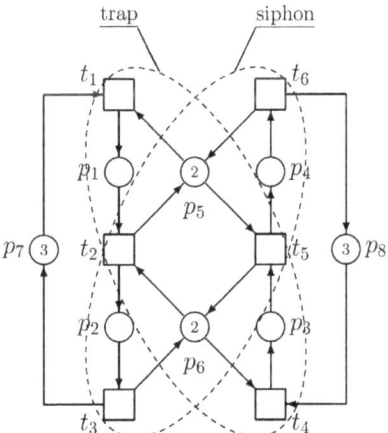

Figure 4. The siphon S and trap T in the PN model.

4.2. Invariant-Controlled Siphons and Setting the Marking of Monitors in the Siphon-Based Approach

The control places p_c creating the supervisor are frequently named as monitors. Denote them as V_{S_i}, $i = 1, \ldots, n_m$ (n_m is a number of monitors). Now it is important to find a suitable marking of the monitors V_{S_i}. Namely, an inadequate setting of marking of monitors may cause other deadlocks in the controlled plant. In general, for setting the marking of monitors V_{S_i}, $i = 1, n_m$ are valid the following general rules.

Let $S = \{p_i, p_j, \ldots, p_k\}$ be a strict minimal siphon (SMS) of an original (uncontrolled) ordinary net system (N_0, M_0), where $N_0 = (P_0, T_0, F_0)$. Add a monitor V_S to N_0 to make the vector $\mathbf{I} = (0, \ldots, 1i, \ldots, 1j, \ldots, 1k, \ldots, 0, -1)^T$ be a P-invariant of a new (controlled) net system (N_1, M_1). Here, $\forall p \in P_0 \backslash S$, $I(p) = 0$, $I(V_S) = -1$, $\forall p \in P_0$, $M_1(p) = M_0(p)$, and $\mathbf{N}_1 = [\mathbf{N}_0^T | \mathbf{L}_{V_s}^T]^T$, where $\mathbf{L}_{V_s}$ is a row vector corresponding to adding the place V_S. Let $M_1(V_S) = M_0(S) - \xi_S$, where $1 \leq \xi_S \leq M_0(S)$. Then S is an invariant-controlled SMS. Hence, it is always marked at any reachable marking of the net system (N_1, M_1). Namely, $\mathbf{I}$ is a P-invariant and $\forall p \in (P_0 \cup \{V_S\}) \backslash S$, $I(p) < 0$. Note than $\mathbf{I}^T.\mathbf{M}_1 = \mathbf{I}^T.\mathbf{M}_0 = M_0(S) - M_1(V_S) = \xi_S > 0$. Thus, S is an invariant-controlled siphon.

A siphon S is controlled in a net (N, M_0) iff $\forall M \in R(N, M_0), M(S) > 0$. Thus, any siphon that contains a marked trap is controlled. Namely, the marked trap can never be emptied. In ordinary PN a controlled siphon does not cause any deadlock.

A siphon S in an ordinary PN (N, M_0) is [7] invariant-controlled by P-invariant I under M_0 iff $\mathbf{I}^T.\mathbf{M}_0 > 0$ and $\forall p \in P \backslash S, I(p) \leq 0$, or equivalently $\mathbf{I}^T.\mathbf{M}_0 > 0$ and $||I||^+ = p \in P|I(p)$ is the positive support of I.

More succinctly said, a siphon S is controlled if it can never be emptied, and invariant-controlled by P-invariant I if $\mathbf{I}^T.\mathbf{M}_0 > 0$ and $||I||^+ \subseteq S$.

So that, to guarantee that a siphon S is always marked in a net system, it is necessary to keep at least one token being present at S at any reachable marking of the net system. Suppose that it was found such a control of a siphon S that S will never be emptied. Let ξ_S is the least number of tokens being present at S. Such ξ_S is called the siphon control depth variable. It is clear that the larger ξ_S is, the more behavior of the modeled system will be restricted. However, it may means that more reachable states will be forbidden than it is necessary. Therefore, it is suitable when the siphon control depth variable is as small as possible, i.e., 1, if possible.

Setting the Marking of Monitors in Example 2

It is easy to check from Figure 3 with taking into account Figure 4 that $I = \{p_2, p_4, p_5, p_6\} - V_S$ is P-invariant of N_1. Clearly, $S = \{p_2, p_4, p_5, p_6\}$ is invariant-controlled by I, since $||I||^+ = S$ and $M_0(S) - M_1(V_S) = 4 - 2 > 0$. Here, $||I||^+$, is the positive support of I.

5. More Complicated Examples
5.1. Example 3

Consider a PN model in the form presented in Figure 5.

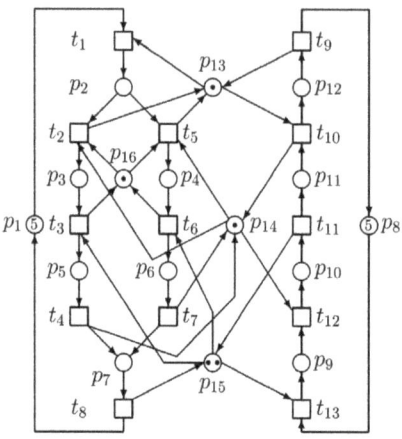

Figure 5. The bigger PN model.

This PN model has RT with 77 nodes (including $\mathbf{M}_0$). There are three deadlocks in the PN, namely

$$\mathbf{M}_{33} = (3, 1, 1, 0, 0, 0, 0, 3, 2, 0, 0, 0, 0, 0, 0, 0)^T \tag{34}$$
$$\mathbf{M}_{36} = (3, 1, 0, 1, 0, 0, 0, 3, 2, 0, 0, 0, 0, 0, 0, 0)^T \tag{35}$$
$$\mathbf{M}_{44} = (4, 1, 0, 0, 0, 0, 0, 2, 2, 0, 1, 0, 0, 0, 0, 1)^T \tag{36}$$

Because of the large RT it is difficult or practically impossible (by commonly available means) to analyze RT in order to find the matrix $\mathbf{L}$ and the vector $\mathbf{b}$ in (5). It remains to use the approach based on siphon and traps. Using the Matlab-based tool in [30] we obtain the following minimal siphons and traps

$\cancel{S_1 = \{p_3, p_4, p_{16}\}}$ $\cancel{Tr_1 = \{p_3, p_4, p_{16}\}}$
$\cancel{S_2 = \{p_2, p_{12}, p_{13}\}}$ $\cancel{Tr_2 = \{p_2, p_{12}, p_{13}\}}$
$\cancel{S_3 = \{p_8, p_9, p_{10}, p_{11}, p_{12}\}}$ $Tr_3 = \{p_2, p_{10}, p_{11}, p_{13}, p_{14}\}$
$\cancel{S_4 = \{p_5, p_6, p_7, p_9, p_{10}, p_{15}\}}$ $\cancel{Tr_4 = \{p_8, p_9, p_{10}, p_{11}, p_{12}\}}$
$\cancel{S_5 = \{p_1, p_2, p_3, p_4, p_5, p_6, p_7\}}$ $\cancel{Tr_5 = \{p_5, p_6, p_7, p_9, p_{10}, p_{15}\}}$
$S_6 = \{p_3, p_4, p_5, p_6, p_{12}, p_{13}, p_{14}\}$ $\cancel{Tr_6 = \{p_1, p_2, p_3, p_4, p_5, p_6, p_7\}}$
$\cancel{S_7 = \{p_3, p_4, p_5, p_6, p_{10}, p_{11}, p_{14}\}}$ $\cancel{Tr_7 = \{p_3, p_4, p_5, p_6, p_{10}, p_{11}, p_{14}\}}$
$S_8 = \{p_5, p_6, p_7, p_{10}, p_{11}, p_{14}, p_{15}\}$ $Tr_8 = \{p_2, p_9, p_{10}, p_{13}, p_{14}, p_{15}, p_{16}\}$
$S_9 = \{p_5, p_6, p_7, p_{10}, p_{12}, p_{13}, p_{14}, p_{15}\}$ $Tr_9 = \{p_2, p_5, p_6, p_9, p_{10}, p_{13}, p_{14}, p_{15}\}$
     $Tr_{10} = \{p_3, p_4, p_5, p_6, p_9, p_{10}, p_{14}, p_{15}\}$

Because $S_1 = Tr_1$, $S_2 = Tr_2$, $S_3 = Tr_4$, $S_4 = Tr_5$, $S_5 = Tr_6$, and $S_7 = Tr_7$, there are three minimal siphons where emptying must be prevented, namely S_6, S_8, and S_9. Rename S_6 to be S_1, S_8 to be S_2 and S_9 to be S_3. Consequently, we have

$$S = \begin{pmatrix} 0 & 0 & 1 & 1 & 1 & 1 & 0 & 0 & 0 & 0 & 0 & 1 & 1 & 1 & 0 & 0 \\ 0 & 0 & 0 & 0 & 1 & 1 & 1 & 0 & 0 & 1 & 1 & 0 & 0 & 1 & 1 & 0 \\ 0 & 0 & 0 & 0 & 1 & 1 & 1 & 0 & 0 & 1 & 0 & 1 & 1 & 1 & 1 & 0 \end{pmatrix} \quad (37)$$

$$N_c = S.N = \begin{pmatrix} -1 & 1 & 0 & 0 & 1 & 0 & 0 & 0 & 0 & 1 & 0 & -1 & 0 \\ 0 & -1 & 0 & 1 & -1 & 0 & 1 & 0 & 0 & 0 & 1 & 0 & -1 \\ -1 & 0 & 0 & 1 & 0 & 0 & 1 & 0 & 0 & 1 & 0 & 0 & -1 \end{pmatrix} \quad (38)$$

where the incidence matrix of the PN model is the following

$$N = \begin{pmatrix} -1 & 0 & 0 & 0 & 0 & 0 & 0 & 1 & 0 & 0 & 0 & 0 & 0 \\ 1 & -1 & 0 & 0 & -1 & 0 & 0 & 0 & 0 & 0 & 0 & 0 & 0 \\ 0 & 1 & -1 & 0 & 0 & 0 & 0 & 0 & 0 & 0 & 0 & 0 & 0 \\ 0 & 0 & 0 & 0 & 1 & -1 & 0 & 0 & 0 & 0 & 0 & 0 & 0 \\ 0 & 0 & 1 & -1 & 0 & 0 & 0 & 0 & 0 & 0 & 0 & 0 & 0 \\ 0 & 0 & 0 & 0 & 0 & 1 & -1 & 0 & 0 & 0 & 0 & 0 & 0 \\ 0 & 0 & 0 & 1 & 0 & 0 & 1 & -1 & 0 & 0 & 0 & 0 & 0 \\ 0 & 0 & 0 & 0 & 0 & 0 & 0 & 1 & 0 & 0 & 0 & 0 & -1 \\ 0 & 0 & 0 & 0 & 0 & 0 & 0 & 0 & 0 & 0 & -1 & 1 \\ 0 & 0 & 0 & 0 & 0 & 0 & 0 & 0 & 0 & -1 & 1 & 0 \\ 0 & 0 & 0 & 0 & 0 & 0 & 0 & 0 & -1 & 1 & 0 & 0 \\ 0 & 0 & 0 & 0 & 0 & 0 & 0 & -1 & 1 & 0 & 0 & 0 \\ -1 & 1 & 0 & 0 & 1 & 0 & 0 & 0 & 1 & -1 & 0 & 0 & 0 \\ 0 & -1 & 0 & 1 & -1 & 0 & 1 & 0 & 0 & 1 & 0 & -1 & 0 \\ 0 & 0 & -1 & 0 & 0 & -1 & 0 & 1 & 0 & 0 & 1 & 0 & -1 \\ 0 & -1 & 1 & 0 & -1 & 1 & 0 & 0 & 0 & 0 & 0 & 0 & 0 \end{pmatrix} \quad (39)$$

The uncontrolled PN model together with its supervisor is displayed in Figure 6. This form of the mutual interaction between the supervisor and the PN model is used in order to avoid intricate interconnections between the uncontrolled model and the supervisor in the same figure. Marking of monitors $V_{S_1} - V_{S_3}$ were established by the relation $M_0(S_i) - M_1(V_{S_i}) > 0$ for $i = 1, 2, 3$. Because $M_0(S_1) = 2$ it is sufficient to put $M_1(V_{S_1}) = 1$. Similarly, because $M_0(S_2) = 3$ it is sufficient to put $M_1(V_{S_2}) = 2$ and because $M_0(S_3) = 4$ it is sufficient to put $M_1(V_{S_3}) = 2$. In such a way controlled PN model (30) has RT with 56 nodes (it creates the state space of reachable markings) and no deadlocks. In case of putting $M_1(V_{S_3}) = 3$ a new deadlock would occur in controlled system, namely $M_{14} = (4, 1, 0, 0, 0, 0, 0, 3, 2, 0, 0, 0, 0, 1, 0, 1, 0, 0, 0)^T$.

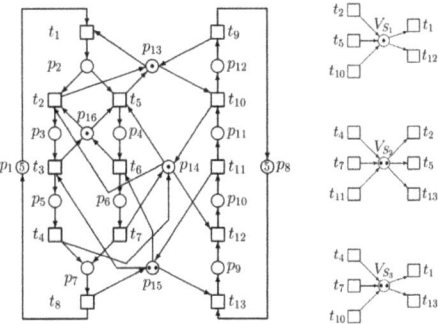

Figure 6. The PN model (**left**) with its supervisor (**right**) created by three monitors and their interconnections with the uncontrolled model.

5.2. Example 4

Consider the PN model given in Figure 7. There are 16 places and 12 transitions.

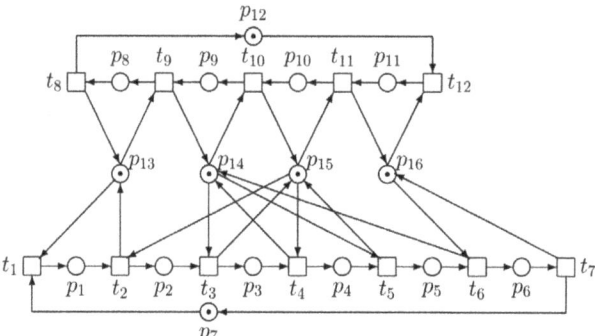

Figure 7. The PN model.

The transpose of the incidence matrix is the following

$$\mathbf{N}^T = \begin{pmatrix} 1 & 0 & 0 & 0 & 0 & 0 & -1 & 0 & 0 & 0 & 0 & -1 & 0 & 0 & 0 \\ -1 & 1 & 0 & 0 & 0 & 0 & 0 & 0 & 0 & 0 & 0 & 1 & 0 & -1 & 0 \\ 0 & -1 & 1 & 0 & 0 & 0 & 0 & 0 & 0 & 0 & 0 & 0 & -1 & 1 & 0 \\ 0 & 0 & -1 & 1 & 0 & 0 & 0 & 0 & 0 & 0 & 0 & 0 & 1 & -1 & 0 \\ 0 & 0 & 0 & -1 & 1 & 0 & 0 & 0 & 0 & 0 & 0 & 0 & -1 & 1 & 0 \\ 0 & 0 & 0 & 0 & -1 & 1 & 0 & 0 & 0 & 0 & 0 & 0 & 1 & 0 & -1 \\ 1 & 0 & 0 & 0 & 0 & -1 & 0 & 0 & 0 & 0 & 0 & 0 & 0 & 0 & 1 \\ 0 & 0 & 0 & 0 & 0 & 0 & -1 & 0 & 0 & 0 & 1 & 1 & 0 & 0 & 0 \\ 0 & 0 & 0 & 0 & 0 & 0 & 1 & -1 & 0 & 0 & 0 & -1 & 1 & 0 & 0 \\ 0 & 0 & 0 & 0 & 0 & 0 & 0 & 1 & -1 & 0 & 0 & 0 & -1 & 1 & 0 \\ 0 & 0 & 0 & 0 & 0 & 0 & 0 & 0 & 1 & -1 & 0 & 0 & 0 & -1 & 1 \\ 0 & 0 & 0 & 0 & 0 & 0 & 0 & 0 & 0 & 1 & -1 & 0 & 0 & 0 & -1 \end{pmatrix}$$

The siphons and traps are the following.

$\cancel{S_1 = \{p_{11}, p_{16}, p_6\}}$ $\qquad$ $\cancel{Tr_1 = \{p_{11}, p_{16}, p_6\}}$
$\cancel{S_2 = \{p_1, p_{13}, p_8\}}$ $\qquad$ $\cancel{Tr_2 = \{p_1, p_{13}, p_8\}}$
$S_3 = \{p_{10}, p_{15}, p_2, p_4\}$ $\qquad$ $Tr_3 = \{p_{10}, p_{14}, p_{15}, p_2\}$
$\cancel{S_4 = \{p_{14}, p_3, p_5, p_9\}}$ $\qquad$ $Tr_4 = \{p_{10}, p_{15}, p_2, p_4\}$
$S_5 = \{p_{14}, p_{15}, p_5, p_9\}$ $\qquad$ $\cancel{Tr_5 = \{p_{14}, p_3, p_5, p_9\}}$
$S_6 = \{p_{14}, p_{15}, p_{16}, p_6, p_9\}$ $\qquad$ $Tr_6 = \{p_1, p_{10}, p_{13}, p_{14}, p_{15}\}$
$\cancel{S_7 = \{p_{10}, p_{11}, p_{12}, p_8, p_9\}}$ $\qquad$ $Tr_7 = \{p_{11}, p_{14}, p_{15}, p_{16}, p_2\}$
$S_8 = \{p_{13}, p_{14}, p_{15}, p_5, p_8\}$ $\qquad$ $\cancel{Tr_8 = \{p_{10}, p_{11}, p_{12}, p_8, p_9\}}$
$S_9 = \{p_{13}, p_{14}, p_{15}, p_{16}, p_6, p_8\}$ $\qquad$ $Tr_9 = \{p_1, p_{11}, p_{13}, p_{14}, p_{15}, p_{16}\}$
$\cancel{S_{10} = \{p_1, p_2, p_3, p_4, p_5, p_6, p_7\}}$ $\qquad$ $\cancel{Tr_{10} = \{p_1, p_2, p_3, p_4, p_5, p_6, p_7\}}$

Here, $S_1 = Tr_1$, $S_2 = Tr_2$, $S_4 = Tr_5$, $S_7 = Tr_8$, $S_{10} = Tr_{10}$. Consequently, S_1, S_2, S_4, S_7, S_{10} cannot be emptied. It is sufficient to prevent S_3, S_5, S_6, S_8, S_9 before emptying. Rename them to be, respectively, S_1, S_2, S_3, S_4, S_5. Hence,

$$S = \begin{pmatrix} 0 & 1 & 0 & 1 & 0 & 0 & 0 & 0 & 1 & 0 & 0 & 0 & 0 & 1 & 0 \\ 0 & 0 & 0 & 0 & 1 & 0 & 0 & 1 & 0 & 0 & 0 & 0 & 1 & 1 & 0 \\ 0 & 0 & 0 & 0 & 0 & 1 & 0 & 0 & 1 & 0 & 0 & 0 & 1 & 1 & 1 \\ 0 & 0 & 0 & 0 & 1 & 0 & 0 & 1 & 0 & 0 & 0 & 1 & 1 & 1 & 0 \\ 0 & 0 & 0 & 0 & 0 & 1 & 0 & 1 & 0 & 0 & 0 & 1 & 1 & 1 & 1 \end{pmatrix} \qquad (40)$$

$$\mathbf{N}_c = \mathbf{S} \cdot \mathbf{N} = \begin{pmatrix} 0 & 0 & 0 & 0 & 0 & 0 & 0 & 0 & 0 & 0 & 0 \\ 0 & -1 & 0 & 0 & 1 & 0 & 0 & 0 & 0 & 1 & -1 & 0 \\ 0 & -1 & 0 & 0 & 0 & 1 & 0 & 0 & 0 & 1 & 0 & -1 \\ -1 & 0 & 0 & 0 & 1 & 0 & 0 & 0 & 1 & 0 & -1 & 0 \\ -1 & 0 & 0 & 0 & 0 & 1 & 0 & 0 & 1 & 0 & 0 & -1 \end{pmatrix} \quad (41)$$

Thus, we obtain five monitors $V_{S_1} - V_{S_5}$ (creating the supervisor) and their interconnections with the uncontrolled PN model. In order to establish marking of these monitors the following settings are necessary: $M_0(S_i) - M_1(V_{S_i}) > 0$, $i = 1, \ldots, 5$. Because $M_0(S_1) = 1$, $M_1(V_{S_1}) = 0$. Analogically, $M_0(S_2) = 2$, $M_1(V_{S_2}) = 1$; $M_0(S_3) = 3$, $M_1(V_{S_3}) = 2$; $M_0(S_4) = 3$, $M_1(V_{S_4}) = 2$; $M_0(S_5) = 4$, $M_1(V_{S_5}) = 3$. With markings of monitors set in such a way, we obtain the controlled PN model without any deadlocks. RT of the controlled PN model has 54 nodes including the initial marking $\mathbf{M}_0 = (0, 0, 0, 0, 0, 0, 1, 0, 0, 0, 0, 1, 1, 1, 1, 1 \,|\, 0, 1, 2, 2, 3)^T$. These nodes represent the space of reachable markings of the controlled PN model. The interconnection between original uncontrolled PN model and the supervisor represented by the set of monitors is realized by means of the incidence matrix $\mathbf{N}_c$, namely by $\mathbf{N}_c^+$ and $\mathbf{N}_c^-$. The supervisor is displayed in Figure 8 (right) together with the uncontrolled system (left).

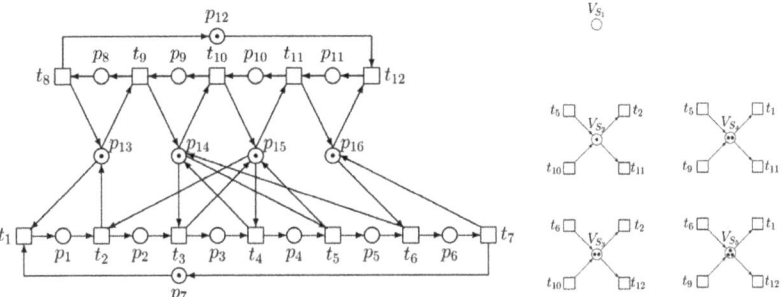

Figure 8. The PN model (**left**) with its supervisor (**right**) created by five monitors and their interconnections with the uncontrolled model. The monitor V_{S_1} is not connected as it is clear from the incidence matrix $\mathbf{N}_c$ in (41).

5.3. Example 5

Consider the PN model displayed in Figure 9.

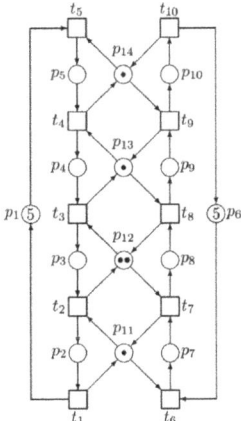

Figure 9. The PN model.

Its RT has 119 nodes (reachable markings) including the initial marking $\mathbf{M}_0 = (5, 0, 0, 0, 0, 5, 0, 0, 0, 0, 1, 2, 1, 1)^T$. There are five deadlocks in the model, namely $\mathbf{M}_{76}$, $\mathbf{M}_{85}$, $\mathbf{M}_{91}$, $\mathbf{M}_{96}$, $\mathbf{M}_{100}$ as follows,

$$\mathbf{M}_{76} = (3, 0, 0, 1, 1, 2, 1, 2, 0, 0, 0, 0, 0, 0)^T \qquad (42)$$
$$\mathbf{M}_{85} = (2, 0, 1, 1, 1, 3, 1, 1, 0, 0, 0, 0, 0, 0)^T \qquad (43)$$
$$\mathbf{M}_{91} = (4, 0, 0, 0, 1, 1, 1, 2, 1, 0, 0, 0, 0, 0)^T \qquad (44)$$
$$\mathbf{M}_{96} = (1, 0, 2, 1, 1, 4, 1, 0, 0, 0, 0, 0, 0, 0)^T \qquad (45)$$
$$\mathbf{M}_{100} = (3, 0, 1, 0, 1, 2, 1, 1, 1, 0, 0, 0, 0, 0)^T \qquad (46)$$

and the following siphon and traps

$\cancel{S_1 = \{p_2, p_7, p_{11}\}}$ $\cancel{Tr_1 = \{p_2, p_7, p_{11}\}}$
$\cancel{S_2 = \{p_3, p_8, p_{12}\}}$ $\cancel{Tr_2 = \{p_3, p_8, p_{12}\}}$
$\cancel{S_3 = \{p_4, p_9, p_{13}\}}$ $\cancel{Tr_3 = \{p_4, p_9, p_{13}\}}$
$\cancel{S_4 = \{p_5, p_{10}, p_{14}\}}$ $\cancel{Tr_4 = \{p_5, p_{10}, p_{14}\}}$
$S_5 = \{p_2, p_8\, p_{11}, p_{12}\}$ $Tr_5 = \{p_3, p_7, p_{11}, p_{12}\}$
$S_6 = \{p_3, p_9, p_{12}, p_{13}\}$ $Tr_6 = \{p_4, p_8, p_{12}, p_{13}\}$
$S_7 = \{p_4, p_{10}, p_{13}, p_{14}\}$ $Tr_7 = \{p_5, p_9, p_{13}, p_{14}\}$
$\cancel{S_8 = \{p_1, p_2, p_3, p_4, p_5\}}$ $\cancel{Tr_8 = \{p_1, p_2, p_3, p_4, p_5\}}$
$S_9 = \{p_2, p_9, p_{11}, p_{12}, p_{13}\}$ $Tr_9 = \{p_4, p_7, p_{11}, p_{12}, p_{13}\}$
$S_{10} = \{p_3, p_{10}, p_{12}, p_{13}, p_{14}\}$ $Tr_{10} = \{p_5, p_8, p_{12}, p_{13}, p_{14}\}$
$\cancel{S_{11} = \{p_6, p_7, p_8, p_9, p_{10}\}}$ $\cancel{Tr_{11} = \{p_6, p_7, p_8, p_9, p_{10}\}}$
$S_{12} = \{p_2, p_{10}, p_{11}, p_{12}, p_{13}, p_{14}\}$ $Tr_{12} = \{p_5, p_7, p_{11}, p_{12}, p_{13}, p_{14}\}$

As we can see, $S_1 = Tr_1$, $S_2 = Tr_2$, $S_3 = Tr_3$, $S_4 = Tr_4$, $S_8 = Tr_8$, $S_{11} = Tr_{11}$. As we already know, if a siphon contains a marked trap, it will never become empty. Therefore, we do not have to take the listed siphons into account. When synthesizing the supervisor, it is sufficient to use the remaining six siphons, i.e., S_5, S_6, S_7, S_9, S_{10}, S_{12}. After elimination of siphons being consensual to traps, rename the residual siphons in ascending order starting from S_1, i.e., $S_1 = S_5$, $S_2 = S_6$, $S_3 = S_7$, $S_4 = S_9$, $S_5 = S_{10}$, and $S_6 = S_{12}$. Thus, the matrix of siphons will have the following shape

$$\mathbf{S}_m = \begin{pmatrix} 0 & 1 & 0 & 0 & 0 & 0 & 0 & 1 & 0 & 0 & 1 & 1 & 0 & 0 \\ 0 & 0 & 1 & 0 & 0 & 0 & 0 & 0 & 1 & 0 & 0 & 1 & 1 & 0 \\ 0 & 0 & 0 & 1 & 0 & 0 & 0 & 0 & 0 & 1 & 0 & 0 & 1 & 1 \\ 0 & 1 & 0 & 0 & 0 & 0 & 0 & 0 & 1 & 0 & 1 & 1 & 1 & 0 \\ 0 & 0 & 1 & 0 & 0 & 0 & 0 & 0 & 0 & 1 & 0 & 1 & 1 & 1 \\ 0 & 1 & 0 & 0 & 0 & 0 & 0 & 0 & 1 & 1 & 1 & 1 & 1 \end{pmatrix} \qquad (47)$$

Since the incidence matrix $\mathbf{N}$ of the uncontrolled PN model directly follows from the model structure introduced in Figure 9, the incidence matrix of the supervisor will be as follows

$$\mathbf{N}_c = \mathbf{S}_m \cdot \mathbf{N} = \begin{pmatrix} 0 & 1 & -1 & 0 & 0 & -1 & 1 & 0 & 0 & 0 \\ 0 & 0 & 1 & -1 & 0 & 0 & -1 & 1 & 0 & 0 \\ 0 & 0 & 0 & 1 & -1 & 0 & 0 & -1 & 1 & 0 \\ 0 & 1 & 0 & -1 & 0 & -1 & 0 & 1 & 0 & 0 \\ 0 & 0 & 1 & 0 & -1 & 0 & -1 & 0 & 1 & 0 \\ 0 & 1 & 0 & 0 & -1 & -1 & 0 & 0 & 1 & 0 \end{pmatrix} \qquad (48)$$

To set marking of particular monitors $V_{S_1}, \ldots, V_{S_6}$, we will use the relation $M_0(S_i) - M_1(V_{S_i}) > 0$ for $i = 1, \ldots, 6$. Because $M_0(S_1) = M_0(S_2) = 3$, $M_0(S_3) = 2$, $M_0(S_4) = M_0(S_5) = 4$, and $M_0(S_6) = 5$. Hence, for $M_1(V_{S_1}) = M_1(V_{S_2}) = 2$, $M_1(V_{S_3}) = 1$, $M_1(V_{S_4}) = M_1(V_{S_5}) = 2$, and $M_1(V_{S_6}) = 2$ there are no deadlocks in the supervised PN model. The supervisor (the set of monitors) is displayed in Figure 10 right, in the neighborhood of the unsupervised PN model.

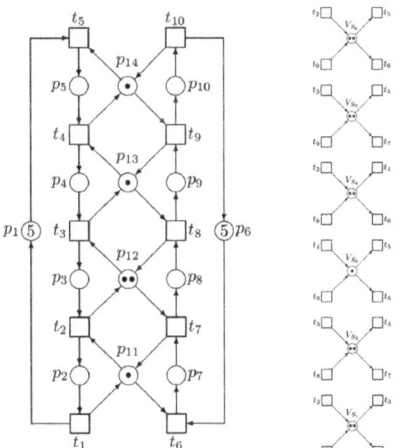

Figure 10. The unsupervised PN model together with its supervisor.

5.4. Example 6

In order to show that there may occur computational problems in case of PN models which need not be neither large nor structurally complicated consider the PN model in Figure 11.

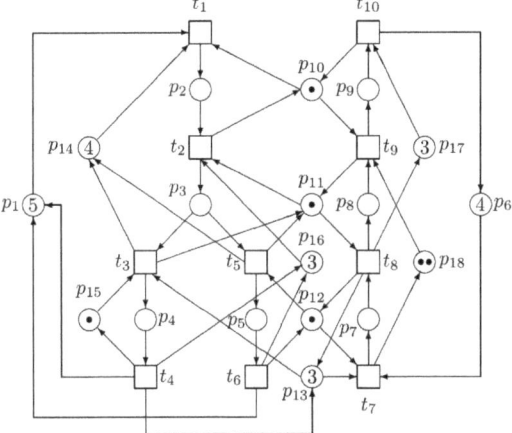

Figure 11. The PN model.

In this case, it was not possible to calculate siphons and traps by the tool offered in [30] on PC (with Intel(R) Core(TM), i7-10700 CPU @ 2.90 GHz 2.90 GHz with 16 GB RAM and 64-bit operating system Windows 11) even after tens of hours (more than 24) of computation. So let us try to go back to the approach based on P-invariants RT of this uncontrolled PN model has 40 nodes (including the initial marking). There is only one deadlock $\mathbf{M}_{17} = (4, 1, 0, 0, 0, 2, 1, 1, 0, 0, 0, 0, 2, 3, 1, 3, 4, 4)^T$, as we can see from the segment of RT displayed in Figure 12.

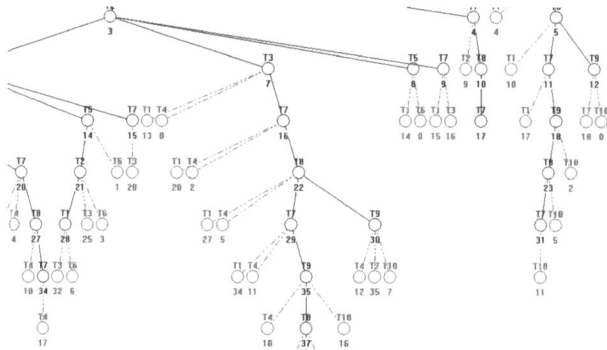

Figure 12. The segment of the PN model RT containing the deadlock and access paths to it.

$$\mathbf{M}_{10} \xrightarrow{t_7} \mathbf{M}_{17} \tag{49}$$

$$\mathbf{M}_4 \xrightarrow{t_8} \mathbf{M}_{10} \xrightarrow{t_7} \mathbf{M}_{17} \tag{50}$$

$$\mathbf{M}_5 \xrightarrow{t_1} \mathbf{M}_{10} \xrightarrow{t_7} \mathbf{M}_{17} \tag{51}$$

$$\mathbf{M}_5 \xrightarrow{t_7} \mathbf{M}_{11} \xrightarrow{t_1} \mathbf{M}_{17} \tag{52}$$

$$\mathbf{M}_{27} \xrightarrow{t_7} \mathbf{M}_{34} \xrightarrow{t_4} \mathbf{M}_{17} \tag{53}$$

Here,

$$\mathbf{M}_4 = (4, 1, 0, 0, 0, 3, 1, 0, 0, 0, 1, 0, 2, 3, 1, 3, 3, 3)^T \tag{54}$$
$$\mathbf{M}_5 = (5, 0, 0, 0, 0, 3, 0, 1, 0, 1, 0, 1, 3, 4, 1, 3, 4, 3)^T \tag{55}$$
$$\mathbf{M}_{10} = (4, 1, 0, 0, 0, 3, 0, 1, 0, 0, 0, 1, 3, 3, 1, 3, 4, 3)^T \tag{56}$$
$$\mathbf{M}_{11} = (5, 0, 0, 0, 0, 2, 1, 1, 0, 1, 0, 0, 2, 4, 1, 3, 4, 4)^T \tag{57}$$
$$\mathbf{M}_{27} = (3, 1, 0, 1, 0, 3, 0, 1, 0, 0, 0, 1, 2, 3, 0, 2, 4, 3)^T \tag{58}$$
$$\mathbf{M}_{34} = (3, 1, 0, 1, 0, 2, 1, 1, 0, 0, 0, 0, 1, 3, 0, 2, 4, 4)^T \tag{59}$$

After a short analysis of RT, we can set the constraints in the form:

$$p_7 + p_{11} <= 2 \tag{60}$$
$$p_7 + p_{18} <= 3 \tag{61}$$
$$p_2 + p_7 <= 1 \tag{62}$$

It means that

$$\mathbf{L} = \begin{pmatrix} 0 & 0 & 0 & 0 & 0 & 0 & 1 & 0 & 0 & 0 & 1 & 0 & 0 & 0 & 0 & 0 & 0 & 0 \\ 0 & 0 & 0 & 0 & 0 & 0 & 1 & 0 & 0 & 0 & 0 & 0 & 0 & 0 & 0 & 0 & 0 & 1 \\ 0 & 1 & 0 & 0 & 0 & 0 & 1 & 0 & 0 & 0 & 0 & 0 & 0 & 0 & 0 & 0 & 0 & 0 \end{pmatrix}; \mathbf{b} = \begin{pmatrix} 2 \\ 3 \\ 1 \end{pmatrix} \tag{63}$$

$$\mathbf{N}_s = -\mathbf{L}.\mathbf{N} = \begin{pmatrix} 0 & 1 & -1 & 0 & -1 & 0 & -1 & 2 & -1 & 0 \\ 0 & 0 & 0 & 0 & 0 & 0 & -2 & 1 & 1 & 0 \\ -1 & 1 & 0 & 0 & 0 & 0 & -1 & 1 & 0 & 0 \end{pmatrix} \tag{64}$$

$$^s\mathbf{M}_0 = \mathbf{b} - \mathbf{L}.\mathbf{M}_0 = \begin{pmatrix} 1 \\ 1 \\ 1 \end{pmatrix} \tag{65}$$

Such supervisor indeed prevents the deadlock but RT of the supervised system has only 16 nodes. It means that its state space is (in comparison with the state space of uncontrolled system having RT with 40 nodes) considerably limited. Unfortunately, the right section (sub-net) in Figure 11 consisting of p_6, p_7, p_8, p_9, p_{17}, p_{18} does not operate because it is eliminated by such supervisor.

Therefore, we have to find another supervisor which will be able to connect also this section in the activity. Consider the following constraints

$$p_2 + p_7 + p_8 + p_9 \leq 1 \tag{66}$$

$$p_2 + p_3 + p_7 + p_8 \leq 1 \tag{67}$$

$$p_2 + p_3 + p_5 + p_7 \leq 1 \tag{68}$$

$$p_2 + p_3 + p_4 + p_7 \leq 3 \tag{69}$$

$$p_2 + p_3 \leq 4 \tag{70}$$

$$p_2 + p_3 + p_4 \leq 1 \tag{71}$$

$$p_2 + p_3 + p_4 + p_5 \leq 3 \tag{72}$$

$$p_7 + p_8 + p_9 \leq 3 \tag{73}$$

$$p_7 + p_8 \leq 2 \tag{74}$$

or in the matrix form

$$\mathbf{L} = \begin{pmatrix} 0 & 1 & 0 & 0 & 0 & 0 & 1 & 1 & 1 & 0 & 0 & 0 & 0 & 0 & 0 & 0 & 0 \\ 0 & 1 & 1 & 0 & 0 & 0 & 1 & 1 & 0 & 0 & 0 & 0 & 0 & 0 & 0 & 0 & 0 \\ 0 & 1 & 1 & 0 & 1 & 0 & 1 & 0 & 0 & 0 & 0 & 0 & 0 & 0 & 0 & 0 & 0 \\ 0 & 1 & 1 & 1 & 0 & 0 & 1 & 0 & 0 & 0 & 0 & 0 & 0 & 0 & 0 & 0 & 0 \\ 0 & 1 & 1 & 0 & 0 & 0 & 0 & 0 & 0 & 0 & 0 & 0 & 0 & 0 & 0 & 0 & 0 \\ 0 & 1 & 1 & 1 & 0 & 0 & 0 & 0 & 0 & 0 & 0 & 0 & 0 & 0 & 0 & 0 & 0 \\ 0 & 1 & 1 & 1 & 1 & 0 & 0 & 0 & 0 & 0 & 0 & 0 & 0 & 0 & 0 & 0 & 0 \\ 0 & 0 & 0 & 0 & 0 & 0 & 1 & 1 & 1 & 0 & 0 & 0 & 0 & 0 & 0 & 0 & 0 \\ 0 & 0 & 0 & 0 & 0 & 0 & 1 & 1 & 0 & 0 & 0 & 0 & 0 & 0 & 0 & 0 & 0 \end{pmatrix} ; \mathbf{b} = \begin{pmatrix} 1 \\ 1 \\ 1 \\ 3 \\ 4 \\ 1 \\ 3 \\ 3 \\ 2 \end{pmatrix} \tag{75}$$

$$\mathbf{N}_s = -\mathbf{L}.\mathbf{N} = \begin{pmatrix} -1 & 1 & 0 & 0 & 0 & -1 & 0 & 0 & 1 \\ -1 & 0 & 1 & 0 & 1 & 0 & -1 & 0 & 1 & 0 \\ -1 & 0 & 1 & 0 & 0 & 1 & -1 & 1 & 0 & 0 \\ -1 & 0 & 0 & 1 & 1 & 0 & -1 & 1 & 0 & 0 \\ -1 & 0 & 1 & 0 & 1 & 0 & 0 & 0 & 0 & 0 \\ -1 & 0 & 0 & 1 & 1 & 0 & 0 & 0 & 0 & 0 \\ -1 & 0 & 0 & 1 & 0 & 1 & 0 & 0 & 0 & 0 \\ 0 & 0 & 0 & 0 & 0 & 0 & -1 & 0 & 0 & 1 \\ 0 & 0 & 0 & 0 & 0 & 0 & -1 & 0 & 1 & 0 \end{pmatrix} ; {}^s\mathbf{M}_0 = \mathbf{b} - \mathbf{L}.\mathbf{M}_0 = \begin{pmatrix} 1 \\ 1 \\ 1 \\ 3 \\ 4 \\ 1 \\ 3 \\ 3 \\ 2 \end{pmatrix} \tag{76}$$

Applying the supervisor to the uncontrolled PN we obtain the controlled model without any deadlocks. Its RT, expressing the space of reachable states, has 11 nodes as it can be seen in Figure 13. In the same Figure right is displayed also the supervisor consisting of 9 monitors. As we can see, both of the sections (sub-nets) are active in this case.

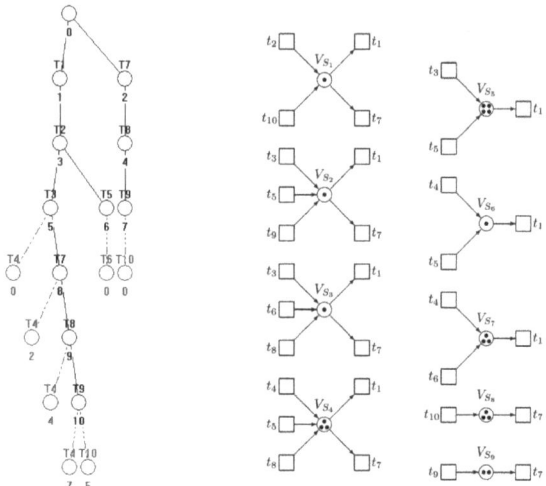

Figure 13. The RT of the controlled PN model (**left**). No deadlocks are there. Both of sections (sub-nets) are active. The supervisor consisting of nine monitors (**right**).

6. Discussion

Two methods (approaches) how to avoid deadlocks in industrial multi-agent systems were presented in this paper, namely: (i) the approach based on P-invariants, and (ii) the approach based on siphons and traps. Let us compare them now.

Both approaches have their advantages and disadvantages.

The former approach represents the procedure in exact analytical terms. The supervisor synthesis is clear and simple. It is suitable especially for the S^3PR paradigm of AMS. Thorough analysis of RT makes possible to find conditions how to mutually eliminate certain states (markings). In such a way it is possible to eliminate deadlocks. However, in a more complicated structure of the PN model with very branched RT the choice of the restriction inequality (5) (especially the matrix **L** and the vector **b**) may be intricate or even impossible. Another disadvantage is that RT depends on the initial marking M_0 of the uncontrolled PN. For another M_0 RT is different.

The latter approach has not so exact analytically expressed procedure. This is due to the fact that siphons and traps are structural entities of the PN model. Their computation (notwithstanding that it may be realized by different algorithms) may sometimes take a very long time, especially in case of structurally complicated PN models. An advantage of this approach is that calculation of siphons and traps does not depend on the initial state of the PN model. This approach is able to deal with both paradigms of AMS—S^3PR and S^4PR.

As a summary it can be said that the weak point (shortcoming, weakness) in both approaches is computational complexity—at computing RT and handling it as well as at computation of siphons and traps—especially at large-scale and structurally complicated PN models.

Despite what has been said, the approach based on siphons and traps seems to be upon the whole more advantageous than the approach based on P-invariants. Apart from the time-consuming calculation of siphons and traps, it is also simpler. However, as it was demonstrated by the Example 6 in the Section 5.4, computational problems may be huge also in relatively simple and not very large PN models.

7. Conclusions

The presented paper is, in a broader sense, an overview paper concerning the deadlock prevention and avoidance in industrial MAS in general. RAS are very important subclass of AMS. Dealing with deadlocks in RAS has been the main topic of this paper. Benefits following from this are that deadlock free RAS can be designed off-line, preliminary to the construction of real manufacturing systems, still before their actual deployment in practice. Hence, this rapidly decreases a risk of defects in operation of AMS/RAS and prevents shutdowns of them. Thus, it is possible to avoid significant economic losses. Of course, another defects unrelated to deadlocks (e.g., some external disturbances) cannot be prevented in such a way. Attention has been paid to the present most frequently used RAS, in particular to their paradigms S^3PR and S^4PR.

A wide review of literature was introduced. A general view on formal methods used in AMS was presented in Section 1.1. A short comment about the agent cooperation and negotiation, as well as on reentering in AMS was introduced in Section 1.2. The most used Petri net-based paradigms of RAS were adduced in Section 2.1. A literature overview about deadlock prevention and avoiding was referred to in Section 2.2. Setting marking of monitors in case of the siphon-based method was described in details in Section 4.2. Two simple illustration examples introduced in Section 3 (Example 1) and in Section 4 (Example 2) were supplemented by four more complicated illustrative examples in Section 5 (Example 3–Example 6).

Two basic deadlock prevention techniques using Petri nets were presented in mathematical details, namely P-invariant-based method and the method based on siphons and traps. Although in Section 6 a rough comparison of both methods was introduced, in this closing section it is necessary to point out the principled difference between them. In Table 1, the main characteristics of both methods are introduced. The ability to address the deadlock prevention in the S^3PR and S^4PR paradigms of RAS is also included there. After comparing those characteristics, the method based on siphons and traps unambiguously appears more advantageous than the method based on P-invariants. The same result follows also from Table 2 (where disadvantageous of both methods are introduced) because long lasting computations can be accelerated, e.g., by using more powerful computing technique and/or by finding algorithms with a less computational complexity.

Table 1. Characteristics of both methods.

P-Invariant-Based Method	Siphon and Trap-Based Method
simple analytic method	Matlab-based computational method
it needs additional elaboration of RT it is more labored	it does need any additional elaboration —
it has analytical setting of the initial marking of monitors	it needs additional setting of the initial marking of monitors
—	it yields a possibility to control elementary siphons and to deal with dependent siphons by means of setting the siphon control depth variables
it is suitable above all for S^3PR paradigm of AMS	it is suitable for S^3PR as well as for S^4PR paradigms of AMS
in the S^4PR paradigm it cannot eliminate the origin of new deadlocks and requires new iterations of the deadlock prevention	it is able to preclude origin of new deadlocks in the S^4PR paradigm

Table 2. Disadvantageous of both methods.

P-Invariant-Based Method	Siphon and Trap-Based Method
possible computational problems at finding RT necessity to additionally analyze RT dependence on the initial state of the PN model	often long lasting computation of siphons — —

However, in spite of all, it must be said that even the method based on P-invariants should not be completely damned, especially in case of S^3PR paradigm of AMS. As it was shown in Example 6 in the Section 5.4 this method has helped us to resolve a case where the siphon-based method was not able to give a result in a reasonable time.

Funding: This research received no external funding.

Data Availability Statement: Not Applicable, the study does not report any data.

Acknowledgments: The author thanks for the partial support of the VEGA Agency (under grant No. 2/0020/21).

Conflicts of Interest: The author declares no conflict of interest.

References

1. Mourtzis, D. Simulation in the Design and Operation of Manufacturing Systems: State of the Art and New Trends. *Int. J. Prod. Res.* **2020**, *58*, 1927–1949. [CrossRef]
2. Mourtzis, D. (Ed.) *Design and Operation of Production Networks for Mass Personalization in the Area of Cloud Technology*; Elsevier Inc.: Amsterdam, The Netherlands, 2022; ISBN 978-0-12-823657-4. [CrossRef]
3. El Maraghy, H.; Monostori, L.; Schuh, G.; El Maraghy, W. Evolution and future of manufacturing systems. *CIRP Ann. Manuf. Technol.* **2021**, *70*, 635–658. [CrossRef]
4. Murata, T. Petri Nets: Properties, Analysis and Applications. *Proc. IEEE* **1989**, *77*, 541–580. [CrossRef]
5. Reisig, W. *Petri Nets*; Springer: Berlin/Heidelberg, Germany, 1985.
6. Iordache, M.V.; Antsaklis, P.J. *Supervisory Control of Concurrent Systems: A Petri Net Structural Approach*; Birkhäuser: Basel, Switzerland, 2006.
7. Li, Z.W.; Zhou, M.C. *Deadlock Resolution in Automated Manufacturing Systems: A Novel Petri Net Approach*; Springer: London, UK, 2009.
8. Wang, Y.; Kelly, T.; Kudlur, M.; Mahlke, S.; Lafortune, S. The Application of Supervisory Control to Deadlock Avoidance in Concurrent Software. In Proceedings of the 9th IEEE/IFAC International Workshop on Discrete Event Systems—WODES'08, Goteborg, Sweden, 28–30 May 2008; pp. 287–292.
9. Iordache M.V. Methods for the Supervisory Control of Concurrent Systems Based on Petri Net Abstractions. Ph.D. Thesis, University of Notre Dame, Notre Dame, IN, USA, 2003.
10. Duhaut, D.; Carrillo, E.; Saint-Aimé, S. Avoiding Deadlock in Multi-agent Systems. In Proceedings of the 2007 IEEE International Conference on Systems, Man and Cybernetics, Montreal, QC, Canada, 7–10 October 2007; pp. 1642–1647. [CrossRef]
11. Mani, N.; Garousi, V.; Far, B.H. Monitoring Multi-Agent Systems for deadlock detection based on UML models. In Proceedings of the 2008 Canadian Conference on Electrical and Computer Engineering (CCECE), Niagara Falls, ON, Canada, 4–7 May 2008; pp. 1611–1616. [CrossRef]
12. Liu, G.Y.; Barkaoui, K. A Survey of Siphons in Petri Nets. *Inf. Sci.* **2016**, *363*, 198–220. [CrossRef]
13. Li, X.Y.; Liu, G.Y.; Li, Z.W.; Wu, N.Q.; Barkaoui, K. Elementary Siphon-Based Robust Control for Automated Manufacturing Systems with Multiple Unreliable Resources. *IEEE Access* **2019**, *7*, 21006–21019. [CrossRef]
14. Yang, Y.; Lu, W.; Xing, W.; Wang, L.; Che, X.; Chen, L. Detecting and Resolving Deadlocks in Mobile Agent Systems. *J. Vis. Lang. Comput.* **2017**, *42*, 23–30. [CrossRef]
15. Luo, J.; Liu, Z.; Zhou, M.; Xing, K.; Wang, X.; Li, X.; Liu, H. Robust deadlock control of automated manufacturing systems with multiple unreliable resources. *Inf. Sci.* **2019**, *479*, 401–415. [CrossRef]
16. Čapkovič, F. Modelling and Control of Resource Allocation Systems within Discrete Event Systems by Means of Petri Nets—Part 1: Invariants, Siphons and Traps in Deadlock Avoidance. *Comput. Inform.* **2021**, *40*, 648–689._3_648. [CrossRef]
17. Ezpeleta, J.; Colom, J.M.; Martinez, J. A Petri Net Based Deadlock Prevention Policy for Flexible Manufacturing Systems. *IEEE Trans. Robot. Autom.* **1995**, *11*, 173–184. [CrossRef]
18. Fanti, M.P.; Maione, B.; Turchiano, B. Comparing Digraph and Petri Net Approaches to Deadlock Avoidance in FMS. *IEEE Trans. Syst. Man Cybern. Part B Cybern.* **2000**, *30*, 783–798. [CrossRef]
19. Gebraeel, N.Z.; Lawley. M.A. Deadlock detection, prevention, and avoidance for automated tool sharing systems. *IEEE Trans. Robot. Autom.* **2001**, *17*, 342–356. [CrossRef]
20. Tricas, F. Deadlock Analysis, Prevention and Avoidance in Sequential Resource Allocation Systems. Ph.D. Thesis, Department of Informatics and System Engineering, University of Zaragoza, Zaragoza, Spain, 2003 [CrossRef]
21. Liu, G.Y. Supervisor Synthesis for Automated Manufacturing Systems Based on Structure Theory of Petri Nets. Ph.D. Thesis, École Doctorale Informatique, Télécommunications et Electronique de Paris, Paris, France, 2014
22. Campos, J.; Seatzu, C.; Xie, X. (Eds.) *Formal Methods in Manufacturing*; CRC Press: Boca Raton, FL, USA; London, UK; Taylor & Francis Group: New York, NY, USA, 2017.
23. Čapkovič, F. Cooperation and Negotiation of Agents by Means of Petri Net-based Models. In Proceedings of the 2012 IEEE 17th Conference Methods and Models in Automation and Robotics (MMAR), Miedzyzdroje, Poland, 27–30 August 2012; pp. 256–261. [CrossRef]

24. Čapkovič, F.; Jotsov, V. A System Approach to Agent Negotiation and Learning. In *Intelligent Systems: From Theory to Practice*; Studies in Computational Intelligence; Sgurev, V., Hadjiski, M., Kacprzyk, J., Eds.; Springer: Berlin/Heidelberg, Germany, 2010; Volume 299, pp. 133–160. [CrossRef]
25. Sindičič, I.; Bogdan, S.; Petrovič, T. Resource Allocation in Free-Choice Multiple Reentrant Manufacturing Systems Based on Machine-Job Incidence Matrix. *IEEE Trans. Ind. Inform.* **2011**, *7*, 105–114.
26. Guan, X.; Li, Y.; Xu, J.; Wang, C.; Wang, S. A Literature Review of Deadlock Prevention Policy Based on Petri Nets for Automated Manufacturing Systems. *Int. J. Digit. Content Technol. Its Appl. (JDCTA)* **2012**, *6*, 426–433. [CrossRef]
27. Yue, H.; Xing, K.Y.; Hu, H.S.; Wu, W.M.; Su, H.Y. Petri-Net-Based Robust Supervisory Control of Automated Manufacturing Systems. *Control Eng. Pract.* **2016**, *54*, 176–189. [CrossRef]
28. Farooq, A.; Huang, H.; Wang, X.L. Petri Net Modeling and Deadlock Analysis of Parallel Manufacturing Processes with Shared-Resources. *J. Syst. Softw.* **2010**, *83*, 675–688. [CrossRef]
29. Hu, H.; Liu, Y.; Yuan, L. Supervisor Simplification in FMSs: Comparative Studies and New Results Using Petri Nets. *IEEE Trans. Control Syst. Technol.* **2016**, *24*, 81–95. [CrossRef]
30. Davidrajuh, R. *Modeling Discrete-Event Systems with GPenSIM: An Introduction*; SpringerBriefs in Applied Sciences and Technology; Springer: Cham, Switzerland, 2018; 155p, ISBN 978-3-319-73102-5. Available online: https://link.springer.com/content/pdf/10.1007/978-3-319-73102-5.pdf?pdf=button (accessed on 3 January 2023). [CrossRef]
31. Iordache, M.V.; Antsaklis, P.J. Supervision Based on Place Invariants: A Survey. *Discret. Event Dyn. Syst.* **2006**, *16*, 4451–4492. [CrossRef]
32. Moody, J.; Antsaklis, P. Petri Net Supervisors for DES with Uncontrollable and Unobservable Transitions. *IEEE Trans. Autom. Control* **2000**, *45*, 462–476. [CrossRef]
33. Wang, Y.; Lafortune, S. The Theory of Deadlock Avoidance via Discrete Control. In Proceedings of the 36th Annual ACM SIGPLAN-SIGACT Symposium on Principles of Programming Languages—POPL'09, Newsletter ACM SIGPLAN Notices, Savannah, GA, USA, 21–23 January 2009; Volume 44, pp. 252–263. [CrossRef]
34. Reveliotis, S. Implicit Siphon Control and its Role in the Liveness Enforcing Supervision of Sequential Resource Allocation Systems. *IEEE Trans. Syst. Man Cybern. Part A* **2007**, *37*, 319–328.
35. Chao, D.Y. Max'-controlled Siphons for Liveness of S^3PGR2. *IET Control Theory Appl.* **2007**, *1*, 933–936.:20060275. [CrossRef]
36. Chao, D.Y.; Pan, Y.L. Uniform Formulas for Compound Siphons, Complementary Siphons and Characteristic Vectors in Deadlock Prevention of Flexible Manufacturing Systems. *J. Intell. Manuf.* **2015**, *26*, 13–23. [CrossRef]
37. Hou, Y.F.; Zhao, M.; Liu, D.; Hong, L. An Efficient Siphon-Based Deadlock Prevention Policy for a Class of Generalized Petri Nets. *Discret. Dyn. Nat. Soc.* **2016**, *2016*, 8219424. [CrossRef]
38. Liu, G.; Li, Z.; Zhong, C. New controllability condition for siphons in a class of generalised Petri nets. *IET Control Theory Appl.* **2010**, *4*, 854–864. [CrossRef]
39. Liu, G.Y.; Barkaoui, K. Necessary and Sufficient Liveness Condition of GS3PR Petri Nets. *Int. J. Syst. Sci.* **2015**, *46*, 1147–1160. [CrossRef]
40. Hu, H.S.; Zhou, M.C.; Li, Z.W. Liveness and Ratio-enforcing Supervision of Automated Manufacturing Systems Using Petri Nets. *IEEE Trans. Syst. Man Cybern.—Part A Syst. Hum.* **2012**, *42*, 392–403. [CrossRef]
41. Hu, H.S.; Zhou, M.C.; Li, Z.W. Supervisor Optimization for Deadlock Resolution in Automated Manufacturing Systems with Petri Nets. *IEEE Trans. Autom. Sci. Eng.* **2011**, *8*, 794–804. [CrossRef]
42. Hu, H.S.; Liu, Y. Supervisor Synthesis and Performance Improvement for Automated Manufacturing Systems by Using Petri Nets. *IEEE Trans. Ind. Inform.* **2015**, *11*, 450–458. [CrossRef]
43. Wu, W.H.; Chao, D.Y. Controllability of Weakly Dependent Siphons under Elementary-Siphon Control. *Trans. Inst. Meas. Control* **2016**, *38*, 941–955. [CrossRef]
44. Yan, M.M.; Zhu, R.M.; Li, Z.W.; Wang, A.; Zhou, M.C. A Siphon-based Deadlock Prevention Policy for a Class of Petri Nets—S^3PMR. In Proceedings of the 17th World Congress of the International Federation of Automatic Control (IFAC), Seoul, Republic of Korea, 6–11 July 2008; Volume 6, pp. 3352–3357. Available online: http://toc.proceedings.com/04672webtoc.pdf (accessed on 13 February 2023). [CrossRef]
45. Yan, M.M.; Li, Z.W.; Wei, N.; Zhao, M. A Deadlock Prevention Policy for a Class of Petri Nets S^3PMR. *J. Inf. Sci. Eng.* **2009**, *25*, 167–183.
46. Ma, Z.Y.; Li, Z.; Giua, A. Design of Optimal Petri Net Controllers for Disjunctive Generalized Mutual Exclusion Constraints. *IEEE Trans. Autom. Control* **2015**, *60*, 1774–1785. [CrossRef]
47. Ma, Z.Y.; Li, Z.; Giua, A. A Constraint Transformation Technique for Petri Nets with Certain Uncontrollable Structures. In Proceedings of the 12th IFAC/IEEE Workshop on Discrete Event Systems, Cachan, France, 14–16 May 2014; pp. 66–72. [CrossRef]
48. Ma, Z.Y.; Li, Z.; Giua, A. Petri Net Controllers for Disjunctive Generalized Mutual Exclusion Constraints. In Proceedings of the 2013 IEEE 18th Conference on Emerging Technologies and Factory Automation (ETFA), Cagliari, Italy, 10–13 September 2013; pp. 1–8. [CrossRef]
49. Ma, Z.Y.; Li, Z.; Giua, A. Petri net Controllers for Generalized Mutual Exclusion Constraints with Floor Operators. *Automatica* **2016**, *74*, 238–246. [CrossRef]
50. Liu, G.Y.; Barkaoui, K.; Zhou, M.C. On Intrinsically Live Structure of a Class of Generalized Petri Nets Modeling FMS. *IFAC Proc. Vol.* **2012**, *45*, 187–192. [CrossRef]

51. Li, Z.W.; Zhou, M.C. Elementary Siphons of Petri Nets for Efficient Deadlock Control. In *Deadlock Resolution in Computer-Integrated Systems*; Zhou, M.C., Fanti, M.P., Eds.; CRC Press: Boca Raton, FL, USA; London, UK; New York, NY, USA, 2005; pp. 309–348; ISBN: 9781482276534. [CrossRef]
52. Li, Z.W.; Wei, N. Deadlock Control of flexible Manufacturing Systems via Invariant-controlled Elementary Siphons of Petri Nets. *Int. J. Adv. Manuf. Technol.* **2007**, *33*, 24–35. [CrossRef]
53. Li, Z.W.; Wu, N.Q.; Zhou, M.C. Deadlock Control of Automated Manufacturing Systems Based on Petri Nets—A Literature Review. *IEEE Trans. Syst. Man Cybern.—Part C* **2012**, *42*, 437–462. [CrossRef]
54. Liu, G. J; Jiang, C.J. Incidence Matrix Based Methods for Computing Repetitive Vectors and Siphons of Petri Net. *J. Inf. Sci. Eng.* **2009**, *25*, 121–136. [CrossRef]
55. Shi, W.; He, Z.; Gu, C.; Run, N.; Ma, Z. Performance Optimization for a Class of Petri Nets. *Sensors* **2023**, *23*, 1447. [CrossRef]
56. You, D.; Wang, S.; Zhou, M. Supervisory Control of Petri Nets in the Presence of Replacement Attacks. *IEEE Trans. Autom. Sci. Eng.* **2021**, *67*, 1466–1473. [CrossRef]
57. Seatzu, C. Modeling, Analysis, and Control of Automated Manufacturing Systems Using Petri Nets. In Proceedings of the 24th IEEE International Conference on Emerging Technologies and Factory Automation (ETFA), Zaragoza, Spain, 10–13 September 2019; pp. 27–30. [CrossRef]
58. Hou, Y.F.; Li, Z.W.; Zhao, M.; Liu, D. Extended Elementary Siphon-based Deadlock Prevention Policy for a Class of Generalised Petri Nets. *Int. J. Comput. Integr. Manuf.* **2014**, *27*, 85–102. [CrossRef]
59. Miyagi, P.E.; Riascos, L.A.M. Modeling and Analysis of Fault-tolerant Systems for Machining Operations Based on Petri Nets. *Control Eng. Pract.* **2006**, *14*, 397–408. [CrossRef]
60. Stan, A.C.; Oprea, M. Petri Nets Based Coordination Mechanism for Cooperative Multi-Robot System. *J. Electr. Eng. Electron. Control. Comput. Sci.—JEEECCS* **2020**, *6*, 7–14. [CrossRef]
61. Lopez-Grao, J.P.; Colom, J.M. Resource Allocation Systems: Some Complexity Results on the S^4PR Class. In *Formal Techniques for Networked and Distributed Systems—FORTE*; Lecture Notes on Computer Science; Najm, E., Pradat-Peyre, J.F., Donzeau-Gouge, V.V., Eds.; Springer: Berlin/Heidelberg, Germany, 2006; Volume 4229, pp. 323–338; ISBN 978-3-540-46219-4. https://doi.org/10.1007/11888116_24.
62. Liu, G.J. Complexity of the Deadlock Problem for Petri Nets Modeling Resource Allocation Systems. *Inf. Sci.* **2016**, *363*, 190–197. [CrossRef]
63. Dong, Y.Y.; Chen, Y.F.; Li, S.Y.; El-Meligy, M.A.; Sharaf, M. An Efficient Deadlock Recovery Policy for Flexible Manufacturing Systems Modeled with Petri Nets. *IEEE Access* **2019**, *7*, 11785–11795. [CrossRef]

Disclaimer/Publisher's Note: The statements, opinions and data contained in all publications are solely those of the individual author(s) and contributor(s) and not of MDPI and/or the editor(s). MDPI and/or the editor(s) disclaim responsibility for any injury to people or property resulting from any ideas, methods, instructions or products referred to in the content.

MDPI
St. Alban-Anlage 66
4052 Basel
Switzerland
www.mdpi.com

Future Internet Editorial Office
E-mail: futureinternet@mdpi.com
www.mdpi.com/journal/futureinternet

Disclaimer/Publisher's Note: The statements, opinions and data contained in all publications are solely those of the individual author(s) and contributor(s) and not of MDPI and/or the editor(s). MDPI and/or the editor(s) disclaim responsibility for any injury to people or property resulting from any ideas, methods, instructions or products referred to in the content.

www.ingramcontent.com/pod-product-compliance
Lightning Source LLC
LaVergne TN
LVHW070427100526
838202LV00014B/1545